Landor as Critic

The Routledge Critics Series

GENERAL EDITOR: B.C. SOUTHAM, M.A., B.LITT. (OXON.)
*Formerly Department of English, Westfield College,
University of London*

Titles in the series

De Quincey	John E. Jordan
W. D. Howells	Edwin H. Cady
Johnson	John Wain
Orage	Wallace Martin
Richard Simpson	David Carroll
Swinburne	Clyde K. Hyder
Wordsworth	W. J. B. Owen

Landor
as Critic

Edited by

Charles L. Proudfit
Professor of English
University of Colorado

Routledge & Kegan Paul
London and Henley

First published in 1979
by Routledge & Kegan Paul Ltd
39 Store Street,
London WC1E 7DD and
Broadway House, Newtown Road,
Henley-on-Thames,
Oxon RG9 1EN
Printed in Great Britain by
Redwood Burn Ltd
Trowbridge and Esher

British Library Cataloguing in Publication Data

Landor, Walter Savage
Landor as critic. – (The Routledge
critics series).
1. English literature – History and
criticism
I. Proudfit, Charles L
820'.9   PR99

ISBN 0 7100 8988 0

General Editor's Preface

The purpose of the Routledge Critics Series is to provide carefully chosen selections from the work of the most important British and American literary critics, the extracts headed by a considerable Introduction to the critic and his work, to the age in which he was writing, and to the influence and tradition to which his criticism has given rise.

Selections of a somewhat similar kind have always existed for the great critics, such as Johnson, Wordsworth, Arnold, Henry James, and the argument for their appearance in this series is that of reappraisal and re-selection: each age has its own particular needs and desiderata and looks in its especial own way at the writing of the past – at criticism as much as literature. And in the last twenty years or so there has also been a much more systematic and intelligent re-reading of other critics, particularly the lesser-known essayists and reviewers of the Victorian period, some of whose writing is now seen to be criticism of the highest order, not merely of historical interest, but valuable to us now in our present reading of nineteenth-century literature, and so informing us in our living experience of literature as well as throwing light upon the state of literature and criticism at particular moments in the past.

B.C.S.

For
Sharon
Charles
Kerren
and
Sun Yata

Contents

Preface and Acknowledgments

Until now, Landor's literary criticism has remained embed-
ded within the sixteen volumes of his collected works edited by Welby and Wheeler, within the remaining uncollec-
ted works, and within the journals, memoirs, and correspondence of his contemporaries. Among his writings only
a few reviews and Latin essays could be considered formal
criticism. The rest is incorporated within creative
works, especially the Imaginary Conversations and poems,
and within letters, prefaces, and a postscript. Consequently, the process of selection for this volume has been
one of difficult excision. There are many works I should
have liked to have included entire rather than in excerpts; and there are many others I have had to omit
which would merit inclusion, among them the Latin essays
and 'Pericles and Aspasia'. My guiding principles have
been to present contemporary readers with the best and the
most representative of Landor's critical writing, and to
provide examples of the various literary forms in which
his criticism appears. Most of my selections fall naturally into four divisions - Letters Private and Public,
Imaginary Conversations, Reviews, Poems - and I have included the remainder under Prose Commentaries. The selections are arranged chronologically within each division.
     Landor has never been an easily accessible writer.
His works, highly allusive, offer the convolutions of a
mind informed by a thorough knowledge of the classics and
a sustained interest in contemporary literature and politics. I have attempted in the annotations to provide
elucidation and identification and to document quotations
in the hope that Landor may become familiar to the common
reader. These annotations, in conjunction with the headnotes, should provide a useful frame of reference for each
selection.
     I should like to express my indebtedness to those Landor

scholars whose efforts have proved indispensable in the
preparation of this volume.   Foremost among them is
Professor R.H. Super, whose many writings on Landor, particularly his 'Walter Savage Landor: A Biography' (1954),
provide the basis for all future critical studies.   I am
also indebted to John Forster's two-volume 'Walter Savage
Landor. A Biography' (1869) for its preservation of correspondence;   to Charles G. Crump's six-volume edition of
the 'Imaginary Conversations' (1891) and two-volume edition of the 'Longer Prose Works of Walter Savage Landor'
(1893) for useful, though limited, annotations;   to
Stephen Wheeler's four-volume edition of Landor's poetry
(vols 13-16) in 'The Complete Works of Walter Savage
Landor', eds T. Earle Welby and Stephen Wheeler, 16 vols
(1927-36);   to Pierre Vitoux's 'L'Œuvre de Walter Savage
Landor' (1964);   and to Professor A. LaVonne Ruoff for
her annotated edition of 'Landor's Letters to the Reverend
Walter Birch' (1968).

Colleagues and friends have been generous with their
suggestions and time.   I should particularly like to
thank Professor R.H. Super who called my attention to the
1798 Preface to 'Gebir', a selection I might have overlooked since copies of the first edition are rare and the
1798 Preface has never been reprinted.   Professor Super's
interest in the preparation of this volume and his helpful
commentary on the manuscript prior to publication have
been invaluable to me.   I am also grateful for the assistance of Professors Donald Baker, Hazel E. Barnes, Elizabeth Nelson, Anthony W. Shipps, and James Wheelock, and of
Mrs Mary McClanahan.   My deepest gratitude, however, is
to Sharon, my wife and colleague, who has assisted me
throughout this labour.

I wish to thank the staffs of The University of Colorado Norlin Library, the University College London Library, the University of London Library, and the Reading Room
of the British Museum for their help in providing materials necessary for this edition.   I would also like to
thank the Department of English at The University of Colorado for secretarial and financial assistance.   I am particularly indebted to Mrs Aladeen Smith and Mrs Carolyn
Dameron who helped prepare the final typescript for publication.   The award of a Faculty Fellowship for the aca-
demic year 1973-4 by The University of Colorado Council on
Research and Creative Work has provided me with the time
and the funds necessary to complete this book, and for
this I am especially grateful.

Acknowledgments are due to the Armstrong Browning Library, Baylor University, Waco, Texas, for permission to
quote from a Landor letter to Robert Browning, postmarked

12 November 1845 (MS in the library's possession); to The
Bodley Head for permission to quote from 'The Divine
Comedy of Dante Alighieri', tr. John D. Sinclair (1961);
to The Heritage Press, Avon, Connecticut 06001, for per-
mission to quote from Francis Winwar's translation of 'The
Decameron of Giovanni Boccaccio', copyright © 1930, 1958;
to the University of Chicago Press for permission to
quote from 'The Triumphs of Petrarch', tr. Ernest Hatch
Wilkins (1962), copyright © 1962 by the University of
Chicago; to Harvard University Press and to William
Heinemann to quote from The Loeb Classical Library; to Dr
John F. Mariani for permission to quote from his The
Letters of Walter Savage Landor To Marguerite Countess of
Blessington (unpublished PhD dissertation, Columbia Uni-
versity, 1973); to David McKay, Inc., for permission to
quote from 'The Sonnets of Petrarch', tr. Joseph Auslander
(1931); and to Professor A. LaVonne Ruoff and to The John
Rylands University Library of Manchester to quote from
Professor Ruoff's Landor's Letters to the Reverend Walter
Birch, 'Bulletin of the John Rylands Library', 51 (Autumn
1968).

Boccaccio ... To be useful to as many as possible is the especial duty of a critic, and his utility can only be attained by rectitude and precision. He walks in a garden which is not his own; and he neither must gather the blossoms to embellish his discourse, nor break the branches to display his strength. Rather let him point to what is out of order, and help to raise what is lying on the ground.

'The Pentameron'

Introduction

THE LANDORIAN VOICE

Walter Savage Landor has not attracted much attention as a
nineteenth-century literary critic.   This would not surprise him.   He neither wrote as a professional critic for
a specific audience;   nor did he, like his contemporaries
Coleridge, De Quincey, Hazlitt, Hunt, and Lamb, seek the
usual critical forums of the day - the periodical review,
the formal essay, and the lecture platform.   'I shall
have as many readers as I desire to have in other times
than ours', wrote the seventy-five-year-old Walter Savage
Landor in 1850 to his friend and biographer, John Forster.
'I shall dine late;   but the dining-room will be well-
lighted, the guests few and select.   I neither am, nor
ever shall be, popular.   Such never was my ambition'
(Forster, 'Landor', 2, 531).   Devotees of Landor's poetry
and prose have never been numerous, and those who have articulated their praise compose as select a company as
Landor could have wished.   In our own century T.S. Eliot,
Ezra Pound, and W.B. Yeats have acknowledged Landor's literary achievement: Eliot considers Landor 'one of the
very finest poets of the first part of the nineteenth century'; (1)   Pound asserts that the 'Imaginary Conversations' contain 'all culture of the encyclopedists reduced
to manageable size, ... and full of human life ventilated,
given a human body, not merely indexed'; (2)   and Yeats in
'A Vision' (1937) includes himself with Landor in Phase 17
of the Moon. (3)   Among the eminent Victorians Robert
Browning believes Landor to have 'written passages not exceeded in beauty and subtlety by any literature that I am
acquainted with'; (4)   and Algernon Charles Swinburne, who
personally paid his respects to Landor by visiting him in
Florence in the writer's ninetieth year, dedicated
'Atlanta in Calydon' to him and further honoured him with

two poems, In Memory of Walter Savage Landor and Song for
the Centenary of Walter Savage Landor.   Yet in the midst
of all these laudatory remarks lavished upon Landor's
poetry and prose, similar praise of Landor's literary
criticism is noticeably absent.

There is reason for this.   Readers who have turned to
Landor's works to find a consistent application of a set
of carefully determined critical principles have been disappointed.   His biographer, Robert H. Super, has described him as 'one of the most perfect *amateurs* among men of
letters'. (5)   Landor was a private man endowed with an
income sufficient to free him to become one of the most
erudite and well-read literary men of the first half of
the nineteenth century.   He wrote out of enjoyment rather
than necessity, and his lifetime devotion to ancient and
modern authors left behind him a body of critical commentary that demands our respect and repays our attention.
This commentary, however, has never been easily available
to readers.   It has remained essentially to be discovered
within his personal correspondence, suppressed or cancelled prose pieces, Latin essays, poetry, the diaries and
memoirs of those who knew him, and that species of composition upon which rests his reputation as a prose
writer, the 'Imaginary Conversations of Literary Men and
Statesmen'.   On those few occasions when reviews were
solicited from him, late in life, he expressed himself in
a form of personal essay uniquely his own.

It is perhaps this very individuality of expression
which has distinguished Landor among his contemporaries,
has found him friends and enemies, and has prevented
the unlearned from following along with him.   The singularity of his pronouncements characterized his conversation as much as it does his writings.   His acquaintances
all mark the Landorian voice.   Malcolm Elwin recounts a
story of a young man to whom Landor was personally unknown.   The two happened one day to be riding in the same
coach; and overhearing Landor's conversation, the young
man interrupted and said: '"Why! this sounds amazingly
like an Imaginary Conversation"'. (6)   This Landorian
voice expresses the man, his confidence in his own judgment, his vast knowledge of literature and painting, his
extremes in temperament and disposition, and his ability
to convey his thoughts in words and images which are memorable.   Henry Crabb Robinson was one of the first of a
series of notable literary men who called upon Landor at
his villa near Florence, Italy, in the early 1830s.
Robinson's account of this meeting with Landor and his
description of the writer's personal appearance and manner
of expression help to convey his uniqueness: (7)

August 16th. [1830] - Met to-day the one man living in
Florence whom I was anxious to know.   This was Walter
Savage Landor, a man of unquestionable genius, but very
questionable good sense; ....   He was a man of florid
complexion, with large full eyes, and altogether a
leonine man, and with a fierceness of tone well suited
to his name; his decisions being confident, and on all
subjects, whether of taste or life, unqualified;   each
standing for itself, not caring whether it was in harmony with what had gone before or would follow from the
same oracular lips.   But why should I trouble myself
to describe him?   He is painted by a master hand in
Dickens's novel, 'Bleak House', ... where he figures as
Mr. Boythorn.   The combination of superficial ferocity
and inherent tenderness, so admirably portrayed in
'Bleak House', still at first strikes every stranger -
for twenty-two years have not materially changed him -
no less than his perfect frankness and reckless indifference to what he says....

Of his literary judgments the following are specimens: - Of Dante, about a seventieth part is good; of
Ariosto, a tenth; of Tasso, not a line worth anything,
- yes, *one* line.   He declared almost all Wordsworth to
be good.   Landor was as dogmatic on paintings as on
poetry.   He possessed a considerable collection of
pictures.   His judgment was amusingly at variance with
popular opinion.   He thought nothing of Michael Angelo
as a painter; and, as a sculptor, preferred John of
Bologna.   Were he rich, he said, he would not give
£1,000 for 'The Transfiguration', but ten times as much
for Fra Bartolomeo's 'St. Mark'.   Next to Raphael and
Fra Bartolomeo he loved Perugino....

Ralph Waldo Emerson's account of his visit as a young
man to Landor's Florentine villa in May 1833 presents a
similar image of Landor's memorable presence: 'He admired
Washington; talked of Wordsworth, Byron, Massinger, Beaumont and Fletcher ... is decided in his opinions, likes to
surprise, and is well content to impress, if possible, his
English whim upon the immutable past....   [Yet] year
after year the scholar must still go back to Landor for a
multitude of elegant sentences - for wisdom, wit, and indignation that are unforgetable.' (8)   This Landorian
voice, so well described by both Robinson and Emerson, is
perhaps characterized most aptly by a more intimate
acquaintance, Richard Monckton Milnes, who spent several
weeks with the Landors during the summer of 1833: (9)

It was his conversation that left on [his visitors] the
most delightful and permanent impression; so affluent,
animated, and coloured, so rich in knowledge and illustration, so gay and yet so weighty - such bitter irony
and such lofty praise, uttered with a voice fibrous in
all its tones, whether gentle or fierce - it equalled,
if not surpassed, all that has been related of the
table-talk of men eminent for social speech.   It pro-
ceeded from a mind so glad of its own exercise, and so
joyous in its own humour, that in its most extravagant
notions and most exaggerated attitudes it made argument
difficult and criticism superfluous.   And when memory
and fancy were alike exhausted, there came a laughter
so pantomimic, yet so genial, rising out of a momentary
silence into peals so cumulative and sonorous, that all
contradiction and possible affront were merged for
ever.

The Landorian voice repels as well as attracts, and his
critics have varied in their susceptibility to its charm.
When Landor's judgments and opinions emerged in dramatized
and objectified form in the 'Imaginary Conversations' of
1824, his early reviewers were not swayed by the force of
his personality into accepting his unorthodox opinions and
pronouncements.   Although the 'Westminster Review'
praises the writer's 'candour and liberality in the discussion of philosophical questions' in the Philosophical
Dialogues, the reviewer has no sympathy for Landor's
attack on French literature, particularly the works of
Voltaire and Boileau, in the conversation between the Abbé
Delille and the author himself.   He finds Landor's critical approach to be unfair and biased, and criticizes him
for making the Abbé a man of straw, for focusing attention
on obvious faults, and for sometimes failing either to
translate or to quote lines of French verse accurately.
He notes the contemporary English dislike of all things
French, and finds this error repeated in Landor's criticisms. (10)   Both William Hazlitt, in the 'Edinburgh
Review', and Sir Henry Taylor, in the 'Quarterly Review',
voice similar criticisms of this literary conversation. (11)
Landor's opinions on Dante also express his distinct
bias, and when his criticism of Dante's 'Divine Comedy'
appeared in 'The Pentameron' (1837), a five-day Imaginary
Conversation between Boccaccio and Petrarch, the 'British
and Foreign Review' condemned those opinions.   The reviewer particularly stresses Landor's dislike of the metaphysical, his a-historical approach to literature, and his
judgment of Dante's poem 'by a scale taken from [classi-

cal] master-works composed under other circumstances and
with different ends', which must of necessity result in
personal and critical judgments that misrepresent both
Dante's character as a man and his achievement as a poet.
He concludes his incisive review by stating 'that whatsoever Mr. Landor does well he does excellently, and that in
his proper and peculiar path he is second to no living
writer. But there is a circle into which he cannot pene-
trate, and Plato and Dante are among its inmates.' (12)

These criticisms, made by Landor's contemporaries, suggest the qualities which render Landor as critic both
fascinating and frustrating. He does not merely read
books; he lives them. In doing so he brings with him
all of his likes and dislikes, loves and hates, strengths
and weaknesses, perceptions and blind spots. He answers
to no one except himself; he cares for no one's criticism
but his own; he is his own ideal critic. It is little
wonder that criticism of Landor's criticism has seemed so
unsatisfying. Those literary historians who have endeav-
oured to know enough of his works even to generalize about
them have had enormous difficulties. They are attempting
to cope with a man who was born into a literary age that
included Dr Johnson, was educated during the exciting
years of the American and French Revolutions, and was
friend of two generations of Romantic writers and of many
eminent Victorians. They are attempting to cope with a
man responding singularly to a life spent reading,
writing, or talking about reading and writing. We see
the effect of this in the general and insubstantial comments they make. Leslie Stephen finds Landor's criticisms of literature 'often admirably perceptive, [though]
too often wayward and unsatisfactory, because at the mercy
of his prejudices'. (13) George Saintsbury sees Landor
as an example of 'Criticism divorced from Taste'. Although Landor's 'taste, in some directions at least, was
delicate and exquisite', he lacks 'judicial ... qualities'
and his 'critical marks' are usually 'caprice, arbitrary
legislation, [and] sometimes positive blindness and deaf-
ness'. (14) One feels almost a certain gratitude to
Oliver Elton who notices that Landor, 'though captious,
whimsical, and often blind', manages to produce in his
'formal examinations of Wordsworth in "Southey and
Porson", and of Milton in "Southey and Landor"', works
which 'are pieces of sharp, minute, textual comment, often
censorious, always courageous, and again and again pertinent'. (15)

Since the middle of the twentieth century, scholars
have attempted to examine Landor, his life, and his works
with mature observation and thorough documentation. R.H.

Super's definitive biography, 'Walter Savage Landor' (New York, 1954), provides the materials necessary for understanding the life and contains numerous critical insights; and Pierre Vitoux, in his monumental study 'L'OEuvre de Walter Savage Landor' (Paris, 1964), offers the most thorough attempt to catalogue and systematize Landor's literary judgments to date. (16)   Both of these works encourage the modern reader to accept as a challenge the conclusion of Stanley T. Williams, who in 1923 made the first exhaustive examination of Landor's criticism, that 'we encounter everywhere brilliant epigrams on literature', but 'we cannot find [a method or] a body of guiding principles.   Personal ideals are the determinants'. (17) To approach Landor in search of a method or guiding principles can only detract from the pleasure of reading him. There are critical procedures and principles, but they emerge through acquaintance, through the gradual submission to the Landorian voice as it leads one arbitrarily, often quixotically, through a library in which nothing is more meaningless than the dates on books.

II THE MAKING OF THE POET-CRITIC

As the Landorian voice accompanies us through this library, making pronouncements on ancients and contemporaries, on poets loved and poets despised, on critical issues past and present, we are forced to consider whether this is the voice of an opinionated eccentric or a voice which echoes his time.   It was a very long time, 1775-1864.   One hardly knows whether to view him as a Neo-Classic, a Romantic, or a Victorian; and he gives the lie, perhaps more than any single figure, to the periodization of English literature.   Landor not only lived in all three eras, but he also belongs within and without each of them.

Education (1775-98)

Landor's education was definitely within the late Neo-Classical tradition.   He was born at Warwick on 30 January 1775, the eldest son of a well-provided physician; and at the age of eight, in 1783, he entered Rugby School to begin the education of a gentleman's son, first public school followed by the university.   Even though Landor's father was informed by the headmaster, Dr Thomas James, in 1791 that Landor 'was rebellious, and incited others to rebellion', and that unless he removed his son he would

have to expell him, 'much to his sorrow' (Forster,
'Landor', 1, 197), Landor himself often recalled his eight
years at Rugby with particular affection.   It was there
that he developed his life-long interests in classical
literature and in writing Latin poetry, for education at
Rugby in the late eighteenth century was primarily devoted
to the study of the classics.   Although Dr James expected
his scholars to learn some mathematics, read a few scrip-
tural commentaries, and analyse Milton's poetry once a
week, major emphasis was placed upon the reading and
translating of Greek and Latin authors: Demosthenes,
Homer, Pindar, the Greek dramatists and lyric poets,
Cicero, Horace, Juvenal, Livy, Ovid, Tacitus, and Virgil.
Although all of the boys were expected to compose in
Latin, only a few of the brightest, among them Landor,
attempted compositions in Greek.   When Landor left Rugby
prematurely at the age of sixteen, he had achieved distinction as a classical scholar and had begun his preparation as a special kind of literary critic among whose
recognizable characteristics would be the practice of
verbal and textual criticism and the use of classical
models as touchstones in judging both ancient and modern
literary works.

Since Landor was still too young to enter the university, provision was made for him to study privately, first
with an Italian master in London, then with a private
tutor, the Reverend William Langley.   In the Langley home
Landor studied Greek authors, particularly Pindar and
Sophocles, familiarized himself with contemporary British
Latinists, and wrote verses in English and Latin.   He
enjoyed his months in the pleasant Langley household, and
in later years commemorated it with the Imaginary Conversation Walton, Cotton, and Oldways which takes the Langley
home for its setting.

In the autumn of 1792 Landor matriculated at Oxford,
and he entered Trinity College in January 1793.   Much of
his time was spent in the company of two former Rugby
school-fellows, Henry Cary of Christ Church, who later
achieved renown as the translator of Dante and Pindar,
and Walter Birch, Landor's closest friend.   Only Cary and
Birch were allowed to read Landor's Latin compositions,
and neither they nor his tutor Benwell could persuade the
sensitive young poet to enter his poems in university competitions.   Yet his interest in contemporary Latinists
increased during his stay at the university, and he continued to progress in his study of the classics.   He
might well have gone on to a distinguished university
career had not certain temperamental difficulties deterred
him, especially his love of exaggeration and delight in
shocking behaviour.

Although not serious in itself, Landor's tendency to exaggerate was, particularly at this time, a bane to nearly all who knew him except for Walter Birch. According to Landor's brother Robert, Birch 'often checked Walter's extravagant language by his laughter; and once he asked me how it could have happened that my brother should have met accidently so many ladies, in an evening's walk or two with him and me, every one of whom was incomparably the most beautiful creature whom he had ever seen? how each of twenty fools could be by much the greatest fool upon earth? and, above all, how Mr. Pitt could be the greatest rascal living, if Mr. Canning surpassed Mr. Pitt, and Lord Castlereagh surpassed Mr. Canning, and all three were infinitely exceeded as brutes and fools by their gracious sovereign king George the Third?' (Forster, 'Landor', 1, 186-7). This tendency to exaggeration later became a distinguishing characteristic of Landor's literary criticism; and, appropriately enough, informs much of the critical commentary found in Landor's letters to Birch with whom he corresponded until Birch's death in 1829.

The pleasure Landor found in shocking people was partly responsible for his cultivating a reputation for Republicanism at a time when it was most dangerous to do so. He was one of the first students at Oxford to wear his hair plain without powder, and, for effect, had it queue-tied with black ribbon. Robert Southey, whose friendship was later to prove so important to Landor's literary career, wrote these words to a friend several years after he had left Oxford: 'He [Landor] was a contemporary of mine at Oxford, of Trinity, and notorious as a mad Jacobin; his Jacobinism would have made me seek his acquaintance, but for his madness; he was obliged to leave the University for shooting at one of the Fellows through the window.' (18) Although Landor had fired his gun at the closed shutters of his enemy's room and not at the young man himself, an investigation was held, and Landor was rusticated in June 1794 for two terms. He never returned to the university, although he did continue his private study of Greek and Latin authors. Indeed, Landor's classical attainments set him off from other literary men of the early nineteenth century with the exceptions of De Quincey and Shelley. Dr Samuel Parr, Landor's friend, neighbour, and himself an eminent classicist, once described Landor as 'a most excellent Latin scholar with some creditable knowledge of Greek' (Forster, 'Landor', 1, 22).

When Landor's father learned of his son's determination not to return to the university, the two men quarrelled, and the son went to London about Christmas 1794. He devoted himself to the study of French, Italian, and

Greek, and arranged for the publication of 'The Poems of
Walter Savage Landor' in the spring of 1795.   The small
volume contained poems in English and Latin, several imitations from Catullus, and a seventeen-page Latin essay in
defence of writing in the Latin tongue.   The subjects and
verse forms of the English poems were similar to those
found in the volumes of countless other minor poets of the
late eighteenth century; and Landor, soon ashamed of this
volume of juvenilia, had it withdrawn.   Three years later
in the Preface to 'Gebir' (1798), a long heroic idyll inspired by repeated readings of Milton's 'Paradise Lost',
the young poet announced a new poetic aim: he would write
a poem 'descriptive of men and manners ... in blank verse
... because there never was a poem in rhyme that grew not
tedious in a thousand lines' (No. 1).   Although Landor's
poem, published before the 'Lyrical Ballads' of Coleridge
and Wordsworth, had little effect on the course of English
poetry, it does show that Landor also participated in the
revolutionary poetic spirit abroad at the close of the
eighteenth century.

In February 1800 an unfavourable notice of 'Gebir' appeared in the 'Monthly Review'.   Thoroughly annoyed,
Landor retaliated with a lively and disorganized prose
essay entitled Post-Script to 'Gebir'.   Since one of his
remarks pained a very close friend, Landor cancelled the
essay from a forthcoming volume of English and Latin
poetry.   This Post-Script, never published during
Landor's lifetime, is especially important to an understanding of Landor as critic for it contains, in addition
to lively criticisms of contemporary periodical reviews
and reviewers, the origin of his concept of the ideal
poet-critic.   Landor asserts in this Post-Script that the
reader who purports to be a critical reviewer 'must surely
be above what he measures, else how can he measure with
exactness?'   Furthermore, 'he must be greater, *ex
officio*, than the person he brings before him; else how
can he stigmatize with censure, or even dismiss with
praise?' (No. 2).   These assertions define the self-con-
cept Landor brought to bear on all he read and criticized
throughout his life.   It is an attitude he may well have
derived from his favourite English poet, John Milton, who
expresses similar lofty sentiments in 'Paradise Regained':
'Who reads / Incessantly, and to his reading brings not /
A spirit and judgment equal or superior, / (And what he
brings, what needs he elsewhere seek) / Uncertain and un-
settl'd still remains, / Deep verst in books and shallow
in himself' (iv, 322-7).

Finding a form (1798-1824)

With the publication of 'Gebir' in 1798, Landor seems to
have entered the Romantic period.   Certainly he shared
the problems of fathers, finances, and love affairs of
many of his contemporaries; and he formed literary
friendships of the sort which mark this period, especially
among those who chose to make their homes in Italy.
Along with many other English Romantics, Landor visited
France in 1802 following the Peace of Amiens, and he even
joined a revolution, serving as a volunteer soldier in the
Spanish revolt against Napoleon in the autumn of 1808.
    After the death of his father in November 1805, Landor
was endowed with a comfortable independent income which
left him free to engage in a life devoted to study and
writing.   Thus this troubled aspect of his relationship
with his family was settled.   His affairs of the heart
were a different matter.   Jane Sophia Swift, the Ianthe
of his poems with whom he was deeply in love, married
another.   Thus, his passion for her, like so many of his
emotional attachments to women, remained unrequited and
became for him an ideal.   Landor's only successful loves
were his idealized ones.   His marriage to Julia Thullier
whom he met in Bath in 1811, when she was about seventeen
and he almost thirty-six, was a disaster.   Although they
managed to live together for twenty-four years and had
four children, their temperaments were very different.
She enjoyed a gay social life, and he a life of study.
They shared no companionship, and his inability to manage
finances only exacerbated a most uncomfortable relationship.   They finally separated in 1835, assuredly to the
great relief of all concerned.
    Landor's most significant literary friendship was that
with the poet Robert Southey whom he met at Bristol in
April 1808.   It lasted from their first meeting until
Southey's death thirty-five years later, and it had an
important bearing on the personal lives and literary
careers of both men.   Southey, a much more practical man
than Landor, on several occasions intervened in matters of
publication for his friend.   Assuredly in 1812 Southey
saved Landor from a libel suit by joining his publisher in
urging him to suppress his printed 'Commentary on Memoirs
of Mr. Fox' (1812).   Landor had written this work, actually a collection of extended marginalia, in response to
the publication of John Bernard Trotter's 'Memoirs of the
Later Years of the Right Honourable Charles James Fox'
(1811), a personal account of the English statesman's
opinions on politics and literature by his private secretary.   Landor's 'Commentary' contains lively political

remarks and is dedicated to the President of the USA.   It
was a most inflammatory work for publication on the eve of
the war of 1812 with America.

Even more important for Landor than Southey's practical
assistance, however, was his role as inspiration and
sounding-board.   It was Southey who kindled Landor's enthusiasm for Wordsworth's poetry by sending him copies of
the 'Excursion' (1814), 'Collected Poems' (1815), and the
'White Doe of Rylstone' (1815).   After reading these
works, Landor was one of the first to recognize and extol
Wordsworth's greatness formally, in both his Latin essay
'De Cultu atque Usu Latini Sermonis' (1820) and in the
first Imaginary Conversation between Southey and Porson
(1823).   In later years Landor and Wordsworth, who had
developed an initial friendship based on their common interest in poetry, quarrelled and became estranged.   When
one reads Landor's vituperative attacks on Wordsworth
written after their falling out, 'A Satire on Satirists,
and Admonition to Detractors' (1836) and Southey and
Porson II (1842), one feels grateful that Southey's introduction of Wordsworth's poetry to Landor resulted in the
positive and worthy judgments of an earlier period.

It was also a chance remark in a letter from Southey
dated 14 August 1820 concerning his writing of dialogues
that inspired Landor likewise to attempt this form of
prose composition.   By March 1822 Landor had written fifteen dialogues and had discovered the literary form so
perfectly suited to him for expressing his opinions on his
favourite subjects, literature and politics.   The number
of major Imaginary Conversations devoted to literature in
which Southey appears as one of the interlocutors in
itself speaks for the importance Landor's exchange of
ideas with Southey had for him.

Indeed, it is in the intellectual and emotional relationship with Southey that Landor's concept of the ideal
poet-critic and of himself as that poet-critic develops.
Landor and Southey actually only met five times during
their lifetimes, and altogether spent no more than three
weeks in each other's company.   Yet in his letters to
Southey Landor first affirmed through practice the role
of the poet-critic he had articulated and defined in the
1800 Post-Script to 'Gebir'.   At his first meeting with
Southey in 1808, Landor encouraged his new friend to proceed with a series of epic poems which he had decided to
abandon.   Consequently, between 1808 and 1814 Southey
regularly sent Landor for criticism sections of 'The Curse
of Kehama' (1810) and 'Roderick, the Last of the Goths'
(1814).   In his criticisms Landor adopts the position of
the ideal critic, offering commentary either on textual

matters or on the emotional response of the reader.   His
verbal criticisms consist of detailed discussion of diction, grammar, metre, rhyme, and harmony; and they are
those of the practising poet, of the craftsman of words
for whom the slightest blemish in a line of poetry affects
the sensitive reader's intellectual and emotional response
to the poem as a whole.   Landor's assessments of the
emotive effects of Southey's poetry on the reader are
those of the superior critic who recognizes as the best
poetry that 'which, by its own powers, produces the
greatest and most durable emotion on generous, well-informed, and elevated minds' (No. 16).   After reading
through one section of 'Roderick', for example, Landor
notes how few readers will be able to 'feel at heart what
Pelayo feels, and fewer still who will follow up with intensity all the vicissitudes of Roderigo'.   He then
quotes several lines that describe Roderick's noble demeanour following his abdication of his throne (vii, 183-
8) and remarks that 'the language is so plain and the
sentiment so natural that I am the only man in England who
knows the full value of them' (No. 4).   Landor's view of
the ideal critic, therefore, through this early practice
on Southey's poems, becomes an idealized projection of
himself.

Landor maintained in the Preface to the first volume of
his 'Imaginary Conversations' (1824) that the opinions expressed by the interlocutors are not his own.   One of the
earliest reviewers, however, recognized his voice: (19)

He does not employ the real dramatic magic of trans-
forming himself into the character of his selection or
creation; he only produces a compound being of which a
tenth may be Milton or Marvel, and the remaining nine-
tenths are Walter Savage Landor.   The result, however,
is far more valuable than it would have been had even
the most successful imitation been the distinguishing
merit of the book....

We may never lose sight of the author, but then we
never wish to lose sight of him; nay, we like the company into which he leads us all the better for their
bearing evident marks of being animated by his spirit.

More recently, R.H. Super observes that 'from the start
[the 'Imaginary Conversations'] appeared to Landor as personal essays (political, literary, and of many other
sorts) in dialogue form.   In a few instances (and generally not in the earlier Conversations) Landor attempted
to make his dialogues genuinely dramatic and his characters expressive of emotions and attitudes they actually

might have held; for the most part, the Conversations
were Landor's own reflections on a wide variety of subjects and their relevance was contemporary, not historical' (Super, 'Landor', p. 159).   Even if we had not evidence to support this view in the annotations to two
recent editions of selected 'Imaginary Conversations', (20) we could derive it from those Conversations
in which Landor introduces Southey, either in conversation
with himself or with Porson.   Landor, who so much delígh-
ted in literary conversation with this friend who shared
his knowledge and interests, frequently has Southey speak
with a voice which echoes his own.   And in the Southey
and Landor Conversations in which they discuss Milton's
poetry, the two poet-critics speak, with a few minor exceptions, with one critical voice, and that voice is
Landor's.

Although the first volumes of the 'Imaginary Conversations' were the most significant literary achievement of
Landor's middle years, they were not his only activity.
In 1815 Landor and his wife fled to Italy to escape financial disaster after a rash investment in an estate in
Wales, Llanthony Abbey.   They joined many of their countrymen who found that they could live well on limited
means in Italy at this time.   This was also a period of
enthusiasm for Italian travel, and a large number of English writers, painters, and young men and women of the
upper classes flocked to Italy after the Napoleonic Wars.
Byron, Shelley, Hazlitt, Hunt, Southey, and Wordsworth are
only a few of the writers who travelled in Italy, and many
found a friendly welcome at Landor's villa.

Landor's interest in writing Latin verse did not abate,
and in 1820 he published 'Idyllia Heroica Decem Librum
Phaleuciorum Unum', a volume of Latin verse containing ten
idylls, fifty-three shorter poems, and a ninety-page essay
on the cultivation and use of the Latin tongue.   'De
Cultu atque Usu Latini Sermonis', the work mentioned
earlier for its praise of Wordsworth's poetry, is also of
interest because in it Landor castigates the Edinburgh reviewers who had attacked Southey and Wordsworth and admon-
ishes Byron, though not by name.   Wordsworth expressed
his gratitude for the defence with a letter, thus initiat-
ing a direct correspondence, and Southey included Landor's
strictures on Byron in his attack on the 'Satanic School'
in 'A Vision of Judgment' (1821).   Landor soon found himself involved in this famous literary quarrel. (21)

Literary recognition (1824-64)

Nearly a year after the publication of the first two volumes of the 'Imaginary Conversations' (1824), William
Hazlitt called on Landor in Florence. Through Hazlitt,
Landor was introduced to a small group of writers and
artists then living in Florence, among then Charles Brown
and Leigh Hunt. Hunt had personally known Keats and
Shelley, and Landor's interest in these poets dates from
this period. Landor was delighted with his new circle of
friends, and they remained a source of pleasure to him for
the rest of his life. In 1827 Landor made the acquaintance of the Countess of Blessington whose gatherings in
Florence and later in London at Gore House enabled the
writer to meet numerous artists, statesmen, and literary
men. She was also to become Landor's agent in London as
well as one of his closest friends, and his correspondence
with her contains numerous interesting literary anecdotes
and judgments on writers ancient and modern.

In 1832 Landor returned to England for a visit of
several months and was welcomed as a man of literary distinction. He not only renewed his friendship with
Southey with whom he had corresponded regularly, but he
also met Wordsworth, Lamb, and Coleridge. After he returned to his villa outside Florence, he was complimented
in May of 1833 by a visit from a serious young American,
Ralph Waldo Emerson. About this time Landor's domestic
situation began to worsen, and in July 1835 he left his
wife and children and returned to England. Both Coleridge and Lamb had died since his last visit, and the literary scene which welcomed him included many new writers
who were to become his friends, a veritable roll-call of
eminent Victorians - Robert Browning, Elizabeth Barrett,
Charles Dickens, John Forster, Thomas Carlyle, Alfred
Tennyson, and Thomas Babington Macaulay.

The most important of these new friends for him was the
young literary critic and later editor, John Forster.
The two men met in May 1836, and Forster, like Lady Blessington, soon became friend, confidant, and literary
agent. As editor of the 'Examiner', Forster was able to
provide Landor with an outlet for the publication of English and Latin poetry, Imaginary Conversations, and letters to the editor on a variety of subjects and concerns.
As editor of the 'Foreign Quarterly Review' he elicited
from Landor two masterpieces of critical writing, one on
the Idylls of Theocritus (1842) and another on the life
and writings of Petrarch (1843). Forster was also responsible for the publication of Landor's collected writings in English (1846) and Latin (1847). In 1869 he pub-

lished his two-volume 'Walter Savage Landor: A Biography', and in 1876, the year of his own death, published
'The Works and Life of Walter Savage Landor' in eight volumes.   Forster was truly Landor's Boswell, and the 1869
biography presents us with a first-hand account of the
later years of Landor's life among the great literary personages of the Victorian era.   It also contains excerpts
from letters Landor wrote to Forster that provide a fascinating commentary on Landor's literary opinions in his
declining years.

Landor did not spend his years among the Victorian writers luxuriating in the achievement of the 'Imaginary Conversations'.   His seventh decade produced several of his
most significant works of literary criticism.   'Pericles
and Aspasia' (1836), for example, is the culmination of
Landor's lifelong interest in classical Greece, and scattered throughout this epistolary work are numerous criticisms of Greek poets, tragedians, and historians as well
as poems that re-create the classical spirit in contemporary verse.   'The Pentameron' (1837) is the fruit of the
writer's twenty-year immersion in Italian life, art, and
literature, and contains extended criticisms of Boccaccio's 'Decameron', Dante's 'Divine Comedy', and detailed
analyses of the poetry of Horace and Vergil.   Between
1842 and 1843 Landor wrote three critical essays for
Forster, solicited by him as reviews, on recent editions
of the works of Catullus, Theocritus, and Petrarch.   In
1842 Landor published his second Conversation between
Southey and Porson in 'Blackwood's Edinburgh Magazine',
important more for the presentation of Southey as the
example of the ideal poet-critic and for the literary
criticism in the digressions than for the hostile verbal
criticism of Wordsworth's poetry.   Between 1844 and the
publication of his collected 'Works' (1846), Landor completed the two Imaginary Conversations between Southey and
himself that contain a sustained critical analysis of
Milton's poetry, and in the 'Morning Chronicle' for 22
November 1845, Landor published To Robert Browning, his
finest literary tribute in verse.

Landor's last years were spent in Italy.   After leaving his family in 1835, he had lived primarily in Bath
where Dickens and Forster often came to celebrate his
birthday with him.   In 1858, in his middle eighties,
Landor became involved in an uncomfortable libel suit, and
the only solution appeared to be flight to Italy.   He
could not tolerate life with his family; and when Robert
Browning found the old man wandering destitute in the
streets of Florence, he took him to his home and cared for
him until his English relatives made financial provision

for his last years.   He died on 17 September 1864, and
was buried in Florence.

III   THE POET-CRITIC AT WORK

The critic of Landor as critic soon finds himself in con-
flict with traditional expectations.   If Landor is to be
justified as a literary critic, then it seems that one
ought to be able to identify his basic principles, describe his method, and place him in a historical critical
tradition.   Landor, however, was a unique literary man,
not a professional literary critic;   and his method for
approaching literature is so much an extension of Landor
the man that attempts to describe it in the usual ways are
doomed either to superficiality or to failure.   Our final
view of him as a convincing literary critic must be determined by the force and substance of his personality and
the enthusiasm and intellectual vigour he brought to his
reading of literature.   To describe his method is to describe his mental behaviour with all of its singular turns
and twists and tastes.   How does Landor behave as a
critic?   He behaves as a highly-trained reader of literature for whom the past and present are one, who respects
his own judgment completely, and who considers himself
especially endowed to judge since he, too, is a practising
poet and prose writer.   He is his own ideal poet-critic,
and he has extraordinary self-confidence.   Thus, he makes
pronouncements;   he makes a-historical comparisons;   he
offers opinions sustained by his likes and dislikes;   and
his sensitivity and temperament are such that he is sus-
ceptible to what we might call sentimental but he would
call the pathetic.   If his love for literature had a
rival, it was painting.   Thus, his imagination is visual.
He thinks in images and metaphors, and his criticism binds
together for us all of the senses as he entices our imagi-
nations either with the pictures he himself creates or
those of artists he chooses to compare.   We may not agree
with his opinions, but we can never read Boccaccio, Petrarch, Milton, Dante, or Spenser again in quite the same
way after reading Landor.
   One definite advantage gained from extracting passages
of literary criticism from Landor's numerous writings is
that his views can finally be examined in chronology and
in perspective, and the elements of his behaviour as
critic which might be deemed critical method can be dis-
cerned.   His method is based upon his justification for
his subjective evaluations.   In the first Imaginary Conversation between Southey and Porson in which the two

poet-critics discuss Wordsworth's new poetry, Porson asks
how they can approach it without 'scales and weights',
that is, without recourse to classical models for comparison. Southey replies: '[Nothing] more is necessary ...
than to interrogate our hearts in what manner they have
been affected. If the ear is satisfied; if at one
moment a tumult is aroused in the breast, and tranquillised at another, with a perfect consciousness of equal
power exerted in both cases; if we rise up from the
perusal of the work with a strong excitement to thought,
to imagination, to sensibility; above all, if we sat down
with some propensities toward evil and walk away with much
stronger toward good' (No. 10). Earlier Porson has
offered advice for the training and practice of literary
critics, and while humorous and ironic, it defines
Landor's own approach:

> I would seriously recommend to the employer of our
> critics, young and old, that he oblige them to pursue a
> course of study such as this: that under the superin-
> tendence of some respectable student from the univer-
> sity, they first read and examine the contents of the
> book; a thing greatly more useful in criticism than is
> generally thought; secondly, that they carefully write
> them down, number them, and range them under their
> several heads; thirdly, that they mark every beauti-
> ful, every faulty, every ambiguous, every uncommon ex-
> pression. Which being completed, that they inquire
> what author, ancient or modern, has treated the same
> subject; that they compare them, first in smaller,
> afterward in larger portions, noting every defect in
> precision and its causes, every excellence and its
> nature; that they graduate these, fixing *plus* and
> *minus*, and designating them more accurately and dis-
> criminately by means of colours, stronger or paler.
> For instance, purple might express grandeur and majesty
> of thought; scarlet, vigour of expression; pink,
> liveliness; green, elegant and equable composition:
> .... The same process may be used where authors have
> not written on the same subject, when those who have
> are wanting, or have touched it but incidentally.
> Thus Addison and Fontenelle, not very like, may be com-
> pared in the graces of style, in the number and degree
> of just thoughts and lively fancies: thus the dia-
> logues of Cicero with those of Plato, his ethics with
> those of Aristoteles, his orations with those of Demos-
> thenes. It matters not if one be found superior to
> the other in this thing, and inferior in that; the
> exercise is taken; the qualities of the two authors

are explored and understood, and their distances laid
down, as geographers speak, from accurate survey (No.
10).

Assuredly, in the context of the Conversation, Porson
is ironically exposing the careless and often virulent
criticism of the early nineteenth-century periodical reviews, particularly the criticism directed towards Wordsworth's poetry which Southey and Porson are about to discuss.   The irony does not, however, detract from the
obvious fact that Landor is here describing both his early
education and his own critical practice, in spite of the
humorous exaggeration implied by the assigning of colours.
In this Conversation, first published in 1823 in the
'London Magazine', Porson is outlining a practice of
criticism which Landor had begun to employ as early as
1800 in his Post-Script to 'Gebir', a judicial, evaluative
criticism evolved from his late eighteenth-century classical education and training.   In the Post-Script Landor
advises young reviewers to practise judicial criticism,
the enquiry into faults and beauties: 'In works of stamp
and character, would it not improve the public taste much
more, if in general a few short passages were selected,
and the defects and excellencies pointed out' (No. 2).
The critic has the right to act as arbiter of taste in
such matters because 'he must surely be above what he
measures, else how can he measure with exactness?   He
must be greater, *ex officio*, than the person he brings
before him;   else how can he stigmatize with censure, or
even dismiss with praise?' (No. 2).   It is Landor's sense
of his own superiority which enables him to practise evaluative criticism throughout his lifetime, and his choice
of the word 'measure' in this early work is significant,
for he constantly measures through classification.
We notice that Porson's advice to critics includes a
very close verbal analysis of the text.   Landor learned
to approach literature in this way during his years at
Rugby.   In his early letters to Southey, responding to
his reading manuscript versions of 'Kehama' and 'Roderick', he extended and developed this kind of analysis,
apt preparation for the poetry of Milton which he treated
in the Imaginary Conversations between Southey and himself.   The importance of the ear in criticism emerges
when Landor responds to Southey's metrical experiments in
'Kehama': 'Is it not reasonable to prefer those kinds of
versification which the best poets have adopted and the
best judges have cherished for the longest time?...
[Furthermore,] poetry is intended to soothe and flatter
our prepossessions, not to wound or irritate or contradict

them' (No. 4). In another letter Landor objects to the
words '"painter"' and '"pourtray"' in the line '"Eye hath
not seen nor painter's hand pourtrayed"' because he has
'an insuperable hatred to such words ... in grave heroic
poetry: add to which, if "eye hath not seen", it is
superfluous to say the rest' (No. 4).

The submission of the text to verbal analysis is fundamental to Landor's approach to the reading and criticism
of literature, but this in itself presents a problem in
methodology. When does Landor's verbal criticism cease
to be that and become marginalia? The two do seem to
overlap for him. He seems more to participate in a text
than merely to read it. Consequently, much of his criticism exists in the form of marginalia: some in books he
once owned, some in his personal correspondence and public
letters, most notably his 'Letter to Emerson' (1856); and
some in his Imaginary Conversations where we would hono-
rifically label it digression. Such marginalia preserves
Landor's wit and humour for us more than his formal writings, as for instance when he finds Dryden's prose 'vigorous and natural' but his poetry partly 'composed in a
brothel, the remainder in a gin-shop' (No. 3). Such is
the highly individualized personal taste of Landor. However much he may desire critics to list faults and beauties and to make formal comparisons, Landor's own criticism is frequently marked by an enthusiasm which links him
with the impressionistic Romantic critics Hazlitt and
Lamb. This tendency can be endearing in him, as for instance when he says: 'I love Goldsmith. The poet never
transgresses into the province of the historian. There
is nothing profound or important in him; but his language
is gracefully familiar, everything about him is sufficiently correct and well-placed, his style is polished
enough, and he invites us by an ingenious and frank simplicity' (No. 3). Such personal enthusiasm did sometimes
mislead Landor, especially in his later years when he
would lavish praise indiscriminately on writers as different as Robert Browning and Felicia Dorthea Hemans.

A certain tension is established in Landor's criticism
between his concept of himself as an ideal critic, his
eighteenth-century notions about how a textual critic
ought to proceed, and his energetic, enthusiastic, imaginative, voracious habit of mind. Even his most successful literary form, the Imaginary Conversation, in which he
attempts to re-create the natural movement of actual conversation, precludes the failure for him of the consistent
application of the kind of thorough and extended critical
analysis suggested in the Porson plan. Landor's thought
is consistently interrupted by numerous digressions. His

success rests in fulfilling the task of the critic as he
describes it in 'The Pentameron':

> *Boccaccio* ... To be useful to as many as possible is
> the especial duty of a critic, and his utility can only
> be attained by rectitude and precision. He walks in a
> garden which is not his own; and he neither must
> gather the blossoms to embellish his discourse, nor
> break the branches to display his strength. Rather
> let him point to what is out of order, and help to
> raise what is lying on the ground (No. 15).

This metaphor of the literary work as a garden in which
the critic as gardener must remove the weeds and briars
without disturbing the 'blossoms' and 'branches' and must
'raise' those beautiful plants that lie 'on the ground' is
a favourite of Landor and figuratively describes his view
that the critic's primary attention should be devoted to
pointing out faults and to praising the beauties of literary works.

Landor's own practice often involves a greater concern
for faults than for beauties. Yet it develops naturally
from the high standards he demanded of himself as a creative artist and the high esteem in which he held verbal
criticism:

> *Alfieri* ... There are those who would persuade us that
> verbal criticism is unfair, and that few poems can re-
> sist it. The truth of the latter assertion by no
> means establishes the former: all good criticism hath
> its foundation on verbal. Long dissertations are
> often denominated criticisms, without one analysis;
> instead of which it is thought enough to say: 'There
> is nothing finer in our language - we can safely rec-
> ommend - imbued with the true spirit - destined to im-
> mortality, &' ('Complete Works', 3, 109).

Although such practice of verbal and textual criticism is
occasionally carried to excessive lengths by Landor, as in
his criticism of Milton's poetry in the Southey and Landor
Conversations, he continually defends verbal criticism,
particularly fault-finding; and when confronted with Dr
Johnson's question: 'What Englishman can take delight in
transcribing passages, which, if they lessen the reputation of Milton, diminish in some degree the honour of our
country?', (22) Landor replies:

> I hope the honour of our country will always rest on
> truth and justice. It is not by concealing what is
> wrong that anything right can be accomplished. There

is no pleasure in transcribing such passages, but there
is great utility.   Inferior writers exercise no interest, attract no notice, and serve no purpose.   Johnson has himself done great good by exposing great
faults in great authors.   His criticism on Milton's
highest work is the most valuable of all his writings (No. 17).

One of the most unique and characteristic features of
Landor's practice as a literary critic is his use of metaphorical criticism.   Vivian Mercier has observed that
'Landor thinks naturally in images, ... [and] if one considers the use of imagery out of place in critical discussion, one had better not read Landor at all'. (23)   Landor's use of imagery in his literary criticism is func-
tional rather than decorative;   that is, his images, similes, and metaphors are integral to his critical thinking
and are not window-dressing.   Furthermore, his metaphorical criticism is given an extra dimension when one reali-
zes that his approach to literature is not unlike his approach to representational art.   After reading a manuscript portion of Southey's 'Roderick', Landor writes
(1809?):   'I have read, and I know not when I shall cease
reading, the incomparable description of Roderick's wanderings and agony [i, 104ff].... The story of Adosinda
is heart-rending [iii, 218ff].   When I have looked long
enough at the figures of great painters, I dwell on the
landscape.   It is only the great ones who make it strikingly peculiar and appropriate.   We wish for more, yet
are conscious that we ought not to wish it.   In the
beginning of the sheet [iii, 1-8], the scene of the pine-
forest is a perfect example of what I mean' (No. 4).
When Landor wishes to blame or praise an author, he
often turns to painting and sculpture for his imagery.
Thus, Dryden is not 'a great poet' because 'there is not
throughout his works one stroke of the sublime or one
touch of the pathetic' (No. 3).   Similarly: 'In Chaucer,
... we recognize the strong homely strokes, the broad and
negligent facility, of a great master' (No. 3).   And the
'chief qualities' of Pindar's poetry are 'rejection of
what is light and minute, disdain of what is trivial, and
selection of those blocks from the quarry which will bear
strong strokes of the hammer and retain all the marks of
the chisel' (No. 20).
On some occasions his choice of imagery is either grotesque or realistic in the extreme.   For example, Landor
closes the first Conversation between Southey and himself
with this grotesque image: 'A rib of Shakespeare would
have made a Milton: the same portion of Milton, all poets

born ever since' (No. 17). One of Landor's most successful realistic descriptions appropriately suggests the
poetry of Crabbe: '[He] wrote with a twopenny nail, and
scratched rough truths and rogues' facts on mud walls....
Young moralized at a distance on some external appearances
of the human heart; Crabbe entered it *on all fours*, and
told the people what an ugly thing it is inside' (No. 16).

Landor is particularly fond of similes and extended
comparisons, and he employs them in a variety of ways.
He may use a simple comparison to praise a certain quality
of a writer: '[Theocritus'] reflections are frequent, but
seasonable; soon over, like the shadows of spring clouds
on flowery meadows, and not hanging heavily upon the
scene, nor depressing the vivacity of the blythe antagonists' (No. 20). Or he may use a simile to excuse a
fault in a favourite author, such as the licentious tales
in Boccaccio's 'Decameron': 'Their levities and gaieties
are like the harmless lightnings of a summer sky in the
delightful regions they were written in' (No. 21). Sometimes he suggests the difference between two writers by
comparing the styles of two painters. For example,
Landor says of Catullus: 'In relation to Virgil, he
[Catullus] stands as Correggio in relation to Raffael: a
richer colourist, a less accurate draftsman; less capable
of executing grand designs, more exquisite in the working
out of smaller' (No. 19). He condemns the use by
Shakespeare of clowns in serious drama by asserting 'a
picture by Morland or Frank Hals ought never to break a
series of frescoes by the hand of Raphael, or of senatorial portraits animated by the sun of Titian' (No. 17).
His image of Dante's great poem is similarly founded in
comparison: 'The *Inferno*, the *Purgatorio*, the *Paradiso*
are pictures from the walls of our churches and chapels
and monasteries, some painted by Giotto and Cimabue, some
earlier. In several of these we detect not only the
cruelty, but likewise the satire and indecency of Dante.
Sometimes there is also his vigour and simplicity, but
oftener his harshness and meagreness and disproportion.
I am afraid the good Alighieri, like his friends the
painters, was inclined to think the angels were created
only to flagellate and burn us; and Paradise only for us
to be driven out of it' (No. 15).

Just as Landor is more successful in pointing out
faults than in noting beauties, so is he especially effective in using simile and metaphor to negative ends, rang-
ing from mild displeasure to fierce indignation. In a
letter to his friend Southey, Landor writes that Wordsworth's 'Lyrical Ballads' have 'sometimes disappointed me,
just as an Æolian harp has done when I expected a note

more' (No. 4).   On another occasion he asserts in a
letter to the Reverend Walter Birch: 'Between genuine
poetry and that of Byron there is the same difference as
between roses and attar of roses.   He smells of the
spirit, not of the flower, you are over-powered and not
satisfied' (No. 5).   When Landor wishes to convey his
view that Tasso's characters are more 'vivid', 'distinct',
and 'interesting' than Virgil's, he creates an extended
comparison: 'The heroes of the "Aeneid" are like the
half-extinct frescoes of Raphael; but what is wanting in
the frescoes of the painter is effaced by time, what is
wanting in the figures of the poet was wanting to his
genius' (No. 11).   Landor's extended comparisons can also
be effective as a weapon of attack in critical discussion,
as demonstrated in his strictures on Voltaire's criticism
of Milton and Shakespeare in the Conversation between the
Abbé Delille and himself: 'He stuck to them as a woodpecker to an old forest-tree, only for the purposes of
picking out what was rotten: he has made the holes deeper
than he found them, and, after all his cries and chatter,
has brought home but scanty sustenance to his starveling
nest' (No. 11).
   Landor even defines in metaphors, approaching one of
the more discussed issues of the day, the distinction between the Fancy and the Imagination, in this way.   In an
Imaginary Conversation between Archdeacon Hare and himself, Hare asks his friend if he can draw 'a strait boundary line between the domains of Fancy and those of Imagination' (No. 18).   Landor's reply contrasts with the
philosophical and metaphysical definitions of these terms
offered by Coleridge in the 'Biographia Literaria'.   He
describes Fancy and Imagination as different aspects of
the same general process through personification:

   Fancy is Imagination in her youth and adolescence.
   Fancy is always excursive; Imagination, not seldom, is
   sedate.   It is the business of Imagination, in her
   maturity, to create and animate such Beings as are
   worthy of her plastic hand; certainly not by invisible
   wires to put marionettes in motion, nor to pin butterflies on blotting-paper.   Vigorous thought, elevated
   sentiment, just expression, development of character,
   power to bring man out from the secret haunts of his
   soul and to place him in strong outline against the
   sky, belong to the Imagination.   Fancy is thought to
   dwell among the Faeries and their congeners (No. 18).

Landor the critic and Landor the man meet in his metaphors, and much that is memorable in his criticism derives

from this. It is especially notable when metaphor be-
comes epigram, as in his observation that 'the strength of
[Dr] Johnson is the strength of twists and knots' (No. 5).
His images are likewise powerful when they convince us
that he has captured the essential quality of his subject.
For instance, he summarizes his preference for Scott over
Byron: 'Give me his massy claymore, and keep in the cabinet or the boudoir the jewelled hilt of the oriental dirk'
(No. 16). He compares Dante's 'Divine Comedy' with
Ariosto's 'Orlando Furioso': 'In the gloomy deserts of
Dante, some scenes are stupendous both from their grandeur
and their solitude, and lose nothing of their distinctness
by their elevation; in Ariosto, if there are a few misshapen ornaments, yet every thing around them is smiling
in sunshine and fertility!' (No. 3). And finally he re-
creates for us the atmosphere of Spenser's 'Faery Queene':
'Spenser's is a spacious but somewhat low chamber, hung
with rich tapestry, on which the figures are mostly disproportioned, but some of the faces are lively and beautiful; the furniture is part creaking and worm-eaten, part
fragrant with cedar and sandalwood and aromatic gums and
balsams; every table and mantelpiece and cabinet is covered with gorgeous vases, and birds, and dragons, and
houses in the air' (No. 16).

IV LANDOR AMONG HIS FAVOURITES

One can analyse certain aspects of Landor's approach as a
practising critic through a general survey of his comments
as they come to us throughout his various writings. But
in order to gain an understanding of how his method func-
tions in conjunction with his basic criteria for determin-
ing great poetry from mediocre, we must look to those
poets whom he chose most often to discuss and whose works
he has celebrated in extended prose pieces. Among them
we find Boccaccio, Dante, Petrarch, Spenser, Shakespeare,
and Milton. Although he constantly refers to the classics, to Homer, Aeschylus, Pindar, Sophocles, Virgil,
Horace, and Ovid for his touchstones in comparing poets,
to only Catullus and Theocritus does he give full studies;
and those were written in response to the solicitation of
John Forster. Wordsworth and Southey among his contemporaries receive detailed criticism; and Southey he over-
values through the sentiments of friendship,and Wordsworth
he treats unjustly in his later criticism through personal
dislike. Landor does not ignore the other poets of his
period. Indeed, he says of them 'our field of poetry at
the present time is both wider and better cultivated than

it has ever been' ('Complete Works', 6, 34), and he pays
poetic tribute to Keats, Shelley, and Browning along with
Southey and Wordsworth.   Yet if we wish to understand
Landor's definition of the sublime and the pathetic, of
the truly great and the truly disgusting in poetry, then
we must turn to those writers he singled out most for
praise and for blame.

Among the Italian writers who most engage Landor's attention, Boccaccio is his favourite.   He ranks him second
only to Dante and considers the 'Divine Comedy' and the
'Decameron' 'the two most admirable works the continent
has produced from the restoration of learning to the
present day' (No. 21).   Landor wrote two Imaginary Conversations in which Boccaccio appears as an interlocutor,
and in both Boccaccio tells a tale that reflects the tone,
style, and subject matter of the *novelle* in the 'Decameron'.   Landor is particularly delighted and moved by
those *novelle* that appeal to his sense of humour and his
feelings of pity and tenderness; but he objects, as did
many of his contemporaries, to the licentious and immoral
aspects of the *novelle*.   He especially criticizes Boccaccio for the over-realistic description of Lisabetta
'cutting off the head of her [dead] lover, "*as well as she
could*" with a clasp-knife' (No. 15).   Yet Landor's enthusiasm for Boccaccio overcomes his few dislikes, and he
asserts through Petrarch in 'The Pentameron' that there is
'more character, more nature, more invention, [in the
"Decameron"] than [in] either modern or ancient Italy, or
than [in] Greece, from whom she derived her whole inheri-
tance' (No. 15).   Landor's appreciation for Boccaccio was
voiced by many of his contemporaries.   Coleridge, for
instance, praised 'the happy art of narration, and the
still greater merit of a depth and fineness in the workings of the passions' and 'the wild and imaginative character of the situations'. (24)   Hazlitt's enthusiasms
appear to match Landor's: 'The only writer among the
Italians I can pretend to any knowledge of, is Boccaccio,
and of him I cannot express half my admiration.   His
story of the Hawk I could read and think of from day to
day, just as I would look at a picture of Titian's!' (25)
And one of Keats's most popular poems, 'Isabella or, the
Pot of Basil' (1820), is based on Boccaccio's fifth tale
of the Fourth Day.

When Landor turns to Dante's 'Divine Comedy', he finds
little that 'delights' and much that 'disgusts'.   Dante
is, for Landor, the 'great master of the disgusting' (No.
15).   Although he remarks critically on all three parts
of Dante's poem, most of his criticism, like that of his
contemporaries, is devoted to the 'Inferno'.   Landor

acknowledges the beauties of Dante's versification and
recognizes him as the father of the Italian language;
however, his praise is reserved almost exclusively for the
Paolo and Francesca of Rimini and the Ugolino episodes in
the 'Inferno'. Appropriately, it is Boccaccio who
quotes Francesca's description of the sinful lovers' fall,
comments on Dante's poetic artistry, and concludes: 'Such
a depth of intuitive judgment, such a delicacy of perception, exists not in any other work of human genius; and
from an author who, on almost all occasions, in this part
of the work, betrays a deplorable want of it' (No. 15).
Landor also praises through Boccaccio 'the simple, vigorous, clear narration' of Count Ugolino's horrible fate,
though he is repelled to find 'the features of Ugolino
reflected full in Dante' (No. 15). Indignation and
hatred have no place in great literature for Landor, and
this belief partially accounts for his dislike of most of
the 'Inferno'. With the exceptions of Paolo, Francesca,
and Ugolino among Dante's shades in Hell, Landor finds
that 'no heart swells here, either for overpowered valour
or for unrequited love. In the shades alone, but in the
shades of Homer, does Ajax rise to his full loftiness: in
the shades alone, but in the shades of Virgil, is Dido the
arbitress of our tears' (No. 15).

Landor's weaknesses as a literary critic are evident
when he confronts a symbolic poem like Dante's 'Divine
Comedy'. His a-historical approach prevents him from
viewing the poet and his poem in their proper historical
and literary perspectives, and his application of classical standards derived from Greek epic and tragedy cause
him to condemn the poem for its 'loose and shallow foundation, ... its unconnectedness; its want of manners, of
passion, of action, consistently and uninterruptedly at
work toward a distinct and worthy purpose' (No. 15). His
rejection of metaphysical systems and speculations in
poetry informs this viewpoint, but so also does his general distaste for allegory. Landor believes that allegory
should teach through delight, and in his opinion neither
Spenser's 'Faery Queene' nor Dante's 'Divine Comedy' do
this. He asserts 'the "Faery Queene" is rambling and
discontinuous, full of every impropriety, and utterly deficient in a just conception both of passion and of character' (No. 3). How similar is this to his criticism of
Dante's great work. And just as he finds the images in
Spenser's 'Faery Queene' disgusting, so does he dislike
much of Dante's realistic imagery. Landor concludes that
in the light of Dante's 'hatred against the whole human
race!', his 'exultation and merriment at eternal and immitigable sufferings!', that he 'can not but consider the

"Inferno" as the most immoral and impious book that was
ever written' (No. 15). Spenser with his 'lowness of
spirits and a peevish whine that he could not have every
thing he wanted' (No. 3) fares little better. Several of
Landor's criticisms of Dante were expressed by such contemporaries as Coleridge, Hazlitt, Hunt, and Wordsworth,
so he is in part expressing views current at the
time. (26) His personal dislike of the metaphysical,
however, informs his judgment consistently; and it prevents him from appreciating the high beauties in the works
of Plato and Wordsworth as well.

Francesco Petrarch speaks in two of Landor's Imaginary
Conversations (1829) and in 'The Pentameron' (1837).
Landor considers him 'certainly the very best man that
ever was a very vain one' (No. 21). He was moved to
present a copy of Petrarch's Sonnets inscribed with some
lines of verse (see 'Complete Works', 15, 370) to his beloved Ianthe, Jane Sophia Swift, prior to her marriage;
and Landor's biographical and critical essay, Francesco
Petrarca (1843), is written with a wit and compassion sug-
gesting that his own frustration in love and domestic
tragedy enabled him to sympathize with the famous lover of
Laura. Landor, indeed, seems to recognize the value of
such frustration when he notes that 'perhaps it is well
for those who delight in poetry that [Laura] was inflexible and obdurate; for the sweetest song ceases when the
feathers have lined the nest' (No. 21). Landor writes
mostly of Petrarch's Italian sonnets in his essay. Although he considers the sonnet an inferior form of poetry,
he does allow Boccaccio to remark in 'The Pentameron' that
the sonnet 'seems peculiarly adapted to the languor of a
melancholy and despondent love, the rhymes returning and
replying to every plaint and every pulsation' (No. 15).
Landor's primary demand for the writer of poetry is that
he feel the emotion he expresses, and he criticizes Petrarch's 'Rime' for their occasional failure in sincerity.
Landor's criticisms, presented as marginal comments on
faults and beauties, are concerned with anything that
either interferes with the conveyance of Petrarch's emotion in the 'Rime' or with anything that disrupts the harmony of the verse. Thus he criticizes catalogues of
names; quibbles in the midst of serious thoughts; extravagant ideas, descriptions, invocations, and conceits;
redundancy of words; repeated rhymes; puns on Laura's
name (laurel); and intricate verse forms such as the
sestina. While admittedly Landor's fault-finding criticism of Petrarch's poetry is in the tradition of the in-
fluential early nineteenth-century literary historian
Sismonde de'Sismondi who discusses the Italian poet in his

'De la littérature du Midi de l'Europe' (1813), Landor's
wit, heart, and ear give his analysis of the 'Rime' its
unique flavour. We see how genuinely he responded to
Petrarch in his final comment in the essay about a moving
passage from 'The Triumph of Death': 'He who, the twentieth time, can read unmoved this canzone, never has experienced a love which could not be requited, and never
has deserved a happy one' (No. 21).

Landor seems to have submitted those writers whose
spirit, temperament, and emotions most moved him to his
own unique form of verbal and textual analysis. This is
definitely true of John Milton whom Landor idealized both
as a great Republican and as a poet. He is strongly
attracted to the harmonious quality of Milton's blank
verse of which he said: 'I had read the "Iliad" twice
over before I had well studied "Paradise Lost". Then
the hexameter, even Homer's, fell upon my ear as a ring
of fine bells after a full organ' (No. 7). Landor's remarks on his literary and political hero are scattered
throughout his numerous writings, yet such hero-worship
in no wise blinded Landor to what he considered to be
faults in Milton's poetry. In the two Imaginary Conversations between Southey and himself, published forty-eight
years after he had first praised Milton in the 1798 Preface to 'Gebir', the two poet-critics meet in order to
devote an entire day to collecting 'all the graver faults'
they can find in this English poet, 'not in the spirit of
Johnson, but in our own' (No. 17). This does not imply
that Landor was unmoved by Johnson's critical biography of
Milton which elicited such a 'massive response' from other
Romantic poets and critics. (27)   Landor took issue with
Johnson's criticisms of Milton's blank verse, but he
agreed with Johnson's dislike of the allegorical Sin and
Death and the non-materiality of Satan. As we might also
expect, Landor accepted Johnson's method of fault-finding
as essential to any critical estimate of an author, and he
considered Johnson's 'Milton' to be 'the most valuable of
all his writings' (No. 17).

Southey and Landor proceed in the Conversations, each
with his own text of Milton's poetry, taking turns reading
individual lines and passages before commenting upon them.
We soon become aware that although Landor has created two
speakers, both are expressing his views. Landor's response to this reading of Milton is auditory. Whatever
pleases his ear is a beauty, and his criticism is replete
with expressions such as 'beautiful line', 'admirable
pause', 'a flood of harmony', and 'a torrent of eloquence'. Conversely, whatever displeases Landor's ear is
a fault. Much of the verbal criticism is, therefore,

devoted to those aspects of Milton's blank verse that
either lessen the harmony or that produce prosaic lines -
to rhymes, rhythms, wordiness, puns, Latinisms, ungramma-
tical expressions, and catalogues of names.   Landor does
not hesitate to condemn a fault even in the midst of an
otherwise harmonious passage; nor is he afraid to take
issue with Milton's commentators in the notes of the
volume he has before him, particularly the infamous
Richard Bentley.   Indeed, Landor has the audacity to
offer his own emendation for improving Milton's verse, a
practice provoking De Quincey's humorous attention in an
article entitled Milton *versus* Southey and Landor. (28)
The emendations Landor suggests include the deletion of
lines that either deaden the harmony or contribute nothing
to the meaning; alteration of punctuations either to
remove confusion over meaning or to improve the scansion
of a line.   Almost all of these suggested emendations are
derived from the ear of the poet-critic.

Landor's criticisms of Milton do range beyond the
verbal and textual.   Among Milton's other faults are his
historical anacronisms, his pedantic display of knowledge,
his use of unseemly metaphors, and his placing coarse in-
vectives on women in Adam's mouth that are more appropriate to the poet than to his character.   Landor credits
Milton, however, with the appropriateness of certain descriptions and with imaginative metaphorical power.   He
also gives special praise to the sublime descriptions of
Satan (i, 589-621) and the approach of the Son of God
(vi, 760-84); and he asserts that with Eve 'the great
poet is always greatest at this beatific vision' (No.
17).   He is entranced by the subtle psychology of guilt
evident in Eve's behaviour after eating the forbidden
fruit, and he finds 'a brief union of the sublime and the
pathetic' at the close of Book Twelve when Adam and Eve
are led out of Paradise by the Angel Michael (No. 17).

However much Landor admired Milton, as he wrote to
Forster in 1850, '"Othello" had agonized my heart before
Milton had reacht my ear' (No. 7).   Landor placed
Shakespeare far above all other English poets, yet he
devotes little extended criticism to him.   One of his
most developed comments occurs, curiously enough, within
his review of Doering's revised edition of Catullus'
'Carmina', and the essential contribution of the review
for Landor's Shakespearean criticism is in his application
to Shakespeare of the qualities which constitute greatness
in a poet.   These qualities are 'creativeness, constructiveness, the sublime, the pathetic' (No. 19).   Shakespeare is the great exemplar of these characteristics.
His ability to take Hamlet and Ophelia and Othello and

Desdemona and transform his given into new worlds demonstrates his creative and constructive qualities.   Landor
also considers Shakespeare capable of great moments of
sublimity and pathos.

No two terms used by Landor are perhaps more difficult
to define than the sublime and the pathetic.   The 'sublime', he asserts in the essay on Catullus, is essential
for great poetry; the 'pathetic' may be 'the very summit
of sublimity', though it is usually found in the poets of
the second order since 'tears are more easily drawn forth
than souls are raised' (No. 19).   Landor, like Dr Johnson
in his 'Milton', finds sublimity to be the prevailing
characteristic of 'Paradise Lost'.   Both critics note
examples of two forms of sublimity: the rhetorical sublime, produced by heightened imagery, style, and harmony
of the verse; and the emotional sublime, created by an
awareness of the awful greatness in man and nature.
Landor, unlike Johnson, finds the pathetic elevated to
sublimity in Book Twelve of 'Paradise Lost'. (29)

We come best to know what Landor meant by the sublime
and the pathetic from his accounts of the scenes in literature which moved him most, such as the 'impassioned,
and therefor so sublime ... last hour of Dido in the
Aeneid' (No. 19).   He finds other examples of the pathetic sublime in Theseus' abandonment of Ariadne in Catullus' poem lxiv, the expulsion of Adam and Eve from Paradise, and the scene between Achilles and Priam in the
'Iliad'.   Often his response is to the pathetic alone, a
response we should consider sentimental today.   He found
the Little Nell of Dickens' 'The Old Curiosity Shop' to
be as interesting and pathetic a heroine as either Juliet
or Desdemona, and he wept over the story of Elinor
Forester in Mary Lamb's 'Mrs Leicester's School' (No. 6).
One can only speculate within the confines of this brief
introduction upon the emotional forces motivating Landor's
subjective responses to certain scenes in literature.   It
does not seem unwarranted, however, to observe that Landor
- a man who left home and mother to attend school at an
early age, who never enjoyed a close relationship with his
father, who knew only idealized and unrequited love, and
who suffered all the indignities of domestic disharmony
including rejection by his own children - was moved to
tears by those scenes in literature which most dramatical-
ly express the inadequacies of his own life.   These he
called either the pathetic or the pathetic sublime, and
to the latter he offered his highest praise.

V   AFTERWORD

Landor's interest in literature is that of an epicure, and
quite properly one of his favourite Imaginary Conversations is that between Epicurus, the Greek philosopher, and
two of his female disciples, Leontion and Ternissa.   Epicurus is an idealized portrait of Landor himself, and it
is Landor who speaks when Epicurus informs his young
friends: 'All the imitative arts have delight for the
principal object: the first of these is poetry: the
highest of poetry is tragic' (No. 14).   Literature is
life to Landor, and the characters of Achilles and Priam,
Dido and Aeneas, Satan and Eve, and Othello and Desdemona
were as real to him as the paintings that hung on his
walls in his villa outside Florence and the deep and
abiding friendships he formed with such men and women as
Robert Southey, John Forster, Charles Dickens, Robert and
Elizabeth Barrett Browning, and the Countess of Blessington.   The very restrained and classical quality of his
verse and short dramatic Imaginary Conversations suggests
the emotional man behind them, and perhaps the poet
Yeats's great admiration for Landor is partly due to his
recognition of the battle between the emotional artist
and the suggestive though impersonal work of art: the man
and the mask: 'Landor has been examined in "Per Amica
Silentia Lunae".   The most violent of men, he uses his
intellect to disengage a visionary image of perfect sanity
("Mask" at Phase 3) seen always in the most serene and
classic art imaginable'. (30)
    We do not turn to Landor today in search of a new ap-
proach to literature which will foster volumes of re-
evaluations.   We turn to Landor for his living appreciation of all he read and contemplated.   So long as we
cherish learning;   so long as harmony in poetry is important to us;   so long as we expect poetry to express the
greatest ideas and the most sincere emotions;   and so long
as we value singularity of response, confidence in informed opinion, and an epigrammatical, imagistic turn of
mind;   so long will Landor have an important place for us
in literary criticism, not as a professional literary
critic, but as a most unique and impressive literary man.

NOTES

1   T.S. Eliot, 'The Use of Poetry and the Use of Criti-
    cism', 2nd ed., London, 1964, 88.
2   Ezra Pound, 'ABC of Reading', London, 1934, 174.
3   W.B. Yeats, 'A Vision', rev. and amp., London, 1937,
    140-5.

4   'Robert Browning and Julia Wedgwood, a Broken Friend-
    ship as Revealed by Their Letters', ed. Richard Curle,
    New York, 1937, 78.

5   R.H. Super, The Fire of Life, 'Cambridge Review', 86
    (16 January 1965), 172.

6   Malcolm Elwin, 'Landor: A Replevin', London, 1958,
    360.

7   'Diary, Reminiscences, and Correspondence of Henry
    Crabb Robinson', ed. Thomas Sadler, 3rd ed., London,
    1872, 2, 100-2.

8   R.W. Emerson, 'English Traits', London, 1856, 3, 5.

9   R.M. Milnes, 'Monographs, Personal and Social',
    London, 1873, 64.

10 'Westminster Review', 1 (April 1824), 431-53.

11 See 'Edinburgh Review', 40 (March 1824), 67-92, and
    'Quarterly Review', 30 (January 1824), 508-19.

12 'British and Foreign Review', 7 (October 1838), 501-
    21.

13 'Dictionary of National Biography', sv. Walter Savage
    Landor.

14 George Saintsbury, 'A History of Criticism and Lite-
    rary Taste in Europe', 3rd ed., Edinburgh and London,
    1917, 3, 276, 279.

15 Oliver Elton, 'A Survey of English Literature 1780-
    1830', London, 1912, 2, 40.

16 See ch. II, 'La critique littéraire', 189-260.

17 Stanley T. Williams, Walter Savage Landor as a Critic
    of Literature, 'PMLA', 38 (December 1923), 906, 909.

18 'Fragmentary Remains, Literary and Scientific, of Sir
    Humphrey Davy', ed. John Davy, London, 1858, 48.

19 'Westminster Review', 1 (April 1824), 433.

20 See Alice LaVonne Prasher, Walter Savage Landor's
    'Imaginary Conversations': A Critical Edition of the
    First Eight Conversations in Volume One ... 1824,
    unpublished PhD dissertation, Northwestern University,
    1966, and 'Selected Imaginary Conversations of Lite-
    rary Men and Statesmen, by Walter Savage Landor', ed.
    Charles L. Proudfit, Lincoln, Nebraska, 1969.

21 See R.H. Super, Landor and the 'Satanic School',
    'Studies in Philology', 42 (October 1945), 793-810.

22 Milton in 'Lives of the English Poets', ed. George B.
    Hill, Oxford, 1905, 1, 181.

23 Vivian Mercier, The Future of Landor Criticism, 'Some
    British Romantics: A Collection of Essays', eds J.V.
    Logan, J.E. Jordan and N. Frye, Columbus, 1966, 55.

24 'The Literary Remains of Samuel Taylor Coleridge', ed.
    H.N. Coleridge, London, 1836, 1, 82.

25 'The Complete Works of William Hazlitt', ed. P.P.
    Howe, London and Toronto, 1931, 12, 227.

26   See Werner P. Frederich, 'Dante's Fame Abroad: 1350-
     1850', Rome, 1950, 241-6, 270-4.
27   See 'The Romantics on Milton', ed. J.A. Wittreich, Jr,
     Cleveland and London, 1970, ix.
28   See 'De Quincey as Critic', ed. John E. Jordan, London
     and Boston, Routledge & Kegan Paul, 1973, 465-82.
29   See Jean H. Hagstrum, 'Samuel Johnson's Literary
     Criticism', Minneapolis and London, 1952, 137-9.
30   Yeats, 'A Vision' (1937), 144-5.

Note on the Text

Selections from the Imaginary Conversations, periodical
reviews, public letters, and poetry are reprinted from the
last texts published during Landor's lifetime. Two exceptions are the 1798 Preface to 'Gebir' and a poem on the
death of Charles Lamb that first appeared in a letter to
Lady Blessington dated 10-13 April? 1835. Since Landor
revised many of his published works, particularly the
'Imaginary Conversations' (1824-9), before reprinting them
in the collected 'Works of Walter Savage Landor' (1846)
and in several later volumes, I have compared my texts
with earlier versions and noted the more important changes
in the headnotes and annotations. Selections from the
private letters and writings unpublished prior to the
author's death are reproduced from the most authoritative
texts. Salient bibliographical information is provided
in the headnotes.

Because Landor's published writings have appeared under
a variety of circumstances and conditions, I have made the
following textual alterations to achieve greater clarity
and uniformity. Landor's eccentric spellings have been
normalized in all the selections except for his personal
correspondence and those poems published after 1846.
Quotation marks have been regularized with punctuation,
proper names have been capitalized when necessary, and
obvious typographical errors have been silently corrected.
Errata lists have been consulted. I have, however, retained Landor's use of capitals and italics for emphasis.
To conform with practice in this series, however, titles
have been given in roman in quotation marks, not italics.
His sources and references have been replaced when my
notes provide more complete information; his notes to the
text, when deleted, are recorded in the annotations; and
omissions within the selections are indicated by ellipses
preceded or followed by line spaces where the omission is

substantial.   Except for these changes and omissions, the texts are faithfully reproduced.

I have employed interpolated material set off by brackets in a variety of ways.   Letter dates are those provided by the editor of the letters;   undated letters are indicated by a question mark.   Untitled Landor poems are given titles.   Landor's notes to the text are signed with the capital L;   my annotations are unsigned.   At times I have provided transitions and/or clarifications within the body of the text and within quotations.   Misquoted material is usually indicated immediately after the error;   if the error is extensive, the original quotation is given in the annotations.   Brackets are also used to set off translations of foreign languages, their sources, and, in certain instances, the translator's initials.

Landor's writings are replete with quotations from foreign languages, particularly Greek, Latin, and Italian. I have provided literal translations of unfamiliar phrases and all lines from foreign literatures that the author quotes in his texts and notes.   All translations from Greek and Latin works are taken from the Loeb Classical Library except for those by Professor Hazel E. Barnes (H.B. in text).   All translations from Dante's 'Divina Commedia' are by John D. Sinclair.   Translations from Petrarch's 'Rime' are by various individuals and are indicated by their initials in the text: Joseph Auslander, Lady Dacre, Major Macgregor, James Wheelock, Ernest H. Wilkins, and Thomas Wyatt.   T.H. Croker, translator of Ariosto's 'Orlando Furioso', and Francis Winwar, translator of Boccaccio's 'Decameron', are also credited by initials following their translations in the text. Translations from the French are my own.

Since I make numerous references to the Landor biographies by John Forster and Robert H. Super and to the Welby and Wheeler edition of Landor's 'Complete Works', short forms of reference are used for these throughout.

Prose Commentaries

I Preface to 'Gebir'

1798, 1803

In July 1798 Landor published 'Gebir', a long Heroic Idyll
written in blank verse.   Two of the earliest examples of
Landor's literary criticism surround the publication of
this poem.   Its Preface announces a poetic aim and practice sharing the revolutionary mood of Wordsworth and
Coleridge, for in this poem he rejects the rhymed verse
forms and poetic diction fashionable at the close of the
eighteenth century which he himself employed in a volume
of juvenilia, 'The Poems of Walter Savage Landor' (1795).
Of these early poems Landor remarks: 'Before I was twenty
years of age I had imprudently sent into the world a
volume, of which I was soon ashamed.   It every-where met
with as much commendation as was proper, and generally
more.   For, tho' the structure was feeble, the lines were
fluent: the rhymes shewed habitual ease, and the personi-
fications fashionable taste....   So early in life, I had
not discovered the error into which we were drawn by the
Wartons.   I was then in raptures with what I now despise'
(Post-Script to 'Gebir', 'Complete Works', 13, 352-3).
His intention in 'Gebir' is to write a different type of
poem, one 'descriptive of men and manners', composed in
blank verse 'because there never was a poem in rhyme that
grew not tedious in a thousand lines'.
     When 'Gebir' was reviewed unfavourably in the 'Monthly
Review' (February 1800), Landor responded with a Post-
Script denouncing the unfair criticism of a reviewer who
had not read his poem with sufficient care, asserting his
independence from conventional poetic diction, defending
his poetic practice, and offering advice and instruction
to his adversary.   His call to his own defence is not
unlike Wordsworth's in the Preface to the second edition
of the 'Lyrical Ballads' (1800).
     Although Landor suppressed the publication of the Post-
Script in 1800 and it was not published during his life-

time, many of the thoughts expressed here found their way
into several of the Imaginary Conversations. Indeed,
certain of these became preoccupations of Landor: his
great admiration for Milton, his denunciation of irrespon-
sible critics, his suggestion of a critical method for
those who seek to improve the public taste, and his definition of what constitutes successful literary borrowing.

The 1798 text of the Preface to 'Gebir' is reprinted
here since several important critical remarks are omitted
from the revised 1803 Preface to the second edition of
'Gebir'. The selection from the Post-Script to 'Gebir',
which is about a third of the whole, is reprinted from
the 1933 text edited by Stephen Wheeler in 'Complete
Works', 13, 350-63.

It may possibly save some trouble, and obviate some
errors, if I take a cursory review of my own performance.
Not that I would prevent others from criticising it, but
that I may explain at large, and state distinctly, its
origin and design. This Poem, the fruit of Idleness and
Ignorance - for had I been a botanist or mineralogist it
never had been written - was principally written in Wales.
The subject was taken, or rather the shadow of the subject, from a wild and incoherent, but fanciful, Arabian
Romance. On the shelf of a circulating library, I met
with a Critique on the various Novels of our Country. (1)
Though the work itself had nothing remarkable in it,
except indeed we reckon remarkable the pertness and petulance of female criticism, yet it presented to me, at the
conclusion, the story of 'Gebirus and Charoba'. (2)   A
Poem, like mine, descriptive of men and manners, should
never be founded totally on fiction. But that which is
originally fiction may cease in effect to be so: - the
tears of Andromache are as precious as those of
Sapphira. (3)

I have availed myself merely of the names, and taken
but few bare circumstances. I have followed no man
closely; nor have I turned from my road because another
stood in it: though perhaps I have momentarily, in passing, caught the object that attracted him. I have written in blank verse, because there never was a poem in
rhyme that grew not tedious in a thousand lines. My
choice is undoubtedly the most difficult of the two: for,
how many have succeeded in rhyme, in the structure at
least; how few comparatively in blank verse. There is
Akenside, there is Armstrong, there is, above all, the
poet of our republic. (4)   But in most others we meet
with stiffness instead of strength, and weakness instead
of ease. I am aware how much I myself stand in need of

favor.   I demand some little from Justice;   I entreat
much more from Candor.   If there are, now in England, ten
men of taste and genius who will applaud my Poem, I
declare myself fully content: I will call for a division;
I shall count a majority.

NOTES

1 Clara Reeve, 'The Progress of Romance' (1785).
2 For a discussion of Landor's use of Clara Reeve's
   History of Charoba Queen of Egypt in the writing of
   'Gebir', see Super, 'Landor', 42.
3 Andromache, in Greek mythology, is the Trojan woman
   whose father, brothers, and husband Hector were slain
   by Achilles in the Trojan war, and whose son, Astyanax, was put to death by the victorious Greeks after
   the fall of Troy.   Sapphira, wife of Ananias, fell
   dead at the rebuke of St Peter about three hours after
   her husband suffered a similar fate (Acts 5:1-10).
4 Mark Akenside (1721-70), author of 'Pleasures of the
   Imagination' (1757);   John Armstrong (1709-79), author
   of 'Art of Preserving Health' (1744);   and John Milton
   (1608-74), author of 'Paradise Lost' (1667), 'Paradise
   Regained' (1671), and 'Samson Agonistes' (1671).

2 Post-Script to 'Gebir'
1800, 1933

See headnote to No. 1.

'Gebir' in different quarters has been differently received. I allude not to those loyal critics, who, recently mounted on their city-war-horse, having borrowed
the portly boots and refurbished the full-bottomed perukes
of the ancient French chevaliers, are foremost to oppose
the return of that traitor, whom, while he was amongst
them, Englishmen called Freedom, but now they have expel-
led him, Anarchy: since, the very first 'Reviews' of
this Association were instituted, not merely for parade
but for hostility: not for exercise, correctness, and
precision, so adventurous and impetuous were these con-
scripts, but for actual and immediate battle. (1)   The
'Critical' and 'Monthly', (2) as being of the old establishment, are those on which at present I would fix attention.   In respect to 'Gebir', the one perhaps is conducted by a partial, but certainly by a masterly, hand. (3)
It objects, and indeed with reason, to a temporary and
local obscurity, which I have not been able, or I have not
been willing, or I have not been bold enough, to remove:
but never on the whole, since its first institution, has a
poem been more warmly praised.   The other's account is
short: containing one quotation and two mis-statements.
'That the poem was nothing more than the version of an
Arabic tale; and that the author, not content with borrowing the expressions, had made the most awkward attempts
to imitate the phraseology of Milton.' (4)
   The Review is not before me.   I believe I have softened, but I have not perverted, nor have I deteriorated
his style.   No man would make or meditate so rash inde-
fensible an attack, unless he were certain that, if not
already stationed there, he could speedily drop into

obscurity.   I repeat to him in answer, what I before asserted in my preface, that, so far from a *translation*,
there is not a single sentence, nor a single sentiment, in
common with the tale.   Some characters are drawn more at
large, some are brought out more prominent, and several
are added.   I have not changed the scene, which would
have distorted the piece, but every line of appropriate
description, and every shade of peculiar manners, is originally and entirely my own.
   Now, whether this gentleman has or has not read the
poem, whether he has or has not read the romance, his
account is equally false and equally malicious.   For the
romance is in English, therefore he could have read it;
the poem is in English, and therefore he could have compared it.   There is no disgrace in omitting to read them:
the disgrace is, either in pretending to have done what he
had not done, or in assuming a part which he was incompetent to support.   But there *is* a disgrace in omitting to
read Milton;   there is a disgrace in forgetting him.   The
critic has not perused or not remembered him: it would be
impossible, if he had, that he should accuse me of borrowing his expressions.   I challenge him to produce them.
If indeed I *had* borrowed them, so little should I have re-
alized by the dangerous and wild speculation, that I might
have composed a better poem and not have been a better
poet.   But I feared to break open, for the supply of my
games or for the maintenance of my veteran heroes, the
sacred treasury of the great republican.   Although I
might enjoy, not indeed the extorted, but the unguarded
praise of an enemy, if my vanity could stoop so low and
could live on so little, - of an enemy who, throughout so
long a journey, and after so many speeches, and those on
such various occasions, pertinaciously took me for Milton
- I will add, for the information of my young opponent,
what a more careful man would conceal, but what in his
present distress will relieve him greatly, that this,
which amongst the vulgar and thoughtless might currently
pass for praise, is really none at all.   For, the language of 'Paradise Lost' ought not to be the language of
'Gebir'.   There should be the softened air of remote antiquity, not the severe air of unapproachable sanctity.
I devoutly offer up my incence at the shrine of Milton.
Woe betide the intruder that would steal its jewels!   It
requires no miracle to detect the sacrilege.   The crime
will be found its punishment.   The venerable saints, and
still more holy personages, of Rapheal or Michael-Angelo,
might as consistently be placed among the Bacchanals and
Satyrs, bestriding the goats and bearing the vases of
Poussin, (5) as the resemblance of that poem, or any of
its component parts, could be introduced in mine.

I have avoided high-sounding words.   I have attempted
to throw back the gross materials, and to bring the figures forward....

   After all, I do not wonder that they [the critics]
barked at 'Gebir' - he came disguised and in tatters.
Still there was nothing to authorize the impertinence with
which the publication was treated by the Monthly Reviewer.
These are not the faults which he complains of; though
these might, without his consciousness, have first occasioned his ill-humour.   I pity his want of abilities, and
I pardon his excess of insolence.   The merit is by no
means small of a critic who speaks with modesty.   For,
his time being chiefly occupied, at first, in works funda-
mentally critical, at least if we suppose him desirous to
learn before he is ambitious to *teach*, he thinks when he
has attained their expressions and brevity, he has attained their solidity and profoundness.   He must surely
be above what he measures, else how can he measure with
exactness?   He must be greater, *ex officio*, than the
person he brings before him; else how can he stigmatize
with censure, or even dismiss with praise?....

   I should rest awhile here, if my sole or even principal
object were chastisement or correction.   But I intend to
give advice, and I hope instruction.   It is possible too
that I may present an opportunity of making some repri-
sals.   For, having overthrown the works of an enemy, and
offered him battle on *my* ground, I now venture forth and
offer it on *his*.   Let him detect any error of judgment,
or any corruption of taste, in plans and observations entirely new, as mine are, and I will forgive him the blun-
ders which he has committed, for the most part rather
through stupidity than haste, and without the excuse of
novelty.
   It is the custom of such people, and a very convenient
one it is, to speak in general language: it saves them
much trouble, and gives them much importance.   In passing
sentence they are chancellors at once, they would become
mere barristers by examination and enquiry.   It has been
observed, I think, that almost every writer has taken up
some word or other which he cherishes with peculiar fondness.   The word '*considerable*' (6) is the favourite here:
it is the stoutest ally of ignorance and indifference, and
is the most insurmountable enemy of acuteness and precision.   '*This volume possesses considerable merit.*'   Such
decisions have I often witnessed on productions the most

strongly marked - decisions not very improper, though
rather too favorable, for poems like 'Leonidas', (7) &c.
- where the faults are rare and the beauties faint, but
where is an even tenor of language, by courtesy and common
acception held poetic, and an equal dilation of appropriate thoughts, hardly anywhere trivial and nowhere exquisite.   But in works of stamp and character, would it not
improve the public taste much more, if in general a few
short passages were selected, and the defects and excellencies pointed out.   Somewhat should be allowed rather
above desert than under it, unless the boon be withheld to
check the first prancings of presumption, wantonly and
dangerously pushing on, ungoaded by injury or severity.
But particularly should evidence and instances be adduced
where accusations of plagiarism are preferred.   Plagiarism, imitation, and allusion, three shades, that soften
from blackness into beauty, are, by the glaring eye of the
malevolent, blended into one.   For the instruction of the
learner, lines should be drawn between them by the dispassionate critic.
    I shall exemplify my idea in passages which, I appre-
hend, have not hitherto been remarked, from two poets the
most regular and accurate.   In comparison with others,
they seem greater than they really are: their lustre is
clear and pure, but borrowed and reflected.   Such are
Racine and Pope. (8)   Opening a translation of Montaigne, (9) I found, within few pages, two sentiments
which the latter, I think, has taken and used.   They are
both quotations: but as they come so near together, and
as Pope was a reader of modern more than of ancient literature, I am of opinion that he is indebted for them exclusively of Montaigne.

    Why may not the goose say thus.   'All the parts of the
    universe I have an interest in: the earth serves me to
    walk upon, the sun to light me & c. is it not man that
    treats, lodges, and serves me.'
    [Montaigne, 'Essays', ii, 12: Apology for Raimonde de
    Sebonde.]

    Seas roll to waft me, Suns to light me, rise,
    My footstool earth - ...
    [Pope, 'Essay on Man', i, 139-40.]

    While man exclaims, 'see all things for my use,'
    'See man for mine,' replies a pamper'd goose.
    [Ibid., iii, 45-6.]

Now, the former part of this quotation being set apart

from the remainder, and differently applied, is rather in
favor of my opinion than against it....

We have seen that taking the thoughts, and even the
expressions, he has divided and disposed them in a manner
quite different from the original.   Now, the man who
steals a bag of peas, and scatters them in his garden, is
no less a thief than if he kept them in the bag and hid
them in his chamber; but the criminal laws, and (10)
those of which we are speaking, are widely different in
this particular.   A theft which comes under the cogni-
sance of the former is not excused nor palliated by the
use to which the thing stolen is converted: in the
latter, you may steal wherever you find it convenient, -
on subscribing to these conditions.   First, that the
property stolen be not the principal and most conspicuous
part of your composition: and secondly, as others are to
enjoy it, and not the mere carrier, that it lose nothing
of its weight or of its polish by the conveyance....

Let us now examine Racine, and that not in places where
it is indifferent whether he has borrowed or otherwise,
but in the two most admirable passages of all his works.

Je crains Dieu, cher Abner, et n'ai point d'autre
                                              crainte.

[I fear God, dear Abner, and have no other fear
('Athalie', I, i, 64).]

This very celebrated verse is taken from Godeau. (11)

Qui cherche vraiment Dieu, dans lui seul se repose.
Et qui craint vraiment Dieu, ne craint rien autre
                                              chose.

[Who truly seeks God, in Him alone finds rest.
And who truly believes in God, fears no other thing
('Poesies Chrestiennes' [Paris, 1660-3]).]

Et laver dans le sang vos bras ensanglantés.

[And wash in blood your blood-stained arms
('Britannicus', IV, iii, 1346).]

This lies on the boundaries of plagiarism, but belongs
to imitation; for, the scene and action (and consequently

some of the principal words) are varied.   I shall present
the counterpart in the language of Mr. Potter.

> Wide thro' the *house* a tide of blood
> Flows where a former tide had flow'd. (12)
> [Aeschylus, 'Choephoroe', 11. 650-1.]

I could produce from the Tragedies of Racine, many more
verses in the same predicament.   Indeed it may be said of
him, that, wherever you trace the steps of genius you lose
the vestige of originality;   for, wherever he is great, he
is great by the existence of others.   Those who have borrowed the most have always been treated the best: whether
it be, that men are gratified by their own ingenuity in
finding out what they imagine is hidden from their neigh-
bours, and the good humour resulting from it expands
itself all around and easily remounts to its source;   or,
by indulging malignity in the discovery of any thing which
lessens the merits of their superiors, they feel a quiet
composure and plenary satisfaction....

NOTES

1 The conservative 'British Critic' (1793-1826) published a damning notice of 'Gebir' in February 1800.
   This review had also attacked Landor's 'Poems' (1795)
   in September 1795.
2 The 'Critical Review' (1756-1817);   the 'Monthly
   Review' (1749-1845).
3 Robert Southey (1774-1843) was the anonymous reviewer
   of 'Gebir' in the 'Critical Review', 27 (September
   1799), 29-39.
4 See the 'Monthly Review', 31 (February 1800), 206-8.
   Landor's recollection of the reviewer's criticisms is
   generally correct.   He does not mention, however,
   the critic's observation that Landor's 'performance
   ... manifests occasionally some talent for description'.
5 Raphael (1483-1520) and Michelangelo (1475-1564),
   Italian Renaissance artists, famous for their paintings of religious subjects;   Nicholas Poussin (1593/4-
   1665), greatest French painter of the seventeenth century, often depicted scenes taken from classical antiquity and mythology.
6 Perhaps it never occurred so often in the same space
   as in the first twenty pages of the 'Life of Mary
   Wollstonecraft' - not seldomer, I believe, than seventeen or eighteen times - This I wonder at, extreme-

ly, as few writers are by habit and course of study
less vague and indefinite than Godwin.   [L]   See
William Godwin, 'Memoirs of the Author of a Vindica-
tion of the Rights of Woman' (Mary Wollstonecraft),
London, 1798.

7   'Leonidas' (1737) by Richard Glover (1712-85).

8   Jean Racine (1639-99), French dramatist; Alexander
Pope (1688-1744), English poet and critic.

9   Michel de Montaigne (1533-92), French thinker and
author of 'Essais' (1580, 1588, 1595).

10 The law of plagiarism is somewhat on the Spartan
model.   You are punished not because you *steal*, but
because you are detected, through want of spirit and
address, in carrying off your booty.   [L]

11 Antoine Godeau (1605-72), French bishop, poet, and
prose writer, author of numerous sacred and profane
poems, a 'Historie de l'Eglise' (1653-78), and an
epic, 'Saint Paul' (1654).

12 'Tragedies of Aeschylus', tr. R. Potter, Norwich,
1777, 355.

3 'Commentary on Memoirs of Mr. Fox'
1812, 1907

Landor's 'Commentary' was occasioned by John Bernard
Trotter's popular 'Memoirs of the Later Years of the Right
Honourable Charles James Fox', London, 1811, a personal
account of the English statesman's political and literary
opinions by his private secretary which went through three
editions in the year of its publication.   The 'Commentary' 'contains', according to Landor's friend, Richard
Monckton Milnes, later Lord Houghton, 'perhaps more fair
and moderate political and literary judgments, delivered
in his own humour, than any work of his earlier or maturer
years' ('Monographs, Personal and Social', 2nd ed.,
London, 1873, 87).   Landor's 'political judgments' were
not viewed as 'moderate', however, by his publisher, John
Murray, and his friend, Robert Southey, who mediated between publisher and author;   for in the 'Commentary',
dedicated to James Madison, President of the USA, and in a
Postscript, Landor fearlessly criticizes English politi-
cians and supports the American position prior to the war
of 1812.   Both Murray and Southey agreed that the work
was too dangerous to publish in 1812, and the printed
copies were accordingly suppressed.   Although parts of
the 'Commentary' were incorporated by Landor in several of
his later prose writings, the work itself was never published in his lifetime.   A transcription of the only
known surviving copy was made by Stephen Wheeler in 1907
for his annotated edition, 'Charles James Fox: A Commentary on His Life and Character by Walter Savage Landor',
2nd ed., London, 1907.

This relatively early work, written when Landor was
thirty-six years old, demonstrates several of the hall-
marks by which Landorian literary criticism was soon to be
recognized, particularly in the Imaginary Conversations:
the obvious depth and breadth of reading in the litera-

tures of classical Greece and Italy, medieval and modern
Europe, and, of course, England; the apparent random
nature of the critical commentary; and the Johnsonian
manner of uttering critical dicta - magisterial, incisive,
sometimes cryptic, and often arbitrary.

The following selection consists of a series of excerpts from the 1907 text edited by Wheeler.   Since each
excerpt must of necessity appear out of context and without the inciting passage from Trotter's 'Memoirs' (many of
Landor's quotations from the 'Memoirs' are augmented for
greater clarity in Wheeler's edition), I have provided in
the notes the appropriate reference to Wheeler's edition
for each of my excerpts.

... Dryden, ... has written on hardly any subject but
poetry, (1) and only a part of his writings was known to
Mr. Fox: (2) the rest has been published since, and is of
little value.   Of his poems, a part seems to have been
composed in a brothel, the remainder in a gin-shop.   His
prose is vigorous and natural.   Those who call him a
copious writer would never have called him so had he not
been a careless one.   In fact, he uses any word that
comes first....

He is never affected: he had not time for dress.   There
is no obscurity, no redundancy; but in every composition,
in poetry or prose, a strength and spirit purely English,
neither broken by labour nor by refinement.   Still, he is
not what Mr. Fox and others have called him, a great poet:
for there is not throughout his works one stroke of the
sublime or one touch of the pathetic, which are the only
true and adequate criteria; nor is there that just description of manners in his dramas, which is very important, though secondary.   For these reasons, he will
never be considered by good judges as equal to Otway, to
Chatterton, to Burns, or even to Cowper. (3)   He was at
repose, and free from all those trifling and pretty inven-
tions and proofs of the truly poetical mind.   There is a
species of these which imposes alike on the undisciplined
and scholastic.   I mean the invention, or rather, the
modification of machinery.   People of an ordinary cast in
the republic of letters grow no less weary at hearing of
just taste, than the vulgar in Athens were at hearing of
Aristides the just. (4)   When our heroic verse was perfected, as it was by Dryden, (5) and others had employed
it with success, something new was demanded.   Poems then
began to contain as much imagery as toy-shops do, and
about as valuable.   'The Rape of the Lock' was admired,

not for its easy and light touches of humour, but for what
was called the *invention* of Pope, his application of the
machinery. (6)   It was not perceived nor suspected, that
there is more real invention in the 'Epistle of Eloise to
Abelard', although so much is copied from the original. (7)   Warton (8) was unable to trace it in the discovery, the arrangement, the concentration of what is
scattered by passion, in the poet's fine tact developing
that idiosyncrasy which is peculiar to one person in one
situation, and his power of enforcing those appeals which
reach in a moment every heart alike.   There was nothing
of this in Dryden, ... (9)

But national characteristics never reach the more elevated
regions of mind; men of genius are not marked by the same
reddle as those on the common of the world. (10)   Do we
find in Pascal (11) anything of the lying, gasconad-
ing, (12) vapouring Frenchman?   On the contrary, do we
not find, in despite of the most miserable language, all
the sober and retired graces of style, all the confident
ease of manliness and strength, with an honest but not
abrupt simplicity, which appeals to the reason, but is
also admitted to the heart?   Let this man, if any, be
compared with Demosthenes. (13)   He was not less, he
hardly could be greater.   The same sincerity, the same
anxiety, the same fervour, was in both, for the only great
objects of a high and aspiring soul, of laudable, perhaps
of pardonable, ambition.   One was for Athens; the other
was not indeed for Paris or for France, but for what most
truly was his country, whose rewards he would lay open to
all men. (14) ...

   Virgil (15) was, at all events, 'worthy the name of
Roman' (16) in poetry.   Never was verse more harmonious,
sentiments more equidistant from flatness and hyperbole,
or touches of nature more true; ... (17)

   Mr. Fox with great reason admired those passages [in
the 'Aeneid'] most which are most pathetic.   In this and
in the harmony of his verse, Virgil is, and will for ever
be, unrivalled.   To blame him or any other poet for his
political opinions is absurd, unless those opinions take
an undue share in his compositions.   Then they are subject to the same censure as anything else would be, doing
the same.   An honourable mind will pay nearly an equal
tribute of admiration and applause to Sir Philip Sidney

and to Algernon. (18)   My heart is as much with the one
as with the other; my reason not.... (19)

I have always had a strong and irresistible curiosity
to discover what opinions were entertained on the first
appearance of works which afterwards acquired the greatest
celebrity, and have generally found that this celebrity
has been of gradual and slow growth.   In the correspondence of Swift (20) and Pope, 'The Arabian Nights' are
mentioned with contempt. (21)   Gray speaks in like manner
of Rousseau's 'Héloise'. (22)   These works are perhaps
read with more universal delight than any others, ancient
or modern.   Gray himself, and Cowper, the two most popular of our poets, have received abundance both of invective and advice from persons whose alacrity of zeal and
weight of judgment are alike forgotten.   It is amusing
to look into reviews of literature, where a series can be
found, and to see the remarks made at the moment, on Hume,
and Robertson, and Goldsmith. (23)   They are treated as
somewhat less than equals by the lowest order of literary
men, and if any thing should be spoken well of, the commendation is followed by hints and suggestions; instead
of deference and homage, they show encouragement, complacency, and favour. (24) ...

Mr. Fox, ... mentions Homer and Ariosto (25) for 'their
wonderful facility, and the *apparent absence* of all study,
in their expression, which,' he says, 'is almost peculiar
to them'. (26)   How that can be *apparent* which is *absent*
I leave to the second-sighted, but I must remark that in
poetry there are two kinds of facility, and opposite in
their nature; one arises from vigour, the other from negligence.   In Homer and Shakespeare (27) we shall invariably find the best parts remarkable for a facility of expression.   As the purest and noblest of the metals is
also the most plastic, in like manner whatever is in
poetry the noblest and the purest takes a 'form and pres-
sure' the most easily and perfectly.
Ariosto and Ovid (28) are negligent; both are amiable,
both are ingenious, both are good poets, but neither of
them can aspire to the highest rank, or to any comparison
with Homer.   It appears rather strange that Mr. Fox
should not have perceived this easiness in Ovid, and in
Hesiod. (29)   The latter is a very indifferent poet, but
he enjoys no inconsiderable reputation.   His verse is the
most fluent of all, yet his sentences are seldom harmonious.... (30)

Ariosto is almost as far below Homer as he is above
Spenser. (31)   He may be ranked among the first writers
of romance.   His versification is very easy, but also
very negligent.   He bears no resemblance whatsoever to
Virgil or to Homer, and comes nearer to Ovid than to any
other of the ancients.   But, although the language of
Ovid is sometimes too familiar, it hardly ever is prosaic.
There is always a something, however little it may be,
which gives it the character of poetry.   In Ariosto there
are at least a thousand verses which have nothing to distinguish them from prose, except the corresponding rhyme;
perhaps if I said three thousand I should not exceed the
truth.   The description of the palace of Atlantes (32) is
a wonderful type of the French revolution.   Could this
possibly have escaped Mr. Fox?... (33)

There is a splendid confusion in Ariosto, which makes
his imagination seem richer and more extensive than it is.
It certainly is not more vigorous nor more various than
Boccaccio's, (34) to whom he is inferior both in the humorous and the pathetic.   I cannot but think him somewhat,
though little inferior to Ovid.   The latter has not only
more of the true epic, but an equal share of that which
Ariosto most excelled in - variety of subject and exuberance of fancy.   His epistles abound in touches of
nature, equally pure, discriminating, and true, and what
they have been most condemned for, but which is among
their highest merits, that sophistry of argument which
follows inventive love, excusing its errors and exasperat-
ing its grief.   In these, however, there are two verses
which ought rather to have come into the mind of Ariosto
than of Ovid:

Sic ubi fata vocant udis abiectus in herbis
Ad vada Mæandri concinit albus olor.

[Thus, at the sommons of fate, casting himself down
amid the watery grasses by the shallows of Maeander,
sings the white swan
('Heroides', vii, 1-2).]

The epistle of Dido to AEneas, which was perhaps a
school exercise, and is certainly the worst poem attributed to Ovid, begins with this simile; (35)   a most contemptible one indeed.   Even such prose as

Lungo sarà che d'Alda di Sansogna
Narri, o della contessa di Celano,

O di Bianca Maria di Catalogna,
O della figlia del re Siciliano,
O della bella Lippa di Bologna, etc.

[Tedious 'twill be, if Alda of Sansogne
I mention, or the Countess of Celan,
Or Bianca Maria of Catalogne,
Or daughter of the King Sicilian,
And also of fair Lippa of Bologne
(Ariosto, 'Orlando Furioso', xiii, 73, 1-5 tr T.C.).]

is rather more tolerable.   This is utterly unnecessary,
but the other is violently misplaced.   Poetry has lost by
similies more than it has gained.   Where we find one ap-
posite, we find several that tend rather to divert our
attention from the object they mean to illustrate: if
they are bad, they must fall short of it;   if good, they
may go beyond it.
   No two poets who have written on the exploits of
heroes, are so totally and universally different as Virgil
and Ariosto.   If there is a general air of melancholy
pervading the poetry of Virgil, there is, on the contrary,
a levity and playfulness of expression even in the most
solemn and pathetic passages of Ariosto:

Sospirando piangea, tal ch'un ruscello
Parean le guancie, e 'l petto un Mongibello.

[He wept: his cheeks appear'd a river's stream:
He sigh'd: his breast a burning mount did seem
('Orlando Furioso', i, 40, 7-8 tr T.C.).]

Well might Cervantes ridicule the romance-writers. (36)
But Ariosto does not always rise with us into this terrific loftiness without leading us back again, and setting
us down nearer home.   For instance:

E il liberal, magnanimo, sublime -
Gran cardinal de la Chiesa di Roma. (37)

[(He ...) is of the church of Rome great Cardinal,
Sublime, and liberal, and full of grace
('Orlando Furioso', iii, 56, 3-4 tr T.C.).]

I hardly know any book so pleasant to read in, or so
tiresome to read through, as 'Orlando Furioso' - of
course, I except 'The Faery Queene'.   I will never believe that any man has overcome twelve or fifteen thousand
lines of allegory, without long intervals of respite and

repose.   I was seventeen years in doing it, and I never
did any thing which I would not rather do again.

In the gloomy deserts of Dante, (38) some scenes are
stupendous both from their grandeur and their solitude,
and lose nothing of their distinctness by their elevation;
in Ariosto, if there are a few misshapen ornaments, yet
every thing around them is smiling in sunshine and fertility.   No man ever lays his poem down without a determination to resume it, but he lays it down often and negli-
gently.   Let him once be under the guidance of Dante,
and -

Revocare gradum superasque evadere ad auras,
Hoc opus, hic labor est.

['To recall thy steps and pass out to the upper air,
This is the task, this the toil'
(Virgil, 'Aeneid', vi, 128-9).]

He is determined not to desist; he may find another passage as striking as the last; he goes on and reads
through.

It is remarkable and surprising that Mr. Fox, in speaking of Italian literature, never conversed about
Alfieri. (39)   He was incomparably the greatest poet in
Europe at the time of this journey, (40) and there are not
in the whole compass of Italian literature such exquisite
specimens of poetical language and vigorous versification.
He approaches more nearly to the manner of the ancients
than any modern; never swollen like Tasso, (41) nor prosaic like Ariosto, nor puny like Metastasio. (42)   If
the fame of such a man cannot be expected to attain its
full growth in his own age, neither can we find without
astonishment that his productions were overlooked.   He
was a cordial hater of the French; he despised their
morals, manners, government, and literature; he detested
Voltaire, (43) whom indeed he might have considered as an
epitomy of that people; versatile, lively, vain, lying,
shameless, unfeeling, unprincipled, and ambitious.   A
hatred of them on these grounds, or any other, might perhaps have not been countenanced by the liberal spirit of
Mr. Fox. (44) ...

... Chaucer (45) is indeed an admirable poet; until
the time of Shakespeare none equalled him; and perhaps
none after, until ours.   The truth of his delineations,
his humour, his simplicity, his tenderness, how different
from the distorted images and gorgeous languor of Spenser!

The language, too, of Chaucer was the language of his day,
the language of those Englishmen who conquered France;
that of Spenser is a strange uncouth compound of words,
chopped off in some places and screwed out in others.
His poem reminds me of a rich painted window, broken in
pieces, where, amidst a thousand petty images, worked most
laboriously and overlaid with colour, not one is well-
proportioned or entire, where the whole is disfigured and
deranged and darkened by the lead that holds them together.   This, however, is not the principal fault, though
surely a great one: the worst of all is the disgusting
and filthy images on which he rests so frequently, and
which he represents with such minuteness.   He never attempts the terrific but he slips back again into nasti-
ness.   Envy chewing a toad (46) is described with all the
coarseness and laboriousness of the worst Dutch painter.
In satirical poets, such as Juvenal and Swift, (47) we are
somewhat less shocked at indelicacy, because in these
there is no incongruity, however little a way such scenes
and images may conduce towards virtue; but in allegory we
are led to improvement through delight.

    ... Spenser has been treated with peculiar lenity and
favour, because no poet has been found so convenient by
the critics to set up against their contemporaries.   The
days of chivalry seemed to be closing at this period, and
their last lustre was reflected on his gorgeous allegory.
Those who were opposed to Pope and Dryden, such as Blackmore and Addison, and Shadwell and Halifax, and Buckingham
and Roscommon, (48) are quoted as poets, only to show the
instability of a premature and inordinate reputation.
    But I am much mistaken if the time is far distant when
the sound sense and vigour of Dryden, and his majestic
versification, will again come into play, in despite of
the impediments and encumbrances brought together from the
refuse of his genius, not more by the bad taste than by
the greediness of publishers.   That he cannot be read
universally is a grievous fault, particularly as it arises
from his gross immodesty and coarse allusions.   Enough
has been said on this subject.   Ample justice has been
awarded him in the greatest effort of the great Johnson;
such is the 'Life of Dryden'. (49)   He too, like Spenser,
complained of neglect, and much more justly.   In Dryden
there is a degree of anger that his claims were overlooked
and his rights withholden; in Spenser there is a lowness
of spirits and a peevish whine that he could not have
every thing he wanted.   Weaker minds are lulled with his
melancholy, stronger are offended at his unmanly and un-

reasonable discontent. It would be ridiculous to compare
him with Burns, or Chatterton, or Cowper, yet in the attention he experienced, and in the largesses he received
from the powerful, how infinitely more fortunate!

The present reign has produced a greater number of good
poets than any in modern times; but the ears of our kings
are still German, and the Muses have never revelled under
the Georgian star. (50)   This, however disgraceful to our
royal family, is the reason perhaps why poetry of late has
not been degraded and dishonoured by flattery to princes
and ministers, and why we have hardly one instance in our
days of great talents united with great baseness. Some
of our most admired and excellent poems are, like the
'Faery Queene', without much order and arrangement, a deficiency which few, either of readers or of critics, are
capable of observing. But the construction and proportions of a poem require not only much care, but, what
would be less apparent to the ordinary reader, much genius
and much imagination. Fitness and order and convenience,
are terms very applicable to the epic, and if not often
employed, it is because they are not found often. The
'Faery Queene' is rambling and discontinuous, full of
every impropriety, and utterly deficient in a just conception both of passion and of character. In Chaucer, on
the contrary, we recognise the strong homely strokes, the
broad and negligent facility, of a great master. Within
his time and Shakespeare's, there was nothing comparable,
nor, I think, between Shakespeare and Burns, a poet who
much resembles him in a knowledge of nature and manners;
who, in addition to this, is the most excellent of pastoral poets, not excepting Theocritus; (51)   and who in
satire, if that indeed can add any thing to qualities so
much greater, is not inferior to Pope, or Horace, or
Aristophanes. (52) ...

I love Goldsmith. The poet never transgresses into
the province of the historian. There is nothing profound
or important in him; but his language is gracefully familiar, everything about him is sufficiently correct and
well-placed, his style is polished enough, and he invites
us by an ingenuous and frank simplicity. Johnson in his
'Lives of the Poets', Goldsmith, Blackstone, and Sir
Joshua Reynolds, (53) are the best of our later prose
writers. Harris, Warton, (54) etc., etc., disgust by
their frippery and affectation even those whom their reading could have instructed. (55) ...

A few writers have indulged in allegory who have not
been deficient in genius; for instance, it is in allegory, and there alone, that Addison (56) has any; delicacy of humour, in which he also is eminent, can hardly
lay claim to such a quality.   Plato, (57) in addition to
almost every other talent, possessed one for allegory,
but he would not have founded a poem on it, nor have permitted it to superabound in one.   It manifests a want of
higher invention, and those poets who have indulged in it
have shown but little taste or fancy in any thing else,
have seldom reached the sublime, and more seldom the
pathetic.   Collins (58) comes nearest of all to an exception, but though he excels the other allegorical poets in
delicacy and proportions, he appears to greatest advantage
when he has escaped from the trammels of this perverted
taste.   The stanza of Spenser is truly delightful, and
there seems to be something creative in its harmony.
Shenstone, a poor poet in other things, becomes an admirable one in 'The Schoolmistress'. (59)   The languor of
Thomson is graceful in 'The Castle of Indolence', and his
redundancy is kept within some bounds by the
stanza. (60) ...

NOTES

1 John Dryden (1631-1700), English literary critic,
   dramatist, poet, and translator.
2 Charles James Fox (1749-1806), radical British statesman and defender of liberty.
3 Thomas Otway (1652-85), English playwright and poet;
   Thomas Chatterton (1752-70), youthful English poet who
   committed suicide at seventeen; Robert Burns (1759-
   96), most famous of Scottish poets, particularly noted
   for his lyrics, satirical poems, and contributions of
   new or adapted songs to James Johnson's 'Scots Musical
   Museum' (1787-1803); William Cowper (1731-1800), English hymn writer, poet, translator of Homer, and
   author of 'The Task' (1784), a long reflective and
   descriptive poem in blank verse.
4 Aristides 'The Just' (d. c. 468 BC), Athenian soldier
   and statesman, known for his moral integrity, democra-
   tic principles, and practice of moderation.   The
   source of Landor's allusion is Plutarch's 'Life of
   Aristides'.
5 Dryden and others in the seventeenth century believed
   that the most appropriate verse form for tragic or
   heroic drama was the English heroic couplet, pairs of
   iambic pentameter lines rhyming aa bb cc etc.   This

verse form, as perfected by Dryden and Pope, became
the standard measure for all forms of poetry throughout most of the eighteenth century.

6   See Joseph Warton (1722-1800), 'Essay on the Genius
and Writings of Pope', 3rd ed. cor., London, 1772-82,
225.

7   See 'P. Abaelardi ... et Heloissæ ... epistolæ ...
cum codd. MSS. collatæ , cura Ricardi Rawlinson',
London, 1718.

8   Concerning the Epistle of Eloise to Abelard, Warton
says: 'Pope was a most excellent *improver*, if no
great original *inventor*; ...' [ibid., 309].

9   See 'Charles James Fox: A Commentary on His Life and
Character by Walter Savage Landor, ed. Stephen
Wheeler, 2nd ed., London: John Murray, 1907, 47-9.

10 Reddle (red ochre) is used in England to mark sheep.

11 Blaise Pascal (1623-62), French mathematician, phy-
sicist, and author of 'Pensées' (1670), a defence of
the Christian religion.

12 Landor, like many of his English contemporaries,
viewed the French as incorrigible boasters.

13 Demosthenes (384-322 BC), greatest of Athenian
orators.

14 Ibid., 76.

15 Virgil (Publius Vergilius Maro, 70-19 BC), Roman
poet, author of the 'Eclogues', the 'Georgics', and
the Latin epic, the 'Aeneid'.

16 Landor quotes from John Bernard Trotter's 'Memoirs of
the Later Years of the Right Honourable Charles James
Fox', 3rd ed., London, 1811, 130.

17 'Commentary', 128.

18 Sir Philip Sidney (1554-86), English courtier and
poet, author of the prose romance 'Arcadia' (1590),
the sonnet cycle 'Astrophel and Stella' (1591), and
the 'Apologie for Poetrie' (1595); Algernon Sidney
(1622-83), republican, author of 'Discourses Concerning Government' (1698).   The latter fought against
Charles I, lived in exile abroad until 1677 rather
than give his pledge to Charles II at the Restoration
(1660), and was convicted of treason and executed on
Tower Hill on the morning of 7 December 1683.

19 'Commentary', 139.

20 Jonathan Swift (1667-1745), Irish writer, Anglican
divine, and brilliant satirist, author of numerous
political-religious pamphlets, 'Battle of the Books'
and 'A Tale of a Tub' (1704), and 'Gulliver's Travels'
(1726).

21 See the letter from Bishop Francis Atterbury to Alexander Pope, 28 September 1720, in 'Correspondence of

Alexander Pope', ed. George Sherburn, 5 vols, Oxford,
1956, 2, 56.   'The Arabian Nights' Entertainments'
were translated into English in 1839-41.

22   See Thomas Gray's letter to Dr Wharton, 11 January
1762, in 'Correspondence of Thomas Gray', eds Paget
Toynbee and Leonard Whibley, 3 vols, Oxford, 1935, 2,
771.
        Thomas Gray (1716-71) was an English academic and
poet whose Elegy Written in a Country Churchyard
(1750) made him the foremost poet of his day.   'La
Nouvelle Héloïse' (1761), by Jean-Jacques Rousseau
(1712-78), is a novel in which the author discusses
the problems created for the family and for the relationship between the sexes by a return to nature.

23   David Hume (1711-76), philosopher and historian,
author of numerous essays and the 'History of Great
Britain' (1754-61);   William Robertson (1721-93),
author of 'History of Scotland during the Reigns of
Queen Mary and James VI until his Accession to the
Crown of England' (1759), the 'History of Charles V'
(1769), and the 'History of America' (1771);   Oliver
Goldsmith (1730?-74), novelist, poet, dramatist,
author of such popular works as 'The Vicar of Wake-
field' (1766), 'The Deserted Village' (1770), and 'She
Stoops to Conquer' (1773).

24   'Commentary', 143-4.

25   Homer, Greek epic poet, author of the 'Iliad' and the
'Odyssey';   Ludovico Ariosto (1474-1533), author of
'Orlando Furioso' (1532), greatest of Italian romantic
epics.

26   Landor quotes from a letter of Fox to Trotter in
'Memoirs', 493.

27   William Shakespeare (1564-1616), greatest of English
dramatists and poets.

28   Ovid (Publius Ovidius Naso, 43 BC-AD 17), Roman poet,
author of 'Amores', 'Heroides', 'Metamorphoses', and
several other works.

29   Hesiod, like Homer, one of the oldest known Greek
poets;   author of the 'Theogony' and 'Works and Days'.

30   'Commentary', 148-9.

31   Edmund Spenser (1552?-99), English poet, author of
numerous poems foremost among which is the uncompleted
'Faerie Queene' (1589, 1596).   Modelled somewhat upon
Ariosto's 'Orlando Furioso', Spenser's long poem is
written in a stanza form invented by the poet.   Landor's feelings about Spenser's 'Faerie Queene' are
humorously expressed in his poem 'To Chaucer', No. 29
below.

32   Ariosto, 'Orlando Furioso', iv.

33   'Commentary', 151.
34   Giovanni Boccaccio (1313-75), Italian writer and
     humanist, author of the 'Decameron' (1349-51).
35   Landor is referring to Ovid, 'Heroides', vii.
36   See 'Don Quixote de la Mancha' (1605, 1615), a satiri-
     cal romance by the great Spanish novelist and drama-
     tist, Miguel Saavedra de Cervantes (1547-1616).
37   Cardinal Ippolito d'Este.
38   Landor's reference is to the 'Inferno', the first part
     of the three-part 'Divina Commedia' (1310-21) by Dante
     Alighieri (1265-1321).
39   Count Vittorio Alfieri (1749-1803), Italian dramatist
     and poet, was greatly admired by Landor.
40   Mr Fox, his wife, and Mr Trotter visited the Low
     Countries and France in 1802.
41   Torquato Tasso (1544-95), Italian poet of the late Re-
     naissance and author of the epic 'Gerusalemme Liber-
     ata' (1575).
42   Pietro Metastasio (1698-1782), Italian poet and li-
     brettist for 'opera seria'.
43   Voltaire (François-Marie Arouet, 1694-1778), one of
     the greatest and most versatile of French authors:
     dramatist, historian, literary critic, philosopher,
     and poet.
44   'Commentary', 152-5.
45   Geoffrey Chaucer (1345?-1400), English poet, prose
     writer, and translator, author of 'The Canterbury
     Tales' (1400).
46   'Faery Queene', I, iv.
47   Juvenal (b. AD 60-70) was the last of the great
     Roman satiric poets. His 'Satires' often dwell upon
     the seamy side of life, and they are characterized by
     the power of invective and bitter ironical humour.
     Many of Jonathan Swift's satirical poems are Juvena-
     lian in tone and subject matter.
48   Sir Richard Blackmore (d. 1729), physician to Queen
     Anne and voluminous prose and verse writer; Joseph
     Addison (1672-1719), poet, dramatist, and periodical
     writer; Thomas Shadwell (1642?-92), dramatist and
     Poet Laureate; Charles Montagu, Earl of Halifax
     (1661-1715), statesman, minor poet, and patron of
     literature; George Villiers, second Duke of Bucking-
     ham (1628-87), courtier, wit, author, and patron;
     Wentworth Dillon, Earl of Roscommon (1633?-85), trans-
     lator and minor poet.
49   Samuel Johnson (1709-84), English poet, periodical
     writer, literary critic, and author of the famous
     'Johnson's Dictionary' (1755). His Life of Dryden
     first appeared in 'Lives of the Poets' (1779-81).

50   George III (1738-1820), king of Great Britain from
     1760 to 1820, was the third Hanoverian to rule the
     British.   Landor's feelings about England's German
     kings are humorously expressed in his poem entitled
     The Georges: 'George the First was always reckoned /
     Vile, but viler George the Second; / And what mortal
     ever heard / Any good of George the Third? / When from
     earth the Fourth descended / (God be praised!) the
     Georges ended' ('Complete Works', 15, 93).

51   Theocritus (fl. c. 270 BC), Greek poet whose 'Idylls'
     established him as the father of pastoral poetry.

52   Horace (65-8 BC), Roman poet whose reputation as a
     satirist is based upon his 'Epodes' and 'Satires';
     Aristophanes (c. 448-c. 380 BC), great Athenian comic
     dramatist.
        See 'Commentary', 211-15.

53   Sir William Blackstone (1723-80), most famous of Eng-
     lish jurists and author of 'Commentaries on the Laws
     of England' (1765-9);   Sir Joshua Reynolds (1723-92),
     English portrait painter and author of 'Discourses'
     (1769-91).

54   James Harris (1709-80), author of 'Hermes' (1751).
     Landor's reference may be either to Joseph Warton,
     author of the 'Enthusiast' (1744), or to his brother
     Thomas Warton (1728-90), author of 'Pleasures of Mel-
     ancholy' (1747) and 'Poems' (1777).

55   'Commentary', 228-9.

56   For several examples of Addison's allegorical writing,
     see the 'Spectator', numbers 159 (Visions of Mirza),
     164 (Constantia and Theodosius), and 183 (Pleasure and
     Pain).

57   Plato (c. 429-347 BC), Athenian philosopher and author
     of numerous dialogues.

58   See the 'Odes on Several Descriptive and Allegorical
     Subjects' (1746) by William Collins (1721-59).

59   William Shenstone (1714-63) composed 'The Schoolmis-
     tress' (1742) in Spenserian stanzas.

60   'The Castle of Indolence' (1748), a long poem in
     Spenserian stanzas by James Thomson (1700-48).   See
     'Commentary', 233.

Selections from Letters
Private and Public

4 Letters to Robert Southey (excerpts), 1808-22

1869, 1876

The correspondence between Landor and Robert Southey
(1774-1843) extends over a period of thirty years and is
both a monument to their friendship and a valuable source
of literary information.   Neither poet could have fore-
seen the effect their meeting in April 1808 would have on
their respective literary careers.   Southey, author of
'Thalaba' (1801) and 'Madoc' (1805), was encouraged by
Landor to resume the writing of poetry;   and Landor,
grateful for Southey's favourable review of the then anonymous 'Gebir' (1798) in the 'Critical Review' (September
1799), had found a fellow writer who could share his literary interests.   Landor's letters to Southey, written
between 1808 and the publication in 1824 of the first two
volumes of his 'Imaginary Conversations', are of particular importance;   for in them one finds several early examples of Landor's practice as a verbal and textual critic
and encounters many of the literary observations on
ancient and modern authors later incorporated into the
early Imaginary Conversations.   Southey, at regular intervals over a five-year period, sent Landor sections of
his poems 'Curse of Kehama' (1810) and 'Pelayo' (later entitled 'Roderick, the Last of the Goths' [1814]) as they
were being composed.   Five of the following excerpts express Landor's critical response to Southey's work.
Other excerpts indicate their mutual interest in writers,
books, and such literary projects as the composition of
dialogues.
    A large number of Landor's letters to Southey were
first printed in John Forster's 'Walter Savage Landor: A
Biography' (1869).   Many of these were reprinted, usually
in abbreviated form, in Forster's condensed 'Life', the
first volume of his eight-volume edition of the 'Works and
Life of Walter Savage Landor' (1876).   The original

65

letters disappeared after Forster used them.   The following selections, as indicated in the notes, are from Forster's 'Landor' (1869).   Undated letters are indicated by
a question mark enclosed by brackets, and the dates, when
given, are the biographer's.   Unfortunately, Forster
often took unwarranted liberties with the texts of these
letters, and he sometimes loosely or incorrectly dated
them.

Sunday evening, May 8 [1808].

The subject you have chosen is magnificent.   There is
more genius in the conception of this design than in the
execution of any recent poem, however perfect.   Shall I
avow to you that in general I am most delighted with those
passages which are in rhyme, and that when I come into the
blank verse again my ear *repines*? (1)   Are we not a
little too fond of novelty and experiment, and is it not
reasonable to prefer those kinds of versification which
the best poets have adopted and the best judges have cherished for the longest time?   In 'Samson Agonistes' and in
'Thalaba' there are many lines which I could not describe.
There are some in 'Kehama'.   Poetry is intended to soothe
and flatter our prepossessions, not to wound or irritate
or contradict them.   We are at liberty to choose the best
modifications, we are not at liberty to change or subvert.
We are going too far from our great luminaries.   There
must be a period: there must be a return from this aphe-
lion.

You have begun a poem which will be coeval with our
language.   March on: conciliate first, then conquer.
The ears of thousands may be captivated - the mind and
imagination of but few.   If Gray had written his 'Elegy'
in another metre, (2) it would not be the most admired
poem in existence.   Many would see its disproportions
and defects: though proportion has not been studied, or
perhaps known, beyond the drama.   'Kehama' will admit
more diversity than has even been imagined in the works of
PINDAR. (3)

I never could perceive that wildness for which Pindar
has been traditionally remarked.   I could perceive an exquisite taste and an elevation of soul such as never were
united - not even in the historical works of the Jewish
writers, not in the Song of Deborah nor of Moses. (4)
Ch. Burney is of opinion that we have lost the best works
of Pindar. (5)   In a little time however he will teach
people to read the remaining Odes in such a manner as to -
distinguish them from prose!   Is it not humiliating and
painful to reflect that a poet who held the second place

in the ancient world, should have left it a question among
those who know his language the most intimately whether
his verses have any intrinsic melody, or owed it merely to
the music by which they were accompanied?   Meanwhile
every one satisfied his own ear with the despicable trash
of Lycophron and Tryphiodorus. (6)   The opposition of
iambic and trochaic, in antispastics, may have been suited
to opposite choirs and instruments; but I hope the metre
and language of our early ballads, which we have no reason
to retain, will be banished for ever by men of genius from
their more elevated works.

SOUTHEY, we have had too much of the lute and of the
lyre.   We forget that there are louder, graver, more impressive tones.   These indeed are not proper for every
day; nor is it every day, every century, or every millen-
nium, that we shall see such poems as 'Kehama'.   I be-
seech you, Southey, use such materials as have already
stood the test.   Wildness of conception, energy, passion,
character - magnificent but wild profusion - all this you
can give it; and with this you will confer on it neither
a hazardous nor a painful immortality. (7)

                                        FEBRUARY 1809.

When I can read what you send of 'Kehama' more calmly and
dispassionately, which I would hardly wish to do, I will
search it through and through to discover the slightest of
its imperfections.   None of your enemies shall be more
zealous in the labour.   One line not only displeased but
disturbed me,

    Eye hath not seen nor painter's hand pourtrayed.

I have an insuperable hatred to such words as 'painter'
and 'pourtray' in grave heroic poetry: add to which, if
'eye hath not seen', it is superfluous to say the rest.
The first words are serious and solemn - the last put one
in mind of the Exhibition and the French. (8)   Take care
how you 'o'erlay this poem with ornament!'... (9)

                                            [?].

    ... I should like to talk about Spenser with you, and
to have the 'Faery Queen' before us.   Passion can alone
give the higher beauties of versification.   Shakespeare,
who excels all mortals in poetry, excels them all in verse
frequently; but I am convinced he formed erroneous opin-

ions on the subject, and that he preferred a stiff and
strutting step systematically, and was great only when he
was carried off his legs in spite of himself.   In my opinion there is more transcendent poetry in Shakespeare
than in all the other poets that have existed since the
creation of the world, and more passages filled with harmony from its inspiration.   Immeasurably as I prefer
Chaucer to Spenser, I cannot as a poet - a great one is
here understood - because he never comes up to the ideal
so well exprest by Horace: '*meum qui pectas inaniter
angit*', &c. ['who with airy nothings wrings my heart'
('Epistles', ii, 1, 211)].   The language of Chaucer is
the language of his time; but Spenser's is a jargon.
No, I do not think we had little good poetry before
Milton.   Some truly pure grains of gold were carried down
by the streamlets in rude old times, ill exchanged for the
tinsel which we are just removing from ours.   The English
nation was in all respects at its highest pitch of glory
in the times of Shakespeare and Hooker. (10)   Chivalry
had forgotten all the follies of its youth: it retained
its spirit, and had lost only its austerity.   The Tudors,
those blackguard and beastly Welsh, had never infected the
mass of English mind.   People read; and to our national
manliness a little was now added of Roman dignity.   I am
going on as if I had nothing else to do or say. (11)

                                                      [?].

I have read, and I know not when I shall cease reading,
the incomparable description of Roderick's wanderings and
agony. (12)   What are those of Aeneas or Ulysses in comparison?   The story of Adosinda is heart-rending. (13)
When I have looked long enough at the figures of great
painters, I dwell on the landscape.   It is only the great
ones who make it strikingly peculiar and appropriate.   We
wish for more, yet are conscious that we ought not to wish
it.   In the beginning of the sheet, the scene of the
pine-forest (14) is a perfect example of what I
mean.... (15)

                                             November 1812.

I have now received two detachments of 'Pelayo' (16) since
I wrote, which proves that one sits much more quiet and
idle under pleasurable sensations than even under those
which are indifferent.   In the mean time I have written a
score silly things to a score silly people....   The more

I read of 'Pelayo', the more arduous the undertaking seems
to me; but at the same time the strength with which it is
carried on increases.   People have formed their opinions
of heroic poetry from Homer and his successors.   All who
have followed Homer have failed deplorably.   Virgil is
great only where he has not followed him.   You will not
persuade any one that anything is heroic without kicks and
cuffs.   All can enter into the spirit of a battle, and
perhaps the timid man likes it most of all from a consciousness of security: there are very few who will feel
at heart what Pelayo feels, and fewer still who will
follow up with intensity all the vicissitudes of Roderigo. (17)   How many, how nearly all, of our poets and
critics will read these concluding lines as if they were
common ones!

>   Roderick alone appear'd
> Unmoved and calm; for now the royal Goth
> Had offered his accepted sacrifice,
> And therefore in his soul he felt that peace
> Which follows painful duty well perform'd -
> Perfect and heavenly peace - the peace of God. (18)
> [vii, 183-8].

The language is so plain and the sentiment so natural that
I am the only man in England who knows the full value of
them.... (19)

                                                    [?].

Certainly this last section of 'Pelayo' is the most masterly of all.   I could not foresee or imagine how the
characters would unfold themselves.   I could have done
but little with Florinda and with Egilona, taking your
outline; (20) yet I could have done a good deal more with
them than any other man except yourself.   For I delight
in the minute variations and almost imperceptible shades
of the female character, and confess that my reveries,
from my most early youth, were almost entirely on what
this one or that one would have said or done in this or
that situation.   Their countenances, their movements,
their forms, the colours of their dresses, were before my
eyes.
    One reason why we admire the tragedies of the ancients
is this: we never have had our images broken by the ico-
noclast effort of the actors.   Within my memory we never
have had any worthy of the name; but I feel convinced
that Garrick himself, (21) who was probably the greatest

that ever lived, would not have recompensed me for the
overthrow and ruin of my 'Lear'. (22)

December 1817.

The first of your magnificent books that I took out of the
box was Wordsworth. (23)   I would have given eighty
pounds out of a hundred that he had not written that
verse,

Of *high respect* and gratitude sincere.
['To the Right Honourable William, Earl of Lonsdale,
KG', dedication to 'The Excursion', l. 8].

It is like the verses of the Italians, Spanish, &c. quite
colloquial;   and '*high* respect', an expression borrowed
from the French, is without intrinsic sense.   Wordsworth
has the merit, the rarest of all merits and the most difficult to be certain of, to avoid street-and-house language and to be richly endowed with whatever is most
simple, pure, and natural.   In his Lyrical Ballads (24)
he has sometimes disappointed me, just as an AEolian harp
has done when I expected a note more.   These books have
wakened me up.   I shall feed upon them till I fall asleep
again, but that will not be until I have devoured
all. (25)

9 March 1822.

It is long ago since you first told me that you were writing some dialogues.   I began to do the same thing after
you, having formerly written two or three about the time
when the first income-tax was imposed. (26)   I have now
written fifteen new ones, throwing into the fire one between Swift and Sir William Temple, (27) and another between Addison and Lord Somers; (28)   the former because it
was democratical, the latter because it was composed mali-
ciously, and contained all the inelegancies and inaccura-
cies of style I could collect from Addison.   The number
would surpass belief.   The two earlier ones, the first
between Lord Grenville and Burke, (29) the other between
Henry the Fourth and Sir Arnold Savage, (30) were written
more than twenty years ago, which no person would believe
of the former;   but I gave the substance of it to Robert
Adair (31) to get inserted in the 'Morning Chronicle', and
a part of it (now omitted) was thought too personal, and
it was refused.   I hope your dialogues are printed, (32)

that they may give some credit and fashion to this manner
of composition. (33)

NOTES

1 Landor's objection to Southey's experiments with
   rhymed and unrhymed meters in 'Kehama' finally brought
   a concession from his friend: 'Do not however be at
   the trouble of criticising the first portion which you
   received, for that has been greatly altered since by
   rhyming most of those parts which were rhymeless - a
   task which is yet to be completed' (undated Southey
   letter, Forster, 'Landor', 1, 249).
2 Thomas Gray's meditative poem, Elegy Written in a
   Country Churchyard (1750), is composed in quatrains of
   iambic pentameter.
3 Pindar (518-438 BC), Greek lyric poet.
4 See Judges 5, for the Song of Deborah and Exodus 15
   for the Hymn of Moses.
5 Charles Burney, DD (1757-1817), classical scholar
   whose contemporary reputation exceeded his actual ac-
   complishments. See 'Carminum Pindaricorum fragmen-
   ta', etc., MS Notes [by C. Burney] (1776).
6 Both Lycophron (b. c. 320 BC), Greek tragic poet, and
   the tragedian Lycophron (c. 273 BC), have been credited with writing the 'Alexandra', the most obscure of
   all Greek poems. Tryphiodorus (third or fourth century AD), epic poet and native of Egypt, author of
   'Marathoniaca, The Story of Hippodamea' and 'The Cap-
   ture of Troy'.
7 Forster, 'Landor', 1, 216-17.
8 Southey replied: 'When the obnoxious line was written, I thought of better painters than the exhibition-
   ers - of those whose creative powers entitle them to
   be mentioned anywhere. It is however an ugly word,
   because it always reminds one of the house-painter.
   I set a black mark upon the line. Your remarks shall
   be well weighed, and every passage which I cannot entirely justify shall be altered....' (undated Southey
   letter, Forster, 'Landor', 1, 249).
9 Ibid., 248.
10 Richard Hooker (1554?-1600), theologian, author 'Of
   the Laws of Ecclesiastical Polity' (1594-1662).
11 Forster, 'Landor', 1, 259.
12 Southey's 'Roderick, the Last of the Goths' (1814), an
   epic poem in blank verse, is based on Count Julian's
   betrayal of Spain to the Moors after King Roderick
   seduced his daughter, Florinda. Landor's reference

is to Roderick's penitential wanderings in the garb of
a monk following his military defeat by the Moors (i,
104ff).

13   Ibid., iii, 218ff.   Adosinda, one of Roderick's defeated subjects, meets her disguised king in the midst
of a ruined city and begs him to help her bury her
slaughtered parents, warrior husband, and infant.
She then relates how a Moorish captain saved her from
certain death to be his mistress and how she murdered
him in his sleep in order to escape.   She concludes
her tale with a vow to fight the invader, and her
courage inspires Roderick to seek a way to free his
people.

14   Ibid., ll. 1-8.

15   Forster, 'Landor', 1, 264.

16   An early title for 'Roderick'.

17   Roderick.

18   These lines follow a moving scene in which the disguised Roderick convinces his cousin Pelayo to lead
the Goths in battle against the Moors and then abdi-
cates his throne by addressing Pelayo as his 'Lord and
King'.   Roderick's foster-father, Siverian, does
likewise, and all except Roderick are moved to tears.

19   Forster, 'Landor', 1, 266.

20   Florinda, the dishonoured daughter of Count Julian,
and Egilona, formerly the wife of Roderick, now wife
of Abdalaziz, Moorish governor of Spain.   Landor himself dramatized this human tragedy in 'Count Julian'
(1812).

21   David Garrick (1717-79), famous English actor.
Landor agreed with Charles Lamb that plays such as
Shakespeare's 'King Lear' were better performed in the
theatre of the mind than on the nineteenth-century
stage.   Both objected to the declamatory style of
actors and the lavish staging of plays.

22   Forster, 'Landor', 1, 267-8.

23   William Wordsworth (1770-1850), English poet, author
of numerous shorter poems as well as the long poems
'The Excursion' (1814) and 'The Prelude' (1805, 1850).
He succeeded Robert Southey as Poet Laureate in 1843.

24   Wordsworth and Samuel Taylor Coleridge (1772-1834)
published a collection of their poems in 1798 under
the title 'Lyrical Ballads'.   A second edition containing new poems and Wordsworth's famous Preface appeared in 1800.   A third edition was published in
1802.

25   Forster, 'Landor', 1, 438.

26   1797.

27   Jonathan Swift (1667-1745) was secretary to Sir

William Temple (1628-99), English envoy and man of
culture, from 1689 until the latter's death in 1699.
Swift was an intimate of Temple's household at Moor
Park, Surrey, and it was there that the young Swift
educated himself, tutored Esther Johnson ('Stella'),
edited Temple's correspondence, and wrote the 'Battle
of the Books' and 'A Tale of a Tub' (published together in 1704).

28   Joseph Addison (1672-1719) is known primarily for his
periodical contributions to the 'Tatler' (1709-11) and
'Spectator' (1711-12 and 1714).   John Somers, Baron
(1651-1716), English statesman and Lord Chancellor of
England from 1697 to 1700, used his influence to help
Addison secure a pension from the crown.   That pension enabled him to pursue various literary projects
and to travel on the continent from 1699 to 1703 with
a view to prepare himself for diplomatic service.   In
1835 Landor published an Imaginary Conversation between Addison and Richard Steele.

29   William Wyndham, Baron Grenville (1759-1834) and
Edmund Burke (1729-97), British statesmen.

30   Henry IV (1366-1413), king of England from 1399 to
1413, and Sir Arnold Savage (d. 1410), speaker of the
House of Commons during Henry IV's reign.   'King
Henry IV and Sir Arnold Savage' first appeared in
volume one of the 1824 'Imaginary Conversations'.
     Landor believed himself descended from Sir Arnold
Savage, and he took pride in thinking that it was his
ancestor who asserted the financial independence of
the House by demanding that Henry IV redress grievan-
ces before Parliament granted him money.   Landor
named his eldest son, Arnold Savage Landor, after this
supposed ancestor.

31   Sir Robert Adair (1763-1855), one of the chief suppor-
ters of the English statesman Charles James Fox and
the Whig cause in the early nineteenth century.
Adair was one of several Whig leaders who wanted
Landor to serve the radicals as a political pamphleteer.

32   See Southey's 'Sir Thomas More: or Colloquies on the
Progress and Prospects of Society' (1829).

33   Forster, 'Landor', 1, 510-11.

5 Letters to the Reverend Walter Birch (excerpts), 1819-20

1869, 1876, 1910, 1941, 1954, 1958, 1968

Landor's lifelong friendship with the Reverend Walter
Birch (1774-1829) began at Rugby in 1786 when Birch, a new
arrival, soundly thrashed the young Landor: 'He was a year
older, and a better boxer: we were intimate ever afterwards, till his death' (W.S.L. to Robert Lytton, 23 October 1860; quoted by Forster, 'Landor', 1, 24). Their
student years continued at Oxford, and their separate
lives and careers afterward in no way lessened their
friendship. Landor shared his literary ideas and projects with Birch in much the same way as he did with
Southey. Although Landor's extant letters to Birch are
fewer than those to Southey, they are more detailed and
convey more vividly Landor's erudition, critical turn of
mind, extensive knowledge of ancient and modern literatures, and competence as a writer of modern Latin verse.
Much of the content of these letters appeared later in
Landor's prose and poetry.

Excerpts from Landor's letters to the Reverend Walter
Birch were first printed in Forster's biographies of Landor (1869, 1876), and thereafter in the Rev. E.R. Tatham's
Some Unpublished Letters of W.S. Landor, 'Fortnightly Review' (February 1910), 361-73, and in the Landor biographies of Malcolm Elwin (1941, 1958) and Professor R.H.
Super (1954). Professor A. LaVonne Ruoff has recently
published a definitive edition of the correspondence: Landor's Letters to the Reverend Walter Birch, 'Bulletin of
the John Rylands Library' (Autumn 1968), 200-61. The following excerpts are from Professor Ruoff's text, and the
appropriate references to her edition are given in the
notes. I have followed her dating either of the receipt
or the writing of the letters from which these selections
are taken, and I am indebted to the thoroughness of her
annotation which has helped substantially in my own work.

[Received 20 April 1819.]

Dear Birch

... Your critical friend [?] in respect to Southey, is
partly right and partly wrong: in respect to Byron (1) he
runs into a very common error.
   A *proof* was once offered to me that Horace too, if he
had chosen, could have written an epic poem.   This proof
rested on the lines.

   neque enim quivis horrentia pilis [agmina] &c.
   [not everyone can paint ranks bristling with lances
   ('Satires', ii, 1, 13).]

The verses are good: but ten thousand equally good
would not necessarily make a good epic poem.
   There are at least one thousand in the Iliad without
any kind of beauty either of thought or expression, yet
the poem has been the just admiration of all ages.   Biron
[sic] is incapable of continued and strenuous exertion.
A mind of this structure is radically weak.   It may present, in its changes and movements, some bright *phases*,
but can do no more.   B. has done at thirty all that he
can do at forty, as you will see, if indeed you should
ever read his poems.   All his feelings are of the same
tone, all his characters of the same cast.   A desperately
wicked man, a girl ready to turn whore, and a youth ready
to assist her in her resolution. (2)   Between genuine
poetry and that of Byron there is the same difference as
between roses and attar of roses.   He smells of the
spirit, not of the flower, you are overpowered and not
satisfied. (3)
   Your critical friend is still more deplorably in the
dark, if he prefers B. to Southey for *purity* of style.   A
style less pure than B's is only to be found in Thompson's
[sic], (4) more *pure* than Southey's nowhere.   S. wants
condensation: he wants nothing else.   He has *strong*
sense, strong feeling, and vivid imagination.   No poet
since Homer was ever so rich in language as Southey.
   The style of Wordsworth's Pamphlet, (5) the strongest
piece of composition that exists among the Moderns, is not
without the affectation you mention: yet how very much
superior to Milton's! how abundant in that harmony which
can only arise from fulness [sic] and energy of thought!
Milton appears to me very affected in his English prose.
   Hooker's Ecclesiastical Polity was written half a century earlier, (6) yet the sentences are more harmonious,

and the diction more easy and natural.   Those who write
to influence the people should employ the popular language.   Every other, in such circumstances, must have been
dictated by inconsiderate vanity and perversly bad taste.
Waller and Cowley (7) wrote as we do, but Milton disdained
to use his pen or move his lips like the men he abominated
or dispised.   The same principle, rather than any thing
rancorously heretical, kept him obstinately from
church. (8) ...

Pisa - January 30, 1820

Dear Birch.
Your letter has arrived on my birthday, and I cd. not have
received a more delightful present.   We must talk again
of poetry, for it is almost the only theme at the present
day that can be discussed with any satisfaction.   I
admire Pindar as much as you do, but Wordsworth more than
you do *yet*.   If ever you should read him thirteen or
fourteen times, as I have done, you will find him richer
in poetry (I do not say a greater poet), than any of the
ancients.   I admire in Pindar elevation of soul, and
purity of taste, to a degree that none else has ever
reached.   I believe him to be the only blameless poet
that ever lived.   But he has written nothing more pure or
more elevated than the sonnet (I abhor the name) beginning 'There are two voices'. (9)   My heart exults in the
glory of our country when I think that she has produced
two poets incontestably the greatest that ever lived and a
third who is still contending, and in whose favour the
judges will decide - but the sitting must last three hundred years. - There are half-pages in Dante worth all
Ariosto, He [is] a Carnival poet.   Tasso has the merit of
having formed a more perfect epic plan than any one, but
his poem, (10) if compared with Southey's Roderick, sinks
to nothing.   Southey tells me that Wordsworth is about to
make me a present of a new poem. (11)   Such a present
from W. is like a kingdom given by Alexander or
Cyrus. (12) - I do not think I could have been explicit in
my last about Byron, for I well understood yours.   My
opinion is this, that a man of a heart so rotten, and a
mind so incompact, was never formed for more than secondary greatness.   If he wd. do this, if he wd. do that,
should not be said: it is not his nature. - The taste of
Milton was much injured by his Italian reading.   I never
read a line of their vile poetry.   Except Alfieri I have
not opened an Italian poet these eleven years.   I have
not yet read a fifth of Dante.   About a twentieth part of
what I have read in him is excellent, the rest trash....

What a quantity of rubbish, both greek & latin, is preserved in what we call the classics, and how many rich gems are lost! - It is impossible to talk of the ancients without something of prejudice. They ~~wormed~~ winded themselves about our hearts in youth, when impressions are strongest, and when admiration is traditionary. We do not see the faults which their contemporaries saw in them. Yet surely in reading Euripides, (13) you must have been ready to exclaim now and then 'There are *two* Richards in the field today'. (14) The lyric parts are admirable, but at least one half of the dialogue is improper. There is an eternal barter of proverb for proverb, verse for verse, and a spectator must have rather imagined himself in the school of some profligate sophist than at the theatre. How different both in their nature and in their application are the moral sentences of Pindar. But in the beauty and propriety (the greatest of all beauties), of moral sentences, no poet is superior to Ovid. In Alcestis, the best tragedy of Euripides, Hercules is drunk. (15) This tragedy in some parts is not unworthy of Shakespear. It is curious that Milton and Dante should both have chosen as objects of admiration the very poets to whom they were the most unlike. One Euripides, (16) the other Virgil. But just criticism had not dawned. Wordsworth has *begun* that science, inasmuch as relates to poetry.... (17)

Pisa. June 15. [1820]

Dear Birch
In two or three days a volume of latin poems, which will be finished tomorrow, (18) will be sent to Leghorn for you, and from Leghorn dispatched to Longmans. Your letter arrived this evening. Happy you! who have yet to read the Excursion. (19) - There is nothing so difficult in literature as that which appears to be the easiest and most natural thing in the world, to see with our own eyes. We admire the ancients by tradition. Suppose for a moment that any one had, on the first publication of Gray's poems, called him a better poet than Statius, (20) in the presence of Johnson. (21) This man, who habitually filled the scorner's chair, would have laughed him to scorn, and been supported by Burke and all the rest, except perhaps Reynolds, whose taste (if I must use the word) preceded by a half-century that of others. (22) Yet you or I would rather have written that one stanza 'The boast of heraldry' [Gray, 'Elegy Written in a Country Churchyard', l. 33] than 30,000 such poems as the Thebaid. (23)

The strength of Johnson is the strength of twists and knots.   Examine almost any of his positions, and you will find it unfounded and baseless.   He knew as much of poetry as I know of astrology: he was the great corrupter of our language;   partly from perverseness, and partly from profound ignorance of its rich and multiform and remote origin.   The first divine I ever read was Lucas on Holiness in one work, on Happiness in another. (24)   These do *not strike* so much as Barrow or Jeremy Taylor, (25) but I am inclined to believe, if I may trust the impressions that remain on my mind, that in sound wisdom and fertility of thought, as distinct from fancy, he is not inferior to these immortal men.   After reading him I could hardly swallow the chaff and chopped straw of the fashionable Blair. (26)   The Scotch are determined to write something better than English;   there is no idiom: they are in english [sic] what schoolboys in their themes are in latin.

I admire so much the criticism of Wordsworth, that I intend to give an italian translation of it, omitting only his just resentment against the scoundrels of the Edinburgh Review. (27)   I have often seen small and separate observations, just and *clever*, on particular pieces of poetry;   on poetry little tolerable has been said before. How very jejune a thing is that which some scholar of Aristotle has left us, partly in the very words of his master, (28) and how utterly contemptible is the whole work of Longinus! (29)   What Horace has said is excellent, but he says little. (30)

Poor Hooker! what mortal ever sustained so long an argument so ably or so high? or where shall we find the same exuberant richness and varied harmony of language? - For a hundred and fifty years we have slumbered in mediocrity. Since the Paradise Lost little has been done either in prose or in poetry, except within these ten or fifteen years.   But surely never was England so fertile in tolerably good writers as now, never at one time had she a third part of so many and so good.... (31)

NOTES

1 George Gordon, Lord Byron, sixth Baron (1788-1824), English poet, defender of liberty, and author of the popular poems, 'Childe Harold's Pilgrimage' (1812-18) and 'Don Juan' (1819-24), an epic satire.
2 See Byron's The Bride of Abydos.
3 Landor saw Byron in 1812 when the two men went to a London perfumer's shop to purchase attar of roses. Landor afterwards associated Byron's writing with this

scent (R.H. Super, Landor and the 'Satanic School', 'Studies in Philology' (October 1945), 794).

4   See James Thomson's 'The Seasons' (1730).

5   See Wordsworth's 'Tract on the Convention of Cintra' (1809).

6   Landor's reference is to those books of Hooker's 'Laws of Ecclesiastical Polity' that were published during the author's lifetime: Books One-Four (1594), Book Five (1597).

7   Edmund Waller (1606-87) and Abraham Cowley (1618-67), English poets and Royalists.

8   Ruoff, Letters to Birch, 235-7.

9   Thought of a Briton on the Subjugation of Switzerland, 11. 1-2: 'Two voices are there; one is of the sea, / One of the mountains; each a mighty Voice....'

10 Apparently a reference to Tasso's 'Gerusalemme Conquistata' (1593), a revision of 'Gerusalemme Liberata' (1580, 1581).   The structure of the revised version is more regular than that of the original.

11 'Peter Bell' (1819).   See Southey's letter to W.S.L. dated 'Keswick, May 7, 1819', in 'Selections from the Letters of Robert Southey', ed. John Wood Warter (1856), 3, 133.   When Landor opened Southey's package containing 'Peter Bell', he also found copies of Wordsworth's 'Waggoner' (1819), 'The River Duddon ... and Other Poems' (1820), and a volume of prose.

12 Cyrus the Great (d. 529 BC), founder of the Persian Empire.   Alexander the Great (356-323 BC), king of Macedonia, one of the greatest generals who ever lived.   His empire extended from the Mediterranean Sea to the Indian Ocean.

13 Euripides (c. 485-c. 406 BC), the last of the great Greek tragedians.

14 Cf. 'Richard III', V, iv, 11-12: 'I think there be six Richmonds in the field; / Five have I slain to-day instead of him.'

15 'Alcestis', 11. 773ff.

16 For several of Milton's numerous references to Euripides, see 'Il Penseroso', 1. 99, the prefaces to 'Samson Agonistes' and 'Of Education', and the opening quotations to the 'Areopagitica' and 'Of Tenure of Kings and Magistrates'.

17 Ruoff, Letters to Birch, 240-3.

18 Landor's 'Idyllia Heroica Decem' was published in June 1820 at Pisa.

19 See Letters to Robert Southey, No. 4 above, n. 23.

20 Publius Papinius Statius (c. AD 45-96), Roman poet, author of 'Silvae', a collection of occasional verses, and two epic poems, 'Thebais' and 'Achilleis'.

21 Samuel Johnson was not fond of Gray's odes (see 'The
    Critical Opinions of Samuel Johnson', ed. Joseph E.
    Brown, Princeton, 1926, 361-6.
22 Edmund Burke, Sir Joshua Reynolds and Samuel Johnson
    were original members of the famed 'Literary Club'
    that held its meetings at the Turk's Head in Gerrard
    Street.
23 See n. 20 above.
24 Richard Lucas (1648-1715), English clergyman, author
    of the popular 'Enquiry after Happiness' (1685) and
    'Practical Christianity, or an Account of the Holiness
    which the Gospel Enjoins' (1690).
25 Isaac Barrow (1630-77), English mathematician, classi-
    cal scholar, and Anglican theologian, author of nume-
    rous mathematical works in Latin; Jeremy Taylor
    (1613-67), English clergyman and Royalist, author of
    many devotional writings including 'The Rule and Ex-
    ercises of Holy Living' (1650) and 'The Rule and Ex-
    ercises of Holy Dying' (1651).
26 Hugh Blair (1718-1800), Scottish rhetorician and Pres-
    byterian divine, whose 'Sermons' in five volumes
    (1777-1801) were exceedingly popular.
27 See Wordsworth's 'Letter to a Friend of Robert Burns:
    Occasioned by an Intended Republication of the Life of
    Burns, by Dr. Currie; and of the Selection Made by
    Him from His Letters' (1816).   Landor's Italian
    translation of Wordsworth's critical essays has not
    survived.
28 See the 'Poetics' of the Greek philosopher Aristotle
    (384-322 BC).
29 Longinus' 'On the Sublime'.
30 Horace's 'Ars Poetica'.
31 Ruoff, Letters to Birch, 246-7.

6 Letters to Lady Blessington
(excerpts), 1835-41
1855, 1895, 1972

Landor first made the acquaintance of Marguerite, Countess
of Blessington (1789-1849), in February 1827, at Florence,
Italy. This charming, intelligent, attractive, and weal-
thy Irish woman enjoyed the society of artists, writers,
and political leaders, and Landor was soon a regular visitor to her evening gatherings. When the Blessingtons
left Florence later that year, Landor and Lady Blessington
commenced an exchange of letters that ended only with her
death twenty-two years later. Lady Blessington, in addition to sharing Landor's confidence and literary interests, also served as his literary agent in England after
the publication of the 'Imaginary Conversations' (1824-9).
When she assumed the editorship in 1833 of 'The Book of
Beauty', a gift annual, she requested and received contributions in poetry and prose from Landor. In 1836 Lady
Blessington moved into Gore House, in Kensington, London;
and Landor, who had recently returned to England, was
often numbered among those who frequented her famous literary salons. Unlike Wordsworth, who once refused to meet
Landor at Gore House because of the mistress's scandalous
past and questionable relationship with Count d'Orsay,
Landor, according to John Forster, spent his happiest days
in London there ('Landor', 2, 325-6). The following selections from Landor's letters to Lady Blessington, written
during Landor's sixties, demonstrate that the advancing
years had little, if any, effect on his keen interest in
books, in contemporary writers, and in his own creative
efforts as poet and prosewriter.

Many of Landor's letters to Lady Blessington were first
published by R.R. Madden in 'The Literary Life and Correspondence of the Countess of Blessington' (1855). Madden
produced a second edition, much improved, in the same
year, and an American edition was printed from the first

English edition.   In 1895 Alfred Morrison printed for
private circulation 'The Blessington Papers' ('The Collection of Autograph Letters and Historical Documents Formed
by Alfred Morrison').   This edition is superior editori-
ally to Madden's second edition, although Morrison did not
possess, and therefore could not print, some of the letters that appeared in Madden's volumes.   Dr John F. Mariani's The Letters of Walter Savage Landor to Marguerite
Countess of Blessington, unpublished PhD dissertation,
Columbia University, 1973, is a scholarly edition based
almost entirely on the original manuscripts and supersedes
the editions of Madden and Morrison.   The following excerpts are from Dr Mariani's edition, and proper acknowledgments are made in the notes.   The dates are those
given by Mariani.

---

13 January, 1835

... I have been reading Beckford's Travels and
Vatheck. (1)   The last pleases me less than it did forty
years ago - and yet the Arabian Nights have lost none of
their charms for me.   All the learned and wiseacres in
England cried out against this wonderful work, upon its
first appearance - Gray among the rest. (2)   Yet I doubt
whether any man except Shakespeare has shown so much invention, or afforded so much delight, if we open our
hearts to receive it.   The author was the greatest benefactor the East ever had, not excepting Mahomet. (3)   How
many hours of pure happiness has he bestowed on ten or
twenty millions of hearers.   All the springs of the
desert have less refreshed the Arabs than those delightful
tales, and they cast their gems and genii over our benighted and foggy regions.... (4)

28 Feb.-3 March? 1835

Dear Lady Blessington,
After a year, or more, I receive your reminiscences of
Byron. (5) ... Thanks upon thanks for making me think
Byron a better and a wiser man than I had thought him.
Since this precious volume, I have been reading the English Opium-eaters recollections of Coleridge, (6) a genius
of higher order, even in poetry....   Mr. Robinson, (7)
the soundest man that ever stepped thro' the tramels of
law, gave me a few days ago the sorrowful information that
another of our great writers has joined Coleridge.   Poor
Charles Lamb! (8) what a tender and joyous heart had he!
what playfullness, what purity, of style and thought!

His sister is yet living, much older than himself. (9)
One of her Tales, a Mrs Leicester's school, (10) is, with
the sole exception of the Bride of Lammermoor, (11) the
most beautiful tale in prose composition, in any language,
ancient or modern.   A young girl has lost her mother.
The father marries again, and marries a friend of his
former wife.   The child is ill reconciled to it, but,
being dressed in new cloathes for the marriage, she runs
up to her mothers chamber filled with the idea how happy
that dear mother would be at seeing her in all her glory
... not reflecting, poor soul! that it was only by her
mother's death that she appeared in it.   How natural, how
novel, is all this!   Did you ever imagine that a fresh
source of the pathetick would burst out before us in this
trodden and hardened world?   I never did - and when I
found myself upon it, I pressed my temples with both
hands, and tears ran down to my elbows.   The Opium-eater
calls Coleridge 'the largest and most spacious intellect,
the subtlest and [the] most comprehensive, [in my judgment,] that has yet existed among[st] men.' (12)   Impiety
to Shakspeare! treason to Milton!   I give up the rest,
even Bacon. (13)   Certainly since their days we have seen
nothing *at all* comparable to him.   Byron and Scott were
but as gun-flints to a granite mountain.   Wordsworth has
one angle of resemblance.   Southey has written more, and
all well, much admirably.   Fonblanque (14) has said grand
things about me - but I sit upon earth with my heels under
me, looking up devoutly to this last glorious ascension.
Never ask me about the rest.   If you do, I shall only
answer in the cries that you are very likely to hear at
this moment from your window - 'Ground-ivy! ground-ivy'
ground-ivy.... (15)

                                        10-13 April? 1835

... I do not think you ever knew Charles Lamb who is
lately dead.   Robinson took me to see him.

    Once, and only once, have I seen thy face,
    Elia! once only has thy tripping tongue
    Run oer my heart, yet never has been left
    Impression on it stronger or more sweet.
    Cordial old man! for, what youth was in thy years
    What wisdom in thy levity, what soul
    In every utterance of thy purest breast!
    Of all that ever wore man's form, tis there
    I first Wd. spring to at the gate of heaven. (16)

I say *tripping* tongue, for Charles Lamb stammered and
spoke hurriedly. He did not think it worth his while to
put on a fine new coat to come down and see me in, as poor
Coleridge did, but met me as if I had been a friend of
twenty years standing: indeed he told me I had been so,
and showed me some things I had written much longer ago
and had utterly forgotten. The world will never see
again two such delightful volumes as the Essays of Elia -
no man living is capable of writing the worst twenty pages
of them. The Continent has Zadig and Gil Blas: we have
Elia & Sr. Roger de Coverley.... (17)

13 December?, 1836

... I wish our friend Robinson would shew you my
defence (18) - for I never make any note of what I write,
be the subject what it may. Wordsworth, no doubt, has a
thousand good reasons why there is not a good poet upon
earth: but as there are many who have given me pleasure,
I love them for it - some of them perhaps a little more
than they deserve. All men are liable to error - I particularly, who believe that there may be criticism without
sarcasm, and christianity without deans and chapters. -
The surface of Wordsworth's mind, the poetry, has a good
deal of staple about it, and will bear handling: but the
inner, the conversational and private, has many coarse intractable dangling threads, fit only for the flockbed
equipage of grooms and drovers. (19)   I am glad I praised
him before I knew more of him; else I never should; and
I might have been unjust to the better part had I remarked
the worse sooner. (20)   This is a great fault, to which
we all are liable, from an erroneous idea of consistency.
Beside, there is a little malice, I fear, at the bottom of
our hearts (*men's* I mean of course)
What a fool I must be to have written as I have just
been writing if my own could rise up against me on this
occasion! Alas! It has done on too many. Do not be angry
with me for my severity to Byron. He deserves it. Of
this I find evident proofs in abundance, altho I never red
his dramas, nor any thing beside Don Juan and some short
pieces. One is admirable. I mean 'A change came oer
the spirit of my dream -' (21) this is not the beginning,
as you will recollect. The bosom of Byron never could
hold the urn in which the Muse of Tragedy embalms the
dead. There have been four tragic poets in the World.
We await the fifth monarchy and, like the Jews with the
Messiah; we shall not be aware of it when it comes.
Poets are called improvident in all affairs out-lying from

poetry, but it appears to me that in their poetry they are
most so - forgetful as they are while they are writing,
that they must transcribe it afterward.   Then comes the
hoe - husbandry, the weeding, &c enough to break the back.
- Infinite pains it has always cost me, not to bring together the materials [?], not to weave the tissue, but to
make the folds of my draperies hang becomingly.   When I
think of writing on any subject, I abstain a long while
from every kind of reading, lest the tome should haunt me,
and some of the ideas take the liberty of playing with
mine.   I do not wish the children of my brain to imitate
the gait or learn any tricks of others.... (22)

Saturday Morning, 3 July, 1841

... I am delighted to find how gloriously my friend
Dickens has been received at Edinburgh. (23)   But the
Scotchmen could not avoid ill-placed criticisms, and
oblique comparisons.   One blockhead talked of his deficiency in the female character - the very thing in which
he and Shakespeare most excell.   Juliet herself may for
one moment turn her eyes from Romeo on little Nell, (24)
and Desdemona take to her heart *her* hair-breadth scapes.
I dare not decide which of these three characters is the
most interesting and pathetic.... (25)

NOTES

1 William Beckford (1759-1844), author of 'Vathek, an
   Arabian Tale' (published in French in 1787 although a
   pirated English translation appeared the previous
   year), and three travel books, 'Dreams, Waking
   Thoughts, and Incidents' (1783, revised 1834), 'Italy;
   With Sketches of Spain and Portugal' (1834), and 'Recollections of an Excursion to the Monasteries of Al-
   cobaca and Batalha' (1835).   Apparently Landor had
   just read the new 1834 edition of 'Vathek'.
2 Compare Landor's remarks on initial English reaction
   to 'The Arabian Nights' and Rousseau's 'Héloise' in
   'Commentary on Memoirs of Mr. Fox', No. 3 above.
3 Muhammad (c. 570-632), founder of Islam, the Muslim
   religion.
4 Mariani, 84.
5 'Conversations of Lord Byron' (1834).
6 Thomas De Quincey's Samuel Taylor Coleridge, by the
   English Opium-Eater appeared in four instalments in
   'Tait's Edinburgh Magazine': September 1834, 509-20;

October 1834, 588-96;   November 1834, 685-90;   January
1835, 3-10.   Samuel Taylor Coleridge (1772-1834),
English critic, metaphysician, and poet.

7   Henry Crabb Robinson (1775-1867), traveller, foreign
correspondent, barrister, and acquaintance of many
notable people of his day.

8   Coleridge died 25 July 1834.   Charles Lamb (1775-
1834), English essayist, literary critic, and poet,
author of the 'Essays of Elia' (1823, 1833), died 27
December.

9   Mary Ann Lamb (1764-1847) and Charles collaborated on
the popular 'Tales from Shakespear' (1807), for young
readers, and 'Mrs Leicester's School' (1807).

10   See Elinor Forester in 'Mrs Leicester's School'.

11   A novel by Sir Walter Scott (1771-1832), published in
1819.

12   'Tait's Edinburgh Magazine' (September 1834), 509.

13   Francis Bacon, first Baron Verulam and Viscount St
Albans (1561-1626), English statesman, essayist, and
philosopher.

14   Landor incorrectly attributed a laudatory review of
his 'Citation and Examination of William Shakespeare'
(1834) that appeared in the 30 November 1834 'Examiner' to the editor, Albany Fonblanque (1793-1872).
The piece was actually written by John Forster.

15   Mariani, 88-90, 92-4.

16   Landor's poem was also included in a letter to Southey
early in 1835, printed in Ablett's 'Literary Hours'
(1837), and reprinted with variants in 'Works' (1846).
See 'Complete Works', 15, 145-6, for a list of Landor's changes.

17   'Zadig' (1747), a satirical tale by Voltaire;   'Gil
Blas' (1715-35), a picaresque romance by Le Sage;
'Essays of Elia' (1820-3, 1833), miscellaneous, large-
ly autobiographical essays by Charles Lamb;   Sir Roger
de Coverley, a character who figures in many of the
'Spectator' papers by Joseph Addison and Sir Richard
Steele.   See Mariani, 100-1.

18   Landor's poem, 'Satire on Satirists, and Admonition to
Detractors', written in heroic couplets like Byron's
'English Bards and Scotch Reviewers' and published the
first week in December 1836, contains attacks on
'Blackwood's', Byron, and Wordsworth in particular
(see 'Complete Works', 16, 217-27).   Mutual friends
of Landor and Wordsworth like Henry Crabb Robinson
were deeply upset by Landor's satire.

19   A drover is either one who drives cattle, sheep, etc.
to markets or one who deals in cattle.

20   See Headnote to Southey and Porson II, No. 16 below.

21   Byron, The Dream, 11, 75, 105, 126, 144, 167, 184.
22   Mariani, 165-7.
23   Charles Dickens (1812-70), famous English novelist and
     friend of Landor, was honoured by a public banquet
     held at Edinburgh on the night of 25 June 1841.
24   Dickens conceived the idea of Little Nell for his
     novel 'The Old Curiosity Shop' (1841) during a visit
     to Landor's lodgings at 35 St James's Square, Bath, in
     late February 1840.   She naturally became one of
     Landor's favourite female literary characters.
25   Mariani, 352.

7 Letters to John Forster
(excerpts), 1850-8
1869, 1876

When Landor befriended the young literary critic John
Forster (1812-76) in May 1836, he could hardly have fore-
seen that he had found his 'Boswell'. Forster, then
twenty-four and actively pursuing a literary career in
London, soon became the older man's friend, confidant, and
literary agent. He later edited Landor's collected writings in English, the two-volume 'Works of Walter Savage
Landor' (1846), and in Latin, 'Poemata et Inscriptiones'
(1847); and, five years after Landor's death, published
his two-volume 'Walter Savage Landor: A Biography'
(1869). In 1876, the year of his own death, Forster published 'The Works and Life of Walter Savage Landor' in
eight volumes.

Forster preserved Landor's letters to himself and made
ample use of them in the second volume of his 'Landor'
(1869). Many of these letters appear in shorter form,
some even with textual alterations, in his condensed
'Life' (1876). A large number of the original letters
used by Forster in his biographies are now in the Hunting-
ton Library and in the Library of the University of Chicago. The following excerpts are reprinted from
Forster's 'Landor' (1869), and the appropriate reference
for each selection is given in the notes. Both the ital-
icized headings and the dates in parentheses are
Forster's. He does not adhere to a strict chronological
presentation of his excerpts, and many of them are undated. The letters from which the following selections are
taken were written when Landor was between the ages of
seventy-five and eighty-three, and they suggest, once
again, that age had little effect on Landor's vigorous
response to literature.

All yesterday and all this day (8th January 1850) I have
been reading Southey's 'Life and Letters'. (1) ... If he
had not spoken so favourably of my 'Gebir', (2) I might
venture to say that there had been no one, for a couple of
centuries, so thoroughly conversant and well-informed in
poetry, or so candid and impartial.   Only Addison, with
his gentle eyes, had lookt a little way into the glorious
scenes of 'Paradise'; (3)   for which he now lies upon Milton's bosom, the greatest of God's rewards.   I have been
reading once more Dante's 'Paradiso'.   There are most
beautiful things in it;   much better than the best in
'Paradise Regained', and more of them.   But never will I
concede that he has written so grand a poem as 'Paradise
Lost';   no, nor any man else.   The 'Iliad' in comparison
is Ida to the Andes. (4)   The odes of Pindar to Milton's
lyrics, that is, the sonnets, Allegro, Penseroso, &c. are
Epsom racecourse to the New Forest. (5)   I am not writing
on my knees;   that duty would be an incommodious one.

Of Himself, as he appears in Southey's Letters.

Here I stand, brought to life by a dead man.   Few people
would ever have known that I had written poetry, if
Southey had not given his word that a sort of poetry it
really and truly was.   I must have waited until Pindar
and Aeschylus (6) had taken me between them, and until
Milton had said, 'Commonwealth's man, we meet at last'.
Well, I would rather meet him and Southey hereafter than
any of them;   though I know he will ask me why I have done
so little.   My answer will be, Because I wrote chiefly to
occupy the vacant hour, caring not a straw for popularity,
and little more for fame.

Of the great Masters of our Language. (March 1850.)

Dear Southey, like Julius Hare, (7) was fond of English
hexameters, my abhorrence.   As I see that word it makes me
shudder;   for what could I have written that Southey
should believe I felt it for the gentle Spenser? (8)   I
may have expressed abhorrence for his method, never for
himself.   Partly the dreariness of allegory, and partly
the reduplication of similar sounds in the stanza, made me
as incapable of reading a hundred or half hundred of them
consecutively as of reading two hundred ten-syllable couplets.   Never in my life could I perform that feat.   He
(Southey) represents me as thinking we had little poetry
which was good for anything before Milton. (9)   Not so.

'Othello' had agonised my heart before Milton had reacht
my ear.   For the best poetry, as for the best painters
and statuary, we must be disciplined.   I had read the
'Iliad' twice over before I had well studied 'Paradise
Lost'.   Then the hexameter, even Homer's, fell upon my
ear as a ring of fine bells after a full organ.   There
are a few passages in Lucretius, a few in Catullus, (10)
and very many in Virgil, which it is delightful to read
and repeat; but our heroic measure is fuller and more
varied. (11)   Not only Milton has shown it, but Shakespeare too, as often as strong passion demanded it.
Southey and Wordsworth have caught up the echo from a distance, and repeated the cadence in a feebler voice.   It
is impossible for me to judge fairly of Shakespeare's sat-
ellites. (12)   I have not read, and never shall read, a
tithe of their dramas, such is my abhorrence of dirty cut-
throats and courtly drabs.   Ben Jonson I have studied,
principally for the purity of his English. (13)   Had it
not been for him and Shakespeare, our language would have
fallen into ruin.   Hooker too lent his surpliced shoulder
to its support, and Bacon brought some well-squared massy
stones towards the edifice those masters were building.
Southey also has contributed much to the glorious work.

Of Southey and Cowper.

How could Southey praise such harsh sounds following one
another so closely as in Lamb's line, 'calls strangers
still'?   What an ear-ache they have given me!   Southey's
heart protected his ear.   He always found a little good
poetry in much good feeling.   I would have given Cowper
a hundred pounds for permission to strike out half that
number of verses from the 'Task'.   I hope he and Southey
have met in heaven.   Two such men have seldom met on
earth.   Who is worth the least of them?   None among the
living.   I have been reading also lately (April 1856) the
Life of Cowper (15) for the fourth or fifth time.   No
author's life ever interested me so deeply.   How sublime
must have been the devotion of that man who could sacrifice the purest and tenderest love to gratitude!   A sacrifice in his case of heart and soul, leaving Venus Urania
for morose Saturn.   Ah! why did she who loved Cowper ever
love again? (16)   How could she?

Of William Gifford and other Mistakes.

I am reading (July 1856) another volume of Southey's Letters. What an invidious knave it shows Gifford to have
been, and how much trouble he took to spoil Southey's reviews! (17)   This cobbler cut away so much of leather,
the shoe would neither fit nor hold together. (18)   His
tastes were detestable. He ought to have kept his nose
eternally over Juvenal's full cess-pool. (19)   Cumberland
told me that, one morning when he called on his friend
Lord Farnborough, at that time untitled but in
office, (20) he found Gifford and another hack in the
ante-chamber. They were admitted to the minister, and
soon dismist. He made an apology to Cumberland for de-
taining him, but said 'These fellows must be attended to'.
In fact they came for their pay, and got it. (21) ...

Of Tennyson's Maud.

I am delighted (Aug. 1855) with Tennyson's 'Maud'. In
this poem how much higher and fresher is his laurel than
the clipt and stunted ones of the old gardeners in the
same garden! (22)   Poetry and philosophy have rarely met
so cordially before. I wish he had not written the Wellington ode. (23)   He is indeed a true poet. What other
could have written this verse, worth many whole volumes:
'the breaking heart that will not break'? (24)   Infinite
his tenderness, his thought, his imagination, the melody
and softness as well as the strength and stateliness of
his verse. (25) ...

Of Scott and Keats, our Prospero and Ariel.

I have been reading (24 March 1850) Scott's 'Kenilworth',
and think I shall prefer it, on a second reading, either
to the 'Bride of Lammermoor' or my old favourite 'The
Heart of Mid-Lothian'. (26)   It appears to me now to be
quite a fine epic. We ought to glory in such men as
Scott. The Germans would; and so should we, if hatred
of our neighbour were not the religion of authors, and
warfare the practice of borderers. Keats is our Ariel of
poetry, Scott our Prospero. (27)   The one commands, the
other captivates; the one controls all the elements, the
other tempers and enlivens them. And yet this wonderful
creature Keats, who in his felicities of expression comes
very often near to Shakespeare, (28) has defects which his
admirers do not seem to understand. Wordsworth called

his ode to Pan a very pretty piece of paganism when my
friend Charles Brown read it to him; (29) but Keats was
no more pagan than Wordsworth himself.   Between you and
me, the style of Keats is extremely far removed from the
very boundaries of Greece.   I wish someone had been near
him when he printed his 'Endymion', (30) to strike out, as
ruthlessly as you would have done, all that amidst its op-
ulence is capricious and disorderly.   The truth is, and
indeed I hardly know an exception to it, it is in Selection that we English are most deficient.   We lay our
hands upon all, and manage very badly our dependencies.
A young poet should be bound apprentice to Pindar for
three years, whether his business be the ode or anything
else.   He will find nothing in the workshop which he expected to find, but quite enough of highly-wrought tools
and well-seasoned materials. (31) ...

Of some Novels.

I have been (Aug. 1856) cushioning my old head on the
pillow of novels.   What a delightful book is Bulwer's
'Caxtons'! (32)   I have done him injustice, for I never
thought he could have written such pure Saxon English as
may be found here; and Sterne himself, (33) whom he has
chosen to imitate as to manner, is hardly better in the
way of character.   'Esmond', too, is a novel that has
surprised me.   Never could I have believed that Thackeray, great as his abilities are, could have written so
noble a story as 'Esmond'. (34)   On your recommendation I
have since been reading the whole of 'Humphrey Clinker'.
It seems to me that I must have read a part of it before.
Every letter ends with a *rigmarole*, then much in fashion,
and thought to be very graceful.   By rigmarole I mean
such a termination as this: 'It [... which] had like to
have kindled the flames of discord in the family of yours
always, &c.' (35)   A tail always curls round the back of
the letter-writer, and sticks to his *sincerely*, &c.   How
would Cicero and Pliny and Trajan have laught at this cir-
cumbendibus! (36)   In the main however you are right
about the book.   It has abundant humour; and how admirable are such strokes as where the jailer's wife 'wishes
[wished from her heart,] there was such another good soul,
[like him,] in every jail [gaol] in England'! (37)   But I
find it rather wearisome, and stuffed with oddities of
language.   P. 191.   'I have [make] no doubt but your
parents will, in a little time, bring you into the
world.' (38)   If the parents did not bring her into the
world (one of them at least), I wonder who did?   By the

world he means society; as Young did in saying of the *God*
Sleep, 'He, like the *world*, his ready visit pays' &c.
card-case in hand.   'He [And] lights on lids unsullied by
[with] a tear': (39) but I warrant he squeezed one out.
P. 175.   'Penetrated [into] the *uttermost* [utmost] recesses': (40) he means the *innermost*.   '*Between* vanity,
methodism, and love': (41) between is only for two, *by*
and *twain*.   'Neither seen, heard, nor felt': (42) here
again, *neither* applies to two, not more.   You see I have
been carrying the cross you laid upon my shoulders.   I
must now run to Dickens for refreshment.   He is a never-
failing resource; and what an astonishing genius he is!

Of the Edinburgh Review on his Hellenics.

You know with what feeling I read a review in the 'Edinburgh' four years ago, (43) and here is another which
makes me proud of being reviewed by such a writer (April
1850). (44)   Yet I could not but smile at the imputation
of *mannerism*. (45)   Whose manner?   I resemble none of
the ancients, and still less the moderns.   My merits, if
I have any at all, are variety and simplicity.   Cowper is
the only modern poet who is so little of a mannerist as I
am; and even he has somewhat of it.   A little of sweet
bile rises up in his stomach from the crudity of his religion. (46)   I am obscure; (47) this is too certain;
everybody says it.   But are Pindar and Aeschylus less so?
I am unable to guess what proportion of their poetry the
best poets have cancelled.   Wordsworth and Byron, and
most now living, leave no traces of erasure: I wish they
had.   I have rejected quite as much as I have admitted,
and some of it quite as good.   Order and proportion always were my objects.   My real strength, I believe, lies
in the dramatic, and I think I could have composed a drama
suitable for the stage, if I had willed it: but intricacy, called plot, undermines the solid structure of well-
ordered poetry.   There is nothing of it in the 'Iliad',
or in Aeschylus; once only in Sophocles (48) is there
much of it.   The Spaniards are known for little else;
and they brought over to England these instruments of
mental torture in their poetical Armada. (49)   Only think
that I am suspected of undervaluing Dante! (50)   The proportion of bad poetry to good in him is vast indeed; but
never was man, excepting Shakespeare alone, so *intensely* a
poet....   But one thing is quite certain, and you know it
well.   I shall have as many readers as I desire to have
in other times than ours.   I shall dine late; but the
dining-room will be well-lighted, the guests few and

select.   I neither am, nor ever shall be, popular.   Such
never was my ambition.   Thousands of people, for centuries to come, will look up at the statues of the Duke of
York, George III, Canning, Pitt, and others of that description; (51) but in no centuries to come will fifty in
any one generation feast their eyes in silent veneration
on the marbles from the Parthenon. (52)

Of the Quarterly on Steele. (1855.)

I would rather have written what is here quoted from
Steele (53) than all the criticism and philosophy of all
the Edinburgh Reviewers.   What a good critic he was!   I
doubt if he has ever been surpassed.   Somehow I cannot
but connect Steele and Goldsmith, as I do Cowper and
Southey.   Of all our literary men, they interest me the
most....   Dear good faulty Steele!   The 'Quarterly' was
not sent to me before nine last night.   I would not, I
could not, go to bed until I had read it through.   My
eyes are the weaker for it this morning.

Of the Dramatists of Elizabeth and James.

I have been reading what Lamb and Hazlitt say of these
men, (54) and trying vainly, once more, to read steadily
some of their writings.   I call them *circum-circa* Shakes-
pearians, and find them to be as unlike as possible to
Shakespeare.   There is crudeness on one side of the
fruit, and rottenness or overripeness on the other, in almost every one.   A wineglassful of pure water for me,
rather than a bucket of turbid: one seazon of Catullus
rather than all the poetry of the Shakespearian age -
beside Shakespeare's!   Yet there are strong throbs in
the breasts that heave in those tarnisht spangles, and
there are crevices that let fresh air into those barns and
brothels.   But Shakespeare! who can speak of him!   Antiquity fades away before him, and even Homer is but a
shadow. (55) ...

Of Swift's Tale of a Tub. (1858.)

I am reading once more (he was now 83 years of age) the
work I have read oftener than any other prose work in our
language.   I cannot bring to my recollection the number
of copies I have given away, chiefly to young catholic
ladies.   I really believe I converted one by it uninten-

tionally.   What a writer! not the most imaginative or the
most simple, not Bacon or Goldsmith, had the power of
saying more forcibly or completely whatever he meant to
say!

Of Shelley and Himself.

I have been looking (26 April 1858) into the life of
Shelley. (56)   I could not help smiling at Shelley's
praise of me, and at his Hogg's tossing up 'Gebir' into
the fire. (57)   Poor Shelley got into a scrape about me
with Byron.   Yet, ardent as he was in my favour, I refused his proffered visit.   His conduct towards his first
wife had made me distrustful of him. (58)   Yet, with perhaps the single exception of Burns, he and Keats were inspired with a stronger spirit of poetry than any other
poets since Milton.   I sometimes fancy that Elizabeth
Barrett Browning comes next. (59)   But I must confess I
turn more frequently to Goldsmith.   A very little of what
is strange estranges me.   I hate new dresses, though they
fit close.   Never tell me again of any one who either
praises or dispraises me.   I know what I am.   Shelley
and Southey knew it also.   When poets extol a poet, be
sure it is not too highly.... (60)

NOTES

1   See the Rev. Charles Cuthbert Southey, 'The Life and
    Correspondence of Robert Southey', 6 vols, London,
    1849-50.
2   Southey reviewed the then anonymous 'Gebir' (1798) in
    the September 1799 'Critical Review'.   Southey com-
    ments on the occasion of his review in a letter to
    Landor dated 'April 23, 1809' (ibid., 3, 229-30).
3   Joseph Addison was one of the first English critics to
    praise Milton extensively.   See 'Spectator' no. 267
    and every Saturday thereafter until no. 369.
4   Ida is the classical name of a mountain range in
    north-west Asia Minor, near the site of ancient Troy.
    The highest peak is about 5,800 feet.   The Andes
    mountain range stretches the full length of western
    South America.   Many of its peaks are higher than
    22,000 feet.
5   Epsom racecourse or Epsom Downs, Surrey, England, home
    of the 'Derby' and the 'Oaks', horse races instituted
    in 1780 and 1779 respectively.   The New Forest is a
    heavily forested area in south-west Hampshire,
    England.

6   Aeschylus (525-456 BC), founder of Greek tragedy.
7   Julius Charles Hare (1795-1855). See Headnote to
     Archdeacon Hare and Walter Landor, No. 18 below.
8   See Southey's letter to Landor, dated 'Keswick, Jan.
     11, 1811', in 'Life and Correspondence', 3, 295.
9   Ibid.
10   Titus Lucretius Carus (c. 99-c. 55 BC), Roman philoso-
     phical poet, author of 'De Rerum Natura'; Gaius Val-
     erius Catullus (c. 84-c. 54 BC), Roman poet whose ex-
     tant work includes lyrics, love poems, satires, ele-
     giacs, and epigrams.
11   English blank verse, unrhymed iambic pentameter, was
     first used by Henry Howard Surrey (1517?-47) in his
     translation of books two and four of the 'Aeneid'.
12   Francis Beaumont, George Chapman, John Fletcher, Ben
     Jonson, Thomas Kyd, Christopher Marlowe, John Webster,
     and others. See n. 54 below.
13   Benjamin Jonson (1572-1637), actor, dramatist, and
     poet, author of such classical and popular comedies as
     'Volpone' (1606), 'Epicoene, or the Silent Woman'
     (1609), and 'The Alchemist' (1610).
14   Southey, 'Life and Correspondence', 1, 325: Southey
     letter to C.W.W. Wynn, Esq., dated 'Bath, Nov. 20,
     1797'. Landor quotes from the fifteenth line of
     Lamb's poem, 'Written Soon After the Preceding Poem',
     quoted in full in Southey's letter.
15   See Southey's 'Life of Cowper', vols 1-3 of his edi-
     tion of 'The Works of William Cowper', 15 vols (1835-
     7).
16   The widow Lady Austen, mutual friend of Cowper and
     Mrs Unwin until a falling out in 1783, afterwards mar-
     ried an accomplished Frenchman, M. de Tardiff. For
     Southey's account of the quarrel involving Cowper and
     his two female muses, see 'Works of Cowper', 2, 56-63.
17   See in particular Cuthbert Southey's remarks on the
     editorial liberties taken by William Gifford (1756-
     1826), editor of the Tory 'Quarterly Review', with
     Robert Southey's contributions ('Life and Correspon-
     dence', 3, 184-5). Landor was himself indirectly
     victimized by Gifford who drastically altered
     Southey's review of Landor's 'Count Julian' (1812)
     that appeared in the September 1812 'Quarterly Re-
     view', 86-92. According to John Forster, Southey
     never acknowledged the review either to Landor or to
     anyone else ('Landor', 1, 352).
18   See Southey and Porson I, No. 17 below, n. 10.
19   Gifford published a translation of Juvenal's 'Satires'
     in 1802.
20   George Cumberland (1754-1847?), whom Landor knew in

Bristol in 1835;   Charles Long, Baron Farnborough
(1761-1838), English politician, created a peer in
1826.

21   Forster, 'Landor', 2, 523-5.
22   Alfred Tennyson, first Baron Tennyson (1809-92), English poet, appointed Poet Laureate in 1850.   'Maud'
(1855) is a monodrama composed in sections of different meters.
      Landor's comment about 'old gardeners' is a thinly-
veiled slap at Wordsworth.   See Headnote to Southey
and Porson II, No. 16 below.
23   Although Tennyson's national reputation was confirmed
by his ode on the death of the Duke of Wellington
(1852), the poem was not well-received by critics.
24   Tennyson, 'Ballad of Oriana', l. 64.
25   Forster, 'Landor', 2, 526.
26   Scott's novels were published in 1821, 1819, and 1818
respectively.
27   John Keats (1795-1821), English poet.   Landor's reference is to Shakespeare's 'The Tempest'.
28   See Landor, English Visitor, and Florentine Visitor,
No. 13 below, and n. 8.
29   Walter Jackson Bate in his biography of Keats gives an
authoritative account of this event: Benjamin Robert
Haydon arranged for Keats to meet Wordsworth at the
home of Thomas Monkhouse in late December 1817.   When
Wordsworth asked Keats '"what he had been lately
doing"', Haydon replied that Keats had '"just finished
an exquisite ode to Pan"' and asked Keats to recite it
which he did.   Wordsworth then replied: '"'a Very
pretty piece of Paganism'"'.   Bate notes that Leigh
Hunt, Charles Cowden Clarke, and Joseph Severn, 'none
of whom was present, all gave their accounts'.   See
Bate, 'John Keats' (1963), 264-7.   Charles Armitage
Brown (1786-1842), friend of Keats and Landor, also
has his version.
30   'Endymion' (1818), a poem in four books, characterized
by the author in his Preface as 'a feverish attempt,
rather than a deed accomplished'.
31   Forster, 'Landor', 2, 527.
32   'The Caxtons' (1849), a novel by Edward Bulwer Lytton,
first Baron Lytton (1803-73).
33   Laurence Sterne (1713-68), English clergyman and novelist, author of 'The Life and Opinions of Tristram
Shandy' (1760-7) and 'A Sentimental Journey through
France and Italy by Mr. Yorick' (1768).
34   'The History of Henry Esmond, Esquire' (1852), a novel
by William Makepeace Thackeray (1811-63).
35   See Tobias Smollett (1721-71), 'The Expedition of

Humphry Clinker' (1771), Oxford University Press,
1966, 207.

36   Marcus Tullius Cicero (106-43 BC), Roman orator and
statesman, author of numerous literary, philosophical,
and political writings as well as four collections of
Letters; Pliny the Younger (c. AD 61-c. 112), Roman
lawyer and statesman, author of nine books of Letters;
Trajan (Marcus Ulpius Traianus), Roman Emperor (AD
98-117), a great soldier and able administrator,
friend to Pliny the Younger.

37   Smollett, 'Humphry Clinker', 151.

38   Ibid., 91.

39   Edward Young, 'The Complaint: or, Night Thoughts', i,
2, 5.

40   Smollett, 'Humphry Clinker', 309.

41   Ibid., 259.

42   Ibid., 260.

43   John Forster wrote the anonymous article praising the
as yet un-published two-volume 'Works of Walter Savage
Landor' (June 1846) that appeared in the April 1846
'Edinburgh Review', 486-511.   For an account of the
furor caused by Forster puffing an edition of which he
was rumoured to own the copyright, see Super,
'Landor', 363 and 583-4, n. 85.

44   See the April 1850 'Edinburgh Review', 408-43, for
Aubrey De Vere's appraisal of Landor's poetry as it
appears in 'Works' (1846), 'Hellenics, Enlarged and
Completed' (1847), and 'Poemata et Inscriptiones'
(1847).

45   Ibid., 427.

46   William Cowper was an ardent, evangelical Calvinist
who suffered periodic attacks of melancholia and despair.

47   'Edinburgh Review', 426-8, 430.

48   Sophocles (c. 496-406 BC), second of the great Greek
tragedians.

49   Landor's allusion is to the Spanish Armada, a huge
fleet sent in 1588 by Philip II of Spain, leader of
Catholic Europe, to help in the attempted invasion of
England.

50   'Edinburgh Review', 438.

51   James II (1633-1701), created Duke of York in 1634,
king of Great Britain from 1685 to 1688; George III
(1738-1820), king of Great Britain from 1760 to 1820;
George Canning (1770-1827), Treasurer of the Navy
during William Pitt's last administration (12 May
1804-23 January 1806); William Pitt (1759-1806),
famous English statesman.   These English kings and
statesmen rank high in Landor's list of political vil-

lains.   See Landor's Imaginary Conversation, Mr. Pitt
and Mr. Canning.

52   Henry Crabb Robinson records that Landor stood so long
before the Elgin Marbles (sculptures from the Parthenon) in the British Museum one morning in the spring
of 1836 that he had to leave his friend there ('Henry
Crabb Robinson on Books and Their Writers', ed. Edith
J. Morley, London, 1938, 2, 493-4.

53   See 517-20 of a review of Thomas Babington Macaulay's
'Life and Writings of Addison', London, 1852, in the
March 1855 'Quarterly Review', 509-68.   Sir Richard
Steele (1672-1729), Irish writer and critic, founded
the 'Tatler' in 1709, the 'Guardian' in 1713, and with
Joseph Addison carried on the 'Spectator' (1711-12).

54   See Charles Lamb, 'Specimens of the English Dramatic
Poets who Lived about the Time of Shakespeare' (1808),
and William Hazlitt, 'Lectures on the Dramatic Literature of the Age of Elizabeth' (1820).   See n. 12
above.

55   Forster, 'Landor', 2, 529-32.

56   Percy Bysshe Shelley (1792-1822), English lyrical and
revolutionary poet.

57   Thomas Jefferson Hogg (1792-1862), educated at Oxford
with Shelley and author of a biography of his friend.
Hogg's account of the 'Gebir' episode reads: 'I often
found Shelley reading "Gebir".   There was something
in that poem which caught his fancy.   He would read
it aloud or to himself sometimes, with a tiresome per-
tinacity.   One morning, I went to his rooms to tell
him something of importance, but he would attend to
nothing but "Gebir".   With a young impatience, I
snatched the book out of the obstinate fellow's hand,
and threw it through the open window into the quad-
rangle [at Oxford].   It fell upon the grass-plot, and
was brought back presently by the servant....'
(Thomas Jefferson Hogg, 'The Life of Percy Bysshe
Shelley' (1858), i, 201-2).

58   When Landor heard Leigh Hunt's version of Shelley's
desertion of Harriet, he repented his decision not to
make Shelley's acquaintance when both men resided at
Pisa in 1820.   See Super, 150, 179.

59   Elizabeth Barrett Browning (1806-61), English poetess,
author of 'Sonnets from the Portuguese' (1850), and
wife of Robert Browning (1812-89).   Landor first met
Elizabeth Barrett and Robert Browning in May 1836,
and, twenty-three years later, lived near the Brown-
ings in Florence.   Landor is buried near Mrs Browning
in the Protestant Cemetery at Florence.

60   Forster, 'Landor', 2, 537.

8 To the Reverend Cuthbert Southey on His Father's Character and Public Services
1850, 1853

Landor wrote To the Reverend Charles Cuthbert Southey on His Father's Character and Public Services in an attempt to draw the government's attention to the financial plight of his old friend's son.   The letter was successful, for by the end of a year the son of the former Poet Laureate was awarded a more secure living.   This public letter first appeared in the December 1850 issue of 'Frazer's Magazine' and was reprinted in 'Last Fruit off an Old Tree' (1853).   The following selection, which contains some of Landor's most discriminating criticism of the literature of the Romantic period, is reprinted from the 1853 text.

It is not because I enjoyed your father's friendship, my dear sir, that I am now about to send you my testimony to his worth.   Indeed that very friendship, and the frequent expression of it in his letters for more than forty years, have made me hesitate too long before the public.

Never in the course of my existence have I known a man so excellent on so many points.   What he was as a son, is now remembered by few;   what he was as a husband and a father, shows it more clearly than the best memory could represent it.   The purity of his youth, the integrity of his manhood, the soundness of his judgment, and the tenderness of his heart, they alone who have been blest with the same qualities can appreciate.   And who are they? Many with one, some with more than one, nobody with all of them in the like degree.   So there are several who possess one quality of his poetry;   none who possess the whole variety.

For poetry there must be invention, energy, truth of conception, wealth of words, and purity of diction.   His were indeed all these, excepting one;   and that one often

came when called for; I mean energy. This is the chief
characteristic and highest merit of Byron; it is also
Scott's, and perhaps more than equally. Shelley is not
deficient in it; nor is Keats, whose heart and soul is
sheer poetry, overflowing from its fermentation. Wordsworth is as meditative and thoughtful as your father, but
less philosophical; his intellect was less amply stored;
his heart was narrower. He knew the fields better than
men, and ordinary men better than extraordinary. He is
second to your father alone, of all poets, ancient or
modern, in local description. The practice of the ancients has inculcated the belief that scenery should be
rare and scanty in heroic poetry. Even those among them
who introduce us into pastoral life are sparing of it.
Little is there in Theocritus, hardly a glimpse in Moschus
or Bion: (1) but Virgil has more and better of (what is
called) *description*, in his 'AEneid' than in his 'Eclogues' or 'Georgics'. The other epic poets, whatever the
age or country, are little worth noticing, with the single
and sole exception of Apollonius. (2) I do not call
epic, as I have said before, that which is written in a
lyric meter, nor indeed in any species of rhyme. For,
the cap and bells should never surmount the helmet and
breast-plate. To the epic not only a certain spirit but
also a certain form is requisite, and not only in the main
body, but likewise in the minute articulations. Ariosto
and Tasso are lyric romancers. To call Milton epic or
heroic would degrade him from his dignity. To call
'Paradise Lost' a divine poem is in every sense of the
word to call it rightly. I am inclined to think there is
more of beautiful and appropriate scenery in 'Roderic' (3)
alone, than the whole range of poetry, in all its lands,
contains. Whatever may be the feeling of others in regard to it, I find it a relief from sanguinary actions and
conflicting passions, to rest a while beyond, but within
sight. However, the poet ought not at any time to grow
cool and inactive in the field of battle, nor retire
often, nor long.

The warmest admirers of Wordsworth are nevertheless so
haunted by antiquity, that there are few among them, I
believe, who would venture to call him, what I have no
hesitation in doing, the superior both of Virgil and of
Theocritus in description. And description, let it be
remembered, is not his only nor his highest excellence.
Before I come to look into his defects, I am ready to
assert that he has written a greater number of good sonnets than all the other sonneteers in Europe put together:
yet sometimes in these compositions, as in many others of
the smaller, he is expletive and diffuse; which Southey

never is.   Rural and humble life has brought him occasionally to a comparison with Crabbe. (4)   They who in
their metaphors are fond of applying the physical to the
moral, might say perhaps that Wordsworth now and then
labors under a diarrhoea; Crabbe under a constipation;
each without the slightest symptom of fever or excitement.
Immeasurably above Crabbe, and widely different, less
graphic, less concise, less anatomical, he would come
nearer to Cowper, had he Cowper's humor. (5)   This, which
Wordsworth totally wanted, your father had abundantly.
Certainly the commentator who extolled him for *universality*, intended no irony, although it seems one.   He wanted not only universality, but variety, in which none of
our later poets is comparable to Southey.   His humor is
gentle and delicate, yet exuberant.   If in the composition of Wordsworth there had been this one ingredient, he
would be a Cowper in solution, with a crust of prose at
the bottom, and innumerable flakes and bee-wings floating
up and down loosely and languidly.   Much of the poetry
lately, and perhaps even still in estimation, reminds me
of plashy and stagnant water, with here and there the
broad flat leaves of its fair but scentless lily on the
surface, showing at once a want of depth and of movement.
I would never say this openly, either to the censurers or
favorers of such as it may appear to concern.   For it is
inhumane to encourage enmities and dislikes, and scarcely
less so to diminish an innocent pleasure in good creatures
incapable of a higher.   I would not persuade, if I could,
those who are enraptured with a morrice-dancer (6) and a
blind fiddler, that their raptures ought to be reserved
for a Grisi and a Beethoven, (7) and that if they are very
happy they are very wrong.   The higher kinds of poetry,
of painture, and of sculpture, can never be duly estimated
by the majority even of the intellectual.   The marbles of
the Parthenon and the Odes of Pindar bring many false wor-
shippers, few sincere. (8)   Cultivation will do much in
the produce of the nobler arts, but there are only a few
spots into which this cultivation can be carried.   Of
what use is the plough, or the harrow, or the seed itself,
if the soil is sterile and the climate uncongenial?

Remarks have been frequently and justly made, on the
absurdity of classing in the same category the three celebrated poets who resided contemporaneously, and in fellowship, near the Lakes.   There is no resemblance between
any two of them in the features and character of their
poetry.   Southey could grasp great subjects, and completely master them; Coleridge never attempted it;
Wordsworth attempted it, and failed.   He has left behind
him no poem, no series or collection of his, requiring and

manifesting so great and diversified powers as are exhibited in 'Marmion', or 'The Lady of the Lake', in 'Roderic', or 'Thalaba', or 'Kehama'. (9)   His 'Excursion' (10) is a vast congeries of small independent poems, several very pleasing.   Breaking up this unwieldy vessel, he might have constructed but of its material several eclogues; craft drawing little water.

Coleridge left unfinished, year after year, until his death, the promising 'Christabel'. (11)   Before he fell exhausted from it, he had done enough to prove that he could write good poetry, not enough to prove that he could ever be a great poet.   He ran with spirit and velocity a short distance, then dropped.   Excelling no less in prose than in poetry, he raised expectations which were suddenly overclouded and blank, undertook what he was conscious he never should perform, and declared he was busily employed in what he had only dreamt of.   Never was love more imaginary than his love of truth.   Not only did he never embrace her, never bow down to her and worship her, but he never looked her earnestly in the face.   Possessing the most extraordinary powers of mind, his unsteadiness gave him the appearance of weakness.   Few critics were more acute, more sensitive, more comprehensive; but, like other men, what he could say most eloquently he said most willingly; and he would rather give or detract with a large full grasp, than weigh deliberately.

What a difference there is between the characters of Coleridge and of Southey!   Coleridge was fond of indulging in a soft malignity, while all the energy of Southey lay in his benevolence.   Southey had long and continuous trains of thought; Coleridge was unable to hold together, in poetry or prose, as much as might be contained in half a dozen pages.   Southey often walked upon tenacious clay; Coleridge on deep and sparkling shingle.   Southey valued truth above all things; Coleridge prized the copy far more highly than the original, and would rather see it reflected in the glass than right before him.   He was giddy by the plethora of power, and after a few paces he was constrained to stop.   He wanted not time to finish the finest of his poems, the 'Christabel', but the means he wanted.   I think more highly of his 'Ancient Mariner' (12) than Southey did; but there are several poems of Shelley, Keats, and Wordsworth, incomparably better. Here I speak of poets who write no longer; I might speak it as justly of quite as many who are moving in the same path among us every day.   Several of these have struck as deep a root, but in none of them are there such wide ramifications.   Coleridge would have written a restless and rambling history; part very rich and part very ragged,

its holes stuffed up with metaphysics and disquisition,
without a man's face to be seen throughout: Southey has
shown us he could do more than any other Englishman of our
age had done in this department, until Napier came and won
from him the Peninsula. (13)

Conscience with Southey stood on the other side of Enthusiasm.   What he saw, he said; what he found, he laid
open.   He alone seems to have been aware that criticism,
to be complete, must be both analytical and synthetic.
Every work should be measured by some standard.   It is
only by such exposition and comparison of two, more or
less similar in the prominent points, that correctness of
arbitriment can be attained.   All men are critics; all
men judge the written or unwritten words of others.   It
is not in works of imagination, as you would think the
most likely for it, but it is chiefly in criticism that
writers at the present day are discursive and erratic.
Among our regular bands of critics there is almost as much
and as ill-placed animosity on one side, and enthusiasm on
the other, as there is among the vulgar voters at parlia-
mentary elections, and they who differ from them are pelted as heartily.   In the performance of the ancient drama
there were those who modulated with the pipe the language
of the actor.   No such instrument is found in the ward-
robe of our critics, to temper their animosity or to
direct their enthusiasm.   Your father carried it with him
wherever he sat in judgment; because he knew that his
sentence would be recorded, and not only there.   Obli-
vion is the refuge of the unjust; but their confidence is
vain in the security of that sanctuary.   The most idle
and ignorant hold arguments on literary merit.   Usually,
the commencement is, '*I think with you, but*', &c., or '*I
do not think with you*'.   The first begins with a false
position; and there is probably one, and more than one,
on each side.   The second would be quite correct if it
ended at the word *think*; for there are few who can do it,
and fewer who will.   The kindlier tell us that no human
work is perfect.   This is untrue: many poetical works
are; many of Horace, more of Catullus, still more of La-
fontaine; if indeed fable may be admitted as poetry by
coming in its garb and equipage. (14)   Surely there are
some of Moore's songs, and several of Barry Cornwall's, (15) absolutely perfect: surely there are also a
few small pieces in the Italian and French.   I wonder, on
a renewed investigation, to find so few among the Greeks.
But the fluency of the language carried them too frequently on the shallows; and even in the graver and more sen-
tentious the current is greater than the depth.   The
Ilissus is sometimes a sandbank. (16)   In the elegant and

graceful arrow there is often not only much feather and
little barb, but the barb wants weight to carry it with
steadiness and velocity to the mark.   Milton and Cowper
were the first and last among us who breathed without
oppression on the serene and cloudless highths where the
Muses were born and educated.   Each was at times a truant
from his school; but even the lower of the two, in his
'Task', has done what extremely few of his preceptors
could do.   Alas! his attic honey was at last turned sour
by the leaven of fanaticism. (17) ... Nobody was readier
than Southey to acknowledge that, in his capacity of
laureate, he had written some indifferent poetry; but it
was better than his predecessor's or successor's on similar occasions. (18)   Personages whom he was expected to
commemorate looked the smaller for the elevation of their
position, and their naturally coarse materials crumbled
under the master's hand.   Against these frail memorials
we may safely place his 'Inscriptions', (19) and challenge
all nations to confront them....

NOTES

1 Theocritus (c. 300-c. 260 BC?), Bion (fl. probably c.
   100 BC), and Moschus (fl. probably c. 150 BC), Greek
   pastoral poets.
2 Apollonius Rhodius (c. 295-215 BC), author of the
   'Argonautica'.
3 Southey's 'Roderick, the Last of the Goths' (1814).
   See Letters to Southey, No. 4 above.
4 George Crabbe (1754-1832), English clergyman and
   poet, author of 'The Village' (1783), 'The Borough'
   (1810), and 'Tales in Verse' (1812).
5 See William Cowper's humorous poem, 'John Gilpin's
   Ride' (1782).
6 A Morris-dance, according to the 'Oxford English Dictionary', is 'a grotesque dance performed by persons
   in fancy costume, usually representing characters from
   the Robin Hood legend, esp. Maid Marian and Friar
   Tuck.   Hence, any mumming performance of which fantastic dancing is an important feature'.
7 Giulia Grisi (1811-69), Italian opera singer whose
   brilliant dramatic soprano voice enabled her to reign
   as a prima donna for thirty years.   Ludwig van
   Beethoven (1770-1827), German composer of universal
   renown.
8 See Letters to John Forster, No. 7 above and n. 52.
9 'Marmion, A Tale of Flodden Field' (1808) and 'The
   Lady of the Lake' (1810), poems by Sir Walter Scott;

'Roderick' (1814), 'Thalaba' (1801), and 'Kehama' (1810), epic poems by Robert Southey.

10 Cf. Landor's remark on Wordsworth's 'Excursion' (1814) in Letters to Birch, No. 5 above.

11 Coleridge composed the first part of 'Christabel' in 1797 and the second part in 1800.   The unfinished poem was published in 1816.

12 Coleridge's 'Rime of the Ancient Mariner' was first published in the 'Lyrical Ballads' (1798) of Wordsworth and Coleridge.

13 Southey's 'History of the Peninsular War' (1823-32) proved less successful than Sir William Napier's 'History of the War in the Peninsula ... from 1807 to ... 1814' (1828-40).

14 See 'Les Fables' (1668, 1678-9, 1693) of the French poet Jean de la Fontaine (1621-95).

15 Thomas Moore (1779-1852), Irish poet and singer, author of 'Irish Melodies' (1807-34); Barry Cornwall, pseudonym for Bryan Waller Procter (1787-1874), author of 'English Songs' (1832).

16 The Ilissus is a stream that originates on Mount Hymettus and flows past Athens to the south-east and east.   The stream bed is often dry.

17 See Letters to John Forster, No. 7 above, and n. 46.

18 Southey was Poet Laureate from 1813 until his death in 1843.   He was preceded by Henry James Pye (1745-1813), who held the office from 1790 to 1813, and succeeded by William Wordsworth, Laureate until 1850.

19 Southey's 'Inscriptions' is a collection of forty-five epitaphs and brief commemorative poems composed primarily between 1796 and 1828.   See 'Poetical Works of Robert Southey', London, 1838, 3, 103-78.

9 'Letter from W. S. Landor to R. W. Emerson' (excerpt)
1856, 1869, 1895, 1896

The privately printed 'Letter from W.S. Landor to R.W.
Emerson' was occasioned by the publication of Emerson's
'English Traits', Boston and London, 1856, a small volume
in which the American writer printed observations jotted
down in his journals during his visits to Europe in 1833
and 1847-8. Emerson (1803-82) made the journey of 1833
specifically to meet four authors whom he greatly admired:
Carlyle, Coleridge, Landor, and Wordsworth. Since his
ship landed at Malta, Landor was the first he visited.
On 15 May Emerson, accompanied by the American sculptor
Horatio Greenough, dined with Landor at his Fiesolan
villa:

> I [Emerson] found him [Landor] noble and courteous,
> living in a cloud of pictures at his Villa Gherardesca,
> a fine house commanding a beautiful landscape. I had
> inferred from his books, or magnified from some anec-
> dotes, an impression of Achillean wrath - an untameable
> petulance. I do not know whether the imputation were
> just or not, but certainly on this May day his courtesy
> veiled that haughty mind, and he was the most patient
> and gentle of hosts.... He admired Washington;
> talked of Wordsworth, Byron, Massinger, Beaumont and
> Fletcher. To be sure, he is decided in his opinions,
> likes to surprise, and is well content to impress, if
> possible, his English whim upon the immutable past....
> He has a wonderful brain, despotic, violent, and inex-
> haustible, meant for a soldier, by what chance conver-
> ted to letters, in which there is not a style nor a
> tint not known to him, yet with an English appetite for
> action and heroes.... But year after year the scholar
> must still go back to Landor for a multitude of elegant
> sentences - for wisdom, wit, and indignation that are
> unforgetable ('English Traits', London, 1856, 3-5).

Emerson breakfasted with Landor two days later, and then
journeyed to England where he called upon Carlyle, Coleridge, and Wordsworth.   Landor knew two of these three
men well, and his 'Letter to Emerson' is both an attempt
to correct what he felt were Emerson's false impressions
about Carlyle and Wordsworth and to justify many of his
own remarks uttered twenty-three years before.   This re-
joinder, composed when Landor was eighty-one years old,
contains some of his most trenchant literary criticism.

Landor's 'Letter to Emerson' was nominally published in
1856 by E. Williams, a local newsagent at Bath.   An extract was preserved by Forster in 'Landor' (1869), 2, 266-
70.   The pamphlet was reproduced in 1895 by the Rowfant
Club, Cleveland, Ohio, USA, and reprinted in W.R. Nicoll's
and T.J. Wise's 'Literary Anecdotes of the Nineteenth Century' (1896), 2, 194-216.   The following selection is
from the Rowfant Club reproduction.

MY DEAR SIR,
Your 'English Traits' have given me great pleasure;   and
they would have done so even if I had been treated by you
with less favour.   The short conversations we held at my
Tuscan Villa were insufficient for an estimate of my character and opinions.   A few of these, and only a few, of
the least important, I may have modified since.   Let me
run briefly over them as I find them stated in your pages.
Twenty-three years have not obliterated from my memory the
traces of your visit, in company with that intelligent man
and glorious sculptor, who was delegated to erect a statue
in your capital to the tutelary genius of America. (1)   I
share with him my enthusiastic love of ancient art;   but I
am no *exclusive*, as you seem to hint I am. (2)   In my
hall at Fiesole there are two busts, if you remember, by
two artists very unlike the ancients, and equally unlike
each other;   Donatello and Fiamingo; (3)   surveying them
at a distance is the sorrowful countenance of Germani-
cus. (4)   Sculpture at the present day flourishes more
than it ever did since the age of Pericles; (5)   and
America is not cast into the shade by Europe.   I do prefer Giovanni da Bologna to Michael Angelo, (6) who indeed
in his conceptions is sublime, but often incorrect, and
sometimes extravagant, both in sculpture and painting.   I
confess I have no relish for his prodigious *giblet pie* in
the Capella Sistina, known throughout the world as his
'Last Judgement'.   Grand in architecture, he was no ordinary poet, no lukewarm patriot....

We will now walk a little way out of the gallery.   Let

me say, before we go farther, that I do not think 'the
Greek historians the only good ones'. (7)   Davila, Machiavelli, Voltaire, Michelet, (8) have afforded me much
instruction and much delight.   Gibbon (9) is worthy of a
name among the most enlightened and eloquent of the ancients.   I find no fault in his language; on the contrary, I find the most exact propriety.   The grave, and
somewhat austere, becomes the historian of the Roman Republic; the grand, and somewhat gorgeous, finds its
proper place in the palace of Byzantium.   Am I indifferent to the merits of our own historians? (10) indifferent
to the merits of him who balanced with equal hand Wellington and Napoleon? (11)   No; I glory in my countryman and
friend.   Is it certain that I am indiscriminating in my
judgment on Charron? (12)   Never have I compared him with
Montaigne; (13) but there is much of wisdom, and, what is
remarkable in the earlier French authors, much of sincerity in him.

I am sorry to have 'pestered you with Southey', and to
have excited the inquiry, 'Who is Southey?' (14)   I will
answer the question.   Southey is the poet who has written
the most imaginative poem of any in our own times, English
or Continental; such is the 'Curse of Kahama'.   Southey
is the proseman who has written the purest prose; Southey
is the critic the most cordial and the least invidious.
Show me another, of any note, without captiousness, without arrogance, and without malignity....

I have enjoyed the conversation of Carlyle within the
room where I am writing. (15)   It appeared at that time
less evidently than now that his energy goes far beyond
his discretion.   Perverseness is often mistaken for
strength, and obstinacy for consistency.   There is only
one thing in which he resembles other writers, namely, in
saying that which he can say best, and with most point.
You tell us, 'he [Carlyle] does not read Plato'. (16)
Perhaps there may be a sufficient reason for it.

Resolved to find out what there is in this remarkable
philosopher, I went daily for several weeks into the Mag-
liabechian library at Florence, and thus refreshing my
neglected Greek, I continued the reading of his works in
the original from beginning to end.   The result of this
reading may be found in several of the 'Imaginary Conversations'. (17)   That one of them between Lord Chesterfield and Lord Chatham contains observations on the caco-
phony of some sentences; and many more could have been
added quite as exceptionable.   Even Attic honey hath its
impurities.

'He (Carlyle) took despairing or satirical views of
literature at this moment.' (18)

I am little fond of satire, and less addicted to despair.   It seems to me that never in this country was
there a greater number of good writers than now; and some
are excellent.   Our epic is the novel or romance.   I
dare not praise the seven or eight of both sexes who have
written these admirably; if I do, the *ignavum fuci pecus*
[the drones, a lazy herd ('Aeneid', i, 435)] would settle
on me.   All are glad to hear the censure, few the praise,
of those who labor in the same vineyard.

We are now at Rydal Mount. (19)

Wordsworth's bile is less fervid than Carlyle's: it
comes with more saliva about it, and with a hoarser ex-
pectoration.   'Lucretius he [Wordsworth] esteems a far
higher poet than Virgil.' (20)

The more fool he! 'not in his [Lucretius] system, which
is nothing, but in his power of illustration'. (21)

Does a power of illustration imply the *high* poet?   It
is in his system (which, according to Wordsworth, *is
nothing*) that the power of Lucretius consists.   Where
then is its use?   But what has Virgil in his Eclogues, in
his Georgics, or in his Aeneid, requiring illustration?
Lucretius does indeed well illustrate his subject; and
few even in prose among the philosophers have written so
intelligibly; but the quantity of his poetry does not
much exceed three hundred lines in the whole: one of the
noblest specimens of it is a scornful expostulation
against the fear of death. (22)   Robert Smith, brother of
Sidney, (23) wrote in the style of Lucretius such Latin
poetry as is fairly worth all the rest in that language
since the banishment of Ovid.   Even Lucretius himself nowhere hath exhibited such a continuation of manly thought
and of lofty harmony.

We must now descend to Wordsworth once again. (24)

He often gave an opinion on authors which he never had
red, and on some which he could not read; Plato for instance. (25)   He speaks contemptuously of the
Scotch. (26)   The first time I ever met him, (27) and the
only time I ever conversed with him longer than a few
minutes, he spoke contemptuously of Scott, and violently
of Byron.   He chattered about them incoherently and indiscriminately.   In reality, Scott had singularly the
power of imagination and of construction: Byron little of
either; but this is what Wordsworth neither said nor
knew.   His censure was hardened froth.   I praised a line
of Scott's on the dog of a traveller lost in the snow (if
I remember) on Skiddaw. (28)   He said it was the only
good one in the poem, and began instantly to recite a

whole one of his own upon the same subject. (29) This
induced me afterward to write as follows on a flyleaf in
Scott's poems,

> Ye who have lungs to mount the Muse's hill,
> Here slake your thirst aside their liveliest rill:
> Asthmatic Wordsworth, Byron piping hot.
> Leave in the rear, and march with manly Scott. (30)

I was thought unfriendly to Scott for one of the friend-
liest things I ever did toward an author. Having noted
all the faults of grammar and expression in two or three
of his volumes, I calculated that the number of them, in
all, must amount to above a thousand. Mr. Lockhart, who
married his daughter, was indignant at this, and announced, at the same time (to prove how very wrong I was) that
they were corrected in the next edition. (31) ...

When Hazlitt was in Tuscany he often called on me, (32)
and once asked me whether I had ever seen Wordsworth. I
answered in the negative, and expressed a wish to know
something of his appearance.
'Sir,' said Hazlitt, 'have you ever seen a horse?'
'Assuredly.' 'Then, Sir, you have seen Wordsworth.'
When I met him some years after at a friend's on the
lake of Waswater, (33) I found him extremely civil.
There was *equinity* in the lower part of his face: in the
upper was much of the contemplative, and no little of the
calculating. This induced me, when, at a breakfast where
many were present, he said he 'would not give five shil-
lings for all Southey's poetry', to tell a friend of his
that he might safely make such an investment of his money
and throw all his own in. Perhaps I was too ill-humour-
ed; but my spirit rose against his ingratitude toward
the man who first, and with incessant effort and great
difficulty, brought him into notice. He ought to have
approached his poetical benefactor as he did the

> illustrious peer,
> ....
> With [Of] high respect and gratitude sincere.
> ['To the Right Honourable William, Earl of Lonsdale,
> KG', dedication to 'The Excursion', ll. 1, 8.]

Southey would have been more pleased by the friendliness
of the sentiment than by the intensity of the poetry in
which it is expressed; for Southey was the most equitable, the most candid, the most indulgent of mankind. I

was unacquainted with him for many years after he had commended, in the 'Critical Review', my early poem,
'Gebir'. (34)   In the letters now edited by Mr. Warter, I
find that in the 'Whitehaven Journal' there was inserted a
criticism, in which, on the strength of this poem, I am
compared and preferred to Göthe. (35)   I am not too much
elated.   Neither in my youthful days nor in any other
have I thrown upon the world such trash as 'Werter' and
'Wilhelm Meister', nor flavoured my poetry with the cor-
rugated spicery of metaphysics. (36)   Nor could he have
written in a lifetime any twenty, in a hundred or there-
about, of my 'Imaginary Conversations'.   My poetry I
throw to the Scotch terriers growling at my feet.   Fifty
pages of Shelley contain more of pure poetry than a hundred of Göthe, who spent the better part of his time in
contriving a puzzle, and in spinning out a yarn for a
labyrinth.   How different in features, both personal and
poetical, are Göthe and Wordsworth!   In the countenance
of Göthe there was something of the elevated and august;
less of it in his poetry;   Wordsworth's physiognomy was
entirely rural.   With a rambling pen he wrote admirable
paragraphs in his longer poem, (37) and sonnets worthy of
Milton: for example,

Two voices are there, &c.,
['Thought of a Briton on the Subjugation of Switzerland.]

which is far above the highest pitch of Göthe.   But his
unbraced and unbuttoned impudence in presence of our grand
historians, Gibbon and Napier, must be reprehended and
scouted. (38)   Of Gibbon I have delivered my opinion;   of
Napier too, on whom I shall add nothing more at present
than that he superseded the Duke, (39) who intended to
write the history of his campaigns, and who (his nephew
Capt. William Wellesley tells me) has left behind him
'Memoirs'.
   I never *glorified* Lord Chesterfield; (40)   yet he
surely is among the best of our writers in regard to
style, and appears to have formed Horace Walpole's and
Sterne's, (41) a style purely English....

   I make no complaint of what is stated in the following
page, that 'Landor is strangely undervalued in England'. (42)   I have heard it before, but I never have
taken the trouble to ascertain it.   Here I find that I am
'savagely attacked in the Reviews'. (43)   Nothing more
likely;   I never see them;   my acquaintances lie in a

different and far distant quarter.   Some honors have,
however, been conferred on me in the literary world.
Southey dedicated to me his 'Kehama';   James his
'Attila': (44)   he and Dickens invited me to be godfather
to their sons.   Moreover, I think as many have offered me
the flatteries of verse as ever were offered to any one
but Louis the Fourteenth. (45)

   P. 19.   I think oftener with Alfieri than with any
other writer, and quite agree with him that 'Italy and
England are (46) the only countries worth living in'.
The only time I ever saw Alfieri, was just before he left
this country for ever. (47)   I accompanied my Italian
master, Parachinetti, to a bookseller's, to order the
Works of Alfieri and Metastasio, and was enthusiastic, as
most young men were, about the French Revolution.   'Sir',
said Alfieri, 'you are a very young man;   you are yet to
learn that nothing good ever came out of France, or ever
will.   The ferocious monsters are about to devour one
another;   and they can do nothing better.   They have always been the curse of Italy;   yet we too have fools among
us who trust them'.

   Such were the expressions of the most classical and
animated poet existing in the present or past century, of
him who could at once be a true patriot and a true gentleman.   There was nothing of the ruffianly in his vigour;
nothing of the vulgar in his resentment;   he could scorn
without a scoff;   he could deride without a grimace....

   Accept this memorial, which your name will render of
less brief duration, of the esteem in which you are held
by

                                    WALTER LANDOR. (48)

NOTES

1   Horatio Greenough (1805-52) was commissioned by the
    American government to execute a colossal statue of
    George Washington for the national capital.   It was
    unveiled in 1843.
2   See 'English Traits', London, 1856, 3.
3   Donatello (c. 1386-1466), Italian sculptor, one of the
    founders of Renaissance art;   François Duquesnoy of
    Brussels (1594-1644), known as Il Fiammingo, a clever
    sculptor, French in style, noted for his reliefs in
    ivory of boys and cupids.
4   Probably Nero Claudius Drusus (38-9 BC), popular

Roman general whose victories over the German peoples
earned for him and his descendants the surname German-
icus.

5   During the rule of the great Athenian statesman Pericles (c. 500-429 BC), the various arts, among them
sculpture, flourished.   Phidias (b. c. 490 BC),
sculptor of colossal and life-size figures, painter,
and engraver, made a huge statue of Athene in gold and
ivory for the Parthenon.   He may also have been
largely responsible for the sculptures of the Parthenon, the metopes, frieze, and pedimental figures.
See Letters to John Forster, No. 7 above, and n. 52.

6   Giovanni da Bologna (1529-1608), Flemish sculptor who
lived and worked in Florence from 1557 until his
death;   Michelangelo (1475-1564), Italian sculptor and
painter of the frescoes in the Sistine Chapel in Rome.
His 'Last Judgment' appears on the east wall.   Giovanni da Bologna was considered second only to Michelangelo until recent times.   See 'English Traits',
3-4.

7   Ibid., 4.   Emerson writes: 'The Greek histories he
thought the only good; ...'

8   Enrico Davila (1576-1631), Italian historian, author
of 'Historia delle guerre civili di Francia' (1630);
Niccolò Machiavelli (1469-1527), Florentine statesman
and political theorist, author of 'Il Principe'
(1513), 'Discorsi sopra la prima deca di Tito Livio'
(1513), 'Arte della guerra' (1520), and 'Storia fior-
entina' (1520-5);   Voltaire, author of 'Histoire de
Charles XII' (1731), 'Le Siècle de Louis XIV' (1751),
'L'Essai sur les moeurs' (1756), 'Histoire de la
Russie sous Pierre le Grand' (1759-63), 'Philosophie
de l'histoire' (1765), and 'Précis du siècle de Louis
XV' (1768);   Jules Michelet (1798-1874), French historian, author of the monumental 'Histoire de France'
(1833-43, 1855-67).

9   Edward Gibbon (1737-94), English historian, author of
'History of the Decline and Fall of the Roman Empire'
(1776-88).

10   See 'English Traits', 4.

11   General Sir William Napier (1785-1860), author of the
six volume 'History of the War in the Peninsula and in
the South of France, from ... 1807 to ... 1814' (1828-
40).

12   Pierre Charron (1541-1603), French philosopher, theo-
logian, disciple of Montaigne, author of 'Les Trois
Vérités' (1593) and 'De la Sagesse' (1601).   See
'English Traits', 4.

13   Ibid.   See Postscript to 'Gebir', No. 2 above.

14   Ibid.   Emerson writes: 'He pestered me with Southey;
     but who is Southey?'
15   Thomas Carlyle (1795-1881), Scots author and histor-
     ian, visited Landor in his lodgings at no. 3 Rivers
     Street, Bath, on the last day of July 1850.
16   'English Traits', 9.   Emerson writes: 'Plato he does
     not read, ...'
17   For Landor's most sustained attack upon the person,
     philosophy, and style of Plato, see Diogenes and Plato
     in 'Selected Imaginary Conversations of Literary Men
     and Statesmen by Walter Savage Landor', ed. C.L.
     Proudfit (1969), 155-228.
18   'English Traits', 9.   Landor's parenthetical matter.
19   Rydal Mount was Wordsworth's home from 1813 until his
     death in 1850.   Emerson first visited the poet there
     on 28 August 1833.   See 'English Traits', 10-13.
20   Ibid., 11.   Landor's italics.
21   Ibid.
22   Perhaps a reference to 'De Rerum Natura', iii, 978-
     1052.
23   Robert Percy Smith (1770-1845), advocate-general of
     Bengal, member of the English Parliament, and author
     of Latin verses published by his son under the title
     of 'Early Writings of Robert Percy Smith' (1850).
     His better-known brother, Sydney Smith (1771-1845),
     was one of the founders of the 'Edinburgh Review'.
24   Emerson visited Wordsworth a second time at Rydal
     Mount in March 1848.   See 'English Traits', 165-8.
25   This is Landor's observation, not Emerson's.
26   'English Traits', 166.
27   Landor, accompanied by his friend Joseph Ablett,
     called on Wordsworth and his daughter who were them-
     selves visiting Wordsworth's son and daughter-in-law
     at Moresby, near Whitehaven, Cumberland, about 18
     June 1832.
28   Hellvellyn (1805), a poem by Scott.
29   See Wordsworth's poem Fidelity (1807).
30   Landor's poem was never reprinted during his lifetime.
31   John Gibson Lockhart (1794-1854), who married Sir
     Walter Scott's elder daughter Sophia in 1820, edited
     his father-in-law's poetry in 1833-4, 1841, and 1848,
     and published his 'Memoirs of the Life of Sir Walter
     Scott' in 1837-8.
32   William Hazlitt (1778-1830), English critic, first
     called upon Landor in Florence in the spring of 1825.
33   Landor and Wordsworth spent a day together in July
     1832 at Mr Stansfeld Rawson's home, Wasdale Hall, on
     Wast Water, following their initial meeting at Moresby
     (n. 24 above).   Landor commemorated this occasion
     with verse (Lines, 'Complete Works', 16, 10-11.

34   Southey made Landor's acquaintance in April 1808, nine years after Southey's anonymous review of 'Gebir' in the September 1799 'Critical Review'.

35   See Southey's letter to Landor, dated 'Keswick, May 7, 1819', in 'Selections from the Letters of Robert Southey', ed. John Wood Warter (1856), 3, 135.   De Quincey probably was the author of the favourable criticism noted by Southey in this letter.

36   Johann Wolfgang von Goethe (1749-1832), German author, critic, educationalist, journalist, natural philosopher, poet, statesman, etc., one of the world's greatest literary men.   'The Sorrows of Young Werther' was published in 1774 and 'Wilhelm Meister's Years of Apprenticeship' appeared in 1795-6.

37   Landor elsewhere comments on Wordsworth's 'Prelude' (1850): *'Walter Landor....*   Frequently there are solid knolls in the midst of Wordsworth's morass, but never did I expect to find so much animation, such vigor, such succinctness, as in the paragraph beginning with "All degrees and shapes of spurious form" and ending with "Left to herself, unheard of and unknown" ['Prelude' (1850), iii, 594-611].   Here indeed the waggoner's frock drops off, and shows to our surprise the imperial purple underneath it....'   (Archdeacon Hare and Walter Landor, 'Complete Works', 6, 24-5).

38   See 'English Traits', 166.

39   Arthur Wellesley, first Duke of Wellington (1769-1852), chief architect of Great Britain's victory in the Napoleonic Wars.

40   Philip Dormer Stanhope, fourth Earl of Chesterfield (1694-1773), statesman, diplomatist, and letter writer, principally remembered for 'Letters ... to his Son Philip Stanhope ...', published by Mrs Eugenia Stanhope, 2 vols, London, 1774.   See 'English Traits', 4.   Landor's italics.

41   Horace Walpole (1717-97) and Laurence Sterne (1713-68), English novelists and letter writers.

42   'English Traits', 5.

43   Ibid.

44   G.P.R. James, author of 'Attila' (1837).

45   Louis XIV (1638-1715), king of France 1643-1715, patron of the arts, and builder of Versailles, Les Invalides and Marly-le-Roi.   He personally encouraged such literary men as Boileau, Molière, and Racine.

46   Landor has inserted 'are'.

47   Malcolm Elwin doubts that Landor actually met the Italian poet and dramatist Count Vittorio Alfieri (1749-1803), in London in 1791.   See 'Landor: A

Replevin' (1958), 60-1 and note.   Landor introduced
this literary hero into two Imaginary Conversations:
Alfieri and Solomon the Florentine Jew (1824) and
Alfieri and Metastasio (1856).
48 Landor's 'P.S.' omitted.

Imaginary Conversations

10 Southey and Porson I
1823, 1824, 1826, 1846

This Imaginary Conversation between the poet-critic Robert
Southey (1775-1843) and the eminent Greek scholar and textual critic Richard Porson (1759-1808) is the first of two
such imaginary meetings devoted primarily to a discussion
of Wordsworth's poetry.   Although Landor speaks through
both interlocutors, Porson, who had a reputation among his
colleagues at Cambridge for his incisive criticism and
brusque manner, is the mouthpiece for the majority of the
author's criticisms and opinions.   The Dialogue contains
penetrating commentary on Wordsworth's poetry, in general,
and several verbal criticisms of 'Laodamia', in particular;   a sustained attack on the periodical critics and
their practices;   numerous observations on writers ancient
and modern;   and one of Landor's early attempts to formu-
late his conception of the ideal poet-critic.

We owe the existence of Southey and Porson I to Landor's decision not to dedicate his 'Imaginary Conversations' to Wordsworth for fear that his friend might be
embarrassed by the political opinions contained in several
of the dialogues.   Landor chose, instead, to honour him
by making his poetry the subject of an Imaginary Conversation.   He took several critical remarks on Wordsworth's
poetry that he had previously jotted down on an old letter
and developed them into what finally became Southey and
Porson.

This Dialogue first appeared in the July 1823 'London
Magazine' to announce the forthcoming publication of the
two-volume 'Imaginary Conversations' (1824).   Although
the conversation was little-changed when it reappeared in
volume one of the 'Imaginary Conversations' (1824), it was
revised for the second edition (1826) and underwent further revision before its inclusion in the 'Works of Walter
Savage Landor' (1846).   For a definitive critical and

textual study of these three versions of Southey and
Porson I, see Alice LaVonne Prasher, Walter Savage Landor's 'Imaginary Conversations': A Critical Edition of
the First Eight Conversations in Volume One. [with] 'Imaginary Conversations of Literary Men and Statesmen'. By
Walter Savage Landor, Esq. The First Volume. 1824, unpublished PhD dissertation, Northwestern University, 1966.
The selection below, which represents about two-thirds of
the Conversation, is reprinted from the 1846 'Works'.

Porson. I suspect, Mr. Southey, you are angry with me for
the freedom with which I have spoken of your poetry and
Wordsworth's. (1)
    Southey. What could have induced you to imagine it, Mr.
Professor?   You have indeed bent your eyes upon me, since
we have been together, with somewhat of fierceness and de-
fiance;   I presume you fancied me to be a commentator.
You wrong me, in your belief that any opinion on my poetical works hath molested me;   but you afford me more than
compensation in supposing me acutely sensible of injustice
done to Wordsworth.   If we must converse on these topics,
we will converse on him.   What man ever existed who spent
a more inoffensive life, or adorned it with nobler
studies?
    Porson. None;   and they who attack him with virulence
are men of as little morality as reflection.   I have demonstrated that one of them, he who wrote the 'Pursuits of
Literature', could not construe a Greek sentence or scan a
verse; (2)   and I have fallen on the very *Index* from which
he drew out his forlorn hope on the parade.   This is incomparably the most impudent fellow I have met with in the
course of my reading, which has lain, you know, in a province where impudence is no rarity.   I am sorry to say
that we critics who write for the learned, have sometimes
set a bad example to our younger brothers, the critics who
write for the public: but if they were considerate and
prudent, they would find out that a deficiency in weight
and authority might in some measure be compensated by deference and decorum.   Not to mention the refuse of the
literary world, the sweeping of booksellers' shops, the
dust thrown up by them in a corner to blow by pinches on
new publications;   not to tread upon or disturb this
filth, the greatest of our critics now living are only
great comparatively.   They betray their inconsiderateness
when they look disdainfully on the humbler in acquirements
and intellect.   A little wit, or, as that is not always
at hand, a little impudence instead of it, throws its ram-
pant briar over dry lacunes: a drop of oil, sweet or
rancid, covers a great quantity of poor broth.   Instead

of anything in this way, I would seriously recommend to
the employer of our critics, young and old, that he oblige
them to pursue a course of study such as this: that under
the superintendence of some respectable student from the
university, they first read and examine the contents of
the book; a thing greatly more useful in criticism than
is generally thought; (3) secondly, that they carefully
write them down, number them, and range them under their
several heads; thirdly, that they mark every beautiful,
every faulty, every ambiguous, every uncommon expression.
Which being completed, that they inquire what author, ancient or modern, has treated the same subject; that they
compare them, first in smaller, afterward in larger portions, noting every defect in precision and its causes,
every excellence and its nature; that they graduate
these, fixing *plus* and *minus*, and designating them more
accurately and discriminately by means of colours, stronger or paler. For instance, purple might express grandeur
and majesty of thought; scarlet, vigour of expression;
pink, liveliness; green, elegant and equable composition:
these however and others, as might best attract their
notice and serve their memory. The same process may be
used where authors have not written on the same subject,
when those who have are wanting, or have touched it but
incidentally. Thus Addison and Fontenelle, (4) not very
like, may be compared in the graces of style, in the
number and degree of just thoughts and lively fancies:
thus the dialogues of Cicero with those of Plato, his
ethics with those of Aristoteles, his orations with those
of Demosthenes. It matters not if one be found superior
to the other in this thing, and inferior in that; the
exercise is taken; the qualities of two authors are explored and understood, and their distances laid down, as
geographers speak, from accurate survey. The *plus* and
minus, of good and bad and ordinary, will have something
of a scale to rest upon; and after a time the degrees of
the higher parts in intellectual dynamics may be more
nearly attained, though never quite exactly.
   Southey. Nothing is easier than to mark and number the
striking parts of Homer: it is little more difficult to
demonstrate why they are so: the same thing may then be
done in Milton: these pieces in each poet may afterward
be collated and summed up. Every man will be capable or
incapable of it in proportion as his mind is poetical:
few indeed will ever write anything on the subject worth
reading; but they will acquire strength and practice.
The critic of the trade will gain a more certain livelihood and a more reputable one than before, and no great
matter will be spent upon his education....

Southey. For my own part, I should be well contented
with that share of reputation which might come meted out
and delivered to me after the analytical and close comparison you propose.   Its accomplishment can hardly be
expected in an age when everything must be done
quickly....
     Porson.... Dwarfs are in fashion still; but they are
the dwarfs of literature.   These little zanies are invited to the assemblies of the gay world, and admitted to
the dinners of the political. (5)   Limbs of the law, par-
alysed and laid up professionally, enter into association
with printers, and take retaining fees from some authors,
to harangue against others out of any brief before
them. (6)
     Southey. And they meet with encouragement and success!
We stigmatise any lie but a malignant one, and we repel
any attack but against fame, virtue, and genius.   Fond of
trying experiments on poison, we find that the strongest
may be extracted from blood; and this itself is rejected
as unworthy of our laboratory, unless it be drawn from a
generous and a capacious heart.
     Porson. No other country hath ever been so abundant in
speculation as ours; but it would be incredible if we did
not see it, that ten or fifteen men, of the humblest attainments, gain a comfortable livelihood by periodical
attacks on its best writers.   Adverse as I have declared
myself to the style and manner of Wordsworth, I never
thought that all his reviewers put together could compose
anything equal to the worst paragraph in his volumes.   I
have spoken vehemently against him, and mildly against
them; because he could do better, they never could.   The
same people would treat me with as little reverence as
they treat him with, if anything I write were popular, or
could become so.   It is by fixing on such works that they
are carried with them into the doorway.   The porter of
Cleopatra would not have admitted the asps if they had not
been under the figs. (7)   Show me, if you can, Mr.
Southey, a temperate, accurate, solid exposition, of any
English work whatever, in any English review.
     Southey. Not having at hand so many numbers as it would
be requisite to turn over, I must decline the challenge....

     Porson. The publications which excite the most bustle
and biting from these fellows, are always the best, as the
fruit on which the flies gather is the ripest.   Periodical critics were never so plentiful as they now are.
There is hardly a young author who does not make his first

attempt in some review; showing his teeth, hanging by his
tail, pleased and pleasing by the volubility of his
chatter, and doing his best to get a penny for his exhi-
bitor and a nut for his own pouch, by the facetiousness of
the tricks he performs upon our heads and shoulders.
From all I can recollect of what I noticed when I turned
over such matters, a well-sized and useful volume might be
compiled and published annually, containing the incorrect
expressions, and omitting the opinions, of our booksellers' boys, the reviewers. Looking the other day by
accident at two pages of *judgments*, recommendatory of new
publications, I found, face to face, the following words,
from not the worst of the species. *Scattering so considerable a degree of interest over the contemplation,
&c....* *The dazzling glitter of intellect,* &c. (8) Now
in what manner can we *scatter a degree*? unless it be one
of those degrees which are scattered at Edinburgh and
Glasgow. Such an expression as *dazzling glitter* may
often be applied to fancy, but never to intellect. These
gentlemen might do somewhat better, if they would read us
for the sake of improvement, and not for the sake of showing off a somewhat light familiarity, which never can ap-
pertain to them. The time however, I am inclined to
believe, is not far distant, when the fashionable will be
as much ashamed of purchasing such wayside publications,
as the learned would be of reading them....

Those who have failed as painters turn picture-clean-
ers, those who have failed as writers turn reviewers. (9)
Orator Henley taught in the last century, that the
readiest-made shoes are boots cut down: (10) there are
those who abundantly teach us now, that the readiest-made
critics are cut-down poets. Their assurance is however
by no means diminished from their ill success.

Southey. Puffy fingers have pelted me long enough with
snowballs, and I should not wonder if some of them reached
the skirts of my great-coat; but I never turned round to
look.

Porson. The little man who followed you in the 'Critical Review', (11) and whose pretensions widen every smile
his imbecility excited, would, I am persuaded, if Homer
were living, pat him in a fatherly way upon the cheek, and
tell him that, by moderating his fire and contracting his
prolixity, the public might ere long expect something from
him worth reading....

Porson.... The plagiary has a greater latitude of
choice than we: and if he brings home a parsnep or tur-
nip-top, when he could as easily have pocketted a nectar-

ine or a pineapple, he must be a blockhead.   I never
heard the name of the *pursuer of literature*, who has
little more merit in having stolen, than he would have had
if he had never stolen at all; (12)   and I have forgotten
that other man's, who evinced his fitness to be the censor
of our age, by a translation of the most naked and impure
satires of antiquity, those of Juvenal, (13) which owe
their preservation to the partiality of the friars.   I
shall entertain an unfavourable opinion of him if he has
translated them well: pray has he?

  Southey. Indeed I do not know.   I read poets for their
poetry, and to extract that nutriment of the intellect and
of the heart which poetry should contain.   I never listen
to the swans of the cess-pool, (14) and must declare that
nothing is heavier to me than rottenness and corruption.

  Porson. You are right, sir, perfectly right.   A translator of Juvenal would open a public drain to look for a
needle, and may miss it.   My nose is not easily offended;
but I must have something to fill my belly.   Come, we
will lay aside the scrip of the transpositor and the pouch
of the pursuer, in reserve for the days of unleavened
bread;   and again, if you please, to the lakes and mountains.   Now we are both in better humour, I must bring
you to a confession that in your friend Wordsworth there
is occasionally a little trash.

  Southey. A haunch of venison would be trash to a Brah-
min, a bottle of burgundy to the xerif of Mecca.

  Porson.... Trash, I confess, is no proof that nothing
good can lie above it and about it.   The roughest and
least manageable soil surrounds gold and diamonds.   Homer
and Dante and Shakspeare and Milton have each many hundred
lines worth little;   lines without force, without feeling,
without fancy;   in short, without beauty of any kind. (15)
But it is the character of modern poetry, as it is of
modern arms and equipments, to be more uniformly trim and
polished.   The ancients in both had more strength and
splendour;   they had also more inequality and rudeness.

  Southey. We are guided by precept, by habit, by taste,
by constitution.   Hitherto our sentiments on poetry have
been delivered down to us from authority;   and if it can
be demonstrated, as I think it may be, that the authority
is inadequate, and that the dictates are often inapplicable and often misinterpreted, you will allow me to remove
the cause out of court.   Every man can see what is very
bad in a poem, almost every one can see what is very good;
but you, Mr. Porson, who have turned over all the volumes
of all the commentators, will inform me whether I am right
or wrong in asserting, that no critic hath yet appeared
who hath been able to fix or to discern the exact degrees
of excellence above a certain point.

Porson. None.

Southey. The reason is, because the eyes of no one have been upon a level with it. (16) ...

Porson.... Returning, Mr. Southey, to the difficulty, or rather to the rarity, of an accurate and just survey of poetical and other literary works, I do not see why we should not borrow an idea from geometricians and astronomers, why we should not have our triangles and quadrants, why, in short, we should not measure out writings by small portions at a time, and compare the brighter parts of two authors page by page. The minor beauties, the complexion and contexture, may be considered at last, and more at large. Daring geniusses, ensigns and undergraduates, members of Anacreontic and Pindaric clubs, will scoff at me. Painters who can draw nothing correctly, hold Raffael in contempt, and appeal to the sublimity of Michaelangelo and the splendour of Titian: (17) ignorant that these great men were great by science first, and employed in painting the means I propose for criticism. Venus and the damned submitted to the same squaring. (18)

Such a method would be useful to critics in general, and even the wisest and most impartial would be much improved by it; although few, either by these means or any, are likely to be quite correct or quite unanimous on the merits of any two authors whatsoever.

Southey. Those who are learners would be teachers; (19) while those who have learnt much would procure them at any price. It is only when we have mounted high, that we are sensible of wanting a hand.

Porson. On the subject of poetry in particular, there are some questions not yet sufficiently discussed: I will propose two. First, admitting that in the tragedies of Sophocles there was (which I believe) twice as much of good poetry as in the 'Iliad', does it follow that he was as admirable a poet as Homer?

Southey. No, indeed: so much I do attribute to the conception and formation of a novel and vast design, and so wide is the difference I see between the completion of one very great, and the perfection of many smaller. Would even these have existed without Homer? I think not.

Porson. My next question is, whether a poet is to be judged from the quantity of his bad poetry, or from the quality of his best?

Southey. I should certainly say from the latter: because it must be in poetry as in sculpture and painting; he who arrives at a high degree of excellence in these arts, will have made more models, more sketches and designs, than he who has reached but a lower; and the con-

servation of them, whether by accident or by choice, can
injure and affect in no manner his more perfect and elaborate works.   A drop of sealing-wax, falling by chance or
negligence, may efface a fine impression: but what is
well done in poetry is never to be effaced by what is ill
done afterward.   Even the bad poetry of a good poet
hath something in it which renders it more valuable, to a
judge of these matters, than what passes for much better,
and what in many essential points is truly so.   I will
however keep to the argument, not having lost sight of my
illustration in alluding to design and sketches.   Many
men would leave themselves penniless to purchase an early
and rude drawing by Raffael;   some arabesque, some nose
upon a gryphon or gryphon upon a nose;   and never would
inquire whether the painter had kept it in his portfolio
or had cast it away.   The same persons, and others whom
we call much wiser, exclaim loudly against any literary
sketch unworthy of a leaf among the productions of its
author.   No ideas are so trivial, so incorrect, so incoherent, but they may have entered the idle fancy, and
have taken a higher place than they ought in the warm
imagination, of the best poets.   We find in Dante, as
you just now remarked, a prodigious quantity of them;   and
indeed not a few in Virgil, grave as he is and stately.
Infantine and pretty there is hardly anything in the
'Iliad', but the dull and drowthy stop us unexpectedly now
and then.   The boundaries of mind lie beyond these writers, although their splendour lets us see nothing on the
farther side.   In so wide and untrodden a creation as
that of Shakespeare's, can we wonder or complain that
sometimes we are bewildered and entangled in the exuberance of fertility?   Dry-brained men upon the Continent, (20) the trifling wits of the theatre, (21) accurate
however and expert calculators, (22) tell us that his
beauties are balanced by his faults. (23)   The poetical
opposition, puffing for popularity, cry cheerily against
them, *his faults are balanced by his beauties*; when, in
reality, all the faults that ever were committed in poetry
would be but as air to earth, if we could weigh them
against one single thought or image, such as almost every
scene exhibits in every drama of this unrivalled genius.
Do you hear me with patience?
    Porson. With more;   although at Cambridge we rather
discourse on Bacon, for we know him better. (24)   He was
immeasurably a less wise man than Shakespeare, (25) and
not a wiser writer: for he knew his fellow-man only as he
saw him in the street and in the court, which indeed is
but a dirtier street and a narrower: Shakespeare, who
also knew him there, knew him everywhere else, both as he
was and as he might be.

Southey. There is as great a difference between Shakespeare and Bacon as between an American forest and a London timber-yard. In the timber-yard the materials are sawed and squared and set across: in the forest we have the natural form of the tree, all its growth, all its branches, all its leaves, all the mosses that grow about it, all the birds and insects that inhabit it; now deep shadows absorbing the whole wilderness; now bright bursting glades, with exuberant grass and flowers and fruitage; now untroubled skies; now terrific thunderstorms; everywhere multiformity, everywhere immensity.

Porson. If after this ramble in the heat you are not thirsty, I would ask another question. What is the reason why, when not only the glory of great kings and statesmen, but even of great philosophers, is much enhanced by two or three good apophthegms, that of a great poet is lowered by them, even if he should invest them with good verse? For certainly the dignity of a great poet is thought to be lowered by the writing of epigrams. (26)

Southey. As you said of Wordsworth, the great poet could accomplish better things; the others could not. People in this apparent act of injustice do real justice, without intending or knowing it. All writers have afforded some information, or have excited some sentiment or idea, somewhere. This alone should exempt the humblest of them from revilings, unless it appear that he hath misapplied his powers through insolence or malice. In that case, whatever sentence may be passed upon him, I consider it no honour to be the executioner. What must we think of those who travel far and wide that, before they go to rest they may burst into the arbour of a recluse, whose weakest thoughts are benevolence, whose worst are purity? On his poetry I shall say nothing, unless you lead me to it, wishing you however to examine it analytically and severely.

Porson. There are folks who, when they read my criticism, say, '*I do not think so*.' It is because they do not think so, that I write. Men entertain some opinions which it is indeed our duty to confirm, but many also which it is expedient to eradicate, and more which it is important to correct. They read less willingly what may improve their understanding and enlarge their capacity, than what corroborates their prejudices and establishes their prepossessions. I never bear malice toward those who try to reduce me to their own dimensions. A narrow mind cannot be enlarged, nor can a capacious one be contracted. Are we angry with a phial for not being a flask? or do we wonder that the skin of an elephant sits unwieldily on a squirrel?

Southey. Great men will always pay deference to
greater: little men will not: because the little are
fractious; and the weaker they are, the more obstinate
and crooked.
Porson. To proceed on our inquiry.   I will not deny
that to compositions of a new kind, like Wordsworth's, we
come without scales and weights, and without the means of
making an assay.
Southey. Mr. Porson, it does not appear to me that anything more is necessary in the first instance, than to interrogate our hearts in what manner they have been affected.   If the ear is satisfied; if at one moment a tumult
is aroused in the breast, and tranquillised at another,
with a perfect consciousness of equal power exerted in
both cases; if we rise up from the perusal of the work
with a strong excitement to thought, to imagination, to
sensibility; above all, if we sat down with some propensities toward evil and walk away with much stronger toward
good, in the midst of a world which we never had entered
and of which we never had dreamed before, shall we per-
versely put on again the *old man* of criticism, and dissemble that we have been conducted by a most beneficent
and most potent genius?   Nothing proves to me so mani-
festly in what a pestiferous condition are its lazarettos,
as when I observe how little hath been objected against
those who have substituted words for things, and how much
against those who have reinstated things for words.
Porson. I find, however, much to censure in our modern
poets; I mean those who have written since Milton. (27)
But praise is due to such as threw aside the French
models. (28)   Percy was the first: then came the Wartons, and then Cowper; (29) more diversified in his
poetry and more classical than any since.
Southey. I wonder you admire an author so near your own
times, indeed contemporary.
Porson. There is reason for wonder.   Men in general do
so in regard both to liberty and poetry....

Southey. Let Wordsworth prove to the world that there
may be animation without blood and broken bones, and tenderness remote from the stews.   Some will doubt it; for
even things the most evident are often but little perceived and strangely estimated. (30)   Swift ridiculed the
music of Handel and the generalship of Marlborough, (31)
Pope the perspicacity and the scholarship of Bentley, (32)
Gray the abilities of Shaftesbury and the eloquence of
Rousseau. (33)   Shakspeare hardly found those who would
collect his tragedies; (34) Milton was read from godli-

ness; (35) Virgil was antiquated and rustic; Cicero
Asiatic. What a rabble has persecuted my friend! An
elephant is born to be consumed by ants in the midst of
his unapproachable solitudes: Wordsworth is the prey of
Jeffrey. (36) Why repine? Let us rather amuse ourselves with allegories, and recollect that God in the creation left his noblest creature at the mercy of a serpent.

Porson. In our authors of the present day I would recommend principally, to reduce the expenditure of words to
the means of support, and to be severe in style without
the appearance of severity. (37) But this advice is more
easily given than taken. Your friend is verbose; not
indeed without something for his words to rest upon, but
from a resolution to gratify and indulge his capacity.
He pursues his thoughts too far; and considers more how
he may show them entirely than how he may show them advantageously. (38) Good men may utter whatever comes upper-
most, good poets may not. It is better, but it is also
more difficult, to make a selection of thoughts than to
accumulate them. He who has a splendid sideboard, should
have an iron chest with a double lock upon it, and should
hold in reserve a greater part than he displays.

I know not why two poets so utterly dissimilar as your
author and Coleridge should be constantly mentioned together. In the one I find diffuseness, monotony, not indis-
tinctness, but uninteresting expanse, and such figures and
such colouring as Morland's; (39) in the other, bright
colours without form, sublimely void. In his prose he
talks like a madman when he calls Saint Paul's Epistle to
the Ephesians 'the sublimest [divinest] composition of
man.' (40)

Southey. This indeed he hath spoken, but he has not yet
published it in his writings: it will appear in his
'Table Talk', perhaps.

Porson. Such table-talk may be expected to come forth
very late in the evening, when the wine and candles are
out, and the body lies horizontally underneath. He believes he is a believer; but why does he believe that the
Scriptures are best reverenced by bearing false witness to
them?...

Wordsworth goes out of his way to be attacked: he
picks up a piece of dirt, throws it on the carpet in the
midst of the company, and cries *This is a better man than
any of you*. He does indeed mould the base material into
what form he chooses; but why not rather invite us to
contemplate it than challenge us to condemn it? (41)
Here surely is false taste.

Southey. The principal and the most general accusation
against him is, that the vehicle of his thoughts is un-

equal to them. (42)   Now did ever the judges at the Olym-
pic games say, 'We would have awarded to you the meed of
victory, if your chariot had been equal to your horses:
it is true they have won; but the people is displeased at
a car neither new nor richly gilt, and without a gryphon
or sphynx engraved on the axle?'   You admire simplicity
in Euripides; you censure it in Wordsworth; believe me,
sir, it arises in neither from penury of thought, which
seldom has produced it, but from the strength of temper-
ance, and at the suggestion of principle. Some of his
critics are sincere in their censure, and are neither invidious nor unlearned, (43) but their optics have been exercised on other objects, altogether dissimilar, and they
are (permit me an expression not the worse for daily use)
entirely out of their element.   His very clearness
puzzles and perplexes them, and they imagine that
straightness is distortion, as children on seeing a wand
dipped in limpid and still water.   Clear writers, like
clear fountains, do not seem so deep as they are: the
turbid look the most profound....

Southey....   Ignorance has not been single-handed the
enemy of Wordsworth; but Petulance and Malignity have
accompanied her, and have been unremittent in their attacks.   Small poets, small critics, lawyers who have much
time on their hands and hanging heavily, come forward un-
fed against him; such is the spirit of patriotism, rushing everywhere for the public good....
     Take up a poem of Wordsworth's and read it; I would
rather say, read them all; and, knowing that a mind like
yours must grasp closely what comes within it, I will then
appeal to you whether any poet of our country, since
Milton, hath exerted greater powers with less of strain and
less of ostentation.   I would however, by his permission,
lay before you for this purpose a poem which is yet unpublished and incomplete. (44)
     Porson. Pity, with such abilities, he does not imitate
the ancients somewhat more.
     Southey. Whom did they imitate?   If his genius is
equal to theirs he has no need of a guide. He also will
be an ancient; and the very counterparts of those who now
decry him, will extol him a thousand years hence in malignity to the moderns. (45) ...

Porson....   I ought not to have interrupted you so
long, in your attempt to prove Wordsworth shall I say the
rival or the resembler of the ancients?

Southey. Such excursions are not unseasonable in such
discussions, and lay in a store of good humour for them.
Your narrative has amused me exceedingly. (46)   As you
call upon me to return with you to the point we set out
from, I hope I may assert without a charge of paradox,
that whatever is good in poetry is common to all good
poets, however wide may be the diversity of manner.   Nothing can be more dissimilar than the three Greek tragedians: (47) but would you prefer the closest and best
copier of Homer to the worst (whichever he be) among them?
Let us avoid what is indifferent or doubtful, and embrace
what is good, whether we see it in another or not;   and
if we have contracted any peculiarity while our muscles
and bones were softer, let us hope finally to outgrow it.
Our feelings and modes of thinking forbid and exclude a
very frequent imitation of the old classics, not to mention our manners, which have a nearer connexion than is
generally known to exist with the higher poetry.   When
the occasion permitted it, Wordsworth has not declined to
treat a subject as an ancient poet of equal vigour would
have treated it.   Let me repeat to you his 'Laodamia'.
   Porson. After your animated recital of this classic
poem, I begin to think more highly of you both.   It is
pleasant to find two poets living as brothers, and particularly when the palm lies between them, with hardly a
third in sight. (48)   Those who have ascended to the
summit of the mountain, sit quietly and familiarly side by
side;   it is only those who are climbing with briers about
their legs, that kick and scramble.   Yours is a temper
found less frequently in our country than in others. (49)
The French poets indeed must stick together to keep themselves warm.   By employing courteous expressions mutual-
ly, they indulge their vanity rather than their benevolence, and bring the spirit of contest into action gaily
and safely.   Among the Romans we find Virgil, Horace, and
several of their contemporaries, intimately united and
profuse of reciprocal praise.   Ovid, Cicero, and
Pliny, (50) are authors the least addicted to censure, and
the most ready to offer their testimony in favour of abilities in Greek or countryman. (51)   These are the three
Romans, the least amiable of nations, and (one excepted)
the least sincere, with whom I should have liked best to
spend an evening....

   Porson. You have recited a most spirited thing indeed:
and now to give you a proof that I have been attentive, I
will remark two passages that offend me. (52)   In the
first stanza,

> With sacrifice before the rising morn
> *Performed*, my slaughtered Lord *have I required;*
> And in thick darkness, amid shades forlorn,
> Him of the infernal Gods *have I desired.*
> [ll. 1-4, in 'Poems' (1815).]

I do not see the necessity of *Performed,* which is dull and cumbersome. The second line and the fourth terminate too much alike, and express to a tittle the same meaning: *have I required* and *have I desired* are worse than prosaic; beside which there are four words together of equal length in each.

Southey. I have seen a couplet oftener than once in which every word of the second verse corresponds in measure to every one above it.

Porson. The Scotch have a scabby and a frost-bitten ear for harmony, both in verse and prose: (53)   and I remember in 'Douglas' two such as you describe.

> This is the place ... the centre of the grove,
> Here stands the oak ... the monarch of the wood.
> [John Home, 'Douglas', V, i, 1-2.] (54)

After this whiff of vapour I must refresh myself with a draught of pure poetry, at the bottom of which is the flake of tartar I wish away.

> He spake of love, such love as Spirits feel
> In worlds whose course is equable and pure;
> No fears to beat away - no strife to heal -
> The past unsighed for, and the future sure;
> Spake, as a witness, of a second birth
> For all that is most perfect upon earth.
> [ll. 97-102, in 'Poems' (1815).]

How unseasonable is the allusion to *witness* and *second birth!* which things, however holy and venerable in themselves, come stinking and reeking to us from the conventicle.   I desire to find Laodamia in the silent and gloomy mansion of her beloved Protesilaus; (55)   not elbowed by the godly butchers in Tottenham-court-road, nor smelling devoutly of ratafia among the sugar-bakers' wives at Blackfriars. (56)

Mythologies should be kept distinct: the fire-place of one should never be subject to the smoke of another.   The gods of different countries, when they come together unexpectedly, are jealous gods, and, as our old women say, *turn the house out of windows.*

Southey. A current of rich and bright thoughts runs

through the poem. Pindar himself would not on that subject have braced one to more vigour, nor Euripides have
breathed into it more tenderness and passion. The first
part of the stanza you have just now quoted might have
been heard with shouts of rapture in the regions it describes.

   Porson. I am not insensible to the warmly chaste morality which is the soul of it, nor indifferent to the bene-
fits that literature on many occasions has derived from
Christianity. But poetry is a luxury to which, if she
tolerates and permits it, she accepts no invitation: she
beats down your gates and citadels, levels your high
places, and eradicates your groves. For which reason I
dwell more willingly with those authors who cannot mix and
confound the manners they represent....

NOTES

1 Although there seems to be no evidence that Porson
   ever read and criticized Wordsworth's poetry, Landor
   believed that he had. In a letter to Wordsworth
   dated 'Florence April 24 [1825]' Landor writes: '... I
   have rceived [*sic*] and redd [*sic*] several times over
   yr. Memorials of a Tour on the Continent - and my
   thanks are due to you for the present of it, and for
   the many hours of delight it brings and leaves behind
   it. Nothing can be conceived more poetical than the
   Ode to Enterprise. If yr. enemies had hearts, it
   would break them. I wish Porson were alive - Altho
   in the latter part of his days I believe he did re-
   tract the sillier of his observations, both on your
   poetry and on Southey's, he would now be forced to acknowledge that you have beaten his trained bands at
   their own weapons' (R.H. Super, Landor's Letters to
   Wordsworth and Coleridge, 'Modern Philology', 15
   (November 1957), 81).
2 [Thomas J. Mathias (1754?-1835)], 'Pursuits of Literature', 16th ed. (1812). Landor criticizes Mathias'
   knowledge of Greek in Post-Script to 'Gebir' (1800)
   (see 'Complete Works', 13, 358-60) and unfavourably
   alludes to him in several poems.
3 See Landor's remarks on a reviewer in Post-Script to
   'Gebir', No. 2 above.
4 Bernard LeBovier De Fontenelle (1657-1757), French
   scientist and man of letters, author of 'Lettres gal-
   antes' (1683, 1685), 'Nouveaux Dialogues des morts'
   (1683, 1684), 'Entretiens sur la pluralité des mondes'
   (1686), and other writings.

5   Throughout this Conversation Landor lashes out against
    three critics who were physically small of stature and
    who had important political connections: Thomas
    Mathias (see n. 2 above); William Gifford (1756-
    1826), first editor of the Tory 'Quarterly Review'
    (1809); and Francis Jeffrey (1773-1850), editor of
    the 'Edinburgh Review' (1802) from 1803 to 1829.
6   Jeffrey practised law while editor of the 'Edinburgh
    Review'.
7   See Shakespeare, 'Antony and Cleopatra', V, ii, 233-
    81.
8   Landor attacks the critical jargon of reviewers in
    similar terms in Post-Script to 'Gebir', No. 2 above.
9   Gifford published the 'Baviad' (1794) and the 'Mae-
    viad' (1795) together in 1797.   Jeffrey wrote verse
    and two plays.
10 John Henley (1692-1756), an eccentric London clergy-
    man, so advised a large crowd of shoemakers who had
    gathered to learn about a new and easy way to make
    shoes.
11 This is a reference to Robert Fellowes (1771-1847) who
    became editor of the 'Critical Review' (1756) in 1807.
    Southey was a contributor to this review in the 1790s.
    Landor criticizes Fellowes (who had spoken slightingly
    of 'Gebir') in his 'Commentary': 'Reviewers and mag-
    azine-men, the linkboys and scavengers of literature,
    treat them [men of genius] like inferiors and depen-
    dents; and indeed no inconsiderable portion of their
    worldly welfare is affected by the representations of
    these men.   Of late years, if any one had paid any
    attention to such people, one would imagine that Dr.
    Johnson was hardly on a level with Dr. Drake, and that
    Aristotle only kept a box for Mr. Fellowes.
        This reverend gentleman having settled religion to
    his mind, but unhappily ... driven out from among the
    poets, is retaliating on them as their judge.   He
    writes, or did write, for I know not whether the work
    survives his hand, in the "Critical Review"; strange
    successor to the gentle, but high-minded Southey!'
    ('Charles James Fox: A Commentary on His Life and
    Character by Walter Savage Landor', ed. Stephen
    Wheeler, 2nd ed., London, 1907, 146).
12 Mathias' popular satirical poem, 'Pursuits of Litera-
    ture', is replete with quotations from Greek and Roman
    classics as well as from the writings of those authors
    (among them Porson) who are held up for ridicule.
    See n. 2 above.
13 'Satires of D.J. Juvenalis', trans. William Gifford
    (1802).

14   Landor's distaste for Juvenal's 'Satires' and his dis-
     like of Gifford are also expressed in a letter to
     Forster; see No. 7 above.
15   Landor twice utters this opinion in his letters to
     Birch; see No. 5 above.
16   A similar remark on the stature of critics is found in
     Post-Script to 'Gebir', No. 2 above.
17   Titian (c. 1487/90-1576), Italian artist, recognized
     as the greatest painter of the Venetian High Renais-
     sance.
18   Probably Titian's 'Sacred and Profane Love' (c. 1515),
     a painting that has had various names.
19   See Post-Script to 'Gebir', No. 2 above.
20   Both Voltaire and P.-A. de La Place (1707-93), eigh-
     teenth-century French critics, attack Shakespeare.
     See The Abbé Delille and Walter Landor, No. 11 below.
21   Perhaps a reference to John Dennis (1657-1734), eigh-
     teenth-century minor English dramatist and Shakespear-
     ean critic.
22   Editions of Shakespeare's plays were published by
     Alexander Pope in 1725 and by Samuel Johnson in 1765.
23   The faults versus beauties controversy animated both
     the eighteenth-century English and French schools of
     Shakespearean criticism.
24   Both Francis Bacon and Porson had been students at
     Trinity College, Cambridge.
25   Landor develops this thought in a footnote to Essex
     and Bacon (1837), a dramatic scene in verse: 'Bacon
     little knew or suspected that there was then existing
     (the only one that ever did exist) his superior in in-
     tellectual power.   Position gives magnitude.   While
     the world was rolling above Shakspear, he was seen im-
     perfectly: when he rose above the world, it was dis-
     covered that he was greater than the world.   The most
     honest of his contemporaries would scarcely have ad-
     mitted this, even had they known it.   But vast ob-
     jects of remote altitude must be looked at a long
     while before they are ascertained.   Ages are the
     telescope-tubes that must be lengthened out for Shaks-
     pear; and generations of men serve but as single
     witnesses to his claims' ('Complete Works', 13, 263).
26   Both Porson and Landor wrote epigrams.
27   Landor makes a similar remark in a letter to Birch;
     see No. 5 above.
28   This assertion is more characteristic of Landor than
     of Porson.   Landor's aversion to French literature is
     scattered throughout his writings.   See especially
     the Imaginary Conversation The Abbé Delille and Walter
     Landor ('Complete Works', 7, 202-48).

29   Bishop Thomas Percy (1729-1811), whose 'Reliques of
     Ancient English Poetry' (1765) further stimulated in-
     terest in Medieval English literature.   See also
     'Commentary on Memoirs of Mr. Fox', No. 3 above,
     notes 54 and 3.
30   See Landor's 'Commentary', No. 3 above.
31   See Directions for a Birth-day Song, October 30,
     1729, ll. 275-80, in 'Poems of Jonathan Swift', ed.
     Harold Williams, 2nd ed., Oxford, 1958, 2, 469, and
     the 'History of the Four Last Years of the Queen',
     in 'Prose Works of Jonathan Swift', ed. Herbert Davis,
     7, Oxford, 1951.
         George Frederick Handel (1685-1759), Anglo-German
     composer of numerous instrumental and vocal works and
     the greatest English composer of the late baroque
     period.   John Churchill, first Duke of Marlborough
     (1650-1722), English soldier who achieved fame with
     his victories against the French in the War of the
     Spanish Succession (1701-14).
32   Richard Bentley (1662-1742), English classical scholar
     whose editions of Horace (1711) and Milton (1732) fur-
     thered his reputation as a type of verbal critic, is
     attacked as such by Pope in An Epistle from Mr. Pope
     to Dr. Arbuthnot, l. 164, and in First Epistle of the
     Second Book of Horace Imitated, ll. 103-4, in 'Poems
     of Alexander Pope', ed. John Butt, London, 1963, 603,
     639.
33   See Gray's letter to Richard Stonhewer, 18 August
     1758, in 'Correspondence of Thomas Gray', ed. Paget
     Toynbee and Leonard Whibley, Oxford, 1935, 2, 583.
         Anthony Ashley Cooper, third Earl of Shaftesbury
     (1671-1713), English philosopher, author of 'Charac-
     teristics of Men, Manners, Opinions, Times' (1711).
34   The First Folio edition of Shakespeare's plays (1623)
     appeared seven years after the poet's death.
35   This approach to Milton was popular in the eighteenth
     century.
36   See Russell Noyes's 'Wordsworth and Jeffrey in Contro-
     versy', Bloomington, 1941, for an account of this
     famous literary quarrel.
37   Brevity of style was both advocated and practised by
     Landor in his writings.
38   This criticism of Wordsworth's style often appeared in
     contemporary reviews of his poetry.   See Elsie Smith,
     'An Estimate of William Wordsworth by His Contempora-
     ries, 1793-1822', Oxford, 1932, 230.
39   George Morland (1763-1804), English genre, animal, and
     landscape painter, is one of the more memorable of the
     popular painters of English rural scenes.   He is re-

membered for his natural figures and picturesque
country settings.

40 See 'Specimens of the Table Talk of the Late Samuel
    Taylor Coleridge', ed. H.N. Coleridge, New York,
    1835, 1, 107.

41 See Wordsworth's defence of his poetic practices in
    the Preface to the second edition of the 'Lyrical Bal-
    lads' (1800).

42 See Smith, op. cit., 158-67, 302-4.

43 Ibid., 187-96, 300-2.

44 Since Porson died in 1808 and Wordsworth's Laodamia
    was not written until 1814, Landor apparently wishes
    to avoid an anachronism by having Southey speak of the
    poem as incomplete and unpublished.   Landor was not
    always this careful.

45 Landor praises Wordsworth's poetry in his letters to
    Southey and Birch;   see Nos 4 and 5 above.

46 The passage omitted above which has to do with Por-
    son's recollection of one of his nights on the town is
    both in keeping with what is known of his habits and
    with Landor's view of the importance of digression in
    the writing of Imaginary Conversations.

47 Aeschylus, Sophocles, and Euripides.

48 Landor makes a similar statement in a letter to Birch;
    see No. 5 above.

49 Landor comments on the mutual esteem found between
    'men of talents' in foreign countries and the lack of
    it in England in Post-Script to 'Gebir', 'Complete
    Works', 13, 357.

50 Either Pliny the Elder (AD 23/24-79), Roman soldier
    and author of 'Naturalis Historia' (AD 77), or Pliny
    the Younger (c. AD 61-112), Roman lawyer and orator,
    author of 'Letters' (AD 100-9).

51 That Porson's remarks on Roman authors are Landor's is
    demonstrated by this recollection of Leigh Hunt:
    'Speaking of the Latin poets of antiquity, I was
    struck with an observation of his;   that Ovid was the
    best-natured of them all.   Horace's perfection that
    way he doubted.   He said, that Ovid had a greater
    range of pleasurable ideas, and was prepared to do
    justice to every thing that came in his way.   Ovid
    was fond of noticing his rivals in wit and genius, and
    has recorded the names of a great number of his
    friends;   whereas Horace seems to confine his eulogies
    to such as were rich or in fashion, and well received
    at court' ('Lord Byron and Some of His Contempora-
    ries', 2nd ed., London, 1828, 2, 381).

52 Wordsworth replied to Landor's criticism in a letter
    dated 'Rydal Mount, Janry 21, 1824':   'When at Mr

Southey's last summer, my eyes being then in a very
bad state, he read me part of that dialogue of yours,
in which he is introduced as a speaker with Porson.
It had appeared (something I must say to my regret) in
a Magazine, and I should have had the pleasure to hear
the whole, but we were interrupted.   I made out part
of the remainder myself.   You have condescended to
minute criticism upon the 'Laodamia'.   I concur with
you in the first stanza, and had several times attempted to alter it upon your grounds.   I cannot, however, accede to your objection to the 'second birth',
merely because the expression has been degraded by
Conventiclers.   I certainly meant nothing more by it
than the *eadem cura*, and the *largior æther*, etc., of
Virgil's 6th AEneid.   All religions owe their origin
or acceptation to the wish of the human heart to
supply in another state of existence the deficiencies
of this, and to carry still nearer to perfection whatever we admire in our present condition; so that
there must be many modes of expression, arising out of
this coincidence, or rather identity of feeling, common to all Mythologies; and under this observation I
should shelter the phrase from your censure; but I
may be wrong in the particular case, though certainly
not in the general principle' ('Letters of William and
Dorothy Wordsworth: The Later Years, 1821-1830', ed.,
Ernest De Selincourt, Oxford, 1939, 1, 134).   Although Wordsworth defended ll. 101-2, he revised both
passages in the 1827 edition of the poem.

53 A similar critical remark on Scottish writers is found
in a letter to Birch; see No. 5 above.

54 John Home (1722-1808), Scottish minister and author of
several tragedies, 'Douglas' (1756) the most popular.

55 For Landor's poetic tribute to Wordsworth and to Laodamia, see To Wordsworth, No. 23 below and n. 1.

56 Tottenham Court Road is a main thoroughfare in St
Pancras, a northern metropolitan borough of London.
Blackfriars Road is a main thoroughfare in Southwark,
London.

II The Abbé Delille and Walter Landor
1824, 1826, 1846

This imaginary meeting between Landor and Abbé Jacques
Delille (1738-1813), renowned French poet, translator of
Milton, and professor of Latin poetry at the Collège de
France, could conceivably have occurred when Landor visited Paris in July/August 1802.   The two men probably met
the previous year in London when Delille, then a political
refugee, and Landor, who was in training to be a Whig
pamphleteer, moved in the same Whig society.   More than
twenty years later Landor selected the witty Abbé as an
appropriate audience for his magisterial and sometimes in-
accurate criticisms of the verse of the French poet
Nicolas Boileau (1636-1711) in particular and French literature in general.   Although Wordsworth rightly judged
the Dialogue as a whole the dullest of the 'Imaginary Conversations' (1824), many of the digressions contain interesting literary observations.   The Abbé Delille and
Walter Landor first appeared in volume one of the 'Imaginary Conversations' (1824), and was successively revised
for both the second edition (1826) and the 'Works of
Walter Savage Landor' (1846).   About one-fourth of the
Conversation, taken from the 1846 text, is reprinted here.

Delille. I owe to Voltaire my first sentiment of admiration for Milton and Shakespeare. (1)
   Landor. He stuck to them as a woodpecker to an old
forest-tree, only for the purpose of picking out what was
rotten: he has made the holes deeper than he found them,
and, after all his cries and chatter, has brought home but
scanty sustenance to his starveling nest....

   Delille. There often are quickness and spirit in the
criticisms of Voltaire: but these, I acknowledge, do not

constitute a good critic, although a good critic will not
have been such without them.   His versatility and variety
are more remarkable than his correctness.   On subjects
where religion was not concerned, he was more accurate and
dispassionate.

Landor. The physical world seemed a vast thing to him:
for it must be a vast thing to contain Paris.   He could
not imagine that the earth had ever been covered by the
sea, but that the shells on mountains were tossed there by
Nature in her hours of idleness, (2) to excite, no doubt,
the curiosity of English travellers.   Never did it once
occur to him that changes are taking place eternally in
every particle of our solar system, and of other solar
systems far remote from ours: never did it occur to him
that the ocean and the world within it are less in the
hand of God than a bowl of milk with a morsel of bread
within it are in a child's, where the one is soon dissol-
ved and dislocates the other.   But his taste in high
poetry is no better than his judgment in high philosophy.
Among the number of his futile and rash remarks, he
declares that nothing in Homer is equivalent to Hesiod's
description of Pandora. (3)   The homely and somewhat dull
poem of Hesiod is indeed to a certain degree enlivened by
it.   But if Voltaire could have read a sentence of Greek,
even without understanding one word, the music of those
verses in the Odyssea, imitated so well by Lucretius, on
the habitations of the gods, (4) and of those others where
the mother of Ulysses tells him the cause of her decease, (5) would have checked him in the temerity of his
decision.   Nothing can excel the harmony of these passages, and the poetry they contain is equally perfect.
How contemptible then is that critic, and how greatly more
that poet, who prefers an indifferent piece of satire not
only to these, but to the parting of Hector and Andromache
and to the interview of Priam and Achilles. (6)

Delille. Acknowledge at least that in tales and in history he has done something.

Landor. Yes, he has united them very dexterously.   In
the lighter touches of irony and derision he excels Rabelais and rivals Molière; (7) but in that which requires
vigour of conception, and there is a kind which does require it, he falls short of Cervantes and Swift....

Landor....   We have lost the greater and (some believe) the better part of Pindar's poetry: what remains
is more distinguished for an exquisite selection of topics
than for enthusiasm.   There is a grandeur of soul which
never leaves him, even in domestic scenes; and his genius

does not rise on points or peaks of sublimity, but pervades the subject with a vigorous and easy motion, such as the poets attribute to the herald of the Gods. (8) He is remarkable for the rich economy of his ideas and the temperate austerity of his judgment; and he never says more than what is proper, nor otherwise than what is best....

Landor.... The business of the higher poetry is to chasten and elevate the mind by exciting the latter passions, and to impress on it lessons of terror and of pity by exhibiting the self-chastisement of the worse. There should be as much of passion as is possible, with as much of reason as is consistent with it....

Delille. You are very fastidious for one so little advanced in years.

Landor. I was more fastidious when I was younger, and I could detect a fallacy in composition as readily as now. I had been accustomed to none but the best models. I had read Pindar and the great tragedians more than once before I had read half the plays of Shakespeare. My prejudices in favour of ancient literature began to wear away on 'Paradise Lost'; and even the great hexameter sounded to me tinkling when I had recited aloud in my solitary walks on the seashore (9) the haughty appeal of Satan and the deep penitence of Eve. I was above twenty-five years old when I first looked at Dante; (10) one cyclopian corner of the great quaternion.

Delille. You studied much, however; and study sharpens criticism.

Landor. I doubt it; unless by references and comparisons. Only four years of my life were given up much to study; and I regret that I spent so many so ill. Even these debarred me from no pleasure; for I seldom read or wrote withindoors, excepting a few hours at night. The learning of those who are called the learned is learning at secondhand: the primary and most important must be acquired by reading in our own bosoms; the rest a deep insight into other men's. What is written is mostly an imperfect and unfaithful copy.

Delille. You have taken little from others.

Landor. When I had irrigated my field from the higher sources of literature, I permitted the waste water to run off again. Few things remained in my memory as they entered; more encumbered it; many assumed fresh combinations....

Delille. This satire contains the line which has been so often quoted,

Et le clinquant du Tasso à tout l'or de Virgile,

[And (prefer) the tinsel of Tasso to all the gold of
                                                    Virgil
('Satire', ix, 176).]

in which Boileau has scarcely his wonted discrimination. Surely Tasso is a superb poet.

Landor. A few remarks on that foolish verse.   Your poets have always felt a violent jealousy of the Italian. If Virgil had lived in the age of Tasso, and Tasso in the age of Virgil, Boileau would have transferred and commuted the designation, and have given the tinsel to Virgil, the gold to Tasso.   There is little of tinsel in the 'Gierusalemme', (11) and much of gold.   The poet fails whenever he attempts the sublime, generally so called; but he seldom overloads his descriptions with idle words or frivolous decorations.   His characters are more vivid and more distinct than Virgil's, and greatly more interesting. The heroes of the 'AEneid' are like the half-extinct frescoes of Raphael; but what is wanting in the frescoes of the painter is effaced by time, what is wanting in the figures of the poet was wanting to his genius.   No man ever formed in his mind an idea of Dido, or perhaps ever wished to form it; particularly on finding her memory so extensive and her years so mature, that she could recollect the arrival of Teucer at Sidon. (12)   Mezentius is called a despiser of the Gods; (13) yet the most pious speech in the 'AEneid' comes from the lips of Mezentius, the most heroical of all the characters in that poem, and the most resigned to the will of Heaven:

    Ast de me divom pater atque hominum rex
Viderit.

[Let the sire of gods and king of men see to me
('Aeneid', x, 743-4).]

Virgil has blemishes like Tasso, and Tasso has beauties like Virgil.   The 'AEneid', I venture to affirm, is the most misshapen of epics; an epic of episodes: for these constitute the greater and better part.   The 'Gierusalemme Liberata' is, of all such compositions, the most perfect in its plan.   In regard to execution, read any one book attentively, and I am persuaded, M. l'Abbé, that

you would rather have written it than all the poetry of
Voltaire and Boileau....

Delille. I cannot well believe that if Boileau, to say
nothing of Racine, was a poet so faulty as you represent
him, he would have escaped the censure of such sound
critics and elegant writers as Johnson and Warton. (14)...

Landor.... Johnson had no feeling for poetry; and
Warton was often led astray by a feverish and weak enthusiasm.
   Delille. Some of his observations are very just.
   Landor. Others are trivial and superficial.   He seldom
demonstrates his objections, or ascends to the sources of
his admiration.   Johnson is practised in both; sometimes
going wrong from an obliquity in his view of poetry,
rarely from his ratiocination.   Neither of them saw the
falsity of Pope's inference at the commencement of the
'Essay on Man'.

   Let us, since life can little more supply
   Than just to look around us and to die,
   Expatiate free o'er all this maze [scene] of man.
   [i, 3-5.]

If human life is so extremely contracted, there is
little encouragement to expatiate in all its maze, and
little power to expatiate *freely*, which can only mean *leisurely*, for freedom of will or purpose is not in question.
   Delille. Johnson may not have been quite so learned as
some whose celebrity is less; for I believe that London
is worse furnished with public libraries of easy access
than any city in Europe, not excepting Constantinople;
and his private one, from his contracted circumstances,
must have been scanty.
   Landor. He was studious; but neither his weak eyes nor
many other infirmities, on which a severe mental disquie-
tude worked incessantly, would allow him all the reading
he coveted: beside, he was both too poor and too wise to
collect a large body of authors.
   Delille. Ignorant men are often more ambitious than the
learned of copious libraries and curious books, as the
blind are fonder of sunshine than the sighted.   Surely
the judgment of Johnson was correct, the style elegant.
   Landor. I have spoken of his judgment in poetry.   In
regard to elegance of style, it appears to me that a sentence of Johnson is like that article of dress which your

nation has lately made peace with; divided into two
parts, equal in length, breadth, and substance, with a
protuberance before and behind.   Warton's 'Essay on Pope'
is a cabinet of curiosities, in which are many trifles
worth looking at, nothing to carry about or use.

Delille. That Racine and Boileau were great borrowers
is undeniable.

Landor. And equally that they were in the habit of
paying a small portion of the debt.

Delille. Even your immortal Shakespeare borrowed from
others.

Landor. Yet he was more original than the originals.
He breathed upon dead bodies and brought them into life.

Delille. I think however I can trace Caliban, that
wonderful creature, (15) when I survey attentively the
Cyclops of Euripides.

Landor. He knew nothing of Euripides or his Cyclops.
That poet, where he is irregular, is great; and he presents more shades and peculiarities of character than all
other poets of antiquity put together.   Yet in several
scenes he appears to have written principally for the purpose of inculcating his political and moral axioms: almost every character introduces them, and in almost every
place.   There is a regular barter of verse for verse; no
credit is given for a proverb, however threadbare;   the
exchange is paid on the nail for the commodity.   The
dogmas, like *valets de place*, serve any master and run to
any quarter.   Even when new, they nevertheless are mis-
erably flat and idle: how different from the striking
sentences employed unsparingly by Pindar, which always
come recommended by some appropriate ornament.   Virgil
and Ovid have interspersed them with equal felicity.   The
dialogue of Euripides is sometimes dull and heavy;   the
construction of his fable infirm and inartificial;   and in
the chorus I can not but exclaim

There be *two* Richards in the field to-day. (16)

Aristophanes, who ridicules him in his Comedies, (17)
treats him disdainfully as the competitor of Sophocles,
and speaks probably the sense of the Athenians in the meridian of their literature.   If however he was not considered by them as the equal of Sophocles in dramatic power,
or in the continuous train of poetical expression, yet
sensible men in all ages will respect him, and the more
because they fancy they discover in him greater wisdom
than others have discovered: for while many things in his
tragedies are direct, and many proverbial, others are allusive and vague, occurring in various states of mind and

temperatures of feeling.   There is little of the theatri-
cal in his works; and his characters are more anxious to
show their understanding than their sufferings.

Euripides came down farther into common life than
Sophocles, and he farther down than AEschylus: one would
have expected the reverse.   But the marvellous had carried AEschylus from the earth, and he filled with light
the whole region in which he rested.   The temperate
greatness and pure eloquence of Pericles formed the moral
constitution of Sophocles, who had exercised with him a
principal magistracy in the republic; (18) and the demon
of Socrates, not always unimportunate, followed Euripides
from the school to the theatre. (19)   The decencies of
the *boudoir* were unknown to him: he would have shocked
your chambermaids.   Talthybius calls Polyxena a calf;
her mother had done the same; and Hercules, in 'Alceste',
is drunk. (20)

Delille. This is horrible, if true.   Virgil (to venture nothing further about Racine), Virgil is greatly more
judicious in his Dido.

Landor. The passion of Dido is always true to Nature.
Other women have called their lovers cruel: she calls
AEneas so, not chiefly for betraying and deserting her,
but for hazarding his life by encountering the tempests of
a wintry sea. (21) ...

Landor....   My admiration of the author of the
'AEneid', as you see, is not inferior to yours: but I
doubt whether he has displayed *on the whole* such poetical
powers as the author of 'Alcestis', (22) who excels in
variety and peculiarity of character all the ancient
poets.   He has invented, it is true, nothing so stupendous nor so awful as the Prometheus: (23) but who has?
The Satan of Milton himself sinks below it; for Satan, if
he sometimes appears with the gloomy grandeur of a fallen
Angel, and sometimes as the antagonist of Omnipotence, is
often a thing to be thrown out of the way, among the rods
and foolscaps of the nursery. (24)

Virgil is not so vigorous as Lucretius, so elegant and
graceful as Catullus, so imaginative and diversified as
Ovid.   All their powers united could not have composed
the 'AEneid'; but in the 'AEneid' there is nothing so
epic as the contest of Ulysses and Ajax in the 'Metamorphoses'. (25)   This, in my opinion, is the most wonderful
thing in the whole range of Latin poetry; for it unites
(what appears incompatible) two pieces of pleading never
excelled by Roman or Athenian orator with exquisitely dis-
criminated characters and unparalleled heroic composition.

The 'Iliad' itself has nothing in the *contentional* so interesting or so animated.   When Ajax hath ended, who can
doubt of his having gained the cause?   Ulysses rises,
slowly, modestly; and our enthusiasm subsides just sufficiently to allow him a patient hearing.   By degrees he
engages, moves, and almost convinces us.   At last, when
we hesitate and waver, he displays the Palladium before
us: (26) and we are gained by that which gained the city,
by that which terminates our toils, by that which restores
to us our country and our home.
    Delille. Ah! you fancy yourself among them.   You
should have been there.
    Landor. I was; I am; I have been often, and shall be
often yet....

    Landor....   We have in England, at the present time,
many poets far above what was formerly thought mediocrity;
but our national taste begins to require excitement.   Our
poems must contain *strong things*: we call for essences,
not for flowers: we run across from the old grove and
soft meadow, into the ruined abbey, the Albanian fortress,
and the Sultan's garden: we cut down our oaks and plant
cypresses: we reprove our children for not calling a *rose
a gul*: (27) we kick the first shepherd we meet, and shake
hands with the first cut-throat: we are resolved to
excite tears, but we conjure them forth at the point of
the dagger: and, if they come slower than we wish, we
bully and blaspheme.
    Nothing is easier than to catch the air of originality
now blowing: do not wonder that it pleases the generali-
ty.   You and I perhaps have stopped, like the children
and the servants, to look at a fine transparency on a
staircase, while many who call themselves professors have
passed a Raphael by, and have never noticed it.   Let us
censure no one for being easily pleased, but let *us* do the
best we can.   Whenever I find a critic or satirist vehe-
ment against the writers of his age and country, I attribute more of his inspiration to vanity than to malignity,
much as I may observe of this.   No good writer was ever
long neglected; no great man overlooked by men equally
great.   Impatience is a proof of inferior strength, and a
destroyer of what little there may be.   Whether, think
you, would Shakespeare be amused or mortified, if he were
sitting in the pit during the performance of his best
tragedy, and heard no other exclamation from one beside
him, than, 'How beautifully those scenes are painted! what
palaces, waterfalls, and rocks!
    Delille. I wish he were more dramatic.

Landor. You would say, more observant of certain rules established for one species of the drama. Never was poet so dramatic, so intelligent of stage effect. I do not defend his anachronisms, nor his confusion of modern customs with ancient; nor do I willingly join him when I find him with Hector and Aristoteles, arm in arm, among knights, esquires, and fiddlers. (28) But our audiences and our princes in those days were resolved that all countries and all ages should be subservient at once, and perceived no incongruity in bringing them together.

Delille. Yet what argument can remove the objection made against your poet, of introducing those who in the first act are children, and grown-up men in the last? (29)

Landor. Such a drama I would not call by the name of tragedy: nevertheless it is a drama; and a very beautiful species of it. Delightful in the first degree are those pieces of history in verse and action, as managed by Shakespeare.

Delille. We must contend against them: we must resist all barbarous inroads on classic ground, all innovations and abuses.

Landor. You fight against your own positions. Such a work is to Tragedy what a forest is to a garden. Those alone are wrong who persist in calling it a garden rather than a forest; who find oaks instead of tulips; who look about the hills and dales, the rocks and precipices, the groves and waterfalls, for flues and balusters and vases, and smooth marble steps, and shepherdesses in hoops and satin. There are some who think those things as unnatural as that children should grow into men, and that we should live to see it.

Delille. Live to see it! but in one day or night!

Landor. The same events pass before us within the same space of time whenever we look into history.

Delille. Ay, but here they act.

Landor. So they do there, unless the history is an English one. And indeed the histories of our country read by Shakespeare held human life within them. (30) When we are interested in the boy, we spring forward to the man, with more than a poet's velocity. We would interrogate the oracles; we would measure the thread around the distaff of the Fates; yet we quarrel with him who knows and tells us all.

Glory to thee in the highest, thou confidant of our Creator! who alone hast taught us in every particle of the mind how wonderfully and fearfully we are made.

Delille. Voltaire was indeed too severe upon him.

Landor. Severe? Is it severity to throw a crab or a pincushion at the Farnese Hercules or the Belvedere

Apollo? (31)   It is folly, perverseness, and impudence,
in poets and critics like Voltaire, whose best composition
in verse is a hard mosaic, sparkling and superficial, of
squares and parallelograms, one speck each.   He, whose
poems are worth all that have been composed from the Creation to the present hour, was so negligent or so secure
of fame as to preserve no copy of them.   Homer and he
confided to the hearts of men the treasures of their
genius, which were, like conscience, unengraved words....

   Landor. We have wandered (and conversation would be
tedious unless we did occasionally) far from the subject:
but I have not forgotten our Cyclops and Caliban.   The
character of the Cyclops is somewhat broad and general,
but worthy of Euripides, and such as the greatest of Roman
poets was incapable of conceiving;   that of Caliban is
peculiar and stands single;   it is admirably imagined and
equally well-sustained.   Another poet would have shown
him spiteful: Shakespeare has made the infringement of
his idleness the origin of his malice.   He has also made
him grateful;   but then his gratitude is the return for an
indulgence granted to his evil appetites.   Those who by
nature are grateful are often by nature vindictive: one
of these properties is the sense of kindness, the other of
unkindness.   Religion and comfort require that the one
should be cherished and that the other should be suppressed.   The mere conception of the monster without these
qualities, without the sudden impression which bring them
vividly out, and the circumstances in which they are displayed, would not be to considerate minds so stupendous as
it appeared to Warton, who little knew that there is a *nil
admirari* (32) as requisite to wisdom as to happiness.
   Delille. And yet how enthusiastic is your admiration of
Shakespeare.
   Landor.

   He lighted with his golden lamp on high
   The unknown regions of the human heart,
   Show'd its bright fountains, show'd its rueful wastes,
   Its shoals and headlands;   and a tower he rais'd
   Refulgent, where eternal breakers roll,
   For all to see, but no man to approach. (33)

The creation of Caliban, wonderful as it is, would excite
in me less admiration than a single sentence, or a single
sentiment, such as I find in fifty of his pages....

NOTES

1 Voltaire's earliest remarks on Milton and Shakespeare
   appeared first in English and later French editions:
   see 'Essay upon the Civil Wars of France ... and upon
   the Epick Poetry of the European Nations from Homer
   down to Milton' (1727) and 'Letters concerning the
   English Nation' (1733). For a definitive edition of
   Voltaire's collected criticism of Shakespeare, see
   Theodore Besterman, Voltaire on Shakespeare, 'Studies
   on Voltaire and the Eighteenth Century', 54, Geneva,
   1967.
2 See Des Singularitiés de la nature, 'OEuvres complètes
   de Voltaire', ed. Louis Moland, new ed., Paris, 1877-
   85, 27, 140-9.
3 See Il faut prendre un parti ou le principe d'action,
   'OEuvres complètes de Voltaire', 28, 538, and Hesiod,
   'Theogony', 570-90.
4 See 'Odyssey', vi, 42-6, and Lucretius, 'De Rerum
   Natura', iii, 18-22.
5 See 'Odyssey', xi, 197-203, for Anticlea's story.
6 Landor alludes to those moving scenes in Homer's
   'Iliad' where the Trojan hero, Hector, bids farewell
   to his wife Andromache prior to his death at the hands
   of the Greek hero Achilles ('Iliad', vi, 391-493), and
   the sorrowful meeting between the Trojan king Priam
   and Achilles at which time Priam requests the body of
   his son, Hector, whom Achilles has abused (xxiv, 471-
   601).
7 François Rabelais (c. 1494-1553), French physician,
   humanist, and writer, author of the comic and satirical 'Gargantua et Pantagruel' (1552). Jean Baptiste
   Poquelin Molière (1622-73), French comic dramatist,
   author of many plays, including 'L'École des femmes'
   (1662), 'Le Misanthrope' (1666), and 'Le Malade imag-
   inaire' (1673).
8 Mercury (Hermes).
9 Landor spent much time in South Wales between 1794 and
   1797: 'Never were my spirits better than in my twentieth year, when I wrote "Gebir," and did not exchange
   twelve sentences with men. I lived among woods,
   which are now killed with copper works, and took my
   walk over sandy sea-coast desarts, then covered with
   low roses and thousands of nameless flowers and
   plants, trodden by the naked feet of the welsh peasan-
   try, and trackless....'   (W.S.L. to Lady Blessington,
   16? November 1839 (Dr John F. Mariani, The Letters of
   Walter Savage Landor to Marguerite Countess of Blessington [unpublished PhD dissertation, Columbia University, 1973], 319)).

10   Dante Alighieri (1265-1321), Italy's greatest poet,
     author of the 'Vita Nuova' (c. 1293), the 'Convivio'
     (1304-8), and the 'Divina Commedia', completed shortly
     before his death.
11   'Gerusalemme Liberata' or 'Jerusalem Delivered', an
     epic poem by Torquato Tasso (1544-95).
12   'Aeneid', i, 619-22.
13   Ibid., vii, 647-8.
14   Joseph Warton (1722-1800), author of 'Essay on the
     Genius and Writings of Pope' (1756 and 1782).
15   Shakespeare's Caliban ('The Tempest') was admired by
     eighteenth-century critics as a tremendous effort of
     the creative imagination.
16   Cf. 'Richard III', V, iv, 11-12: 'I think there be
     six Richmonds in the field; / Five have I slain to-day
     instead of him.'
17   See Aristophanes, 'Acharnians', 394-490; 'Knights',
     18-20; 'Clouds', 1371-7; 'Wasps', 61, 1414;
     'Peace', 146-50; 'Frogs', 53-82, 96-105; 'Lysis-
     trata', 283-5, 368-9.
18   Sophocles (c. 496-406 BC) was one of the generals who
     served with Pericles (c. 500-429 BC) in the Samian War
     (440-439 BC).
19   Although there is no proof that Euripides (c. 485-
     c. 406 BC) personally knew Socrates (469-399 BC), he
     was certainly involved in contemporary intellectual
     movements.
20   See Euripides, 'Hecuba', 484ff, and 'Alcestis', 773ff.
21   'Aeneid', iv, 309-13.
22   Euripides.
23   Aeschylus, 'Prometheus Bound'.
24   Cf. Shelley's remarks on Prometheus and Milton's Satan
     in his Preface to 'Prometheus Unbound' (1820).
25   Ovid, 'Metamorphoses', xiii, 1-398.
26   According to Greek belief, Troy could not be taken as
     long as the Palladium, an ancient image of Pallas
     Athene, remained safely within the city walls. Odys-
     seus wins his listeners' support by pointing out that
     it was he who stole the Palladium from the temple
     inside Troy ('Metamorphoses', xiii, 339-49), thus en-
     abling the Greeks to ravage Troy.
27   'Gul' is the Persian word for 'rose'. Byron popular-
     ized the term in 1813 with these lines from 'The Bride
     of Abydos': 'Know ye the land ... / Where the light
     wings of Zephyr, oppress'd with perfume, / Wax faint
     o'er the gardens of Gúl in her bloom' (i, 1, 7-8).
        Landor's comments in this paragraph and the next
     are thinly veiled criticisms of Byron's popular works.
28   See Shakespeare's 'Troilus and Cressida' (1609), pro-
     duced 1602-3.

29 See 'Henry VI, Part I' (1623), produced 1591-2.
30 Shakespeare's chief historical sources for the 'Chron-
    ical plays' were: 'The newe Cronycles of Englande and
    of Fraunce' (1516, 1533, 1542, 1559), by Robert Fabyan
    (d. 1513);   'The Union of the Two Noble and Illustre
    Famelies of Lancastre and Yorke' (1548, 1550), by
    Edward Hall (c. 1498-1547);   and the 'Chronicles of
    England, Scotland, and Ireland' (1577), by Raphael
    Holinshed (d. c. 1580).
31 The Farnese Hercules stands ten feet two inches high
    and is located in the Museo Nazionale at Naples,
    Italy.   The Apollo Belvedere, the most famous statue
    of this Greek god, is housed in the Vatican at Rome.
32 'Nil admirari:' 'to wonder at nothing'.
33 Landor added this poem to the Conversation in 1846.

12 Lord Chesterfield and Lord Chatham
1824, 1826, 1846

Lord Chesterfield and Lord Chatham is one of several Imaginary Conversations devoted primarily to an unrelenting
and biased attack by Landor on the character, philosophy,
and writings of Plato.   Landor's devotion to individual
freedom, his hatred of tyranny in whatever form, and his
dislike of metaphysical speculation made his clash with
Plato inevitable.   Landor also saw himself as a rival of
Plato in the matter of writing dialogues: 'Before I wrote
this conversation [Marcus Tullius and Quinctus Cicero], I
would on no account open Plato.   I have since read twice
over his dialogue [?] of Socrates, and am not so discour-
aged as I might have been' (W.S.L. to Robert Southey, 31
May 1823; quoted in Forster, 'Landor', 2, 113).   Charles
G. Crump, editor of 'Imaginary Conversations', 6 vols
(1891), attributes Landor's erroneous judgments on the
thought and style of Plato's writings in this conversation
either to an inadequate understanding of the Greek or to a
failure to grasp the meaning within the proper context.
Although the following excerpt substantiates Crump's
latter assertion (see n. 1 below), it is the literary
criticism elicited from Landor's reading of Plato that is
of value here.
     Had such a meeting occurred between Lord Chesterfield
(Philip Dormer Stanhope, fourth Earl, 1694-1773) and Lord
Chatham (William Pitt, first Earl, 1708-78), it would have
taken place shortly before Lord Chesterfield's death.
That Lord Chatham is Landor's mouthpiece for this attack
on Plato is evident both by the tone and content of his
remarks.   This Dialogue first appeared in volume two of
'Imaginary Conversations' (1824), and was successively revised for the second edition (1826) and the 'Works of
Walter Savage Landor' (1846).   The selection below is
taken from the 1846 text.

Chatham.... I am reminded by the mention of poetry, that
Plato is offended in the 'Iliad' at the undignified grief
of Achilles and of Priam. (1) To clasp the knee is going
too far: and to roll in the dust is beastly. I am certain that he never was a father or a friend: not that
among us the loss of friends is accompanied by such violence of affliction, but because I have observed that
grief is less often in proportion to delicacy, and even to
tenderness, than to the higher energies of our nature and
the impetuosity of our nobler passions. The intemperate
and wild resentment of Achilles at the injustice of Agamemnon, (2) and his self-devotion, certain as he was of
his fate, (3) prepare us for intensity and extravagance of
feeling, and teach us that in such a character diversity
is not incongruity. This censure of the philosopher on
the poet, convinces me that the wisest of his works was
the burning of his tragedies. (4) Heroism, as Plato
would have had it, would be afraid to soil his robe, and
Passion would blush to unfold her handkerchief. He who
could censure the two most admirable passages in Homer,
could indeed feel no reluctance at banishing the poets
from his republic: (5) and we can not wonder that he
strays wide from sound philosophy, who knows so little of
the human heart, as to be ignorant that the poet is most a
poet in the midst of its varieties and its excesses.
Only with God can greatness exist without irregularity:
that of Achilles was a necessary and essential part of
him. Without it, no resentment at Agamemnon, no abandonment of his cause and of his countrymen, no revenge for
Patroclus, no indignity to the body of his bravest enemy,
no impatience at the first sight of Priam, no effusion of
tears at his paternal sorrows, no agony stronger than his
vows or than his vengeance forcing him to deliver up the
mangled hero; (6) in short, no Iliad, no Homer. We all
are little before such men, and principally when we censure or contend with them. Plato on this occasion stands
among the ringers of the twelve unchangeable French bells;
among the apes who chatter as they pick out the scurf of
Shakespeare. These two poets divide the ages of the
world between them, and will divide the ages of eternity.
Prudent men, who wish to avoid the appearance of pygmies,
will reverently keep at some distance, laying aside here
their cruet of vinegar and here their cake of honey.
Plato is the only one of the ancients who extols the
poetry of Solon; of whom he says that, if he had written
his poem on the war of the Athenians against the island of
Atalantis, undistracted by the business of the state, he
might have rivalled the glory of *Hesiod and Homer*. (7)
No man of sound judgment ever placed these names together,

unless as contemporaries;   and he must possess a very unsound one indeed, who calculates thus on the contingency
of Homer's rival in any statesman.

'Poetical expression', Plato tells you, 'is a copy of
the poet's own conception of things;   and things, of the
archetype existing in the divine mind;   thus the poet's
expression is a copy at the third hand'.   (8)   And this
argument he adduces to prove that poetry is far distant
from truth.   It proves no such thing;   and if it did, it
would not prove that poetry is not delightful;   and
delight, we know, is its aim and end.   But that truths
also, and most important ones, are conveyed by poetry, is
quite as certain as that fallacies, and the most captious
and quibbling fallacies, are conveyed by Plato: more certain nothing can be.   If the poet has a conception of
things as they emanate from the divine mind, whether it is
at third hand or at thirtieth, so long as nothing distorts
or disturbs them, what matters it?   The image or archetype is God's: he impresses it on things: the poet represents the things as they are impressed on his mind by
the hand of the Creator.   Now, if this is done, the distance from truth is not remote.   But there is a truth,
accommodated to our nature, which poetry best conveys.
There is a truth for the reason;   there is a truth for the
passions;   there is a truth for every character of man.
Shakespeare has rendered this clear and luminous, over all
the stumps and stumbling-blocks and lighter brushwood and
briars thrown across the path by the puerile trickery of
Plato. (9)...

NOTES

1   Plato, 'Republic', iii, 388a-b.   Plato would reject as
    unsuitable examples of human behaviour for those in-
    tended to be future guardians of the Republic Homer's
    descriptions of Achilles' grief on learning of Patro-
    clus' death ('Iliad', xviii, 23-4), his subsequent
    mourning (xxiv, 10-12), and Priam's agony as Achilles
    maltreated Hector's corpse befo-e Troy (xxii, 414-15).
2   Agamemnon seized Achilles' prize, Briseis, for himself
    when the Greeks compelled him to relinquish the
    daughter of Chryses ('Iliad', i, 180-7, 318-47).
3   Achilles knew an early death awaited him if he re-
    mained with the Greek expeditionary force against Troy
    ('Iliad', i, 413-18).
4   See Diogenes Laertius, 'Lives of Eminent Philoso-
    phers', iii, 5-6.
5   Plato, 'Republic', viii, 568b;   x, 595a, 607a.

6   See 'Iliad', i, 188ff, 488ff; xix, 199ff; xxii,
    395ff; xxiv, 483ff, 507ff, 559ff.
7   Plato, 'Timaeus', 21b-d.   Solon (c. 640-c. 558 BC),
    famed Athenian statesman, lawgiver, and poet.   Only
    fragments of his elegiacs and iambics have survived.
8   Plato, 'Republic', x, 597e ff.
9   See 'Letter from W.S. Landor to R.W. Emerson', No. 9
    above, n. 17.

13 Landor, English Visitor, and Florentine Visitor

1828, 1846

This meeting between Landor, an English visitor, and a
Florentine visitor is imagined to have taken place in June
1824 at one of Landor's Florentine residences, apartments
in the palace of the Marchese de'Medici-Tornaquinci, in
the Borgo degli Albizi. Although most of the Conversation is devoted to political and personal matters, the
digressions contain some perceptive remarks on character
portrayal in the 'Imaginary Conversations', poetic style,
and several of the English Romantic poets. Landor, English Visitor, and Florentine Visitor first appeared in
volume three of the 'Imaginary Conversations' (1828), and
was revised before its inclusion in the 'Works of Walter
Savage Landor' (1846). About an eighth of the Conversation, taken from the 1846 text, is given here.

English Visitor. One objection to your 'Imaginary Conversations' is, that you represent some living characters as
speaking with greater powers of mind than they possess,
vile as they are in conduct.

Landor. It can not be expected, by those who know of
what materials the cabinets of Europe are composed, that
any person in them should reason so conclusively, and with
such illustrations, as some who are introduced. This, if
it is a blemish in a book, is one which the book would be
worse without. The practice of Shakespeare and Sophocles
is a better apology for me than I could offer of my own.
If men were to be represented as they show themselves,
encrusted with all the dirtiness they contract in public
life, in all the debility of ignorance, in all the distortion of prejudice, in all the reptile trickery of partis-
anship, who would care about the greater part of what are
called the greatest? Principles and ideas are my objects: they must be reflected from high and low, but they

must also be exhibited where people can see them best, and
are most inclined to look at them....

Landor....   Poetry, like wine, requires a gentle and
regular and long fermentation.   What is it if it can buoy
up no wisdom, no reflection? if we can throw into it none
of our experience? if no repository is to be found in it
for the gems we have collected, at the price sometimes of
our fortunes, of our health, and of our peace?...   The
first thing a young person who wishes to be a poet has to
do, is, to conquer his volubility;   to compress in three
verses what he had easily thrown off in twelve;   and to be
an hour about what cost him a minute.   If he has a *knack*
for verses, he must break it and forget it.   Both the
poet and the painter should acquire facility and frankness;   but they must be exercised with discretion;   they
must be sternly regulated, and in great part suppressed.
The young poet will remonstrate, and more often scoff: he
will appall you by placing before you the *deep mouth* of
Pindar and his mountain torrents.   Tell him, and tell
older ones too, that Pindar of all poets is the most accurate and the most laborious....

Landor....   Since the time of Chaucer there have been
only two poets who at all resemble him;   and these two
are widely dissimilar one from the other, Burns and Keats.
The accuracy and truth with which Chaucer has described
the manners of common life, with the foreground and back-
ground, are also to be found in Burns, who delights in
broader strokes of external nature, but equally appropriate.   He has parts of genius which Chaucer has not in the
same degree;   the animated and pathetic.   Keats, in his
'Endymion', is richer in imagery than either: and there
are passages in which no poet has arrived at the same excellence on the same ground.   Time alone was wanting to
complete a poet, who already far surpassed all his contemporaries in this country, in the poet's most noble attributes.   If anything could engage me to visit Rome, to
endure the sight of her scarred and awful ruins, telling
their stories on the ground in the midst of bell-ringers
and pantomimes;   if I could let charnel-houses and opera-
houses, consuls and popes, tribunes and cardinals, senatorial orators and preaching friars, clash in my mind;   it
would be that I might afterward spend an hour in solitude,
where the pyramid of Cestius stands against the wall, and
points to the humbler tombs of Keats and Shelley. (1)
Nothing so attracts my heart as ruins in deserts, or so

repels it as ruins in the circle of fashion. What is so
shocking as the hard verity of Death swept by the rustling
masquerade of Life!...

Florentine Visitor. I wish, sir, you would favour us
with a Latin inscription for the tombs of the gentlemen
whose names you mentioned, since the pathetic is not requisite in that species of composition.

Landor. Although I have written at various times a
great number of such inscriptions, as parts of literature,
yet I think nothing is so absurd if you only inscribe them
on a tomb. Why should extremely few persons, the least
capable perhaps of sympathy, be invited to sympathise,
while thousands are excluded from it by the iron grate of
a dead language? Those who read a Latin inscription are
the most likely to know already the character of the de-
funct, and no new feelings are to be excited in them: but
the language of the country tells the ignorant who he was
that lies under the turf before them; and, if he was a
stranger, it naturalises him among them; it gives him
friends and relations; it brings to him and detains about
him some who may imitate, many who will lament him. We
have no right to deprive anyone of a tender sentiment, by
talking in an unknown tongue to him, when his heart would
listen and answer to his own: we have no right to turn a
chapel into a library, locking it with a key which the
lawful proprietors can not turn.

Italian Visitor. It is rarely we find an epitaph in
which the thought, if novel, is not superficial. Where
there is only one, it should be striking or affecting.

Landor. But it is an error to imagine that every
thought must be either. Truth, in these documents and
appeals, should oftener be remarkable for simplicity than
force. It sinks deeplier into the mind by insinuating
than by striking, and is more acceptable for grace than
for novelty....

Landor. It was not my fortune (shall I call it good or
bad now they are dead?) to know those young men who,
within so short a space of time, have added two more immortal names to the cemeteries of Rome. Upon one of them
I have written what by no means satisfies me.

English Visitor. Pray let me hear it, if you retain it
in your memory.

Landor. I rarely do retain anything of my own: and
probably you will never find a man who has heard me repeat
a line. But here it is: you may read it yourself.

English Visitor.

Fair and free soul of poesy, O Keats!
O how my temples throb, my heart-blood beats,
   At every image, every word of thine!
Thy bosom, pierced by Envy, drops to rest,
Nor hearest ! thou the friendlier voice, nor seest
   The sun of fancy climb along thy line.

But under it, although a viperous brood
That stung an Orpheus (in a clime more rude
   Than Rhodope and Haernus frown upon) (2)
Still writhes and hisses, and peers out for more
Whose buoyant blood they leave concreted gore,
   Thy flowers root deep and split the creviced stone.

Ill may I speculate on scenes to come,
Yet I would dream to meet thee at our home
   With Spenser's quiet, Chaucer's livelier ghost,
Cognate to thine ... not higher, and less fair ...
And Madalene and Isabella there
   Shall say, *without thee half our loves were lost.*(3)

Here indeed is little of the pathetic. You must rather
have been thinking on the depravity of those who exerted
their popularity to depress him, heedless that it precipi-
tated him to the tomb.
   Landor. If I bore malice toward any man I should wish
him to write against me: but poor Keats, sinking under
the blow, perceived not the incurable ignominy it inflicted by its recoil on the executioner.
   English Visitor. Such people as Gifford (4) are to be
acquitted: for how could they feel his poetry or estimate his virtues? Gifford is the Harriet Wilson (5) of
our literary world; the witherer of young names. With
the exception of Mathias (6) he is the dullest, as Byron
is the sharpest, of our satirists.
   Landor. I have no recollection of anything written by
the couple you mentioned with Byron; but of him and of
his sharpness we think alike. He has not exerted all his
force, or he has not experienced all his felicity, on me.
Rather than the world should have been a loser in this
part of his poetry, I would have corrected and enlarged
for him what he composed about me, and I would have furnished him with fresh materials. I only wish I could
have diverted his pen from Southey. While he wrote or
spoke against me alone, I said nothing of him in print or
conversation: but the taciturnity of pride gave way immediately to my zeal in defence of my friend. (7) What I

write is not written on slate: and no finger, not of Time
himself, who dips it in the clouds of years, can efface
it.   To condemn what is evil and to commend what is good
is consistent.   To soften an asperity, to speak all the
good we can after worse than we wish, is *that*, and more.
If I must understand the meaning of consistency as many
do, I wish I may be inconsistent with all my enemies.
There are many hearts which have risen higher and sunk
lower at his tales, and yet have been shocked and sorrowed
at his untimely death a great deal less than mine has
been.   Honour and glory to him for the extensive good he
did! peace and forgiveness for the partial evil!...

English Visitor. But certainly there are blemishes in
Keats, which strike the most incurious and inobservant
beholder.
Landor. If so, why expose them? why triumph over them?
In Keats, I acknowledge, there are many wild thoughts, and
there are expressions which even outstrip them in extravagance: but in none of our poets, with the sole exception
of Shakespeare, do we find so many phrases so happy in
their boldness. (8)
English Visitor. There is a more vivid spirit, more
genuine poetry, in him than in any of his contemporaries;...

English Visitor. You appear more interested about this
youth than about Burns, whom I have known you extol to the
skies.
Landor. I do not recollect what I wrote on Burns, for I
seldom keep a copy of anything, but I know that I wrote it
many years after his decease, which was hardly less deplorable than Keats's.   One would imagine that those who,
for the honour of our country, ought to have guarded and
watched over this prodigy of genius, had considered only
how they could soonest despatch him from the earth.   They
gave him a disreputable and sordid place, exactly of the
kind in which he would indulge his only bad propensity. (9)
English Visitor. And I now remember that you allude to
this propensity, not without an acknowledgment that you
yourself would have joined him in its excess.
Landor. How so?   If you can recollect it, the critics
will thank you for it.
English Visitor. These, I think, are the verses.

Had we two met, blithe-hearted Burns,
   Tho' water is my daily drink,
   May God forgive me but I think
We should have roared out toasts by turns.

Inquisitive low whispering cares
   Had found no room in either pate,
   Until I asked thee, rather late,
Is there a hand-rail to the stairs? (10)

Landor. My Bacchus is, I protest, as innocent as Cowley's mistress: (11) but, with a man like Burns, I do not know whether I should have cried out very anxiously

Quo me Bacche rapis?

[Whither, O Bacchus, dost thou hurry me?
(Horace, 'Odes', iii, 25, 1).]...

English Visitor. There was something in his [Byron] mind not ungraceful nor inelegant, although from a deficiency of firmness, it wanted dignity. He issued forth against stronger and better men than himself, partly through wantonness and malignity, partly through ignorance of their powers and worth, and partly through impatience at their competition. He could comprehend nothing heroic, nothing disinterested. Shelley, at the gates of Pisa, threw himself between him (12) and the dragoon, whose sword in his indignation was lifted and about to strike. Byron told a common friend, (13) some time afterward, that he could not conceive how any man living should act so. 'Do you know, he might have been killed! and there was every appearance that he would be'! The answer was, 'Between you and Shelley there is but little similarity, and perhaps but little sympathy: yet what Shelley did then, he would do again, and always. There is not a human creature, not even the most hostile, that he would hesitate to protect from injury at the imminent hazard of life. And yet life, which he would throw forward so unguardedly, is somewhat more with him than with others: it is full of hopes and aspirations, it is teeming with warm feelings, it is rich and overrun with its own native simple enjoyments. In him everything that ever gave pleasure, gives it still, with the same freshness, the same exuberance, the same earnestness to communicate and share it'.
'By God! I can not understand it'! cried Byron. 'A man to run upon a naked sword for another'!

Landor. He [Byron] had drawn largely from his imagination, penuriously from his heart.   He distrusted it:
what wonder then if he had little faith in another's!
Had he lived among the best of the ancient Greeks, he
would have satirised and reviled them: but their characters caught his eye softened by time and distance;   nothing in them of opposition, nothing of rivalry;   where
they are, there they must stand;   they can not come down
nearer.   Of all great poets, for such I consider him,
Byron has borrowed most from others, not excepting Ariosto, of whose description he reminds me:

> Salta a cavallo, e per *diversa strada*
> Va discorrendo, e *molti pone a sacco.*

> [(Orlando) leaps on the horse; by diff'rent roads
>   does stray,
> Wand'ring about, and many puts to sack
> ('Orlando Furios', xxx, 8, 1-2 tr T.C.).]

Not only in the dresses which he puts on expressly for the
ladies, not only in the oriental train and puffy turban,
but also in the tragic pall, his perfumery has somewhat
too large a proportion of musk in it; which so hangs
about those who are accustomed to spend many hours with
him, that they seldom come forth again with satisfaction
into what is fresher and purer.   Yet Byron is, I think,
the keenest and most imaginative of satirists....

Landor....   Innocent and careless as a boy, he
[Shelley] possessed all the delicate feelings of a gentleman, all the discrimination of a scholar, and united, in
just degrees, the ardour of the poet with the patience and
forbearance of the philosopher.   His generosity and
charity went far beyond those of any man (I believe) at
present in existence.   He was never known to speak evil
of an enemy, unless that enemy had done some grievous injustice to another: and he divided his income of only one
thousand pounds with the fallen and afflicted.
This is the man against whom such clamours have been
raised by the religious and the loyal, and by those who
live and lap under their tables: this is the man, whom
from one false story about his former wife, related by
Mackintosh, I had refused to visit at Pisa. (14)   I blush
in anguish at my prejudice, and ought hardly to feel it as
a blessing or a consolation, that I regret him less than
I should have done if I had known him personally.   As to
what remains of him now life is over, he occupies if not

the highest, almost the highest place among our poets of
the present age; no humble station; and is among the
most elegant, graceful, and harmonious of the prose-
writers....

NOTES

1 Landor visited Rome early in 1826, and he may well
   have seen the graves of Keats and Shelley in the Protestant Cemetery.
2 In the Greek myth it is Eurydice, and not her husband
   Orpheus, who is fatally bitten by a snake. Landor's
   allusion is to the then commonly accepted belief that
   the early death of Keats (Orpheus) was caused by
   savage reviews of his poetry. Rhodope and Haemus,
   according to Greek mythology, were a wife and husband
   who presumed to assume the names of Zeus and Hera,
   king and queen of the gods, and were punished by being
   metamorphosed into mountains in Thrace.
3 Madalene and Isabella are the chief female characters
   in Keats's poems The Eve of St Agnes and Isabella or,
   the Pot of Basil (1820). Landor's poem first appeared in the 1828 Conversation and was reprinted with
   two spelling changes in 'Works' (1846).
4 Although William Gifford edited the 'Quarterly Review', John Wilson Croker (1780-1857) wrote the savage
   and unsigned review of Keats's 'Endymion' (1818) that
   appeared in the September 1818 number.
5 Harriet Wilson (fl. 1810-25), a woman of fashion, published her sensational and scandalous 'Memoirs' (1825)
   when her former aristocratic admirers refused to buy
   her silence. The threat of further instalments reme-
   died her financial plight.
6 See Southey and Porson I, No. 7 above, notes 2 and 5.
7 For a detailed account of Landor's involvement in the
   Southey-Byron quarrel, see R.H. Super, Landor and the
   'Satanic School', 'Studies in Philology' 42 (October
   1945), 793-810.
8 Professor E.E. Bostetter has suggested that Landor may
   have been the first critic to observe Keats's close
   affinity with Shakespeare in respect to the latter's
   gift of language. See R.H. Super, 'Landor', 179,
   544, n. 10.
9 In 1789 Robert Burns (1759-96) applied for and received a position as an exciseman, his occupation
   until his death. Contrary to popular belief, Burns
   was never a drunkard and his untimely death was not
   caused by heavy drinking. See David Daiches, 'Robert
   Burns', London: Bell, 1952, 303.

10   Landor's poem first appeared in the 1828 Conversation
     and was reprinted with one spelling change, two alte-
     rations in punctuation, and with the omission of a
     footnote in 'Works' (1846).
11   Abraham Cowley (1618-67), author of 'The Mistress: or
     Several Copies of Love Verses' (1647).
12   Shelley rode his horse between Edward Trelawny (not
     Byron) and an attacking dragoon in the affray outside
     Pisa on 24 March 1822, and was knocked to the ground
     where he lay unconscious for several minutes.
13   The 'common friend' is Leigh Hunt who may well have
     told Landor the story of Shelley's bravery at Pisa
     and Byron's response as early as the spring of 1825.
     Hunt's published recollection is similar to that re-
     lated by Landor's English Visitor: 'Mr. Shelley's
     bravery was remarkable, and was the ultimate ruin of
     him.   In a scuffle that took place on horseback, in
     the streets of Pisa, with a hot-headed dragoon, he be-
     haved with a courage so distinguished, and with so
     much thought for every body but himself, that Lord
     Byron wondered upon what principle a man could be in-
     duced to prefer any other person's life in that
     manner, before his own.   The solution of the diffi-
     culty was to be found in their different views of
     human nature.   Mr. Shelley would have lost his life
     with pleasure, to set an example of disinterested-
     ness: Lord Byron could do striking public things.
     Greece, and an admiring public, still re-echo them.
     But the course of his Lordship's studies had led him
     to require, that they should be mixed up with other
     stimulants' (Leigh Hunt, 'Lord Byron and Some of His
     Contemporaries', 1st ed., London, 1828, 193-4).
14   Sir James Mackintosh (1765-1832), Scottish philoso-
     pher, writer, Whig politician, remembered primarily
     for his 'Vindiciae Gallicae' (1791), a reply to
     Edmund Burke's 'Reflections on the French Revolution'
     (1790).   See Letters to John Forster, No. 7 above,
     and n. 58.

14 Epicurus, Leontion, and Ternissa

1829, 1846, 1853

Epicurus, Leontion, and Ternissa was one of Landor's favourite Imaginary Conversations: 'I received more pleasure
from my Lucullus, my Epicurus, and my Diogenes, than I
could receive from not only extensive popularity, but from
eternal fame. They satisfied my heart, which is larger
than the World's, and nearer home' (W.S.L. to Lady Blessington, 14? October 1838 (Dr John F. Mariani, The Letters
of Walter Savage Landor to Marguerite Countess of Blessington [unpublished PhD dissertation, Columbia University,
1973], 248)). Both Epicurus (341-270 BC) and Leontion,
an Athenian courtesan, are historical personages much
idealized by Landor. The young girl Ternissa is the author's creation. This idyllic, day-long conversation between Epicurus and two of his female disciples takes place
in the philosopher's garden near Athens. In this brief
excerpt Epicurus, Landor's mouthpiece, comments on the
principal object of the imitative arts, the poetic forms
of tragedy and the epic, and the theatre. The Conversation was first published in vol. 2 of the 'Imaginary Conversations' (1829), second series, revised for inclusion
in the 'Works of Walter Savage Landor' (1846) and reprinted, with several minor revisions, in 'Imaginary Conversations of Greeks and Romans' (1853). This selection is
from the 1853 text.

Leontion. Theophrastus would persuade us that, according
to your [Epicurus'] system, we not only should decline the
succour of the wretched, but avoid the sympathies that
poets and historians would awaken in us. (1) ... He says
that, following the guidance of Epicurus, we should altogether shun the theater, and not only when 'Prometheus' and
'OEdipus' and 'Philoctetes' are introduced, (2) but even
where generous and kindly sentiments are predominant, if
they partake of that tenderness which belongs to pity....
167

Epicurus. I would never close my bosom against the
feelings of humanity: but I would calmly and well consider by what conduct of life they may enter it with the
least importunity and violence.   A consciousness that we
have promoted the happiness of others, to the uttermost
of our power, is certain not only to meet them at the
threshold, but to bring them along with us, and to render
them accurate and faithful prompters, when we bend per-
plexedly over the problem of evil figured by the tragedians.   If indeed there were more of pain than of pleasure in the exhibitions of the dramatist, no man in his
senses would attend them twice.   All the imitative arts
have delight for the principal object: the first of these
is poetry: the highest of poetry is tragic.
Leontion. The epic has been called so.
Epicurus. Improperly; for the epic has much more in it
of what is prosaic.   Its magnitude is no argument.   An
Egyptian pyramid contains more materials than an Ionic
temple, but requires less contrivance, and exhibits less
beauty of design.   My simile is yet a defective one;
for, a tragedy must be carried on with an unbroken interest;   and, undecorated by loose foliage or fantastic
branches, it must rise, like the palm tree, with a lofty
unity....
Leontion.... I would rather hear a little about the
theater, and whether you think at last that women should
frequent it; for you have often said the contrary.
Epicurus. I think they should visit it rarely; not because it excites their affections, but because it deadens
them.   To me nothing is so odious as to be at once among
the rabble and among the heroes, and, while I am receiving
into my heart the most exquisite of human sensations, to
feel upon my shoulder the hand of some inattentive and insensible young officer. (3)
Leontion. O very bad indeed! horrible!
Ternissa. You quite fire at the idea.
Leontion. Not I: I don't care about it.
Ternissa. Not about what is very bad indeed? quite
horrible?
Leontion. I seldom go thither.
Epicurus. The theater is delightful when we erect it in
our own house or arbour, and when there is but one spectator. (4)
Leontion. You must lose the illusion in great part, if
you only read the tragedy, which I fancy to be your meaning.
Epicurus. I lose the less of it.   Do not imagine that
the illusion is, or can be, or ought to be, complete.   If
it were possible, no Phalaris or Perillus could devise a

crueller torture. (5)   Here are two imitations: first,
the poet's of the sufferer; secondly, the actor's of
both: poetry is superinduced.   No man in pain ever
uttered the better part of the language used by Sophocles.
We admit it, and willingly, and are at least as much illu-
ded by it as by anything else we hear or see upon the
stage.   Poets and statuaries and painters give us an
adorned imitation of the object, so skilfully treated that
we receive it for a correct one.   This is the only illusion they aim at: this is the perfection of their arts.

Leontion. Do you derive no pleasure from the representation of a consummate actor?

Epicurus. High pleasure; but liable to be overturned
in an instant; pleasure at the mercy of anyone who sits
beside me.   Rarely does it happen that an Athenian utters
a syllable in the midst of it: but our city is open to
the inhabitants of all the world, and all the world that
is yet humanised a woman might walk across in sixty hours.
There are even in Greece a few remaining still so barbarous, that I have heard them whisper in the midst of the
finest scenes of our greatest poets....

NOTES

1 Theophrastus (c. 370-288/5 BC) was the collaborator
   and successor of Aristotle.   Leontion's recollections
   of Theophrastus' remarks on Epicurus' philosophy are
   imaginary.
2 'Prometheus Bound', a tragedy by Aeschylus; 'Oedipus
   Tyrannus' and 'Philoctetes', tragedies by Sophocles.
3 On 14 March 1811 Landor wrote Southey: 'You would
   hardly imagine it, I have not seen a play acted a
   dozen times in my life.   I am not remarkably pure or
   chaste; but to hear generous and pathetic sentiments
   and to behold glorious and grand actions amidst the
   vulgar hard-hearted language of prostitutes and lobby-
   loungers, not only takes away all my pleasure by the
   evident contrast, but seizes me with the most painful
   and insuperable disgust.   Added to which, I cannot
   restrain my tears, sometimes at even an indifferent
   piece.   It is curious that we should be more anxious
   to conceal our best passions than our worst.   Our
   pity and love are profaned by the most casual glance;
   but one would imagine our hatred and vengeance were
   pro bono publico' [Forster, 'Landor', 1, 298].
4 See the excerpt from Landor's undated letter to
   Southey, No. 4 above and n. 18.
5 Perillus (floruit c. BC 560) made the celebrated

bronze bull in which Phalaris, tyrant of Acragas (c. 570-554 BC), is supposed to have incinerated the living victims of his cruelty.

15 'The Pentameron'
1837, 1846

Landor's prose masterpiece, 'The Pentameron', is a five-days' interview between two Italian writers whom he greatly admired: Giovanni Boccaccio (1313-75), 'the most creative genius that the continent has produced since *the* creation', and Francesco Petrarch (1304-74), 'the defender of resuscitated Liberty, and the recoverer of ancient learning' (W.S.L. to Miss Mary Boyle, 12 September 1842; quoted by James Russell Lowell in Some Letters of Walter Savage Landor, 'Century Magazine', February 1888, 520. This extended Imaginary Conversation is the culmination of Landor's reading in Italian literature; and, although the interlocutors are endowed with such characteristic traits as Petrarch's moral gravity and Boccaccio's playful and slightly irreverent turn of mind, both characters serve as mouthpieces for Landor's known sentiments and opinions.

The setting of these imaginary meetings is Boccaccio's villa at Certaldo. Petrarch's visit has been occasioned by a letter from Boccaccio in which the latter has threatened to destroy his 'Decameron' if God should restore him to health. After Petrarch's remonstrances, the two friends engage in a lengthy criticism of Dante's 'Divine Comedy', the intended subject of Boccaccio's forthcoming series of lectures in Florence. The selection below, about one-fifth of the conversation, contains most of Landor's Dante criticism as well as numerous observations on classical authors. 'The Pentameron' first appeared in 1837 with five short, dramatic, blank-verse scenes in a volume entitled 'The Pentameron and Pentalogia'. It was reprinted with minor revisions in the 'Works of Walter Savage Landor' (1846), the text of the following selection.

Petrarca.... You have then been dangerously ill?

171

Boccaccio. I do not know: they told me I was: and truly a man might be unwell enough, who has twenty masses said for him, and fain sigh when he thinks what he has paid for them....   And yet I begin to think God would have had mercy on me, if I had begged it of him myself in my own house.   What think you?

Petrarca. I think he might.

Boccaccio. Particularly if I offered him the sacrifice on which I wrote to you.

Petrarca. That letter has brought me hither.

Boccaccio. You do then insist on my fulfilling my promise, the moment I can leave my bed.   I am ready and willing.

Petrarca. Promise! none was made.   You only told me that, if it pleased God to restore you to your health again, you are ready to acknowledge his mercy by the holocaust of your 'Decameron'.   What proof have you that God would exact it?   If you could destroy the 'Inferno' of Dante, would you?

Boccaccio. Not I, upon my life!   I would not promise to burn a copy of it on the condition of a recovery for twenty years.

Petrarca. You are the only author who would not rather demolish another's work than his own; especially if he thought it better: a thought which seldom goes beyond suspicion.

Boccaccio. I am not jealous of anyone: I think admiration pleasanter.   Moreover, Dante and I did not come forward at the same time, nor take the same walks.   His flames are too fierce for you and me: we had trouble enough with milder.   I never felt any high gratification in hearing of people being damned; and much less would I toss them into the fire myself.   I might indeed have put a nettle under the nose of the learned judge in Florence, when he banished you and your family; (1) but I hardly think I could have voted for more than a scourging to the foulest and fiercest of the party.

Petrarca. Be as compassionate, be as amiably irresolute, toward your own 'Novelle', which have injured no friend of yours, and deserve more affection.

Boccaccio. Francesco! no character I ever knew, ever heard of, or ever feigned, deserves the same affection as you do; the tenderest lover, the truest friend, the firmest patriot, and, rarest of glories! the poet who cherishes another's fame as dearly as his own.

Petrarca. If aught of this is true, let it be recorded of me that my exhortations and intreaties have been successful, in preserving the works of the most imaginative and creative genius that our Italy, or indeed our world, hath in any age beheld.

Boccaccio. I would not destroy his poems, as I told
you, or think I told you. Even the worst of the Florentines, who in general keep only one of God's commandments,
keep it rigidly in regard to Dante.

Love them who curse you. (2)

He called them all scoundrels, with somewhat less courtesy
than cordiality, and less afraid of censure for veracity
than adulation: he sent their fathers to hell, with no
inclination to separate the child and parent: and now
they are hugging him for it in his shroud! Would you
ever have suspected them of being such lovers of justice?
  You must have mistaken my meaning; the thought never
entered my head: the idea of destroying a single copy of
Dante! And what effect would that produce? There must
be fifty, or near it, in various parts of Italy.
  Petrarca. I spoke of you.
  Boccaccio. Of me! My poetry is vile; I have already
thrown into the fire all of it within my reach.
  Petrarca. Poetry was not the question. We neither of
us are such poets as we thought ourselves when we were
younger, and as younger men think us still. I meant your
'Decameron'; in which there is more character, more
nature, more invention, than either modern or ancient
Italy, or than Greece, from whom she derived her whole in-
heritance, ever claimed or ever knew. Would you consume
a beautiful meadow because there are reptiles in it; or
because a few grubs hereafter may be generated by the succulence of the grass?
  Boccaccio. You amaze me: you utterly confound me.
  Petrarca. If you would eradicate twelve or thirteen of
the 'Novelle', and insert the same number of better, which
you could easily do within as many weeks, I should be
heartily glad to see it done. Little more than a tenth
of the 'Decameron' is bad: less than a twentieth of the
'Divina Commedia' is good.
  Boccaccio. So little?
  Petrarca. Let me never seem irreverent to our master.
  Boccaccio. Speak plainly and fearlessly, Francesco!
Malice and detraction are strangers to you.
  Petrarca. Well then: at least sixteen parts in twenty
of the 'Inferno' and 'Purgatorio' are detestable, both in
poetry and principle: the higher parts are excellent
indeed.
  Boccaccio. I have been reading the 'Paradiso' more re-
cently. Here it is, under the pillow. It brings me
happier dreams than the others, and takes no more time in
bringing them. Preparation for my lectures made me

remember a great deal of the poem. I did not request my
auditors to admire the beauty of the metrical version;

Osanna sanctus deus Sabbaoth,
Super-illustrans claritate tuâ
Felices ignes horum Malacoth,

[Hosanna, holy God of hosts, making more resplendent
With thy brightness the happy fires of these realms
('Par.', vii, 1-3).]

nor these, with a slip of Italian between two pales of
Latin;

Modicum, (3) et non videbitis me,
Et iterum, sorelle mie dilette,
Modicum, et vos videbitis me.

[A little while, and ye shall not see me: and again,
(my beloved sisters), a little while, and ye shall see
me (John 16:16; quoted by Dante in 'Purg.', xxxiii,
10-12.)]

I dare not repeat all I recollect of

Pepe Satan, Pepe Satan, aleppe, (4)
['Inf.', vii, 1.]

as there is no holy-water-sprinkler in the room: and you
are aware that other dangers awaited me, had I been so im-
prudent as to show the Florentines the allusion of our
poet. His *gergo* (5) is perpetually in play, and sometimes plays very roughly.
    Petrarca. We will talk again of him presently. I must
now rejoice with you over the recovery and safety of your
prodigal son, the 'Decameron'.
    Boccaccio. So then, you would preserve at any rate my
favourite volume from the threatened conflagration.
    Petrarca. Had I lived at the time of Dante, I would
have given him the same advice in the same circumstances.
Yet how different is the tendency of the two productions!
Yours is somewhat too licentious; and young men, in whose
nature, or rather in whose education and habits, there is
usually this failing, will read you with more pleasure
than is commendable or innocent. Yet the very time they
occupy with you, would perhaps be spent in the midst of
those excesses or irregularities, to which the moralist,
in his utmost severity, will argue that your pen directs
them. Now there are many who are fond of standing on the

brink of precipices, and who nevertheless are as cautious
as any of falling in. And there are minds desirous of
being warmed by description, which, without this warmth,
might seek excitement among the things described.

I would not tell you in health what I tell you in con-
valescence, nor urge you to compose what I dissuade you
from cancelling. After this avowal, I do declare to you,
Giovanni, that in my opinion, the very idlest of your
tales will do the world as much good as evil; not reckon-
ing the pleasure of reading, nor the exercise and recreation of the mind, which in themselves are good. What I
reprove you for, is the indecorous and uncleanly; and
these, I trust, you will abolish. Even these, however,
may repel from vice the ingenuous and graceful spirit, and
can never lead any such toward them. Never have you
taken an inhuman pleasure in blunting and fusing the affections at the furnace of the passions; never, in hardening by sour sagacity and ungenial strictures, that
delicacy which is more productive of innocence and happiness, more estranged from every track and tendency of
their opposites, than what in cold crude systems hath
holden the place and dignity of the highest virtue. May
you live, O my friend, in the enjoyment of health, to substitute the facetious for the licentious, the simple for
the extravagant, the true and characteristic for the indefinite and diffuse.

  Boccaccio. I dare not defend myself under the bad example of any: and the bad example of a great man is the
worst defence of all. Since however you have mentioned
Messer Dante Alighieri, to whose genius I never thought of
approaching, I may perhaps have been formerly the less
cautious of offending by my levity, after seeing him display as much or more of it in hell itself.

  Petrarca. The best apology for Dante, in his poetical
character, is presented by the indulgence of criticism, in
considering the 'Inferno' and 'Purgatorio' as a string of
Satires, part in narrative and part in action; which renders the title of 'Commedia' more applicable. The fil-
thiness of some passages would disgrace the drunkenest
horse-dealer; and the names of such criminals are recorded by the poet as would be forgotten by the hangman in
six months. I wish I could expatiate rather on his in-
judiciousness than on his ferocity, in devising punishments for various crimes; or rather, than on his malignity in composing catalogues of criminals to inflict them
on....

  Boccaccio. I begin to think you are in the right.
Well then, retrenching some of my licentious tales, I must
endeavour to fill up the vacancy with some serious and
some pathetic.

Petrarca. I am heartily glad to hear of this decision;
for, admirable as you are in the jocose, you descend from
your natural position when you come to the convivial and
the festive.   You were placed among the Affections, to
move and master them, and gifted with the rod that sweet-
ens the fount of tears.   My nature leads me also to the
pathetic;   in which, however, an imbecile writer may
obtain celebrity.   Even the hard-hearted are fond of such
reading, when they are fond of any;   and nothing is easier
in the world than to find and accumulate its sufferings.
Yet this very profusion and luxuriance of misery is the
reason why few have excelled in describing it.   The eye
wanders over the mass without noticing the peculiarities.
To mark them distinctly is the work of genius;   a work so
rarely performed, that, if time and space may be compared,
specimens of it stand at wider distances than the trophies
of Sesostris. (6)   Here we return again to the 'Inferno'
of Dante, who overcame the difficulty.   In this vast
desert are its greater and its less oasis;   Ugolino and
Francesca da Rimini. (7)   The peopled region is peopled
chiefly with monsters and moschitoes: the rest for the
most part is sand and suffocation.
Boccaccio. Ah! had Dante remained through life the pure
solitary lover of Bice, (8) his soul had been gentler,
tranquiller, and more generous.   He scarcely hath described half the curses he went through, nor the roads he
took on the journey: theology, politics, and that barbi-
can of the 'Inferno', marriage, surrounded with its

Selva selvaggia ed aspra e forte.

[Wood, savage and harsh and dense
('Inf.', i, 5).]

Admirable is indeed the description of Ugolino, to whoever
can endure the sight of an old soldier gnawing at the
scalp of an old archbishop. (9)
Petrarca. The thirty lines from

Ed io sentj,

[And I heard below the door of the horrible tower
nailed up;   at which I (Ugolino) looked in the faces of
my sons without a word....   ('Inf.', xxxiii, 46-75).]

are unequalled by any other continuous thirty in the whole
dominions of poetry.
Boccaccio. Give me rather the six on Francesca: (10)
for if in the former I find the simple, vigorous, clear

narration, I find also what I would not wish, the features
of Ugolino reflected full in Dante.   The two characters
are similar in themselves; hard, cruel, inflexible, malignant, but, whenever moved, moved powerfully.   In Francesca, with the faculty of divine spirits, he leaves his
own nature (not indeed the exact representative of theirs)
and converts all his strength into tenderness.   The great
poet, like the original man of the Platonists, (11) is
double, possessing the further advantage of being able to
drop one half at his option, and to resume it.   Some of
the tenderest on paper have no sympathies beyond; and
some of the austerest in their intercourse with their
fellow-creatures, have deluged the world with tears.   It
is not from the rose that the bee gathers her honey, but
often from the most acrid and the most bitter leaves and
petals.

Quando leggemmo il disiato viso
   Esser baciato da cotanto amante,
Questi, cha mai da me non fia diviso!
   La bocca mi baciò tutto tremante...
Galeotto fù il libro, e chi lo serisse...
   Quel giorno più non vi leggemmo avante.

[When we read that the longed-for smile (of Queen
Guinevere) was kissed by so great a lover (Sir Lancelot), he who never shall be parted from me, all trem-
bling, kissed my mouth.   A Galeotto (intermediary between Lancelot and Guinevere) was the book and he that
wrote it; that day we read in it no farther ('Inf.',
v, 133-8).]

In the midst of her punishment, Francesca, when she comes
to the tenderest part of her story, tells it with complacency and delight; and, instead of naming Paolo, which
indeed she never has done from the beginning, she now
designates him as

Questi che mai da me non fia diviso!

[He who never shall be parted from me (v, 135).]

Are we not impelled to join in her prayer, wishing them
happier in their union?
   Petrarca. If there be no sin in it.
   Boccaccio. Ay, and even if there be ... God help us!
What a sweet aspiration in each cesura of the verse!
three love-sighs fixed and incorporate!   Then, when she
hath said

> La bocca mi baciò, tutto tremante,
>
> [All trembling, kissed my mouth (v, 136).]

she stops: she would avert the eyes of Dante from her: he looks for the sequel: she thinks he looks severely: she says,

> *Galeotto* is the name of the book [v, 137],

fancying by this timorous little flight she has drawn him far enough from the nest of her young loves. No, the eagle beak of Dante and his piercing eyes are yet over her.

> *Galeotto* is the name of the book.
> What matters that?
> And of the writer [v, 137].
> Or that either?

At last she disarms him: but how?

> *That* day we read no more [v, 138].

Such a depth of intuitive judgment, such a delicacy of perception, exists not in any other work of human genius; and from an author who, on almost all occasions, in this part of the work, betrays a deplorable want of it

Petrarca. Perfection of poetry! The greater is my wonder at discovering nothing else of the same order or cast in this whole section of the poem. He who fainted at the recital of Francesca,

> And he who fell as a dead body falls,
> ['Inf.', v, 142.]

would exterminate all the inhabitants of every town in Italy! What execrations against Florence, Pistoia, Siena, Pisa, Genoa! what hatred against the whole human race! what exultation and merriment at eternal and immitigable sufferings! Seeing this, I can not but consider the 'Inferno' as the most immoral and impious book that ever was written. Yet, hopeless that our country shall ever see again such poetry, and certain that without it our future poets would be more feebly urged forward to excellence, I would have dissuaded Dante from cancelling it, if this had been his intention. Much however as I admire his vigour and severity of style in the description of Ugolino, I acknowledge with you that I do not discover

so much imagination, so much creative power, as in the
Francesca. I find indeed a minute detail of probable
events: but this is not all I want in a poet: it is not
even all I want most in a scene of horror. Tribunals of
justice, dens of murderers, wards of hospitals, schools of
anatomy, will afford us nearly the same sensations, if we
hear them from an accurate observer, a clear reporter, a
skilful surgeon, or an attentive nurse. There is nothing
of sublimity in the horrific of Dante, which there always
is in AEschylus and Homer. If you, Giovanni, had described so nakedly the reception of Guiscardo's heart by Ghismonda, or Lorenzo's head by Lisabetta, (12) we could
hardly have endured it.

Boccaccio. Prythee, dear Francesco, do not place me
over Dante: I stagger at the idea of approaching him.

Petrarca. Never think I am placing you blindly or indiscriminately. I have faults to find with you, and even
here. Lisabetta should by no means have been represented
cutting off the head of her lover, 'as well as she could'
['Il meglio che poté' ('Decameron', iv, 5)] with a clasp-
knife. This is shocking and improbable. She might have
found it already cut off by her brothers, in order to bury
the corpse more commodiously and expeditiously. Nor
indeed is it likely that she should have intrusted it to
her waiting-maid, who carried home in her bosom a treasure
so dear to her, and found so unexpectedly and so lately.

Boccaccio. That is true: I will correct the oversight.
Why do we never hear of our faults until everybody knows
them, and until they stand in record against us?

Petrarca. Because our ears are closed to truth and
friendship for some time after the triumphal course of
composition. We are too sensitive for the gentlest
touch; and when we really have the most infirmity, we are
angry to be told that we have any.

Boccaccio. Ah Francesco! thou art poet from scalp to
heel: but what other would open his breast as thou hast
done! They show ostentatiously far worse weaknesses;
but the most honest of the tribe would forswear himself on
this. Again, I acknowledge it, you have reason to complain of Lisabetta and Ghismonda.

Petrarca. They keep the soul from sinking in such
dreadful circumstances by the buoyancy of imagination.
The sunshine of poetry makes the colour of blood less horrible, and draws up a shadowy and a softening haziness
where the scene would otherwise be too distinct. Poems,
like rivers, convey to their destination what must without
their appliances be left unhandled: these to ports and
arsenals, this to the human heart.

Boccaccio. So it is; and what is terror in poetry is

horror in prose.   We may be brought too close to an
object to leave any room for pleasure.   Ugolino affects
us like a skeleton, by dry bony verity.

Petrarca. We can not be too distinct in our images;
but although distinctness, on this and most other occasions, is desirable in the imitative arts, yet sometimes
in painting, and sometimes in poetry, an object should not
be quite precise.   In your novel of Andrevola and Gabri-
otto, you afford me an illustration.

> Le pareva dal corpo di lui uscire una
> cosa oscura e terribile.

> [It seemed to her she saw a black and fearful thing ...
> exuding from his body ('Decameron', iv, 6 tr. F.W.).]

This is like a dream: this *is* a dream.   Afterward, you
present to us such palpable forms and pleasing colours as
may relieve and soothe us.

> Ed avendo molte rose, bianche e vermi-
> glie, colte, perciocche la stagione era.

> [Many roses white and red she gathered, for their
> season was at its height (iv, 6 tr. F.W.).]

Boccaccio. Surely you now are mocking me.   The roses,
I perceive, would not have been there, had it not been the
season.

Petrarca. A poet often does more and better than he is
aware at the time, and seems at last to know as little
about it as a silkworm knows about the fineness of her
thread.

The uncertain dream that still hangs over us in the
novel, is intercepted and hindered from hurting us by the
spell of the roses, of the white and the red; a word the
less would have rendered it incomplete.   The very warmth
and geniality of the season shed their kindly influence on
us;   and we are renovated and ourselves again by virtue of
the clear fountain where we rest.   Nothing of this poetical providence comes to our relief in Dante, though we
want it oftener.   It would be difficult to form an idea
of a poem, into which so many personages are introduced,
containing so few delineations of character, so few touches that excite our sympathy, so few elementary signs for
our instruction, so few topics for our delight, so few
excursions for our recreation.   Nevertheless, his powers
of language are prodigious;   and, in the solitary places
where he exerts his force rightly, the stroke is irresis-

tible. But how greatly to be pitied must he be, who can find nothing in paradise better than sterile theology! and what an object of sadness and of consternation, he who rises up from hell like a giant refreshed!

Boccaccio. Strange perversion! 'A pillar of smoke by day and of fire by night;'(13) to guide no one. Paradise had fewer wants for him to satisfy than hell had; all which he fed to repletion. But let us rather look to his poetry than his temper.

Petrarca. We will then.

A good poem is not divided into little panes like a cathedral window; which little panes themselves are broken and blurred, with a saint's coat on a dragon's tail, a doctor's head on the bosom of a virgin martyr, and having about them more lead than glass, and more gloom than colouring. A good satire or good comedy, if it does not always smile, rarely and briefly intermits it, and never rages. A good epic shows us more and more distinctly, at every book of it we open, the features and properties of heroic character, and terminates with accomplishing some momentous action. A good tragedy shows us that greater men than ourselves have suffered more severely and more unjustly; that the highest human power hath suddenly fallen helpless and extinct; or, what is better to contemplate and usefuller to know, that uncontrolled by law, unaccompanied by virtue, unfollowed by contentment, its possession is undesirable and unsafe. Sometimes we go away in triumph with Affliction proved and purified, and leave her under the smiles of heaven. In all these consummations the object is excellent; and here is the highest point to which poetry can attain. Tragedy has no by-paths, no resting-places; there is everywhere action and passion. What do we find of this nature, or what of the epic, in the Orpheus and Judith, the Charon and Can della Scala, the Sinon and Maestro Adamo? (14)

Boccaccio. Personages strangely confounded! In this category it required a strong hand to make Pluto and Pepe Satan keep the peace, both having the same pretensions, and neither the sweetest temper. (15)

Petrarca. Then the description of Mahomet is indecent and filthy. (16) Yet Dante is scarcely more disgusting in this place, than he is insipid and spiritless in his allegory of the marriages, between Saint Francesco and Poverty, Saint Dominico and Faith. (17) I speak freely and plainly to you, Giovanni, and the rather, as you have informed me that I have been thought invidious to the reputation of our great poet; for such he is transcendently, in the midst of his imperfections....

Petrarca....   The worst I can recollect to have said
against his poem to others, is, that the architectural
fabric of the 'Inferno' is unintelligible without a long
study, and only to be understood after distracting our
attention from its inhabitants.   Its locality and dimensions are at last uninteresting, and would better have
been left in their obscurity.   The zealots of Dante compare it, for invention, with the infernal regions of Homer
and Virgil.   I am ignorant how much the Grecian poet invented, how much existed in the religion, how much in the
songs and traditions of the people.   But surely our
Alighieri has taken the same idea, and even made his des-
cent in the same part of Italy, as AEneas had done
before. (18)   In the 'Odyssea' the mind is perpetually
relieved by variety of scene and character.   There are
vices enough in it, but rising from lofty or from powerful
passions, and under the veil of mystery and poetry: there
are virtues too enough, and human and definite and practi-
cable.   We have man, although a shade, in his own features, in his own dimensions: he appears before us
neither cramped by systems nor jaundiced by schools;   no
savage, no cit, no cannibal, no doctor.   Vigorous and
elastic, he is such as poetry saw him first;   he is such
as poetry would ever see him.   In Dante, the greater part
of those who are not degraded, are debilitated and distorted.   No heart swells here, either for overpowered
valour or for unrequited love.   In the shades alone, but
in the shades of Homer, does Ajax rise to his full loftiness; (19)   in the shades alone, but in the shades of
Virgil, is Dido the arbitress of our tears. (20)

Boccaccio. I must confess there are nowhere two whole
cantos in Dante which will bear a sustained and close comparison with the very worst book of the 'Odyssea' or the
'AEneid';   that there is nothing of the same continued and
unabated excellence, as Ovid's in the contention for the
armour of Achilles; (21)   the most heroic of heroic
poetry, and only censurable, if censurable at all, because
the eloquence of the braver man (22) is more animated and
more persuasive than his successful rival's. (23)   I do
not think Ovid the best poet that ever lived, but I think
he wrote the most of good poetry, and, in proportion to
its quantity, the least of bad or indifferent.   The 'Inferno', the 'Purgatorio', the 'Paradiso', are pictures
from the walls of our churches and chapels and monasteries, some painted by Giotto and Cimabue, (24) some earlier.   In several of these we detect not only the cruelty, but likewise the satire and indecency of Dante.
Sometimes there is also his vigour and simplicity, but
oftener his harshness and meagreness and disproportion.

I am afraid the good Alighieri, like his friends the painters, was inclined to think the angels were created only
to flagellate and burn us; and Paradise only for us to be
driven out of it.   And in truth, as we have seen it exhibited, there is but little hardship in the case.
   The opening of the third canto of the 'Inferno' has always been much admired.   There is indeed a great solem-
nity in the words of the inscription on the portal of
hell: nevertheless, I do not see the necessity for three
verses out of six.   After

   Per me si va nell' eterno dolore,

   [Through me the way to the eternal pain (iii, 2).]

it surely is superfluous to subjoin

   Per me si va tra la perduta gente;

   [Through me the way among the lost people (iii, 3).]

for, beside the erduta gente, who else can suffer the
eternal woe?   And when the portal has told us that 'Justice moved the high Maker to make it' [iii, 4], surely it
might have omitted the notification that his 'divine
power' did it.

   Fecemi la divina potestate.

   [Divine power made me (iii, 5).]

The next piece of information I wish had been conveyed
even in darker characters, so that they never could have
been deciphered.   The following line is,

   La somma Sapienza e 'l primo Amore.

   [(The) supreme Wisdom and primal Love (iii, 6).]

If God's first love was hell-making, we might almost wish
his affections were as mutable as ours are; that is, if
holy church would countenance us therein.
   Petrarca. Systems of poetry, of philosophy, of government, form and model us to their own proportions.   As our
systems want the grandeur, the light, and the symmetry of
the ancient, we can not hope for poets, philosophers, or
statesmen, of equal dignity.   Very justly do you remark
that our churches and chapels and monasteries, and even
our shrines and tabernacles on the road-side, contain in

painting the same punishments as Alighieri hath registered
in his poem: and several of these were painted before his
birth.   Nor surely can you have forgotten that his
master, Brunetto Latini, composed one on the same
plan. (25)

The Virtues and Vices, and persons under their influence, appear to him likewise in a wood, wherein he, like
Dante, is bewildered.   Old walls are the tablets both
copy: the arrangement is the devise of Brunetto.   Our
religion is too simple in its verities, and too penurious
in its decorations, for poetry of high value.   We can not
hope or desire that a pious Italian will ever have the
audacity to restore to Satan a portion of his majesty, or
to remind the faithful that he is a fallen angel.

Boccaccio. No, no, Francesco; let us keep as much of
him down as we can, and as long.

Petrarca. It might not be amiss to remember that even
human power is complacent in security, and that Omnipotence is ever omnipotent, without threats and fulmina-
tions.

Boccaccio. These, however, are the main springs of
sacred poetry, of which I think we already have enough.

Petrarca. But good enough?

Boccaccio. Even much better would produce less effect
than that which has occupied our ears from childhood, and
comes sounding and swelling with a mysterious voice from
the deep and dark recesses of antiquity.

Petrarca. I see no reason why we should not revert, at
times, to the first intentions of poetry.   Hymns to the
Creator were its earliest efforts.

Boccaccio. I do not believe a word of it, unless He
himself was graciously pleased to inspire the singer; of
which we have received no account.   I rather think it
originated in pleasurable song, perhaps of drunkenness,
and resembled the dithyrambic. (26)   Strong excitement
alone could force and hurry men among words displaced and
exaggerated ideas.

Believing that man fell, first into disobedience, next
into ferocity and fratricide, we may reasonably believe
that war-songs were among the earliest of his intellectual
exertions.   When he rested from battle he had leisure to
think of love; and the skies and the fountains and the
flowers reminded him of her, the coy and beautiful, who
fled to a mother from the ardour of his pursuit.   In
after years he lost a son, his companion in the croft and
in the forest: images too grew up there, and rested on
the grave.   A daughter, who had wondered at his strength
and wisdom, looked to him in vain for succour at the approach of death.   Inarticulate grief gave way to passion-

ate and wailing words, and Elegy was awakened.   We have
tears in this world before we have smiles, Francesco! we
have struggles before we have composure; we have strife
and complaints before we have submission and gratitude.
I am suspicious that if we could collect the 'winged
words' of the earliest hymns, we should find that they
called upon the Deity for vengeance.   Priests and rulers
were far from insensible to private wrongs.   Chryses in
the 'Iliad' is willing that his king and country should be
enslaved, so that his daughter be sent back to him. (27)
David in the 'Psalms' is no unimportunate or lukewarm
applicant for the discomfiture and extermination of his
adversaries: and, among the visions of felicity, none
brighter is promised a fortunate warrior, than to dash the
infants of his enemy against the stones. (28)

SECOND DAY'S INTERVIEW

... *Petrarca*. In the whole of the 'Inferno' I find only
the descriptions of Francesca and of Ugolino at all admirable.   Vigorous expressions there are many, but lost in
their application to base objects; and insulated thoughts
in high relief, but with everything crumbling round them.
Proportionally to the extent, there is a scantiness of
poetry, if delight is the purpose or indication of it.
Intensity shows everywhere the powerful master: and yet
intensity is not invitation.   A great poet may do everything but repell us.   Established laws are pliant before
him: nevertheless his office hath both its duties and its
limits.
   Boccaccio. The simile in the third canto, (29) the
satire at the close of the fourth, (30) and the description at the commencement of the eighth, (31) if not highly
admirable, are what no ordinary poet could have produced.
   Petrarca. They are streaks of light in a thundercloud.
You might have added the beginning of the twenty-
seventh, (32) in which the poetry of itself is good, although not excellent, and the subject of it assuages the
weariness left on us, after passing through so many holes
and furnaces, and undergoing the dialogue between Sinon
and Master Adam. (33)
   Boccaccio. I am sorry to be reminded of this.   It is
like the brawl of the two fellows in Horace's 'Journey to
Brundusium. (34)   They are the straitest parallels of bad
wit and bad poetry that ancient and modern times exhibit.
Ought I to speak so sharply of poets who elsewhere have
given me so great delight?
   Petrarca. Surely you ought.   No criticism is less

beneficial to an author or his reader than one tagged with favour and tricked with courtesy.   The gratification of our humours is not the intent and scope of criticism, and those who indulge in it on such occasions are neither wise nor honest....

Petrarca....   Foremost in zeal, in vigour and authority, Alighieri took on himself the same patronage and guardianship of our adolescent dialect, as Homer of the Greek: and my Giovanni hath since endowed it so handsomely, that additional bequests, we may apprehend, will only corrupt its principles, and render it lax and lavish.

Boccaccio. Beware of violating those canons of criticism you have just laid down.   We have no right to gratify one by misleading another, nor, when we undertake to show the road, to bandage the eyes of him who trusts us for his conductor.   In regard to censure, those only speak ill who speak untruly, unless a truth be barbed by malice and aimed by passion.   To be useful to as many as possible is the especial duty of a critic, and his utility can only be attained by rectitude and precision.   He walks in a garden which is not his own;   and he neither must gather the blossoms to embellish his discourse, nor break the branches to display his strength.   Rather let him point to what is out of order, and help to raise what is lying on the ground.

Petrarca. Auditors, and readers in general, come to hear or read, not your opinion delivered, but their own repeated.   Fresh notions are as disagreeable to some as fresh air to others;   and this inability to bear them is equally a symptom of disease....

Petrarca....   Come, ... let us now continue with our Dante.

Ugolino relates to him his terrible dream, in which he fancied that he had seen Gualando, Sismondi, and Lanfranco, killing his children: and he says that, when he awakened, he heard them moan in their sleep. (35)   In such circumstances, his awakening ought rather to have removed the impression he laboured under;   since it showed him the vanity of the dream, and afforded him the consolation that the children were alive.   Yet he adds immediately, what, if he were to speak it at all, he should have deferred,

'You are very cruel if you do not begin to grieve, considering what my heart presaged to me;   and, if you do not weep at it, what is it you are wont to weep at?' ['Inf.', xxxiii, 40-2.]

Boccaccio. Certainly this is ill-timed; and the con-
ference would indeed be better without it anywhere.

Petrarca. Farther on, in whatever way we interpret

Poscia più che 'l dolor potè 'l digiuno,

[Then fasting had more power than grief
('Inf.', xxxiii, 75).]

the poet falls sadly from his sublimity.

Boccaccio. If the fact were as he mentions, he should
have suppressed it, since we had already seen the most
pathetic in the features, and the most horrible in the
stride, of Famine. Gnawing, not in hunger, but in rage
and revenge, the arch-bishop's skull, is, in the opinion
of many, rather ludicrous than tremendous.

Petrarca. In mine, rather disgusting than ludicrous:
but Dante (we must whisper it) is the great master of the
disgusting. When the ancients wrote indecently and
loosely, they presented what either had something alluring
or something laughable about it, and, if they disgusted,
it was involuntarily. Indecency is the most shocking in
deformity....

Petrarca.... We must do then for our poet that which
other men do for themselves; we must defend him by advancing the best authority for something as bad or worse;
and although it puzzle our ingenuity, yet we may almost
make out in quantity, and quite in quality, our spicilege
from Virgil himself. (36)   If younger men were present, I
would admonish and exhort them to abate no more of their
reverence for the Roman poet on the demonstration of his
imperfections, than of their love for a parent or guardian
who had walked with them far into the country, and had
shown them its many beauties and blessings, on his lassi-
tude or his debility. Never will such men receive too
much homage. He who can best discover their blemishes,
will best appreciate their merit, and most zealously guard
their honour. The flippancy with which genius is often
treated by mediocrity, is the surest sign of a prostrate
mind's incontinence and impotence. It will gratify the
national pride of our Florentines, if you show them how
greatly the nobler parts of their fellow-citizen excell
the loftiest of his Mantuan guide.

Boccaccio. Of Virgil?

Petrarca. Even so.

Boccaccio. He had no suspicion of his equality with
this prince of Roman poets, whose footsteps he follows
with reverential and submissive obsequiousness. (37)...

Boccaccio. But surely if there are some very high places in our Alighieri, the inequalities are perpetual and vast: whereas the regularity, the continuity, the purity of Virgil, are proverbial.

Petrarca. It is only in literature that what is proverbial is suspicious: and mostly in poetry. Do we find in Dante, do we find in Ovid, such tautologies and flatnesses as these,

Quam si dura silex .. *aut stet Marpessia cautes.*

[Than if she were set in hard flint or Marpesian rock (Virgil, 'Aeneid', vi, 471).]

Majus adorta nefas .. *majoremque orsa furorem.*

[Essaying a greater sin and launching a greater madness (vii, 386).]

Arma *amens* capio .. nec *sat rationis* in armis.

[Frantic I seize arms; yet little purpose is there in arms (ii, 314).]

Si vescitur aura
AEtheria .. *neque adhuc crudelibus occubat umbris?*

[If he (Aeneas) feeds on the air of heaven and lies not yet in the cruel shades (i, 546-7).]

Omnes .. cælicolas .. omnes supera alta tenentes.

[All denizens of heaven, all tenants of the heights obove (vi, 787).]

Scuta *latentia condunt.*

[(And) bury their shields out of sight (iii, 237).]

Has inter voces .. *media inter talia verba.*

[Amid these cries, amid such words (xii, 318).]

Finem dedit .. *ore loquendi.*

[His lips ceased speaking (vi, 76).]

Insonuere cavae .. *gemitumque dedere cavernae.*

[The vaults rang hollow, sending forth a moan (ii, 53).]

Ferro accisam .. crebrisque *bipennibus*.

[Hacked with many a blow of axe and iron (ii, 627).]

Nec nostri generis puerum .. *nec sanguinis*.

[A child not of our race or blood ('Eclogues', viii, 45).]

Boccaccio. These things look very ill in Latin; and yet they had quite escaped my observation.   We often find, in the 'Psalms of David', one section of a sentence placed as it were in symmetry with another, and not at all supporting it by presenting the same idea.   It is a species of piety to drop the nether lip in admiration; but in reality it is not only the modern taste that is vitiated; the ancient is little less so, although differently.   To say over again what we have just ceased to say, with nothing added, nothing improved, is equally bad in all languages and all times.
Petrarca. But in these repetitions we may imagine one part of the chorus to be answering another part opposite.
Boccaccio. Likely enough.   However, you have ransacked poor Virgil to the skin, and have stripped him clean.
Petrarca. Of all who have ever dealt with 'Winter', he is the most frostbitten.   Hesiod's description of the snowy season is more poetical and more formidable. (38) What do you think of these icicles,

OEraque dissiliunt vulgo; vestesque *rigescunt!*

[Everywhere brass splits, clothes freeze (Virgil, 'Georgics', iii, 363).]

Boccaccio. Wretched falling off.
Petrarca. He comes close enough presently.

Stiriaque hirsutis dependent horrida barbis.

[And the rough icicle hardens on the unkempt beard (iii, 366).]

We will withdraw from the Alps into the city.   And now are you not smitten with reverence at seeing

Romanos rerum dominos; *gentemque togatam?*

The masters of the world .. and *long-tailed coats!*
['Aeneid', i, 282.]

Come to Carthage. What a recommendation to a beautiful queen (39) does AEneas offer, in himself and his
associates!

Lupi ceu
Raptores; atrâ in nebulâ, quos *improba ventris*
Exegit caecos rabies!

[Then, like ravening wolves in a black mist, when the
belly's lawless rage has driven them blindly forth
(ii, 355-7).]

Ovid is censured for his

Consiliis non *curribus* utere nostris.

[Take my counsel, not my chariot ('Metamorphoses',
ii, 146).]

Virgil never for

Inceptoque et *sedibus* haeret in iisdem.

[He refuses, and abides in his purpose and his place
('Aeneid', ii, 654).]

The same in its quality, but more forced.
    The affectation of Ovid was light and playful;
Virgil's was wilful, perverse, and grammatistical. Are
we therefore to suppose that every hand able to elaborate
a sonnet may be raised up against the majesty of Virgil?
Is ingratitude so rare and precious, that we should prefer
the exposure of his faults to the enjoyment of his harmony? He first delivered it to his countrymen in unbroken links under the form of poetry, and consoled them for
the eloquent tongue that had withered on the Rostra. (40)
It would be no difficult matter to point out at least
twenty bad passages in the 'AEneid', and a proportionate
number of worse in the 'Georgics'. In your comparison of
poet with poet, the defects as well as the merits of each
ought to be placed side by side. This is the rather to
be expected, as Dante professes to be Virgil's disciple.
You may easily show that his humility no more became him
than his fierceness.

Boccaccio. You have praised the harmony of the Roman
poet. Now in single verses I think our poetry is sometimes more harmonious than the Latin, but never in whole
sentences. Advantage could perhaps be taken of our metre
if we broke through the stanza. Our language is capable,
I think, of all the vigour and expression of the Latin;
and, in regard to the pauses in our versification, in which
chiefly the harmony of metre consists, we have greatly the
advantage. What for instance is more beautiful than your

Solo .. e pensoso .. i più deserti campi
Vo .. misurando .. a passi tardi .. e lenti.

[Alone, thought-sick, I pace where none has been,
Roaming the desert with dull steps and slow,
('Rime', xxxv, 1-2 tr. J.A.).]

Petrarca. My critics have found fault with the *lenti,*
calling it an expletive, and ignorant that equally in
Italian and Latin the word signifies both *slow* and *languid,* while *tardi* signifies *slow* only.
Boccaccio. Good poetry, like good music, pleases most
people, but the ignorant and inexpert lose half its pleasure, the invidious lose them all. What a paradise lost
is here!
Petrarca. If we deduct the inexpert, the ignorant, and
the invidious, can we correctly say it pleases most
people? But either my worst compositions are the most
admired, or the insincere and malignant bring them most
forward for admiration, keeping the others in the back-
ground! Sonnetteers, in consequence, have started up
from all quarters.
Boccaccio. The sonnet seems peculiarly adapted to the
languor of a melancholy and despondent love, the rhymes
returning and replying to every plaint and every pulsation. Our poetasters are now converting it into the
penfold and pound of stray thoughts and vagrant fancies.
No sooner have they collected in their excursions as much
matter as they conveniently can manage, than they seat
themselves down and set busily to work, punching it neatly
out with a clever cubic stamp of fourteen lines in dia-
meter.
Petrarca. A pretty sonnet may be written on a lambkin
or a parsnip; there being room enough for truth and tenderness on the edge of a leaf or the tip of an ear; but a
great poet must clasp the higher passions breast high, and
compell them in an authoritative tone to answer his inter-
rogatories.
We will now return again to Virgil, and consider in

what relation he stands to Dante.   Our Tuscan and Homer
are never inflated.
   Boccaccio. Pardon my interruption; but do you find
that Virgil is?   Surely he has always borne the character
of the most chaste, the most temperate, the most judicious
among the poets.
   Petrarca. And will not soon lose it....

   Boccaccio. Virgil and Dante are altogether so different
that, unless you will lend me your whole store of ingenuity, I shall never bring them to bear one upon the other.
   Petrarca. Frequently the points of comparison are
salient in proportion as the angles of similitude recede:
and the absence of a quality in one man usually makes us
recollect its presence in another; hence the comparison
is at the same time natural and involuntary.   Few poets
are so different as Homer and Virgil, yet no comparison
has been made oftener.   Ovid, although unlike Homer, is
greatly more like him than Virgil is; for there is the
same facility, and apparently the same negligence, in
both.   The great fault in the 'Metamorphoses' is in the
plan, as proposed in the argument,

                    primaque ab origine mundi
        In mea *perpetuum* deducere tempora carmen.

   [... bring down my song in unbroken strains from the
   world's very beginning even unto the present time
   (i, 2-4).]

Had he divided the more interesting of the tales, and
omitted all the transformations, he would have written a
greater number of exquisite poems than any author of
Italy or Greece.   He wants on many occasions the gravity
of Virgil; he wants on all the variety of cadence; but
it is a very mistaken notion that he either has heavier
faults or more numerous.   His natural air of levity, his
unequalled and unfailing ease, have always made the contrary opinion prevalent.   Errors and faults are readily
supposed, in literature as in life, where there is much
gaiety: and the appearance of ease, among those who never
could acquire or understand it, excites a suspicion of
negligence and faultiness.   Of all the ancient Romans,
Ovid had the finest imagination; he likewise had the
truest tact in judging the poetry of his contemporaries
and predecessors.   Compare his estimate with Quinti-
lian's (41) of the same writers, and this will strike you
forcibly.   He was the only one of his countrymen who
could justly appreciate the labours of Lucretius.

Carmina sublimis tunc sunt peritura Lucreti,
    Exitio terras quum dabit una dies.

[The verses of sublime Lucretius will perish only then
when a single day shall give the earth to doom
(Ovid, 'Amores', i, 15, 23-4).]

And the kindness with which he rests on all the others,
shows a benignity of disposition which is often lamentably
deficient in authors who write tenderly upon imaginary
occasions.

I begin to be inclined to your opinion in regard to the
advantages of our Italian versification. It surely has a
greater variety, in its usual measure, than the Latin, in
dactyls and spondees. We admit several feet into ours:
the Latin, if we believe the grammarians, admits only two
into the heroic; and at least seven verses in every ten
conclude with a dissyllabic word.

Boccaccio. We are taught indeed that the final foot of
an hexameter is always a spondee: but our ears deny the
assertion, and prove to us that it never is, any more than
it is in the Italian. In both the one and the other the
last foot is uniformly a trochee in pronunciation. There
is only one species of Latin verse which ends with a true
inflexible spondee, and this is the *scazon*. Its name of
the *limper* is but little prepossessing, yet the two most
beautiful and most perfect poems of the language are composed in it; the *Miser Catulle* and the *Sirmio*. (42)

Petrarca. This is likewise my opinion of those two
little golden images, which however are insufficient to
raise Catullus on an equality with Virgil: nor would
twenty such. Amplitude of dimensions is requisite to
constitute the greatness of a poet, beside his symmetry of
form and his richness of decoration. We have conversed
more than once together on the defects and oversights of
the correct and elaborate Mantuan, but never without the
expression of our gratitude for the exquisite delight he
has afforded us. We may forgive him his Proteus and his
Pollio, (43) but we can not well forbear to ask him, how
AEneas came to know that Acragas was *formerly* the sire of
high-mettled steeds, (44) even if such had been the fact?
But such was only the fact a thousand years afterward, in
the reign of Gelon. (45)

Boccaccio.... I love beyond measure in Virgil his
kindness toward dumb creatures. Although he represents
his Mezentius as a hater of the Gods, and so inhuman as to
fasten dead bodies to the living, (46) and violates in him
the unity of character more than character was ever viola-
ted before, we treat as impossible all he has been telling

us of his atrocities, when we hear his allocution to
Rhoebus. (47)

   Petrarca. The dying hero, for hero he is transcendently
above all the others in the 'AEneid', is not only the
kindest father, not only the most passionate in his grief
for Lausus, (48) but likewise gives way to manly sorrows
for the mute companion of his warfare.

   Rhoebe diu, res si qua diu mortalibus usquam,
   Viximus.

   [Rhoebus, long have we lived, if to mortal beings
   ought be long ('Aeneid', x, 861-2).]

Here the philosophical reflection addressed to the
worthy quadruped, on the brief duration of human and
equine life, is ill-applied.   It is not the thought for
the occasion; it is not the thought for the man.   He
could no more have uttered it than Rhoebus could have ap-
preciated it.   This is not however quite so great an absurdity as the tender apostrophe of the monster Proteus to
the dead Eurydice. (49)   Beside, the youth of Lausus, and
the activity and strength of Mezentius, as exerted in many
actions just before his fall, do not allow us to suppose
that he who says to his horse

   Diu viximus,

   [Long have we lived (x, 861).]

had passed the meridian of existence....

                    FOURTH DAY'S INTERVIEW

   Petrarca. Do not throw aside your 'Paradiso' for me.
Have you been reading it again so early?
   Boccaccio. Looking into it here and there.   I had
spare time before me.
   Petrarca You have coasted the whole poem, and your
boat's bottom now touches ground.   But tell me what you
think of Beatrice.
   Boccaccio. I think her in general more of the seraphic
doctor than of the seraph.   It is well she retained her
beauty where she was, or she would scarcely be tolerable
now and then.   And yet, in other parts, we forget the
captiousness in which Theology takes delight, and feel our
bosoms refreshed by the perfect presence of the youthful
and innocent Bice.

There is something so sweetly sanctifying in pure love!
Petrarca.

Pure love? there is no other; nor shall be,
Till the worse angels hurl the better down
And heaven lie under hell: if God is one
And pure, so surely love is pure and one. (50)

Boccaccio. You understand it better than I do: you
must have your own way.
     Above all, I have been admiring the melody of the ca-
dence in this portion of the 'Divina Commedia'.   Some of
the stanzas leave us nothing to desire in facility and
elegance.
     Alighieri grows harmonious as he grows humane, and does
not, like Orpheus, play the better with the beasts about
him. (51)
     Petrarca. It is in Paradise that we might expect his
tones to be tried and modulated.
     Boccaccio. None of the imitative arts should repose on
writhings and distortions.   Tragedy herself, unless she
lead from Terror to Pity, has lost her way.
     Petrarca. What then must be thought of a long and
crowded work, whence Pity is violently excluded, and where
Hatred is the first personage we meet, and almost the last
we part from?
     Boccaccio. Happily the poet has given us here a few
breezes of the morning, a few glimpses of the stars, a few
similes of objects to which we have been accustomed among
the amusements or occupations of the country.   Some of
them would be less admired in a meaner author, and are
welcome here chiefly as a variety and relief to the mind,
after a long continuance in a painful posture.   Have you
not frequently been pleased with a short quotation of
verses in themselves but indifferent, from finding them in
some tedious dissertation? and especially if they carry
you forth a little into the open air.
     Petrarca. I am not quite certain whether, if the verses
were indifferent, I should willingly exchange the prose
for them; bad prose being less wearisome than bad poetry:
so much less indeed, that the advantage of the exchange
might fail to balance the account....

     Petrarca.... Among authors, none hath so many
friends as he who is just now dead, and had the most enemies last week.   Those who were then his adversaries are
now sincerely his admirers, for moving out of the way, and
leaving one name less in the lottery.   And yet, poor

souls! the prize will never fall to them. There is something sweet and generous in the tone of praise, which captivates an ingenuous mind, whatever may be the subject of
it; while propensity to censure not only excites suspicion of malevolence, but reminds the hearer of what he can
not disentangle from his earliest ideas of vulgarity.
There being no pleasure in thinking ill, it is wonderful
there should be any in speaking ill. You, my friend, can
find none in it: but every step you are about to take in
the revisal of your Lectures, will require much caution.
Aware you must be that there are many more defects in our
author than we have touched or glanced at: principally,
the loose and shallow foundation of so vast a structure;
its unconnectedness; its want of manners, of passion, of
action, consistently and uninterruptedly at work toward a
distinct and worthy purpose; and lastly (although less
importantly as regards the poetical character) that sple-
netic temper, which seems to grudge brightness to the
flames of hell, to delight in deepening its gloom, in mul-
tiplying its miseries, in accumulating weight upon depres-
sion, and building labyrinths about perplexity.
    Boccaccio.   Yet, O Francesco! when I remember what
Dante had suffered and was suffering from the malice and
obduracy of his enemies; when I feel (and how I do feel
it!) that you also have been following up his glory
through the same paths of exile; I can rest only on what
is great in him, and the exposure of a fault appears to me
almost an inhumanity....

    Petrarca. Posterity will regret that many of those al-
lusions to persons and events, which we now possess in the
pages of Dante, have not reached her. Among the ancients
there are few poets who more abound in them than Horace
does, and yet we feel certain that there are many which
are lost to us.
    Boccaccio. I wonder you did not mention him before.
Perhaps he is no favourite with you.
    Petrarca. Why can not we be delighted with an author,
and even feel a predilection for him, without a dislike to
others?   An admiration of Catullus or Virgil, of Tibullus (52) or Ovid, is never to be heightened by a discharge
of bile on Horace....

    Petrarca. We may indeed think the first ode of little
value, the second of none, until we come to the sixth
stanza.
    Boccaccio. Bad as are the first and second, they are

better than that wretched one, sounded so lugubriously in
our ears at school, as the masterpiece of the pathetic: I
mean the ode addressed to Virgil on the death of Quinctil-
ius Varus.

> Praecipe lugubres
> Cantus, Melpomene, cui liquidam pater
> Vocem cum citharâ dedit.

[Teach me a song of mourning, O Melpomene, thou to
whom the Father gave a liquid voice and music of the
lyre (Horace, 'Odes', i, 24, 2-4).]

Did he want any one to help him to cry?   What man im-
mersed in grief cares a quattrino about Melpomene, (53) or
her father's fairing of an artificial cuckoo and a gilt
guitar?   What man, on such an occasion, is at leisure to
amuse himself with the little plaster images of Pudor and
Fides, of Justitia and Veritas, or disposed to make a comparison of Virgil and Orpheus? (54)   But if Horace had
written a thousandfold as much trash, we are never to forget that he also wrote

> Caelo tonantem, &c.

[We believe that Jove is king in heaven because we hear
his thunders peal (iii, 5, 1-2).]

in competition with which ode, the finest in the Greek
language itself has, to my ear, too many low notes, and
somewhat of a wooden sound.   And give me *Vixi puellis*,
[Till recently I lived fit for Love's battles and served
not without renown (iii, 26, 1-2)] and give me *Quis multa
gracilis*, [What slender youth, bedewed with perfumes, embraces thee amid many a rose, O Pyrrha, in the pleasant
grotto (i, 5, 1-3)] and as many more as you please; for
there are charms in nearly all of them.   It now occurs to
me that what is written, or interpolated,

> Acer et *Mauri* peditis cruentum
> Vultus in hostem,

[And the grim visage of the Moorish foot-soldier facing
his blood-stained foe (i, 2, 39-40).]

should be *manci*; a foot soldier *mutilated*, but looking
with indignant courage at the trooper who inflicted the
wound.   The Mauritanians were celebrated only for their
cavalry.   In return for my suggestion, pray tell me what
is the meaning of

> *Obliquo laborat*
> *Lympha fugax trepidare rivo.*

[(Why) does the hurrying water strive to press onward
in the winding stream (ii, 3, 11-12).]

Petrarca. The moment I learn it you shall have it.
Laborat trepidare! lympha rivo! fugax too!   *Fugacity* is
not the action for hard work, or *labour*.
Boccaccio. Since you can not help me out, I must give
up the conjecture, it seems, while it has cost me only
half a century....

Boccaccio. In the 'Dinner of Nasidienus', I remember
the expression *nosse laboro; I am anxious to know*:
['Satires', ii, 8, 19] this expedites the solution but
little.   In the same piece there is another odd expression:

> Tum in lecto quôque *videres*
> *Stridere* secretâ divisos aure *susurros*.

[Then on each couch you might note the buzz of whispers
in secret ears exchanged (ll. 77-8).]

Petrarca. I doubt Horace's felicity in the choice of
words, being quite unable to discover it, and finding more
evidences of the contrary than in any contemporary or preceding poet; but I do not doubt his infelicity in his
transpositions of them, in which certainly he is more remarkable than whatsoever writer of antiquity.   How
simple, in comparison, are Catullus (55) and Lucretius in
the structure of their sentences! but the most simple and
natural of all are Ovid and Tibullus....

Petrarca.... Alighieri is grand by his lights, not by
his shadows; by his human affections, not by his infernal.   As the minutest sands are the labours of some profound sea, or the spoils of some vast mountain, in like
manner his horrid wastes and wearying minutenesses are the
chafings of a turbulent spirit, grasping the loftiest
things and penetrating the deepest, and moving and moaning
on the earth in loneliness and sadness....

Boccaccio.... Alighieri is the parent of his system,
like the sun, about whom all the worlds are but particles

thrown forth from him.   We may write little things well,
and accumulate one upon another; but never will any be
justly called a great poet unless he has treated a great
subject worthily.   He may be the poet of the lover and of
the idler, he may be the poet of green fields or gay society; but whoever is this can be no more.   A throne is
not built of birds'-nests, nor do a thousand reeds make a
trumpet.

Petrarca. I wish Alighieri had blown his on nobler
occasions.

Boccaccio. We may rightly wish it: but, in regretting
what he wanted, let us acknowledge what he had: and never
forget (which we omitted to mention) that he borrowed less
from his predecessors than any of the Roman poets from
theirs.   Reasonably may it be expected that almost all
who follow will be greatly more indebted to antiquity, to
whose stores we, every year, are making some addition.

Petrarca. It can be held no flaw in the title-deeds of
genius, if the same thoughts reappear as have been exhibited long ago.   The indisputable sign of defect should be
looked for in the proportion they bear to the unquestion-
ably original.   There are ideas which necessarily must
occur to minds of the like magnitude and materials,
aspect and temperature.   When two ages are in the same
phasis, they will excite the same humours, and produce the
same coincidences and combinations.   In addition to
which, a great poet may really borrow: he may even con-
descend to an obligation at the hand of an equal or inferior: but he forfeits his title if he borrows more than
the amount of his own possessions.   The nightingale himself takes somewhat of his song from birds less glorified:
and the lark, having beaten with her wing the very gates
of heaven, cools her breast among the grass.   The lowlier
of intellect may lay out a table in their field, at which
table the highest one shall sometimes be disposed to partake: want does not compell him.   Imitation, as we call
it, is often weakness, but it likewise is often sympathy.

Boccaccio. Our poet was seldom accessible in this quarter.   Invective picks up the first stone on the wayside,
and wants leisure to consult a forerunner.

Petrarca. Dante (original enough everywhere) is coarse
and clumsy in this career.   Vengeance has nothing to do
with comedy, nor properly with satire.   The satirist who
told us that Indignation made his verses for him, (56)
might have been told in return that she excluded him
thereby from the first class, and thrust him among the
rhetoricians and declaimers.   Lucretius, in his vitupera-
tion, is graver and more dignified than Alighieri.   Painful: to see how tolerant is the atheist, how intolerant

the catholic: how anxiously the one removes from among
the sufferings of Mortality, her last and heaviest, the
fear of a vindictive Fury pursuing her shadow across
rivers of fire and tears; (57)   how laboriously the other
brings down Anguish and Despair, even when Death has done
his work.   How grateful the one is to that beneficent
philosopher who made him at peace with himself, and tolerant and kindly toward his fellow-creatures! how importu-
nate the other that God should forego his divine mercy,
and hurl everlasting torments both upon the dead and the
living!...

FIFTH DAY'S INTERVIEW

Boccaccio....   We have had enough of Dante: I believe
few of his beauties have escaped us: and small faults,
which we readily pass by, are fitter for small folks, as
grubs are the proper bait for gudgeons. (58) ...

Petrarca. When I was younger I was fond of wandering in
solitary places, and never was afraid of slumbering in
woods and grottoes.   Among the chief pleasures of my
life, and among the commonest of my occupations, was the
bringing before me such heroes and heroines of antiquity,
such poets and sages, such of the prosperous and the un-
fortunate, as most interested me by their courage, their
wisdom, their eloquence, or their adventures.   Engaging
them in the conversation best suited to their characters,
I knew perfectly their manners, their steps, their voices:
and often did I moisten with my tears the models I had
been forming of the less happy. (59) ...

Boccaccio. Certainly you thus throw open, to its full
extent, the range of poetry and invention;   which can not
but be very limited and sterile, unless where we find displayed much diversity of character as disseminated by
nature, much peculiarity of sentiment as arising from
position, marked with unerring skill through every shade
and gradation;   and finally and chiefly, much intertexture
and intensity of passion.   You thus convey to us more
largely and expeditiously the stores of your understanding
and imagination, than you ever could by sonnets or canzo-
nets, or sinewless and sapless allegories....

NOTES

1 Ser Petracco, Petrarch's father, was exiled from Florence in October 1302.   Petrarch was born two years
  later on 20 July 1304, in Arezzo.
2 Cf. Luke 6:28: '"Bless those who curse you, ..."'
3 It may puzzle an Englishman to read the lines beginning with 'Modicum', so as to give the metre.   The
  secret is, to draw out 'et' into a dissyllable, et-te,
  as the Italians do, who pronounce Latin verse, if possible, worse than we, adding a syllable to such as end
  with a consonant. [L]
4 Plutus' 'clucking' words appear to be a threat against
  Dante and Virgil and a warning to Satan.
5 'Gergo': Italian for 'jargon' or 'slang'.
6 See Herodotus, 'History', ii, 102-3, 106.
7 See 'Inf.', xxxiii, 1-90, and v, 73-142.
8 Beatrice Portinari (AD 1266-90), the Florentine girl
  with whom Dante fell in love when she was eight years
  four months old and he was almost nine.   Dante's
  'Vita Nuova' (1290-4) is a record of this love.   In
  the 'Divine Comedy', Beatrice is the image through
  which the poet perceives Divine Glory, and it is her
  function to bring him to that state where he can perceive God directly.
9 'Inf.', xxxiii, 1-14, 76-8.
10 'Inf.', v, 88-93.
11 See Plato, 'Symposium', 189e-191d.
12 See the First and Fifth tales of the Fourth Day in
   the 'Decameron'.
13 Exodus 13:21.
14 See 'Inf.', iv, 140; 'Par.', xxxii, 10; 'Inf.',
   iii, 82-129, i, 101-10 ['hound'] and 'Par.', xvii,
   76-92; 'Inf.', xxx, 98-130, xxx, 49-129.
15 See 'Inf.', vi, 115-vii, 15, and xxxiv, 1-128 passim.
16 'Inf.', xxviii, 22-63.
17 See 'Par.', xi, and xii.
18 Virgil, 'Aeneid', vi.
19 'Odyssey', xi, 465-70, 541-67.
20 'Aeneid', vi, 450-76.
21 'Metamorphoses', xii, 622-xiii, 398.
22 Ajax.
23 Ulysses.
24 The Florentine painters Cimabue (1240?-1302?) and
   Giotto (1266/7?-1337), traditionally viewed as master
   and pupil respectively, were contemporaries of Dante.
   They are mentioned in 'Purg.', xi, 94-6.
25 Brunetto Latini (c. 1210-94), notary, poet, scholar,
   Guelf leader in Florence, and counsellor and friend to

the young Dante, composed an allegory of his life in
Italian entitled 'Tesoretto' (1262).   Dante offers a
moving tribute to his old master when they meet in the
'Inf.', xv, 79-87.

26   A dithyramb was originally a choral song to Dionysus.
About 600 BC Arion at Corinth developed the dithyramb
into a song that was sung by a regular choir and that
treated definite subjects.

27   Homer, 'Iliad', i, 17-21.

28   Psalm 137:9.

29   'Inf.', iii, 112-17.

30   'Inf.', iv, 94ff.

31   'Inf.', viii, 1-30.

32   'Inf.', xxvii, 1-6.

33   'Inf.', xxx, 49-129.

34   Horace, 'Satires', i, 5.

35   'Inf.', xxxiii, 26-39.   The Guland, Sismund, and
Lanfranc were Ghibelline families of Pisa.

36   Spicilege: a 'gleaning', 'collection', or 'antholo-
gy'.

37   'Inf.', i, 79ff.

38   See Hesiod, 'Works and Days', 503-63.

39   Dido.

40   Although Virgil studied rhetoric in Rome, he appeared
only once in the courts as an advocate.   The 'Rostra'
was the platform in the forum in Rome from which orators addressed the people.

41   See 'Institutio Oratoria', x, 1, 37-130, by Marcus
Fabius Quintilianus (c. AD 35-95), Roman educator and
rhetorician.

42   Catullus, viii, and xxxi.

43   See Virgil, 'Georgics', iv, 387-528, and 'Eclogues',
iv.

44   'Aeneid', iii, 703-4.

45   Gelon (c. 540-478 BC), tyrant of Gela from about 490
BC.   After defeating Syracuse, he made the city in
485 BC the centre of his government, thereby making
Syracuse the greatest Hellenic power of the time.

46   See 'Aeneid', vii, 647-8, and viii, 481-95.

47   'Aeneid', x, 861-6.   Rhoebus, the warhorse of
Mezentius.

48   'Aeneid', x, 841-56.   Lansus, Mezentius' son, is
killed by Aeneas while enabling his father, who has
been wounded by Aeneas, to escape.

49   'Georgics', iv, 506.

50   Landor's poem first appeared in the 'Pentameron and
Pentalogia' (1837), and was reprinted in 'Works'
(1846).

51   Orpheus, a legendary pre-Homeric poet from Thrace, was

Wordsworth.   But higher power produces an intimate consciousness of itself;   and this consciousness is the
parent of tranquillity and repose.   Small poets (observe,
I do not call Wordsworth and Byron small poets) are as
unquiet as grubs, which in their boneless and bloodless
flaccidity, struggle and wriggle and die, the moment they
tumble out of the nutshell and its comfortable drouth.
Shakespeare was assailed on every side by rude and beggar-
ly rivals, but he never kicked them out of his way.

Southey. Milton was less tolerant;   he shrivelled up
the lips of his revilers by the austerity of his scorn.
In our last conversation, I remember, I had to defend
against you the weaker of the two poets you just now
cited, before we came to Milton and Shakespeare.   I am
always ready to undertake the task.   Byron wants no support or setting off, so many workmen have been employed in
the construction of his throne, and so many fair hands in
the adaptation of his cushion and canopy.   But Wordsworth, in his poetry at least, always aimed at....

Porson. My dear Mr. Southey! there are two quarters in
which you can not expect the will to be taken for the
deed: I mean the women and the critics.   Your friend in-
serts parenthesis in parenthesis, and adds clause to
clause, codicil to codicil, with all the circumspection,
circuition, wariness, and strictness, of an indenture.
His client has it hard and fast.   But what is an axiom in
law is none in poetry.   You can not say in your profession, *plus non vitiat;* (1)   *plus* is the worst vitiator and
violator of the Muses and the Graces.

Be sparing of your animadversions on Byron.   He will
always have more partisans and admirers than any other in
your confraternity.   He will always be an especial favourite with the ladies, and with all who, like them, have
no opportunity of comparing him with the modes of antiquity.   He possesses the soul of poetry, which is energy;
but he wants that ideal beauty, which is the sublimer
emanation, I will not say of the real, for this is the
more real of the two, but of that which is ordinarily subject to the senses.   With much that is admirable, he has
nearly all that is vicious;   a large grasp of small
things, without selection and without cohesion.   This
likewise is the case with the other, without the long hand
and the strong fist.

Southey. I have heard that you prefer Crabbe to either.

Porson. Crabbe wrote with a twopenny nail, and
scratched rough truths and rogues' facts on mud walls.
There is, however, much in his poetry, and more in his
moral character, to admire.   Comparing the smartnesses of
Crabbe with Young's, (2) I cannot help thinking that the

reverend doctor must have wandered in his Night Thoughts
rather too near the future vicar's future mother, so
striking is the resemblance.   But the vicar, if he was
fonder of low company, has greatly more nature and sympathy, greatly more vigour and compression.   Young moral-
ised at a distance on some external appearances of the
human heart; Crabbe entered it *on all fours*, and told the
people what an ugly thing it is inside....

   Porson....   There are several things in these volumes
[of Wordsworth's poetry], ... containing just thoughts
poetically expressed.   Few, however, are there which do
not contain much of the superfluous, and more of the prosaic.   For one nod of approbation, I therefore give two
of drowsiness.   You accuse me of injustice, not only to
this author, but to all the living.   Now Byron is living;
there is more spirit in Byron: Scott is living; there is
more vivacity and variety in Scott.   Byron exhibits *disjecti membra poetae*; (3) and strong muscles quiver
throughout; but rather like galvanism than healthy life.
There is a freshness in all Scott's scenery; a vigour and
distinctness in all his characters.   He seems the
brother-in-arms of Froissart. (4)   I admire his 'Marmion'
in particular. (5)   Give me his massy claymore, and keep
in the cabinet or the boudoir the jewelled hilt of the
oriental dirk.   The pages which my forefinger keeps open
for you, contain a thing in the form of a sonnet; a thing
to which, for insipidity, *tripe au naturel* (6) is a
dainty.

     Great men have been among us, hands that penned
     And tongues that uttered wisdom; better none.
     The later Sidney, Marvel, Harrington,
     Young Vane, and others who called Milton friend. (7)
     [Wordsworth, 'Sonnet xv', ll. 1-4.]

   Porson. But ... the sonnet admits not that approach to
the prosaic which is allowable in the ballad, particularly
in the ballad of action.   For which reason I never
laughed, as many did, at

     Lord Lion King at Arms.
     ['Marmion', iv, 7, 31.]

Scott knew what he was about.   In his chivalry, and in
all the true, gaiety is mingled with strength, and facility with majesty.   Lord Lion may be defended by the

practice of the older poets who describe the like scenes
and adventures.   There is much resembling it, for instance, in 'Chevy Chase'. (8)   'Marmion' is a poem of
chivalry, partaking (in some measure) of the ballad, but
rising in sundry places to the epic, and closing with a
battle worthy of the 'Iliad'.   Ariosto has demonstrated
that a romance may be so adorned by the apparatus, and so
elevated by the spirit of poetry, as to be taken for an
epic; but it has a wider field of its own, with outlying
forests and chases.   Spanish and Italian poetry often
seems to run in extremely slender veins through a vast
extent of barren ground....

Porson....   It is much to be regretted that, in re-
solving on simplicity, he [Wordsworth] did not place himself under the tuition of Burns; which quality Burns
could have taught him in perfection; but others he never
could have imparted to such an auditor.   He would have
sung in vain to him

>   Scots wha hae wi' Wallace bled.
>   ['Robert Bruce's March to Bannockburn', l. 1.]

A song more animating than ever Tyrtaeus sang to the fife
before the Spartans. (9)   But simplicity in Burns is
never stale and unprofitable.   In Burns there is no
waste of words out of an ill-shouldered sack; no troublesome running backward and forward of little, idle, ragged
ideas; no ostentation of sentiment in the surtout of
selfishness.   Where was I?

>   Better none ... The later Sidney ... Young Vane ...
>   These moralists could act ... and ... comprehend!
>   [Wordsworth, 'Sonnet xv', ll. 2-5.]

We might expect as much if *'none were better'*.

>   They knew how genuine glory was ... put on!
>   [l. 6.]

What is genuine is not *put on*.

>   Taught us how rightfully ... a nation ...
>   [l. 7.]

Did what?   Took up arms?   No such thing.   *Remonstrated*?
No, nor that.   What then?   Why, *'shone'*!   I am inclined
to take the *shine* out of him for it.   But how did the
nation *'rightfully shine'*?   In *splendour*!

Taught us how rightfully a nation shone
In splendour!
[ll. 7-8.]

Now the secret is out; make the most of it. Another
thing they taught us,

What strength was.
[l. 8.]

They did indeed, with a vengeance. Furthermore, they
taught us what we never could have expected from such
masters,

What strength was ... *that would not bend*
But in magnanimous *meekness.*
[ll. 8-9.]

Brave Oliver! brave and honest Ireton! (10) We know
pretty well where your magnanimity lay; we never could so
cleverly find out your meekness. Did you leave it per-
adventure on the window-seat at Whitehall? (11) The
'later Sidney and young Vane, who could call Milton
friend', and Milton himself, were gentlemen of your
kidney, and they were all as meek as Moses with their
arch-enemy.

Perpetual emptiness: unceasing change.
[l. 11.]

How could the *change* be unceasing if the *emptiness* was
perpetual?

No single volume paramount: no *code:*
[l. 12.]

That is untrue. There is a Code, and the best in Europe:
there was none promulgated under our Commonwealth.

No master spirit, no determined road,
And [But] equally a want of books and men.
[ll. 13-14.]

Southey. I do not agree in this opinion: for although
of late years France hath exhibited no man of exalted
wisdom or great worth, yet surely her Revolution (12) cast
up several both intellectual and virtuous. But, like
fishes in dark nights and wintry weather, allured by de-
ceptive torches, they came to the surface only to be
speared.

Porson. Although there were many deplorable ends in the
French Revolution, there was none so deplorable as the
last sonnet's.   So diffuse and pointless and aimless is
not only this, but fifty more, that the author seems to
have written them in hedger's gloves, on blotting paper.
If he could by any contrivance have added to

Perpetual emptiness unceasing change,

or some occasional change at least, he would have been
more tolerable.
Southey. He has done it lately: he has written, although not yet published, a vast number of sonnets on
Capital Punishment. (13)
Porson. Are you serious?   Already he has inflicted it
far and wide, for divers attempts made upon him to extort
his meaning.
Southey. Remember, poets superlatively great have composed things below their dignity.   Suffice it to mention
only Milton's translation of the Psalms.
Porson. Milton was never half so wicked a regicide as
when he lifted up his hand and smote King David.   He has
atoned for it, however, by composing a magnificent psalm
of his own, in the form of a sonnet.
Southey. You mean on the massacre of the Protestants in
Piedmont.   This is indeed the noblest of sonnets.
Porson. There are others in Milton comparable to it,
but none elsewhere.   In the poems of Shakespeare, which
are printed as sonnets, there sometimes is a singular
strength and intensity of thought, with little of that
imagination which was afterward to raise him highest in
the universe of poetry.   Even the interest we take in
the private life of this miraculous man cannot keep the
volume in our hands long together. (14)   We acknowledge
great power, but we experience great weariness.   Were I a
poet, I would much rather have written the 'Allegro' or
the 'Penseroso', than all those, and moreover than nearly
all that portion of our metre, which, wanting a definite
term, is ranged under the capitulary of lyric.
Southey. Evidently you dislike the sonnet; otherwise
there are very many in Wordsworth which would have
obtained your approbation.
Porson. I have no objection to see mincemeat put into
small patty pans, all of equal size, with ribs at odd distances: my objection lies mainly where I find it without
salt or succulence.   Milton was glad, I can imagine, to
seize upon the sonnet, because it restricted him from a
profuse expression of what soon becomes tiresome, praise.
In addressing it to the Lord Protector, he was aware that

prolixity of speech was both unnecessary and indecorous:
in addressing it to Vane, and Lawrence, and Lawes, (15) he
felt that friendship is never the stronger for running
through long periods: and in addressing it to

>Captain, or Colonel, or Knight-at-Arms,
>['Sonnet viii', l. l.]

he might be confident that fourteen such glorious lines
were a bulwark sufficient for his protection against a
royal army.
   Southey. I am highly gratified at your enthusiasm.   A
great poet represents a great portion of the human race.
Nature delegated to Shakespeare the interests and direc-
tion of the whole: to Milton a smaller part, but with
plenary power over it; and she bestowed on him such fervour and majesty of eloquence as on no other mortal in any
age.
   Porson. Perhaps, indeed, not on Demosthenes himself.
   Southey. Without many of these qualities of which a
loftier genius is constituted, without much fire, without
a wide extent of range, without an eye that can look into
the heart, or an organ that can touch it, Demosthenes had
great dexterity and great force.   By the union of these
properties he always was impressive on his audience: but
his orations bear less testimony to the seal of genius
than the dissertations of Milton do.
   Porson. You judge correctly that there are several
parts of genius in which Demosthenes is deficient, although in none whatever of the consummate orator.   In
that character there is no necessity for stage-exhibitions
of wit, however well it may be received in an oration from
the most persuasive and the most stately: Demosthenes,
when he catches at wit, misses it, and falls flat in the
mire.   But by discipline and training, by abstinence from
what is florid and too juicy, and by loitering with no
idle words on his way, he acquired the hard muscles of a
wrestler, and nobody could stand up against him with success or impunity.
   Southey. Milton has equal strength, without an abate-
ment of beauty: not a sinew sharp or rigid, not a vein
varicose or inflated.   Hercules killed robbers and rav-
ishers with his knotted club; he cleansed also royal
stables by turning whole rivers into them: (16) Apollo,
with no labour or effort, overcame the Python; (17)
brought round him, in the full accordance of harmony, all
the Muses: and illuminated with his sole spendour the
universal world.   Such is the difference I see between
Demosthenes and Milton....

Southey..... When I have been told, as I often have
been, that I shall find very few of my opinion, certainly
no compliment was intended me; yet there are few, comparatively, whom nature has gifted with intuition or exquisite taste; few whose ideas have been drawn, modelled,
marked, chiselled, and polished, in a *studio* well lighted
from above. The opinion of a thousand millions who are
ignorant or ill-informed, is not equal to the opinion of
only one who is wiser. This is too self-evident for argument; yet we hear about the common sense of mankind!
A common sense which, unless the people receive it from
their betters, leads them only into common error. If
such is the case, and we have the testimony of all ages
for it, in matters which have most attracted their attention, matters in which their nearest interests are mainly
concerned, in politics, in religion, in the education of
their families, how greatly, how surpassingly, must it be
in those which require a peculiar structure of understanding, a peculiar endowment of mind, a peculiar susceptibility, and almost an undivided application. In what regards poetry, I should just as soon expect a sound judgment of its essentials from a boatman or a waggoner, as
from the usual set of persons we meet in society; persons
not uneducated, but deriving their intelligence from
little gutters and drains round about. The mud is easily
raised to the surface in so shallow a receptacle, and
nothing is seen distinctly or clearly. Whereas the humbler man has received no false impressions, and may therefore to a limited extent be right. As for books in general, it is only with men like you that I ever open my
lips upon them in conversation. In my capacity of reviewer, dispassionate by temperament, equitable by principle, and, moreover, for fear of offending God and of suffering in my conscience, I dare not leave behind me in my
writings either a false estimate or a frivolous objection.

Porson..... You, Mr. Southey, will always be considered the soundest and the fairest of our English critics;
and indeed, to the present time, you have been the only
one of very delicate perception in poetry. But your admirable good-nature has thrown a costly veil over many defects and some deformities....

Southey. Let us return, if you please, to one among the
partakers of your praise, whose philosophy is neither ob-
trusive nor abstruse. I am highly gratified by your commendation of Cowper, than whom there never was a more virtuous or more amiable man. In some passages, he stands
quit unrivalled by any recent poet of this century; none,

indeed, modern or ancient, has touched the heart more
delicately, purely, and effectively, than he has done in
'Crazy Kate', in Lines on his 'Mother's Picture', in
'Omai', and on hearing 'Bells at a Distance'.

Porson. Thank you for the mention of bells. Mr.
Wordsworth, I remember, speaks, in an authoritative and
scornful tone of censure, on Cowper's 'church-going' bell,
treating the expression as a gross impropriety and absurdity. (18) True enough, the *church-going* bell does not
go to church any more than I do; neither does the
passing-bell pass any more than I; nor does the *curfew*-
bell cover any more fire than is contained in Mr. Wordsworth's poetry: but the church-going bell is that which
is rung for people going to church; the passing-bell for
those passing to heaven; the curfew-bell for the burges-
ses and villagers to cover their fires. He would not
allow me to be called *well-spoken*, nor you to be called
well-read; and yet, by this expression, I should mean to
signify that you have read much, and I should employ another in signifying that you have been much read. Incomparably better is Cowper's 'Winter' than Virgil's, which
is indeed a disgrace to the Georgics; or than Thomson's,
which in places is grand. (19) But would you on the
whole compare Cowper with Dryden?

Southey. Dryden possesses a much richer store of
thoughts, expatiates upon more topics, has more vigour,
vivacity, and animation. He is always shrewd and penetrating, explicit and perspicuous, concise, where conciseness is desirable, and copious where copiousness can yield
delight. When he aims at what is highest in poetry, the
dramatic, he falls below his 'Fables'. However, I would
not compare the poetical power of Cowper with his; nor
would I, as some have done, pit Young against him. Young
is too often fastastical and frivolous; he pins butterflies to the pulpit-cushion; he suspends against the
grating of the charnel house coloured lamps and comic
transparencies, Cupid, and the cat and the fiddle; he
opens a storehouse filled with minute particles of hetero-
geneous wisdom, and unpalatable gobbets of ill-concocted
learning, contributions from the classics, from the
schoolmen, from homilies, and from farces. What you
expect to be an elegy turns out an epigram; and when you
think he is bursting into tears, he laughs in your face.
Do you go with him into his closet, prepared for an admonition or a rebuke, he shakes his head, and you sneeze at
the powder and perfumery of his peruke. Wonder not if I
prefer to his pungent essences the incense which Cowper
burns before the altar.

Porson. Young was, in every sense of the word, an ambi-

tious man.   He had strength, but wasted it.   Blair's
'Grave' (20) has more spirit in it than the same portion
of the 'Night Thoughts'; but never was poetry so ill put
together; never was there so good a poem, of the same
extent, from which so great a quantity of what is mere
trash might be rejected.   The worse blemish in it is the
ridicule and scoffs, cast not only on the violent and
grasping, but equally on the gentle, the beautiful, the
studious, the eloquent, and the manly.   It is ugly enough
to be carried quietly to the grave; it is uglier to be
hissed and hooted into it.   Even the quiet astronomer,

> With study pale, and midnight vigils spent,
> ['The Grave', l. 286.]

is not permitted to depart in peace, but (of all men in
the world!) is called a 'proud man' [l. 292], and is
coolly and flippantly told that

> Great heights are hazardous to the weak head,
> [l. 293.]

which the poet might have turned into a verse, if he had
tried again, as we will:

> To the weak head great heights are hazardous.

In the same funny style he writes

> O that some courteous ghost would blab it out,
> What 'tis they [you] are.
> [ll. 433-4.]

Courtesy and blabbing, in this upper world of ours, are
thought to be irreconcilable; but blabbing may not be
indecorous nor derogatory to the character of courtesy in
a ghost.   However, the expression is an uncouth one; and
when we find it so employed, we suspect the ghost cannot
have been keeping good company....

Cowper plays in the playground, and not in the
churchyard.   Nothing of his is out of place or out of
season.   He possessed a rich vein of ridicule, but he
turned it to good account, opening it on prig parsons, and
graver and worse impostors.   He was among the first who
put to flight the mischievous little imps of allegory, so
cherished and fondled by the Wartons. (21)   They are as
bad in poetry as mice in a cheese-room.   You poets are

still rather too fond of the unsubstantial. Some will
have nothing else than what they call pure imagination.
Now air plants ought not to fill the whole conservatory;
other plants, I would modestly suggest, are worth cultivating, which send their roots pretty deep into the
ground. I hate both poetry and wine without body. Look
at Shakespeare, Bacon, and Milton; were these your pure-
imagination-men? The least of them, whichever it was,
carried a jewel of poetry about him, worth all his tribe
that came after. Did the two of them who wrote in verse
build upon nothing? Did their predecessors? And, pray,
whose daughter was the Muse they invoked? Why, Memory's.
They stood among substantial men, and sang upon recorded
actions. The plain of Scamander, the promontory of
Sigaeum, the palaces of Tros and Dardanus, the citadel in
which the Fates sang mournfully under the image of Miner-
va, seem fitter places for the Muses to alight on, (22)
than artificial rockwork or than faery-rings. But your
great favourite, I hear, is Spenser, who shines in allegory, and who, like an aerolithe, is dull and heavy when
he descends to the ground.

Southey. He continues a great favourite with me still,
although he must always lose a little as our youth de-
clines. Spenser's is a spacious but somewhat low chamber, hung with rich tapestry, on which the figures are
mostly disproportioned, but some of the faces are lively
and beautiful; the furniture is part creaking and worm-
eaten, part fragrant with cedar and sandalwood and aromatic gums and balsams; every table and mantelpiece and
cabinet is covered with gorgeous vases, and birds, and
dragons, and houses in the air.

Porson. There is scarcely a poet of the same eminence,
whom I have found it so delightful to read in, or so tedious to read through. Give me Chaucer in preference.
He slaps us on the shoulder, and makes us spring up while
the dew is on the grass, and while the long shadows play
about it in all quarters. We feel strong with the freshness round us, and we return with a keener appetite,
having such a companion in our walk. Among the English
poets, both on this side and the other side of Milton, I
place him next to Shakespeare; but the word *next*, must
have nothing to do with the word *near*. I said before,
that I do not estimate so highly as many do the mushrooms
that sprang up in a ring under the great oak of
Arden. (23)

Southey. These authors deal in strong distillations for
foggy minds that want excitement. In few places is there
a great depth of sentiment, but everywhere vast exaggeration and insane display. I find the over-crammed

curiosity-shop, with its incommodious appendages, some
grotesquely rich, all disorderly and disconnected.
Rather would I find, as you would, the well-proportioned
hall, with its pillars of right dimensions at right distances; with its figures, some in high relief and some in
lower; with its statues and its busts of glorious men and
women, whom I recognise at first sight; and its tables of
the rarest marbles and richest gems, inlaid in glowing
porphyry, and supported by imperishable bronze. Without
a pure simplicity of design, without a just subordination
of characters, without a select choice of such personages
as either have interested us or must by the power of association, without appropriate ornaments laid on solid
materials, no admirable poetry of the first order can
exist.

Porson. Well, we can not get all these things, and we
will not cry for them. Leave me rather in the curiosity-
shop than in the nursery. By your reference to the noble
models of antiquity, it is evident that those poets most
value the ancients who are certain to be among them. In
our own earlier poets, as in the earlier Italian painters,
we find many disproportions; but we discern the dawn of
truth over the depths of expression. These were soon
lost sight of, and every new comer passed further from
them. I like Pietro Perugino a thousand-fold better than
Carlo Maratta, (24) and Giotto a thousand-fold better than
Carlo Dolce. (25) On the same principle, the daybreak of
Chaucer is pleasanter to me than the hot dazzling noon of
Byron.

Southey. I am not confident that we ever speak quite
correctly of those who differ from us essentially in
taste, in opinion, or even in style. If we cordially
wish to do it, we are apt to lay a restraint on ourselves,
and to dissemble a part of our convictions.

Porson. An error seldom committed.

Southey. Sometimes, however. I for example did not
expose in my criticisms half the blemishes I discovered in
the style and structure of Byron's poetry, because I had
infinitely more to object against the morals it disseminated; and what must have been acknowledged for earnestness
in the greater question, might have been mistaken for
captiousness in the less....

Porson.... That is the best poetry which, by its own
powers, produces the greatest and most durable emotion on
generous, well-informed, and elevated minds. It often
happens that what belongs to the subject is attributed to
the poet. Tenderness, melancholy, and other affections

of the soul, attract us toward him who represents them to
us; and while we hang upon his neck, we are ready to
think him stronger than he is.   No doubt, it is very
natural that the wings of the Muse should seem to grow
larger the nearer they come to the ground!   Such is the
effect, I presume, of our English atmosphere!   But if Mr.
Wordsworth should at any time become more popular, it will
be owing in great measure to your authority and patronage;
and I hope that, neither in health nor in sickness, he
will forget his benefactor.

Southey. However that may be, it would be unbecoming
and base in me to suppress an act of justice toward him,
withholding my testimony in his behalf when he appeals to
the tribunal of the public.   The reader who can discover
no good or indeed no excellent poetry in his manifold
productions, must have lost the finer part of his senses.

Porson. And he who fancies he has found it in all or in
most of them, is just as happy as if his senses were
entire.   A great portion of his compositions is not
poetry, but only the plasma or matrix of poetry, which
has something of the same colour and material, but wants
the brilliancy and solidity.

Southey. Acknowledge at least, that what purifies the
mind elevates it also; and that he does it.

Porson. Such a result may be effected at a small expenditure of the poetical faculty, and indeed without any.
But I do not say that he has none, or that he has little;
I only say, and I stake my credit on it, that what he has
is not of the higher order.   This is proved beyond all
controversy by the effect it produces.   The effect of the
higher poetry is excitement;   the effect of the inferior
is composure....

NOTES

1   'Plus non vitiat':   'he doesn't violate more'.
2   Edward Young (1683-1765), clergyman and poet, author
    of the popular 'Complaint, or Night Thoughts on Life,
    Death, and Immortality' (1742-5);   George Crabbe
    (1754-1832), vicar and poet, author of 'The Village'
    (1783) and numerous verse tales.
3   'Disjecti membra poetae':   'limbs of the dismembered
    poet'.
4   Jean Froissart (1337?-c. 1410), French chronicler of
    the affairs of fourteenth-century Flanders, France,
    Spain, Portugal, and England.
5   'Marmion, a Tale of Flodden Field' (1808), a poem in
    six cantos, by Sir Walter Scott.

6   'Tripe au naturel': 'natural trash'.
7   Algernon Sidney (1622-83), republican and writer;
     Andrew Marvell (1621-78), poet and satirist; James
     Harrington (1611-77), author of 'Oceana'; and Sir
     Henry Vane, the younger (1613-62), statesman and
     writer.
8   Chevy Chase is one of the oldest English ballads.
9   Tyrtaeus (seventh century BC), Spartan general and
     poet, author of war songs and exhortations in elegiac
     verse.
10   Oliver Cromwell (1599-1658), Puritan military leader
     and lord protector of the Commonwealth of England,
     Scotland, and Ireland (1653-8); Henry Ireton (1611-
     51), English parliamentary general who was active in
     bringing Charles I to trial, attended the court regu-
     larly, and signed the king's death-warrant.
11   On 30 January 1649 Charles I, king of England, was
     executed outside the banqueting hall of Whitehall
     palace in London.
12   The French Revolution is usually thought to have begun
     with the May 1879 meeting of the States General.
13   Wordsworth's 'Sonnets upon the Punishment of Death'
     were composed in 1839-40 and published in December
     1841.
14   This is apparently an allusion to Charles Brown's
     'Shakespeare's Autobiographical Poems' (1838), which
     contains a dedicatory epistle to his friend Landor.
15   See Milton's sonnets: 'To the Lord Generall Cromwell
     May 1652' (xvi); 'To Sr Henry Vane the younger'
     (xvii); 'Lawrence of vertuous Father vertuous Son,
     ...' (xx); 'To Mr. H. Lawes, on his Aires' (xiii).
     Edward Lawrence (1633-56), was a member of Parliament
     and son of Henry Lawrence (1600-64), Lord President of
     the Council under Cromwell; Henry Lawes (1595-1662),
     English composer who supplied incidental music for
     Milton's 'Comus' (1634).
16   Heracles' cleaning the Augean Stables is the sixth of
     the twelve labours of Heracles.
17   According to Greek myth, the first feat of the god
     Apollo was to destroy the dragon Python, guardian of
     Delphi. He then made Delphi his abode.
18   See the Appendix, in 'Poetical Works of William Words-
     worth', ed. E. de Selincourt and rev. by H. Darbi-
     shire, 2nd ed. (Oxford: Clarendon Press, 1952), 2,
     408.
19   See Cowper's Winter Evening (iv), Winter Morning Walk
     (v), Winter Walk at Noon (vi), in the 'Task'; Vir-
     gil's 'Georgics', iii, 349ff; Thomson's Winter (iv),
     in the 'Seasons'.

20   'The Grave' (1743), by Robert Blair (1699-1746), is,
     like Young's 'Night Thoughts', a didactic, meditative
     poem in blank verse.
21   See Southey and Porson I, No. 10 above, n. 25.
22   Porson's allusions are to prominent places in Homer's
     'Iliad'.   The plain of Scamander, so-named because of
     the river that flows through it, was the main battle-
     ground for the Greek and Trojan armies.   The promon-
     tory of Sigaeum, the northwestern extremity of Asia
     Minor at the entrance of the Hellespont (Dardanelles),
     was the site of the Greek invaders' camp.   The pal-
     aces of Dardanus, legendary ancestor of the Trojan
     kings, and Tros, an early Trojan king whose people
     assumed his name, are the royal residence of the
     Trojan king Priam.   The citadel of Troy housed the
     Palladium, an ancient sacred image of Pallas, the
     Greek Athene and Roman Minerva, which was supposed to
     have been Zeus' gift to Dardanus, or, according to
     another version of the myth, Dardanus' descendant,
     Ilus.   It was believed that the protection of Troy
     depended on its safe custody.   In Greek legend Dio-
     mede and Odysseus stole this talisman, thus making
     possible the Greek sack of Troy.
23   Shakespeare.   The poet's mother, Mary Arden, claimed
     to belong to the Arden family of Warwickshire who
     owned manors in the Forest of Arden at the time of
     Elizabeth I.
24   Pietro Perugino (c. 1450-1523), chief Italian painter
     of the Umbrian school and master of Raphael;   Carlo
     Maratta (1625-1713), Italian painter who was one of
     the leaders of the late seventeenth-century Roman
     school.
25   Giotto (1266/67?-1337), the first great Italian master
     and father of modern art;   Carlo Dolci (1616-86), one
     of the last Italian representatives of the local
     Florentine school.

'Latterly it has cost me above a month to remark on the
faults of Milton, in an Imaginary Conversation with
Southey, which our friend Forster desired', wrote Landor
to Leigh Hunt on 18 November 1844.   'You know how highly
I venerate the poet of our Republic.   In vain do I attempt to read any verse after his.   My ear rejects even
Homer's.   Never was harmony so perfect, excepting in some
passages of Shakespeare.   What a glorious language is
ours!' (cited by R.H. Super, 'Landor', 579-80, n. 17).

Landor may well be referring to a request by Forster
that he review an edition of Milton's poetry for the
'Foreign Quarterly Review'.   Forster records that as editor he persuaded Landor to write a series of essays on his
favourite poets in the form of reviews of recent editions
of Catullus, Horace, Petrarch, Pindar, and Theocritus
(Forster, 'Landor', 2, 437-45).   Although Forster omits
Milton's name from this list of Landor's favourite poets,
evidence strongly suggests that these two Conversations
between Southey and Landor existed first in the form of
marginal notes intended for a review of the Reverend Henry
Todd's variorum edition of 'The Poetical Works of John
Milton' (1826, 1842).   A thorough comparison of Landor's
critical remarks on the poetry and the commentary on
Milton in these Conversations with the order of presentation of the poetry and the commentary in Todd's 'Milton',
demonstrates beyond question that Landor had Todd's variorum edition before him as he criticized his favourite
English poet (see the notes to this selection and my
Landor on Milton: The Commentators' Commentator, 'The
Wordsworth Circle', 7 (Winter 1976), 3-12).

It is in keeping with Landor's temperament and critical
predilections that he should choose to pursue his most-
extended analysis of Milton's poetry in a day-long imagi-

219

nary meeting with his friend Robert Southey.   The Imaginary Conversation is the literary prose form most congenial to Landor, and Southey was to him representative of
the ideal poet-critic.   It is even likely that when the
two friends did meet, their conversation ran along similar
lines.   The Rev. Cuthbert Southey, who was present during
the last meetings in November 1836 of his father and
Landor, recalls: 'This was a pleasant visit, and my
father's enjoyment was greatly enhanced by the company of
Mr. Savage Landor, who was then residing at Clifton, and
in whose society we spent several delightful days.   He
was one of the few men with whom my father used to enter
freely into conversation, and on such occasions it was no
mean privilege to be a listener' ('Life and Correspondence
of Robert Southey', London, 1849-50, 6, 311).

In reading these two Conversations one must not assume,
however, that Southey speaks for himself, for the two interlocutors actually speak with one voice, and that voice
is Landor's.   He lavishes upon Milton a reading so close
and so specific that only a poet of Milton's stature could
survive it.   The harmonious quality of Milton's verse is
his primary concern, and he demands from Milton the same
high standard that he demanded from himself in his own
writing.

The following excerpts are reprinted from the second
volume of the 'Works of Walter Savage Landor' (1846).
About two-thirds of the first conversation, devoted to
criticism of 'Paradise Lost', is included here since it
affords the unusual opportunity to observe Landor in a
sustained effort as a verbal and textual critic.   The
excerpts from the second conversation, consisting of about
one-seventh of the whole, contain digressions on such miscellaneous subjects as French drama, Elizabethan theatre
audiences, and various English dramatists, poets, and
critics.

Landor....   It would ill beseem us to treat Milton with
generalities.   Radishes and salt are the *pic-nic* quota of
slim spruce reviewers: let us hope to find somewhat more
solid and of better taste.   Desirous to be a listener and
a learner when you discourse on his poetry, I have been
more occupied of late in examining the prose.

Southey. Do you retain your high opinion of it?

Landor. Experience makes us more sensible of faults
than of beauties.   Milton is more correct than Addison,
but less correct than Hooker, whom I wish he had been contented to receive as a model in style, rather than authors
who wrote in another and a poorer language; such, I
think, you are ready to acknowledge is the Latin.

Southey. This was always my opinion.

Landor. However, I do not complain that in oratory and history his diction is sometimes poetical.

Southey. Little do I approve of it in prose on any subject.   Demosthenes and AEschines, Lysias and Isaeus, and finally Cicero, avoided it. (1)

Landor. They did: but Chatham and Burke and Grattan did not; (2) nor indeed the graver and greater Pericles; of whom the most memorable sentence on record is pure poetry.   On the fall of the young Athenians in the field of battle, he said, 'The year hath lost its spring'. (3) But how little are these men, even Pericles himself, if you compare them as men of genius with Livy! (4)   In Livy, as in Milton, there are bursts of passion which can not by the nature of things be other than poetical, nor (being so) come forth in other language.   If Milton had executed his design of writing a history of England, (5) it would probably have abounded in such diction, especially in the more turbulent scenes and in the darker ages....

Southey. Being now alone, with the whole day before us, and having carried, as we agreed at breakfast, each his Milton in his pocket, let us collect all the graver faults we can lay our hands upon, without a too minute and troublesome research; not in the spirit of Johnson, but in our own. (6)

Landor. That is, abasing our eyes in reverence to so great a man, but without closing them.   The beauties of his poetry we may omit to notice, if we can: but where the crowd claps the hands, it will be difficult for us always to refrain.   Johnson, I think, has been charged unjustly with expressing too freely and inconsiderately the blemishes of Milton.   There are many more of them than he has noticed.

Southey. If we add any to the number, and the literary world hears of it, we shall raise an outcry from hundreds who never could see either his excellences or his defects, and from several who never have perused the noblest of his writings.

Landor. It may be boyish and mischievous, but I acknowledge I have sometimes felt a pleasure in irritating, by the cast of a pebble, those who stretch forward to the full extent of the chain their open and frothy mouths against me.   I shall seize upon this conjecture of yours, and say everything that comes into my head on the subject. Beside which, if any collateral thoughts should spring up, I may throw them in also; as you perceive I have frequently done in my 'Imaginary Conversations', and as we always do in real ones.

Southey. When we adhere to one point, whatever the form, it should rather be called a disquisition than a conversation. Most writers of dialogue take but a single stride into questions the most abstruse, and collect a heap of arguments to be blown away by the bloated whiffs of some rhetorical charlatan, tricked out in a multiplicity of ribbons for the occasion. (7)

Before we open the volume of poetry, let me confess to you I admire his prose less than you do.

Landor. Probably because you dissent more widely from the opinions it conveys: for those who are displeased with anything are unable to confine the displeasure to one spot. We dislike everything a little when we dislike anything much. It must indeed be admitted that his prose is often too Latinized and stiff. But I prefer his heavy cut velvet, with its ill-placed Roman fibula, (8) to the spangled gauze and gummed-on flowers and puffy flounces of our present street-walking literature. So do you, I am certain.

Southey. Incomparably. But let those who have gone astray, keep astray, rather than bring Milton into disrepute by pushing themselves into his company and imitating his manner. As some men conceive that if their name is engraven in gothic letters, with several superfluous, it denotes antiquity of family, so do others that a congestion of words swept together out of a corner, and dry chopped sentences which turn the mouth awry in reading, make them look like original thinkers. Milton is none of these: and his language is never a patchwork. We find daily, in almost every book we open, expressions which are not English, never were, and never will be: for the writers are by no means of sufficiently high rank to be masters of the mint. To arrive at this distinction, it is not enough to scatter in all directions bold, hazardous, undisciplined thoughts: there must be lordly and commanding ones, with a full establishment of well-appointed expressions adequate to their maintenance.

Occasionally I have been dissatisfied with Milton, because in my opinion that is ill said in prose which can be said more plainly. Not so in poetry: if it were, much of Pindar and Aeschylus, and no little of Dante, would be censurable.

Landor. Acknowledge that he whose poetry I am holding in my hand is free from every false ornament in his prose, unless a few bosses of Latinity may be called so; and I am ready to admit the full claims of your favourite South. (9) Acknowledge that, heading all the forces of our language, he was the great antagonist of every great monster which infested our country; and he disdained to

trim his lion-skin with lace.   No other English writer
has equalled Raleigh, (10) Hooker, and Milton, in the
loftier parts of their works.

Southey. But Hooker and Milton, you allow, are sometimes pedantic.   In Hooker there is nothing so elevated
as there is in Raleigh.

Landor. Neither he, however, nor any modern, nor any
ancient, has attained to that summit on which the sacred
ark of Milton strikes and rests.   Reflections, such as we
indulged in on the borders of the Larius, (11) come over
me here again.   Perhaps from the very sod where you are
sitting, the poet in his youth sat looking at the Sabrina
he was soon to celebrate. (12)   There is pleasure in the
sight of a glebe which never has been broken; but it delights me particularly in those places where great men
have been before.   I do not mean warriors: for extremely
few among the most remarkable of them will a considerate
man call great: but poets and philosophers and philan-
thropists, the ornaments of society, the charmers of solitude, the warders of civilisation, the watchmen at the
gate which Tyranny would batter down, and the healers of
those wounds which she left festering in the field.   And
now, to reduce this demon into its proper toad-shape
again, and to lose sight of it, open your 'Paradise
Lost'....

Southey. Before we pursue the details of a poem, it is
customary to look at it as a whole, and to consider what
is the scope and tendency, or what is usually called the
moral. (13)   But surely it is a silly and stupid business
to talk mainly about the moral of a poem, unless it pro-
fessedly be a fable.   A good epic, a good tragedy, a good
comedy, will inculcate several.   Homer does not represent
the anger of Achilles as being fatal or disastrous to that
hero; which would be what critics call poetical justice.
But he demonstrates in the greater part of the 'Iliad' the
evil effects of arbitrary power, in alienating an elevated
soul from the cause of his country.   In the 'Odyssea' he
shows that every obstacle yields to constancy and persev-
erance: yet he does not propose to show it: and there
are other morals no less obvious.   Why should the machinery of the longest poem be drawn out to establish an
obvious truth, which a single verse would exhibit more
plainly, and impress more memorably?   Both in epic and
dramatic poetry it is action, and not moral, that is first
demanded.   The feelings and exploits of the principal
agent should excite the principal interest.   The two
greatest of human compositions are here defective: I mean

the 'Iliad' and 'Paradise Lost'. Agamemnon is leader of
the confederate Greeks before Troy, to avenge the cause of
Menelaus: yet not only Achilles and Diomed on his side,
but Hector and Sarpedon on the opposite, interest us more
than the 'king of men', the avenger, or than his brother,
the injured prince, about whom they all are fighting. (14)
In the 'Paradise Lost' no principal character seems to
have been intended. There is neither truth nor wit however in saying that Satan is hero of the piece, unless, as
is usually the case in human life, he is the greatest hero
who gives the widest sway to the worst passions. It is
Adam who acts and suffers most, and on whom the consequences have most influence. This constitutes him the
main character; although Eve is the more interesting,
Satan the more energetic, and on whom the greater force of
poetry is displayed. The Creator and his angels are
quite secondary.

  Landor. Must we not confess that every epic hitherto
has been defective in plan; and even that each, until the
time of Tasso, was more so than its predecessor? Such
stupendous genius, so much fancy, so much eloquence, so
much vigour of intellect, never were united as in 'Paradise Lost'. Yet it is neither so correct nor so varied
as the 'Iliad', nor, however important the action, so interesting. The moral itself is the reason why it wearies
even those who insist on the necessity of it. Founded on
an event believed by nearly all nations, certainly by all
who read the poem, it lays down a principle which concerns
every man's welfare, and a fact which every man's experience confirms; that great and irremediable misery may
arise from apparently small offences. But will any one
say that, in a poetical view, our certainty of moral truth
in this position is an equivalent for the uncertainty
which of the agents is what critics call the hero of the
piece?

  Southey. We are informed in the beginning of the
'Iliad' that the poet, or the Muse for him, is about to
sing the anger of Achilles, with the disasters it brought
down on the Greeks. (15) But these disasters are of
brief continuance, and this anger terminates most prosper-
ously? Another fit of anger, from another motive, less
ungenerous and less selfish, supervenes; and Hector falls
because Patroclus had fallen. (16) The son of Peleus,
whom the poet in the beginning proposed for his hero,
drops suddenly out of sight, abandoning a noble cause from
an ignoble resentment. Milton, in regard to the discon-
tinuity of agency, is in the same predicament as Homer.

  Let us now take him more in detail. He soon begins to
give the learned and less obvious signification to English
words. In the sixth line,

That on the secret top, &c.
[i, 6ff.]

Here *secret* is in the same sense as Virgil's

Secretosque pios, his dantem jura Catonem.

[Far apart, the good, and Cato giving them laws
('Aeneid', viii, 670).]

Would it not have been better to omit the fourth and fifth
verses, as incumbrances, and deadeners of the harmony? -
and for the same reason, the fourteenth, fifteenth, and
sixteenth?

That with no middle flight intends to soar
Above the Aonian mount, while it pursues
Things unattempted yet in prose or rhyme.

Landor. Certainly much better: for the harmony of the
sentence is complete without them, and they make it gasp
for breath.   Supposing the fact to be true, the mention
of it is unnecessary and unpoetical.   Little does it
become Milton to run in debt with Ariosto for his

Cose non dette mai né in prose in rima. (17)

[Things unattempted yet in prose or rhime ('Orlando
Furioso', i, 2, 2 tr T.C.).]

Prosaic enough in a rhymed romance, for such is the
'Orlando' with all its spirit and all its beauty, and far
beneath the dignity of the epic.
Southey. Beside, it interrupts the intensity of the
poet's aspiration in the words,

And chiefly thou, O Spirit!
[i, 17.]

Again: I would rather see omitted the five which follow
that beautiful line,

Dovelike satst brooding on the vast abyss.
[i, 21.]

Landor. The ear, however accustomed to the rhythm of
these sentences, is relieved of a burden by rejecting
them: and they are not wanted for anything they convey.
Southey. I am sorry that Milton (V. 34) did not always

keep separate the sublime Satan and the 'infernal Serpent'.   The thirty-eighth verse is the first hendecasyl-
labic in the poem. (18)   It is much to be regretted, I
think, that he admits this metre into epic poetry.   It is
often very efficient in the dramatic, at least in Shakespeare, but hardly ever in Milton.   He indulges in it much
less fluently in the 'Paradise Lost' than in the 'Paradise
Regained'.   In the seventy-third verse he tells us that
the rebellious angels are

> As far removed from God and light of heaven
> As from the centre thrice to the utmost pole.
> [i, 73-4.]

Not very far for creatures who could have measured all
that distance, and a much greater, by a single act of the
will.
      V. 188 ends with the word *repair*;   191 with *despair*.

> Nor did they not perceive the evil plight
> *In which they were*
> [i, 335-6.]

Landor. We are oftener in such *evil plight* of founder-
ing in the prosaic slough about your neighbourhood than
in Bunhill Fields. (19)

> And Powers that erst in heaven sat on thrones.
> [i, 360.]

Excuse my asking why you, and indeed most poets in most
places, make a monosyllable of *heaven*? (20)   I observe
you treat *spirit* in the same manner;   and although not
peril, yet *perilous*.   I would not insist at all times on
an iambic foot, neither would I deprive these words of
their right to a participation in it.
      Southey. I have seized all fair opportunities of intro-
ducing the tribrachys, (21) and these are the words that
most easily afford one.   I have turned over the leaves as
far as verse 581, where I wish he had written *Damascus·* (as
he does elsewhere) (22) for *Damasco*, which never was the
English appellation.   Beside, he sinks the last vowel in
Meröe in 'Paradise Regained', [iv, 71] which follows;   and
should consistently have done the same in Damasco, following the practice of the Italian poets, which certainly is
better than leaving the vowels open and gaping at one
another.

                    Anon they move
In perfect phalanx to the Dorian mood.
[i, 549-50.]

Thousands of years before there were phalanxes, schools of
music, or Dorians. (23)
    Landor. Never mind the Dorians, but look at Satan:

                    And now his heart
Distends with pride, and, hardening in his strength,
Glories!
[i, 571-3.]

What an admirable pause is here.   I wish he had not ended
one verse with '*his* heart', and the next with '*his*
strength'.
    Southey. What think you of

                    That small infantry
Warred on by cranes.
[i, 575-6.]

    Landor. I think he might easily have turned the flank
of *that small infantry.*   He would have done much better
by writing, not

                    For never since created man
Met such imbodied force as *named with these*
Could merit more than that small infantry
Warred on by cranes, though all the giant-brood, &c.
[i, 573-6ff.]

but leaving behind him also these heavy and unserviceable
tumbrils, it would have been enough to have written,

                    Never since created man,
Met such imbodied force;   though all the brood
Of Phlegra with the Heroic race were joined.

But where, in poetry or painting, shall we find anything
that approaches the sublimity of that description, which
begins v. 589 and ends in v. 620?   What an admirable
pause at

    Tears such as angels weep, burst forth!
    [i, 620.]

    V. 642.   But *tempted* our *attempt.*   Such a play on
words would be unbecoming in the poet's own person, and

even on the lightest subject, but is most injudicious and
intolerable in the mouth of Satan, about to assail the
Almighty.

>   *Undoubted* sign
>   That in *his* womb was hid metallic ore.
>   [i, 672-3.]

I know not exactly which of these words induces you to
raise your eyes above the book and cast them on me: perhaps both.   It was hardly worth his while to display in
this place his knowledge of mineralogy, or his recollection that Virgil, in the wooden horse before Troy, had
said,

>   *Uterumque* armato milite complent.

>   [Fill the huge cavern with armed soldiery ('Aeneid',
>   ii, 20).]

and that some modern poets had followed him.

>   *Southey*.
>   As when bands
>   Of pioneers, with spade and pick-axe armed,
>   Fore-run the royal camp to trench a field
>   Or cast a rampart.
>   [i, 675-8.]

Nothing is gained to the celestial host by comparing it
with the terrestrial.   Angels are not promoted by brigad-
ing with sappers and miners.   Here we are entertained with

>   *Dulcet* symphonies .. and voices *sweet*,
>   [i, 712.]

among 'pilasters ... and *Doric* pillars'.   [i, 713-14.]
V. 745 is that noble one on Vulcan, (24) who

>   Dropt from the zenith like a falling star.

Landor. The six following are quite superfluous.   Instead of stopping where the pause is so natural and so
necessary, he carries the words on,

>   Dropt from the zenith, like a falling star,
>   On Lemnos, the AEgean isle.   Thus they relate,
>   Erring; for he, with this rebellious rout,
>   Fell long before; nor aught avail'd him now

To have built in Heaven high towers, nor did he scape
By all his engines, but was headlong *sent*
With his *industrious* crew to build in hell.
[i, 745-51.]

My good Milton! why in a passion?   If he was sent to
build in hell, and *did* build there, give the Devil his
due, and acknowledge that on this one occasion he ceased
to be rebellious.
   Southey. The verses are insufferable stuff, and would
be ill placed anywhere.
   Landor. Let me remark that in my copy I find a hyphen
before the first letter in *scape.*
   Southey. The same in mine.
   Landor. Scaped is pointed in the same manner at the
beginning of the fourth book.   But Milton took the word
directly from the Italian *scappare*, and committed no muti-
lation.   We do not always think it necessary to make the
sign of an elision in its relatives, as appears by *scape-
grace.*   In v. 752 what we write *herald* he more properly
writes *harald*; in the next *sovran* equally so, following
the Italian rather than the French. (25)
   Southey. At verse 768 we come to a series of twenty
lines, which, excepting the metamorphosis of the Evil
Angels [x, 504ff.] would be delightful in any other situation.   The poem is much better without these.   And in
these verses I think there are two whole ones and two
hemistichs (26) which you would strike out:

                        As bees
In spring-time, when the sun with Taurus rides,
Pour forth their populous youth about the hive
In clusters: they among fresh dews and flowers
Fly to and fro, or on the smoothed plank,
The suburb of their straw-built citadel,
New rubbed with balm, expatiate and confer
Their state affairs.   So thick the aery crowd, &c.
[i, 768-75ff.]

   Landor. I should be sorry to destroy the suburb of the
straw-built citadel, or even to remove the smoothed plank,
if I found them in any other place.   Neither the harmony
of the sentence, nor the propriety and completeness of the
simile, would suffer by removing all between '*to and fro*',
and '*so thick*', &c.   But I wish I had not been called
upon to '*Behold a wonder*' [i, 777]
   Southey. (Book II.)

     High on a throne of royal state, which far

Outshone the wealth of Ormus and of Ind,
Or where the gorgeous east, &c.
[ii, 1-3ff.]

Are not Ormus and Ind within the gorgeous East?   If so,
would not the sense be better if he had written, instead
of '*Or* where', '*There* where'.
Landor. Certainly.
Southey. Turn over, if you please, another two or three
pages, and tell me whether in your opinion the 150th
verse,

In the wide womb of uncreated night,

might not also have been omitted advantageously.
Landor. The sentence is long enough and full enough
without it, and the omission would cause no visible gap.
Southey.

Thus Belial, with words clothed in reason's garb,
Counsel'd *ignoble ease and peaceful sloth,*
Not peace.
[ii, 226-8.]

These words are spoken by the poet in his own person;
very improperly: they would have suited the character of
any fallen angel; but the reporter of the occurrence
ought not to have delivered such a sentence.

Which when Beelzebub perceived (than whom,
Satan except, none higher sat) with grave
Aspect he rose, and in his rising seemed
A pillar of state.   Deep on his front engraven
Deliberation sat and public care;
And princely counsel in his face yet shone
Majestic, though in ruin: sage he stood,
With Atlantean shoulders, fit to bear
The weight of mightiest monarchies.
[ii, 299-307.]

Often and often have these verses been quoted, without a
suspicion how strangely the corporeal is substituted for
the moral.   However Atlantean his shoulders might be, the
weight of monarchies could no more be supported by them
than by the shoulders of a grasshopper. (27)   The verses
are sonorous, but they are unserviceable as an incantation
to make a stout figure look like a pillar of state.
Landor. We have seen pillars of state which made no
figure at all, and which are quite as misplaced as

Milton's.   But seriously;   the pillar's representative,
if any figure but a metaphorical one could represent him,
would hardly be brought to represent the said pillar by
rising up;   as

Beelzebub in his *rising* seem'd, &c.

His fondness for Latinisms induces him to write,

What sit we then projecting peace and war?
[ii, 329.]

For '*Why sit we*'? as *quid* for *cur*.   To my ear
sounds less pleasingly than *why sit*.
I have often wished that Cicero, who so delighted in
harmonious sentences, and was so studious of the closes,
could have heard,

So was his will
Pronounced among the God's, and, by an oath
That shook heaven's whole circumference, confirm'd.
[ii, 351-3.]

Although in the former part of the sentence two cadences
are the same.

So was his will,
And by an oath.

This is unhappy.   But at 412 bursts forth again such a
torrent of eloquence as there is nowhere else in the regions of poetry, although *strict* and *thick*, in v. 412,
sound unpleasantly.

The parching air
Burns frore, *and cold performs the effect of fire!*
[ii, 594-5.]

The latter part of this verse is redundant, and ruinous to
the former.
Southey. Milton, like Dante, has mixed the Greek mythology with the Oriental.   To hinder the damned from tast-
ing a single drop of the *Lethe* they are *ferried* over,

Medusa with Gorgonian terror guards
The ford.
[ii, 611-12.]

It is strange that until now they never had explored the
banks of the other four infernal rivers.

Landor. It appears to me that his imitation of Shakespeare,

> From beds of raging fire to starve in ice, (28)
> [ii, 600.]

is feeble.   Never was poet so little made to imitate another.   Whether he imitates a good or a bad one, the of-
fence of his voluntary degradation is punished in general
with ill success.   Shakespeare, on the contrary, touches
not even a worthless thing but he renders it precious.
    Southey. To continue the last verse I was reading,

> And of itself the water flies
> All taste of living wight, as *once* it fled
> The lip of Tantalus.
> [ii, 612-14.]

No living wight had ever attempted to taste it;   nor was
it *this* water that fled the lip of Tantalus (29) at any
time;   least of all can we imagine that it had already
fled it.   In the description of Sin and Death, and
Satan's interview with them, [ii, 648-870] there is a
wonderful vigour of imagination and of thought, with such
sonorous verse as Milton alone was capable of composing.
But there is also much of what is odious and intolerable.
The terrific is then sublime, and then only, when it fixes
you in the midst of all your energies, and not when it
weakens, nauseates, and repels you.

> God and his son except,
> Created thing nought valued he.
> [ii, 678-9.]

This is not the only time when he has used such language,
evidently with no other view than to defend it by his
scholarship.   But no authority can vindicate what is
false, and no ingenuity can explain what is absurd.   You
have remarked it already in the 'Imaginary Conversations',
referring to

> *The fairest of her daughters, Eve*. (30)
> [iv, 324.]

Landor. I must now be the reader.   It is impossible to
refuse the ear its satisfaction at

> Thus roving on

In confused march forlorn, the adventurous bands
With shuddering horror pale and eyes aghast,
View'd first their lamentable lot, and found
No rest.   Through many a dark and dreary vale
They past, and many a region dolorous;
O'er many a frozen, many a fiery Alp,
Rocks, caves, lakes, fens, bogs, dens, and shades of
                                        death,
A universe of death.
[ii, 614-22.]

Now who would not rather have forfeited an estate, than
that Milton should have ended so deplorably,

            Which God by curse
Created evil, *for evil only good,*
Where all life dies, death lives.
[ii, 622-4.]

Southey. How Ovidian!   This book would be greatly improved, not merely by the rejection of a couple such as
these, but by the whole from verse 647 to verse 1007. (31)
The number would still be 705;   fewer by only sixty-four
than the first would be after its reduction.
    Verses 1008 and 1009 could be spared.   Satan but
little encouraged his followers by reminding them that, if
they took the course he pointed out, they were

    So much the nearer danger,

nor was it necessary to remind them of the obvious fact by
saying,

    Havoc and spoil and ruin are my gain. (32)

Landor. In the third book the Invocation extends to
fifty-five verses;   of these however there are only two
which you would expunge.   He says to the 'Holy Light',

                    But thou
Revisit'st not these eyes, that roll in vain
To find thy piercing ray, and find no dawn,
So thick a *drop serene* hath quencht their orbs,
Or dim suffusion veiled.   Yet not the more, &c.
[iii, 22-6ff.]

The fantastical Latin expression *gutta serena,* (33) for
amaurosis, was never received under any form into our
language, and a *thick drop serene* would be nonsense in
any.   I think every reader would be contented with

To find thy piercing ray.   Yet not the more
Cease I to wander where the Muses haunt, &c.

Southey. Pope is not highly reverent to Milton, or to
God the Father, whom he calls a *school divine*. (34)   The
doctrines, in this place (V. 80) more scripturally than
poetically laid down, are apostolic.   But Pope was un-
likely to know it; for while he was a papist he was forbidden to read the Holy Scriptures, and when he ceased to
be a papist, he threw them overboard and clung to nothing.
The fixedness of his opinions may be estimated by his
having written at the commencement of his 'Essay', first

A mighty maze, a maze without a plan, (35)
['Essay on Man', i, 1, 6.]

And then,

A mighty maze, *but not* without a plan. (36)

After the seventy-sixth verse I wish the poet had abstained from writing all the rest until we come to 345:   and
that after the 382d from all that precede the 418th.
Again, all between 462 and 497.   This about the Fool's
Paradise,

Indulgences, dispenses, pardons, bulls,
[iii, 492.]

is too much in the manner of Dante, whose poetry, admirable as it often is, is at all times very far removed from
the dramatic and the epic.
Landor. Verse 586 is among the few inharmonious in this
poem.

Shoots invisible virtue even to the deep.

There has lately sprung up among us a Vulcan-descended
body of splay-foot poets, who, unwilling

Incudi reddere versus,

[To return the verses to the anvil (Horace, 'Ars
Poetica', 441).]

or unable to hammer them into better shape and more solidity, tell us how necessary it is to shovel in the dust of
a discord now and then.   But Homer and Sophocles and
Virgil could do without it.

What a beautiful expression is there in v. 546, which I
do not remember that any critic has noticed,

Obtains the brow of some *high-climbing* hill.

Here the hill itself is instinct with life and activity.
    V. 574.   '*But up or down*' in '*longitude*' are not worth
the parenthesis.

Farewell remorse! all good to me is lost.
[iv, 109.]

Nothing more surprises me in Milton than that his ear
should have endured this verse.
    Southey. How admirably contrasted with the malignant
spirit of Satan, in all its intensity, is the scene of
Paradise which opens at verse 131.   The change comes
naturally and necessarily to accomplish the order of
events.
    The Fourth Book contains several imperfections.   The
six verses after 181 efface the delightful impression we
had just received.

At one slight *bound* high overleapt all *bound*.

Such a play on words, so grave a pun, is unpardonable;
and such a prodigious leap is ill represented by the feat
of a wolf in a sheepfold;   and still worse by

        A thief bent to unhoard the *cash*
Of some rich burgher, whose substantial doors,
Cross-barr'd and bolted fast, fear no assault,
In at the window climbs, or o'er the tiles.
[iv, 188-91.]

Landor. This 'in at the window' is very unlike the
'bound high above all bound': and *climbing* 'o'er the
tiles' is the practice of a more deliberate burglar.

So since into his church lewd hirelings climb.
[iv, 193.]

I must leave the lewd hirelings where I find them;
they are too many for me.   I would gladly have seen omitted all between v. 160 and 205.

Southey.

Betwixt them lawns or level downs, and flocks
Grazing the tender herb.
[iv, 252.]

There had not yet been time for flocks, or even for one
flock.
Landor. At two hundred and ninety-seven commences a
series of verses so harmonious, that my ear is impatient
of any other poetry for several days after I have read
them.   I mean those which begin,

For contemplation he and valour formed,
For softness she and sweet attractive grace,

and ending with,

And sweet, reluctant, amorous, delay.
[iv, 297-311.]

Southey. Here indeed is the triumph of our language,
and I should say of our poetry, if, in your preference of
Shakespeare, you could endure my saying it.   But, since
we seek faults rather than beauties this morning, tell me
whether you are quite contented with,

She, as a veil, down to the slender waist
Her unadorned golden tresses wore,
Dishevel'd, but in wanton ringlets waved
As the vine curls her tendrils; *which implied*
Subjection, but required with gentle sway,
And by her yielded, by him best received.
[iv, 304-9.]

Landor. Stopping there, you break the link of harmony
just above the richest jewel that Poetry ever wore:

Yielded with coy submission, modest pride,
And sweet, reluctant, amorous, delay.
[iv, 310-11.]

I would rather have written these two lines than all
the poetry that has been written since Milton's time in
all the regions of the earth.   We shall see again things
equal in their way to the best of them: but here the
sweetest of images and sentiments is seized and carried
far away from all pursuers.   Never tell me, what I think
is already on your lips, that the golden tresses in their
wanton ringlets implied nothing like subjection....

Southey. It is very amusing to read Johnson for his
notions of harmony. (37)   He quotes these exquisite
verses, and says, 'There are two lines in this passage
more remarkably inharmonious'. (38)

> This delicious place,
> For us too large, *where thy* abundance wants
> Partakers, and uncropt *falls to* the ground.
> [iv, 729-31.]

There are few so dull as to be incapable of perceiving the
beauty of the rhythm in the last.   Johnson goes out of
his way to censure the best thought and the best verse in
Cowley. (39)

> And the soft wings of Peace *cover him* round.
> ['Virgil's 'Georgics', Lib. II, A Translation', l. 16.]

Certainly it is not iambic where he wishes it to be.
Milton, like the Italian poets, was rather too fond of
this cadence, but in the instances which Johnson has
pointed out for reprobation, it produces a fine effect.
So in the verse

> Not Typhon huge, ending in snaky twine.
> ['On the Morning of Christ's Nativity', l. 226.]

It does the same in Samson Agonistes:

> Retiring from the popular noise, I seek
> This unfrequented place, to find some ease,
> Ease to the body some, *none* to the mind.
> [ll. 16-18.]

Johnson tells us that the third and seventh are weak syllables, and that the period leaves the ear unsatis-
fied. (40)   Milton's ear happened to be satisfied by
these pauses;   and so will any ear be that is not (or was
not intended by nature to be) nine fair inches long.
Johnson is sensible of the harmony which is produced by
the pause on the sixth syllable;   but commends it for no
better reason than because it forms a complete verse of
itself. (41)   There can be no better reason against it.
    In regard to the pause at the third syllable, it is
very singular and remarkable that Milton never has paused
for three lines together on any other.   In the 327th,
328th, and 329th of 'Paradise Lost' are these.

> His swift pursuers from heaven's gates discern

The advantage, and descending tread us down,
Thus drooping, or with linked thunderbolts
Transfix us to the bottom of this gulf.
[i, 326-9.]

Another, whose name I have forgotten, has censured in
like manner the defection and falling off in the seventh
syllable of that very verse, which I remember your quoting
as among the innumerable proofs of the poet's exquisite
sensibility and judgment,

And toward the gate *rolling* her bestial train,
[ii, 873.]

where another would have written

And rolling toward the gate, &c.

On the same occasion you praised Thomson very highly for
having once written a most admirable verse where an ordinary one was obvious.

And tremble [shiver] every feather with desire.
[Spring, 'The Seasons', l. 630.]

Pope would certainly have preferred

And every feather trembles with desire.

So would Dryden probably. Johnson, who censures some of
the most beautiful lines in Milton, praises one in Virgil
with as little judgment. He says, 'We hear the passing
arrow' (42)

Et fugit *horrendum stridens* elapsa sagitta.

[With awful whirr speeds forth the tight-drawn shaft
('Aeneid', ix, 632).]

Now there never was an arrow in the world that made a
horrible stridor in its course. The only sound is a very
slight one occasioned by the feather. Homer would never
have fallen into such an incongruity.
How magnificent is the close of this fourth book, from,

Then when I am thy captive.
[iv, 970.]

Landor. I do not agree to the use of golden scales, not

figurative but real jewellers' gold, for weighing events,

> *Battles* and realms.   In these he put two *weights,*
> The sequel each of parting and of fight;
> The latter *quick* up-flew and *kicked* the beam.
> [iv, 1002-4.]

To pass over the slighter objection of *quick* and *kick* as displeasing to the ear, the vulgarity of *kicking the beam* is intolerable: he might as well, among his angels, and among sights and sounds befitting them, talk of *kicking the bucket.*   Here again he pays a penalty for trespassing.

Southey. I doubt whether (Fifth Book) there ever was a poet in a warm or temperate climate, who at some time or other of his life has not written about the nightingale. But no one rivals or approaches Milton in his fondness or his success.   However, at the beginning of this book, in a passage full of beauty, there are two expressions, and the first of them relates to the nightingale, which I disapprove,

> Tunes sweetest his *love-laboured* song.
> [v, 41.]

In *love-laboured,* the ear is gained over by the sweetness of the sound: but in the nightingale's song there is neither the reality nor the appearance of labour.

> *Sets off* the face of things.
> [v, 43.]

is worthier of Addison than of Milton.

> But know that in the soul, &c.
> [v, 100ff.]

This philosophy on dreams, expounded by Adam, could never have been hitherto the fruit of his experience or his reflection.
Landor.

> These are thy glorious works, &c.
> [v, 153ff.]

Who could imagine that Milton, who translated the Psalms worse than any man ever translated them before or since, should in this glorious hymn have made the 148th so much better than the original? (43)   But there is a wide dif-

ference between being bound to the wheels of a chariot and
guiding it.   He has ennobled that more noble one,

O all ye works of the Lord, &c.

But in

Ye mists and exhalations that now rise
From hill or steaming lake, dusky or gray,
Till the sun *paint* your fleecy skirts with *gold*, &c.
[v, 185-7ff.]

Such a verse might be well ejected from any poem whatsoever: but here its prettiness is quite insufferable.
Adam never knew anything either of paint or gold.   But,
casting out this devil of a verse, surely so beautiful a
psalm or hymn never rose to the Creator.
Southey. 'No fear lest dinner cool', v. 396, might as
well never have been thought of: it seems a little too
jocose.   The speech of Raphael to Adam, on the subject of
eating and drinking and the consequences [v, 404-33], is
neither angelic nor poetical: but the Sun *supping* with
the Ocean [v, 423-6] is at least Anacreontic, and not very
much debased by Cowley. (44)

So *down they sat*
And to their viands *fell*.
[v, 433-4.]

Landor.

Meanwhile the eternal eye, whose sight discerns
Abstrusest thoughts, from forth his holy mount
And from within the golden lamps that burn
Nightly before him, saw without their light
Rebellion rising, &c.
And smiling to his only son thus said, &c.
[v, 711-15ff., 718ff.]

Bentley, and several such critics of poetry, are sadly
puzzled, perplexed, and irritated at this. (45)   One
would take refuge with the first grammar he can lay hold
on, and cry *pars pro toto*: (46)   another strives hard for
another suggestion.   But if Milton by accident had written both *Eternal* and *Eye* with a capital letter at the beginning, they would have perceived that he had used a
noble and sublime expression for the Deity.   No one is
offended at the words, 'It is the will of Providence', or,
'It is the will of the Almighty'; yet Providence is that

which *sees before;* and *will* is different from *might.*
True it is that Providence and Almighty are qualities converted into appellations, and are well known to signify
the Supreme Being: but, if the Eternal Eye is less well
known to signify him, or not known at all, that is no
reason why it should be thought inapplicable. It might
be used injudiciously: for instance, the *right hand* of
the Eternal Eye would be singularly so; but *smiles* not.
The Eternal Eye *speaks* to his only Son. This is more in-
comprehensible to the critics than the preceding. And
truly if that eye were like ours, and the organ of speech
like ours also, it might be strange. Yet the very same
good people have often heard without wonder of a *speaking*
eye in a very ordinary person, and are conversant with
poets who precede an expostulation, or an entreaty for a
reply, with 'Lux mea'. (47) There is a much greater
fault, which none of them has observed, in the beginning
of the speech.

Son! thou in whom my glory I behold
In full resplendence! *heir* of all my might.
[v, 719-20.]

Now an *heir* is the future and not the present possessor;
and he to whom he is heir must be extinct before he comes
into possession. But this is nothing if you compare it
with what follows, a few lines below:

Let us advise and to this hazard draw
With speed what force is left, and all employ
In our defence, *lest unawares we lose*
This our high place, our sanctuary, our hill.
[v, 729-32.]

Such expressions of derision are very ill applied, and
derogate much from the majesty of the Father. We may
well imagine that far different thoughts occupied the
Divine Mind at the defection of innumerable angels, and
their inevitable and everlasting punishment....

Landor.... Beautiful as are many parts of the Invocation at the commencement of the Seventh Book, I should
more gladly have seen it without the first forty lines,
and beginning,

The affable archangel.
[vii, 41.]

Southey.

> But knowledge is as food, and needs no less
> Her temperance over appetite.
> [vii, 126-7.]

He might have ended here: he goes on thus:

>   To know
> In measure what the mind may well contain.
> [vii, 127-8.]

Even this does not satisfy him: he adds,

> Oppresses else with surfeit, and soon turns
> Wisdom to folly, as *nourishment to wind.*
> [vii, 129-30.]

Now certainly Adam could never yet have known anything
about the meaning of surfeit, and we may suspect that the
angel himself must have been just as ignorant on a section
of physics which never had existed in the world below, and
must have been without analogy in the world above.
    Landor. His supper with Adam was unlikely to produce a
surfeit.

> *At least* our envious foe hath fail'd.
> [vii, 139.]

There is no meaning in *at least;* 'at *last*' would be
little better.   I would not be captious nor irreverent;
but surely the words which Milton gives as spoken by the
Father to the Son, bear the appearance of boastfulness
and absurdity.   The Son must already have known both the
potency and will of the Father.   How incomparably more
judicious, after five terrific verses, comes at once,
without any intervention,

> Silence, ye troubled waves! and thou, deep, peace.
> [vii, 216.]

If we can imagine any thought or expression at all worthy
of the Deity, we find it here.   In v. 242 we have another
specimen of Milton's consummate art:

> And earth, self-balanced, on her centre hung.

Unhappily he permitted his learning to render him verbose
immediately after:

Let there be light, said God, and forthwith light
Ethereal, first of things, quintessence pure,
Sprung from the deep.
[vii, 243-5.]

The intermediate verse is useless and injurious; beside,
according to his own account, light was not 'first of
things'. He represents it springing from 'the deep'
after the earth had 'hung on her centre', and long after
the waters had been apparent. We do not want philosophy
in the poem, we only want consistency.

Southey. There is no part of Milton's poetry where harmony is preserved, together with conciseness, so remarkably as in the verses beginning with 313, and ending at
338: but in the midst of this beautiful description of
the young earth, we find

And bush with *frizzled* hair *implicit*.
[vii, 323.]

But what poet or painter ever in an equal degree has
raised our admiration of beasts, fowls, and fish? I know
you have objected to the repetition of *shoal* in the word
scull.

Landor. Shoal is a corruption of *scull*, which ought to
be restored, serving the other with an ejectment to another place. Nor do I like *fry*. (48) But the birds
never looked so beautiful since they left Paradise. Let
me read however three or four verses in order to offer a
remark.

Others, on silver lakes and rivers, bathed
Their downy breast: the swan with arched neck
Between her white wings mantling proudly, rows
Her state with oary feet, yet oft they quit
The dank, and rising on stiff pennons, tower, &c.
[vii, 437-41ff.]

Frequently as the great poet pauses at the ninth syllable,
it is incredible that he should have done it thrice in the
space of five verses. For which reason, and as nothing
is to be lost by it, I would place the comma after *mantling*. No word in the whole compass of our language has
been so often ill applied or misunderstood by the poet as
this.

Southey.

Speed to describe whose swiftness number fails.
[viii, 38.]

Adam could have had no notion of swiftness in the
heavenly bodies or the earth: it is among the latest and
most wonderful of discoveries.
   Landor. Let us rise to Eve, and throw aside our alge-
bra.   The great poet is always greatest at this beatific
vision.   I wish however he had omitted the 46th and 47th
verses, and also the 60th, 61st, 62nd, and 63d.   There is
a beautiful irregularity in the 62d,

And from about her shot darts of desire

But when he adds, 'Into *all* eyes' [viii, 63], as there
were but four, we must except the angel's two: the angel
had no occasion for wishing to see what he was seeing.

        He his fabric of the heavens
   Hath left to their disputes, *perhaps to move*
   His laughter.
   [viii, 76-8.]

I can not well entertain this opinion of the Creator's
risible faculties and propensities.   Milton here carries
his anthropomorphism much farther than the poem (which
needed a good deal of it) required....

   Southey. We are come to the Ninth Book, ...

   Landor....   But although we met together for the purpose of plucking out the weeds and briars of this boundless and most glorious garden, and not of overlauding the
praises of others, we must admire the wonderful skill of
Milton in this section of his work.   He represents Eve
as beginning to be deceitful and audacious; as ceasing to
fear, and almost as ceasing to reverence the Creator; and
shuddering not at extinction itself, until she thinks

   And Adam wedded to another Eve.
   [ix, 828.]

   Southey. We shall lose our dinner, our supper, and our
sleep, if we expatiate on the innumerable beauties of the
volume: we have scarcely time to note the blemishes.
Among these,

           In her face excuse
   Came prologue and apology to prompt.
   [ix, 853-4.]

There is a levity and impropriety in thus rushing on the stage.   I think the vv. 957, 958, and 959, superfluous, and somewhat dull; beside that they are the repetition of 915 and 916, in his [Adam] soliloquy.
    Landor. I wish that after 1003,

Wept at completing of the mortal sin,

every verse were omitted, until we reach the 1121st.

They sat them down to weep.

A very natural sequence.   We should indeed lose some fine poetry; in which however there are passages which even the sanctitude of Milton is inadequate to veil decorously. At all events, we should get fairly rid of 'Herculean Samson' [ix, 1060].
    Southey. But you would also lose such a flood of harmony as never ran on earth beyond that Paradise.   I mean,

                    How shall I behold the face
    Henceforth of God or angel, erst with joy
    And rapture so oft beheld?   Those heavenly shapes
    Will dazzle now this earthly with their blaze,
    Insufferably bright.   O! might I here
    In solitude live savage! in some glade
    Obscured, where highest woods, impenetrable
    To star or sunlight, spread their umbrage broad
    And brown as evening.   Cover me, ye pines,
    Ye cedars, with innumerable boughs,
    Hide me, where I may never see them more.
    [ix, 1080-90.]

    Landor. Certainly, when we read these verses, the ear is closed against all others, for the day, or even longer. It sometimes is a matter of amusement to hear the sillinesses of good men conversing on poetry; but when they lift up some favourite on their shoulders, and tell us to look at one equal in height to Milton, I feel strongly inclined to scourge the more prominent fool of the two, the moment I can discover which it is.
    Southey.

Long they sat, as *strucken mute*.
    [ix, 1064.]

Stillingfleet says, 'This vulgar expression may owe its origin to the stories, in Romances, of the effect of the magical wand'. (49)   Nothing more likely.   How many

modes of speech are called vulgar, in a contemptuous
sense, which, because of their propriety and aptitude,
strike the senses of all who hear them, and remain in the
memory during the whole existence of the language. This
is one, and although of daily parlance, it is highly
poetical, and among the few flowers of romance that retain
their freshness and odour....

   Landor.... How divinely beautiful is the next passage! It is impossible not to apply to Milton himself
the words he has attributed to Eve:

                              From thee
   How shall I part? and whither wander down
   Into a lower world?
   [xi, 281-3.]

My ear, I confess it, is dissatisfied with everything, for
days and weeks after the harmony of 'Paradise Lost'.
Leaving this magnificent temple, I am hardly to be paci-
fied by the fairy-built chambers, the rich cupboards of
embossed plate, and the omnigenous images of Shakespeare....

   Landor....

                     Sea covered sea,
   Sea without shore.
   [xi, 749-50.]

This is very sublime: and indeed I could never heartily
join with those who condemn in Ovid

   Omnia pontus erant; deerant quoque litora ponto. (50)

   [All is sea, but a sea without a shore ('Metamorphoses', i, 292).]

It is true, the whole fact is stated in the first hemi-
stych; but the mind's eye moves from the centre to the
circumference, and the pleonasm carries it into infinity.
If there is any fault in this passage of Ovid, Milton has
avoided it, but he frequently falls into one vastly more
than Ovidian, and after so awful a pause as is nowhere
else in all the regions of poetry.

   How didst thou grieve then, Adam, to behold

> The end of all thy offspring! end so sad!
> Depopulation!
> > *Thee another flood,*
> *Of tears and sorrow a flood, thee also drowned,*
> *And sunk thee as thy sons.*
> [xi, 754-8.]

It is wonderful how little reflection on many occasions, and how little knowledge on some very obvious ones, is displayed by Bentley. To pass over his impudence in pretending to correct the words of Milton (whose handwriting was extant) just as he would the corroded or corrupt text of any ancient author, here in vv. 894-5. 'To drown the world, / With man therein, or *beast*'; he tells us that *birds are forgot,* and would substitute 'With man or beast or *fowl*'. (51) He might as well have said that *fleas* and *forgot*. Beast means everything that is not man. It would be much more sensible to object to such an expression as *men and animals,* and to ask, are not men animals? and even more so than the rest, if *anima* has with men a more extensive meaning than with other creatures. Bentley in many things was very acute; but his criticisms on poetry produce the same effect as the water of a lead mine on plants. He knew no more about it than Hallam knows, (52) in whom acuteness is certainly not blunted by such a weight of learning.

Southey. We open the Twelfth Book: we see land at last.

Landor. Yes, and dry land too. Happily the twelfth is the shortest. In a continuation of six hundred and twenty-five flat verses, we are prepared for our passage over several such deserts of almost equal extent, and still more frequent, in 'Paradise Regained'. But at the close of the poem now under our examination, there is a brief union of the sublime and the pathetic for about twenty lines, beginning with 'All in bright array' [xii, 627ff.]

We are comforted by the thought that Providence had not abandoned our first parents, but was still their guide; that, although they had lost Paradise, they were not debarred from Eden; that, although the angel had left them solitary and sorrowing, he left them 'yet in peace' [xi, 117.] The termination is proper and complete.

In Johnson's estimate I do not perceive the unfairness of which many have complained. (53) Among his first observations is this: 'Scarcely any recital is wished shorter for the sake of quickening the [progress of the] main action'. (54) This is untrue: were it true, why remark, as he does subsequently, that the poem is mostly read as a duty; not as a pleasure. (55)   I think it unnecessary to say a word on the moral or the subject; for it requires no genius to select a grand one.   The heaviest poems may be appended to the loftiest themes.   Andreini (56) and others, whom Milton turned over and tossed aside, are evidences.   It requires a large stock of patience to travel through Vida; (57) and we slacken in our march, although accompanied with the livelier singsong of Sannazar. (58) Let any reader, who is not by many degrees more pious than poetical, be asked whether he felt a very great interest in the greatest actors of 'Paradise Lost', in what is either said or done by the angels or the Creator; and whether the humblest and weakest does not most attract him.   Johnson's remarks on the allegory of Milton are just and wise; (59)   so are those on the non-materiality or non-immateriality of Satan. (60)   These faults might have been easily avoided: but Milton, with all his strength, chose rather to make Antiquity his shield-bearer, and to come forward under a protection which he might proudly have disdained.

Southey. You will not countenance the critic, nor Dryden whom he quotes, in saying that Milton 'saw Nature, ... *through the spectacles of books*'. (61)

Landor. Unhappily both he and Dryden saw Nature from between the houses of Fleet-street.   If ever there was a poet who knew her well, and described her in all her loveliness, it was Milton.   In the 'Paradise Lost' how profuse in his descriptions, as became the time and place! in the 'Allegro' and 'Penseroso', how exquisite and select!

Johnson asks, 'What Englishman can take delight in transcribing passages, which, if they lessen the reputation of Milton, diminish in some degree the honour of our country?' (62)   I hope the honour of our country will always rest on truth and justice.   It is not by concealing what is wrong that anything right can be accomplished. There is no pleasure in transcribing such passages, but there is great utility.   Inferior writers exercise no interest, attract no notice, and serve no purpose.   Johnson has himself done great good by exposing great faults in great authors.   His criticism on Milton's highest work is the most valuable of all his writings.   He seldom is erroneous in his censures, but he never is sufficiently excited to admiration of what is purest and highest in poetry.   He has this in common with common minds (from which however his own is otherwise far remote), to be pleased with what is nearly on a level with him, and to drink as contentedly a heady beverage with its discoloured froth, as what is of the best vintage.   He is morbid, not only in his weakness, but in his strength.   There is much

to pardon, much to pity, much to respect, and no little to
admire in him.

After I have been reading the 'Paradise Lost', I can
take up no other poet with satisfaction.   I seem to have
left the music of Handel for the music of the streets, or
at best for drums and fifes.   Although in Shakespeare
there are occasional bursts of harmony no less sublime,
yet, if there were many such in continuation, it would be
hurtful, not only in comedy, but also in tragedy.   The
greater part should be equable and conversational.   For,
if the excitement were the same at the beginning, the
middle, and the end; if consequently (as must be the
case) the language and versification were equally elevated
throughout; any long poem would be a bad one, and, worst
of all, a drama.   In our English heroic verse, such as
Milton has composed it, there is a much greater variety of
fact, of movement, of musical notes and bars, than in the
Greek heroic; and the final sounds are incomparably more
diversified.   My predilection in youth was on the side of
Homer; for I had read the 'Iliad' twice, and the 'Odyssea' once, before the 'Paradise Lost'.   Averse as I am to
everything relating to theology, and especially to the
view of it thrown open by this poem, I recur to it incessantly as the noblest specimen in the world of eloquence,
harmony, and genius.

Southey. Learned and sensible men are of opinion that
the 'Paradise Lost' should have ended with the words
'Providence their guide' [xii, 647]. (63)   It might very
well have ended there; but we are unwilling to lose sight
all at once of our first parents.   Only one more glimpse
is allowed us [xii, 648-9] we are thankful for it.   We
have seen the natural tears they dropped; we have seen
that they wiped them *soon* [xii, 645].   And why was it?
Not because the world was all before them, but because
there still remained for them, under the guidance of Providence, not indeed the delights of Paradise, now lost for
ever, but the genial clime and calm repose of Eden.

Landor. It has been the practice in late years to sup-
plant one dynasty by another, political and poetical.
Within our own memory no man had ever existed who preferred Lucretius, on the whole, to Virgil, or Dante to Homer.
But the great Florentine, in these days, is extolled high
above the Grecian and Milton.   Few, I believe, have studied him more attentively or with more delight than I have;
but beside the prodigious disproportion of the bad to the
good, there are fundamental defects which there are not in
either of the other two.   In the 'Divina Commedia' the
characters are without any bond of union, any field of
action, any definite aim.   There is no central light

above the Bolge; (64) and we are chilled in Paradise even
at the side of Beatrice.

Southey. Some poetical Perillus (65) must surely have
invented the *terza rima*.   I feel in reading it as a
school-boy feels when he is beaten over the head with a
bolster.

Landor. We shall hardly be in time for dinner.   What
should we have been if we had repeated with just eulogies
all the noble things in the poem we have been reading?

Southey. They would never have weaned you from the
Mighty Mother who placed her turreted crown on the head of
Shakespeare.

Landor. A rib of Shakespeare would have made a Milton:
the same portion of Milton, all poets born ever since.

SOUTHEY AND LANDOR
SECOND CONVERSATION

Landor. I do not believe that anything short of your
friendship would induce me to read a third time during my
life the 'Paradise Regained': and I now feel my misfor-
tune and imprudence in having given to various friends
this poem and many others, in which I had marked with a
pencil the faults and beauties.   The dead level lay wide
and without a fingerpost: the highest objects appeared,
with few exceptions, no higher or more ornamental than
bulrushes.   We shall spend but little time in repeating
all the passages where they occur, and it will be a great
relief to us.   Invention, energy, and grandeur of design,
the three great requisites to constitute a great poet, and
which no poet since Milton hath united, are wanting here.
Call the design a grand one, if you will; you can not
however call it his.   Wherever there are thought, imagination, and energy, grace invariably follows; otherwise
the colossus would be without its radiance, and we should
sail by with wonder and astonishment, and gather no roses
and gaze at no images on the sunny isle.

Southey. Shakespeare, whom you not only prefer to every
other poet, but think he contains more poetry and more
wisdom than all the rest united, is surely less grand in
his designs than several.

Landor. To the eye.   But 'Othello' was loftier than
the citadel of *Troy*; and what a 'Paradise' fell before
him!   Let us descend; for from 'Othello' we *must* descend, whatever road we take; let us look at 'Julius
Caesar'.   No man ever overcame such difficulties, or produced by his life and death such a change in the world we
inhabit.   But that also is a grand design which displays

the interior workings of the world within us, and where we
see the imperishable and unalterable passions depicted *al
fresco* on a lofty dome.   Our other dramatists painted
only on the shambles, and represented what they found
there; blood and garbage.   We leave them a few paces behind us, and step over the gutter into the green-market.
There are however men rising up among us endowed with ex-
quisiteness of taste and intensity of thought.   At no time
have there been so many who write well in so many ways.

   Southey. Have you taken breath? and are you ready to go
on with me?

   Landor. More than ready, alert.   For we see before us
a longer continuation of good poetry than we shall find
again throughout the whole poem, beginning at verse 153,
and terminating at 224.   In these however there are some
bad verses, such as

> Among daughters of men the fairest found,
> ....
> And made him bow to the gods of his wives.
> ['Paradise Regained', ii, 154, 171.]

V. 180,

> Cast wanton eyes on the daughters of men,

is false grammar; 'thou *cast* for thou *castedst*'.   I find
the same fault where I am as much surprised to find it, in
Shelley.

> Thou lovest, but ne'er *knew* love's sad satiety.
> ['To a Skylark', l. 80.]

Shelley in his 'Cenci' has overcome the greatest difficulty that ever was overcome in poetry, although he has not
risen to the greatest elevation. (66)   He possesses less
vigour than Byron, and less command of language than
Keats; but I would rather have written his

> Music, when soft voices die,
> ['To ———', l. 1.]

than all that Beaumont and Fletcher ever wrote, together
with all of their contemporaries, excepting Shakespeare. (67) ...

   Landor. Milton took but little time in forming the plan
of his 'Paradise Regained', doubtful and hesitating as he

had been in the construction of 'Paradise Lost'.   In composing a poem or any other work of imagination, although
it may be well and proper to lay down a plan, I doubt
whether any author of any durable work has confined himself to it very strictly.   But writers will no more tell
you whether they do or not, than they will bring out before you the foul copies, or than painters will admit you
into the secret of composing or of laying on their colours.   I confess to you that a few detached thoughts and
images have always been the beginnings of my works.
Narrow slips have risen up, more or fewer, above the surface.   These gradually became larger and more consolida-
ted: freshness and verdure first covered one part, then
another;   then plants of firmer and of higher growth,
however scantily, took their places, then extended their
roots and branches;   and among them and round about them
in a little while you yourself, and as many more as I
desired, found places for study and for recreation.

     Returning to 'Paradise Regained'.   If a loop in the
netting of a purse is let down, it loses the money that is
in it;   so a poem by laxity drops the weight of its contents.   In the animal body, not only nerves and juices
are necessary, but also continuity and cohesion.   Milton
is caught sleeping after his exertions in 'Paradise Lost',
and the lock of his strength is shorn off; (68) but here
and there a prominent muscle swells out from the vast mass
of the collapsed.

     Southey. The 'Samson Agonistes', now before us, is less
languid, but it may be charged with almost the heaviest
fault of a poem, or indeed of any composition, particularly the dramatic, which is, there is insufficient coheren-
cy, or dependence of part on part.   Let us not complain
that, while we look at Samson and hear his voice, we are
forced to think of Milton, of his blindness, of his abandonment, with as deep a commiseration.   If we lay open
the few faults covered by his transcendant excellencies,
we feel confident that none are more willing (or would be
more acceptable were he present) to pay him homage.   I
retain all my admiration of his poetry;   you all yours,
not only of his poetry, but of his sentiments on many
grave subjects....

     Southey. Passing Milton's oversights, we next notice
his systematic defects.   Fondness for Euripides made him
too didactic when action was required.   Perhaps the
French drama kept him in countenance, although he seems to
have paid little attention to it, comparatively.
     Landor. The French drama contains some of the finest

didactic poetry in the world, and is peculiarly adapted
both to direct the reason and to control the passions.
It is a well-lighted saloon of graceful eloquence, where
the sword-knot is appended by the hand of Beauty, and
where the snuff-box is composed of such brilliants as,
after a peace or treaty, kings bestow on diplomatists.
Whenever I read a French alexandrine, I fancy I receive a
box on the ear in the middle of it, and another at the
end, sufficient, if not to pain, to weary me intolerably,
and to make the book drop out of my hand. Molière and La
Fontaine (69) can alone by their homoeopathy revive me.
Such is the power of united wit and wisdom, in ages the
most desperate!   These men, with Montaigne and
Charron, (70) will survive existing customs, and probably
existing creeds.   Millions will be captivated by them,
when the eloquence of Bossuet (71) himself shall interest
extremely few.   Yet the charms of language are less liable to be dissipated by time than the sentences of
wisdom.   While the incondite volumes of more profound
philosophers are no longer in existence, scarcely one of
writers who enjoyed in a high degree the gift of eloquence, is altogether lost.   Among the Athenians there
are indeed some, but in general they were worthless men,
squabbling on worthless matters: we have little to
regret, excepting of Phocion and of Pericles. (72)   If we
turn to Rome, we retain all the best of Cicero; and we
patiently and almost indifferently hear that nothing is to
be found of Marcus Antonius or Hortensius; (73) for the
eloquence of the bar is, and ought always to be, secondary.

Southey. You were remarking that our poet paid little
attention to the French drama.   Indeed in his preface (74) he takes no notice of it whatsoever, not even as
regards the plot, in which consists its chief excellence,
or perhaps I should say rather its superiority.   He holds
the opinion that 'a [the] plot, whether intricate or explicit [which] is nothing [indeed] but such economy, or
disposition of the fable, as may stand best with verisim-
ilitude and decorum'. (75)   Surely the French tragedians
have observed this doctrine attentively.

Landor. It has rarely happened that dramatic events
have followed one another in their natural order.   The
most remarkable instance of it is in the 'King OEdipus' of
Sophocles.   But Racine (76) is in general the most skilful of the tragedians, with little energy and less invention.   I wish Milton had abstained from calling 'AEschylus, Sophocles, and Euripides, the three tragick poets
unequalled *yet* by any'; (77) because it may leave a suspicion that he fancied he, essentially undramatic, could

equal them, and had now done it; and because it exhibits
him as a detractor from Shakespeare.   I am as sorry to
find him in this condition as I should have been to find
him in a fit of the gout, or treading on a nail with naked
foot in his blindness.

Southey. Unfortunately it is impossible to exculpate
him; for you must have remarked where, a few sentences
above, are those expressions.   'This is mentioned to vindicate [tragedy] from the *small esteem, or rather infamy,*
which in the account of many, it undergoes at this day,
with other common interludes; happening through the
poet's error of intermixing *comick stuff with tragick sadness and gravity;* or intermixing [introducing] trivial
and vulgar persons, which, by all judicious, hath been
counted absurd, and brought in without discretion, cor-
ruptly to gratify the people'. (78)

Landor. It may be questioned whether the people in the
reign of Elizabeth, (79) or indeed the queen herself,
would have been contented with a drama without a smack of
the indecent or the ludicrous.   They had alike been accustomed to scenes of ribaldry and of bloodshed; and the
palace opened on one wing to the brothel, on the other to
the shambles.   The clowns of Shakespeare are still admired by not the vulgar only.

Southey. The more the pity.   Let them appear in their
proper places.   But a picture by Morland or Frank
Hals (80) ought never to break a series of frescoes by the
hand of Raphael, (81) or of senatorial portraits animated
by the sun of Titian. (82)   There is much to be regretted
in, and (since we are alone I will say it) a little which
might without loss or injury be rejected, from, the treasury of Shakespeare.

Landor. It is difficult to sweep away anything and not
to sweep away gold-dust with it! but viler dust lies thick
in some places.   The grave Milton too has cobwebs hanging
on his workshop, which a high broom, in a steady hand, may
reach without doing mischief.   But let children and short
men, and unwary ones, stand out of the way....

Landor.....   But the poem is a noble poem, and the
characters of Samson and Delilah are drawn with precision
and truth.   The Athenian dramatists, both tragic and
comic, have always one chief personage, one central light.
Homer has not in the 'Iliad', nor has Milton in the 'Paradise Lost', nor has Shakespeare in several of his best
tragedies.   We find it in Racine, in the great Corneille,
in the greater Schiller. (83)   In Calderon, (84) and the
other dramatists of Spain, it rarely is wanting; but

their principal delight is in what we call plot or in-
trigue, in plainer English (and very like it) intricacy
and trick.... It may be vain and useless to propose
for imitation the chief excellences of a great author,
such being the gift of transcendent genius, and not an ac-
quisition to be obtained by study or labour: but it is
only in great authors that defects are memorable when
pointed out, and unsuspected until they are distinctly.
For which reason I think it probable that at no distant
time I may publish your remarks, if you consent to it.
    Southey. It is well known in what spirit I made them;
and as you have objected to few, if any, I leave them at
your discretion....

    Landor.... Chaucer, like Shakespeare, like Homer,
like Milton, like every great poet that ever lived, derived from open sources the slender origin of his immortal
works. Imagination is not a mere work-shop of images,
great and small, as there are many who would represent it;
but sometimes *thoughts* also are imagined before they are
felt, and descend from the brain into the bosom. Young
Poets imagine feelings to which in reality they are
strangers.
    Southey. Copy them rather.
    Landor. Not entirely. The copybook acts on the imag-
ination. Unless they felt the truth or the verisimili-
tude, it could not take possession of them. Both feelings and images fly from distant coverts into their little
field, without their consciousness whence they come, and
rear young ones there which are properly their own.
Chatterton hath shown as much imagination in the 'Bristowe
Tragedie', as in that animated allegory which begins,

When Freedom dreste in blood-stain'd veste.
[Chatterton, 'Goddwyn. A Tragedie', l. 196ff.]

Keats is the most imaginative of our poets, after Chaucer,
Spenser, Shakespeare, and Milton.
    Southey. I am glad you admit my favourite, Spenser.
    Landor. He is my favourite too, if you admit the ex-
pression without the signification of precedency. I do
not think him equal to Chaucer even in imagination, and he
appears to me very inferior to him in all other points,
excepting harmony. Here the miscarriage is in Chaucer's
age, not in Chaucer, many of whose verses are highly beautiful, but never (as in Spenser) one whole period. I
love the geniality of his temperature: no straining, no
effort, no storm, no fury. His vivid thoughts burst

their way to us through the coarsest integuments of
language.

The heart is the creator of the poetical world; only
the atmosphere is from the brain.   Do I then undervalue
imagination?   No indeed: but I find imagination where
others never look for it: in character multiform yet consistent.   Chaucer first united the two glorious realms of
Italy and England.   Shakespeare came after, and subjected
the whole universe to his dominion.   But he mounted the
highest steps of his throne under those bland skies which
had warmed the congenial breasts of Chaucer and Boccaccio.

The powers of imagination are but slender when it can
invent only shadowy appearances; much greater are requisite to make an inert and insignificant atom grow up
into greatness; to give it form, life, mobility, and intellect.   Spenser hath accomplished the one; Shakespeare
and Chaucer the other.   Pope and Dryden have displayed a
little of it in their 'Satires'. (85)   In passing, let me
express my wish that writers who compare them in generalities, and who lean mostly toward the stronger, would attempt to trim the balance, by placing Pope among our best
critics on poetry, while Dryden is knee-deep below John
Dennis.   You do not like either: I read both with pleas-
sure, so long as they keep to the couplet.   But 'St.
Cecilia's' music-book is in interlined with epigrams, (86)
and 'Alexander's Feast' smells of gin at second-hand, with
true Briton fiddlers full of native *talent* in the orches-
tra. (87)

Southey. Dryden says, 'It were an easy matter to produce some *thousands* of Chaucer's [his] verses *which* are
lame for want of half [a foot], and sometimes a whole
foot [one], [and] *which* no pronunciation can make otherwise'. (88)

Landor. Certainly no pronunciation but the proper one
can do it.

Southey. On the opposite quarter, comparing him with
Boccaccio, he says, 'He [Chaucer] has refined on the Italian [Boccace], and has mended his [the] stories [which he
has borrowed,] in his way of telling. [...]   Our countryman carries weight, and yet wins the race at disadvan-
tage'. (89)

Landor. Certainly our brisk and vigorous poet carries
with him no weight in criticism.

Southey. Vivacity and shrewd sense are Dyrden's characteristics, with quickness of perception rather than accuracy of remark, and consequently a facility rather than a
fidelity of expression....

NOTES

1 Aeschines (c. 397-c. 322 BC), famous Athenian orator
   and opponent of Desmothenes; Lysias (c. 459-c. 380
   BC), a Syracusan who lived in Athens and who achieved
   renown as an orator; Isaeus (c. 420-350 BC), orator
   and teacher of Demosthenes.
2 William Pitt, first Earl of Chatham (1708-78), famous
   English statesman and orator; Henry Grattan (1746-
   1820), Irish statesman noted for eloquent oratory.
3 See Aristotle, 'Rhetoric', i, 7, 34, and iii, 10, 7.
4 Titus Livius (59 BC-AD 17), Roman historian, author
   of the 'History of Rome'.
5 Milton's unfinished 'History of Britain' (1670) concludes with the Norman Conquest.
6 Both Southey and Landor subscribe to Samuel Johnson's
   assertion that 'the defects and faults of "Paradise
   Lost", for faults and defects every work must have, it
   is the business of impartial criticism to discover'
   (Milton, 'Lives of the English Poets', ed. George B.
   Hill, 3 vols, Oxford: Clarendon Press, 1905, 1, 180).
   Johnson's criticism of 'Paradise Lost' is reprinted by
   the Rev. Henry Todd in his 'Poetical Works of John
   Milton', 2, 558-65.
7 Plato.   See Lord Chesterfield and Lord Chatham, No.
   12 above.
8 A decorative brooch used to fasten the cloak on the
   shoulder.
9 Southey admired the devotional writings of Robert
   South (1634-1716), seventeenth-century divine.
10 Sir Walter Ralegh (155?-1618), English soldier, ad-
   venturer, poet, and prose writer.
11 Lake Como.   Southey spent three days with Landor at
   Como in June 1817.
12 Milton praises the English river Severn (Sabrina) in
   the person of Sabrina, a nymph in 'Comus' (ll. 824ff).
13 The remainder of this paragraph, as well as the following, was printed earlier in a slightly altered form
   in 'Commentary on Memoirs of Mr. Fox' (1812).   See
   'Charles James Fox: A Commentary on His Life and
   Character by Walter Savage Landor', ed. Stephen
   Wheeler, 2nd ed., London, 1907, 133-5.
14 According to Homer, the cause of the Trojan War was
   the abduction of Helen, wife of Menelaus, by the Trojan prince Paris.
15 See 'Iliad', i, 1-7.
16 Ibid., xvi, xxii.
17 Milton's sixteenth line is an ironical paraphrase of
   Ariosto's verse.

18 A verse consisting of eleven syllables.   Verse 38 is
   one of the few lines in the poem ending in an unstres-
   sed, redundant syllable.

19 The allusion is to Wordsworth whose home, Rydal Mount,
   Ambleside, is about fourteen miles from Southey's
   Greta Hall, Keswick, Cumberland.   Milton's final
   residence was in Artillery Walk, Bunhill Fields,
   London.

20 Landor himself did in 'Gebir', ii, 160;   see 'Complete
   Works', 13, 13.

21 A metrical foot consisting of three short syllables.

22 'Paradise Lost', i, 468.

23 According to ancient writers, Spartan soldiers went to
   battle accompanied by the music of the flute.

24 An early Roman deity, later identified with the Greek
   Hephaestus or Mulciber, 'the smelter' of metals.

25 Landor praises Milton's orthography in the Imaginary
   Conversations Samuel Johnson and John Horne (Tooke) I
   and II, and Archdeacon Hare and Walter Landor.   See
   also Charles L. Proudfit, Landor's Hobbyhorse: A
   Study in Romantic Orthography, 'Studies in Romanti-
   cism', 7 (Summer 1968), 207-17.

26 A half or section of a line of verse.

27 Landor's allusion is to Atlas, a Titan, who, according
   to Hesiod, must hold up the sky as a punishment for
   revolting against Zeus ('Theogony', 510-21).

28 Cf. Shakespeare, 'Measure for Measure', III, i, 121-2:
   'To bath in fiery floods, or to reside / In thrilling
   region of thick-ribbed ice'.

29 According to Greek mythology, Tantalus, who sinned
   against the gods, was punished in Hades by being
   placed in a pool of water that always receded when he
   went to drink.

30 See Samuel Johnson and John Horne (Tooke) I, 'Complete
   Works', 5, 37.

31 Southey, unlike Landor, wishes to exclude Satan's
   meeting with Sin and Death and his journey through the
   'wild abyss'.

32 These words are spoken by Chaos, not Satan.

33 'Gutta serena':   'a clear drop'.

34 'Imitations of Horace, Epistle II', i, 102.

35 First edition (1733) reads: 'A mighty maze! of walks
   without a plan'.

36 Dr Johnson also notes this revision in his Pope,
   'Lives', ed. Hill, 3, 162.

37 In The Poems of Catullus Landor writes: 'Warton and
   Johnson are of opinion that Milton is defective in the
   sense of harmony.   But Warton had lost his ear by
   laying it down on low and swampy places, on ballads

and sonnets; and Johnson was a deaf adder coiled up
in the brambles of party prejudices. He was acute
and judicious, he was honest and generous, he was for-
bearing and humane: but he was cold where he was
overshadowed. The poet's peculiar excellence, above
all others, was in his exquisite perception of rhythm,
and in the boundless variety he has given it, both in
verse and prose' ('Complete Works', 11, 189).

38 See Johnson's Rambler no. 86 in the 'Rambler', eds
W.J. Bate and Albrecht B. Strauss, New Haven: Yale
University Press, 1969, 4, 92. Todd reprints Ram-
blers nos 86, 88, 90, 92, and 94 in Observations on
the Versification of Milton, by Dr. Johnson and
Others, 'Poetical Works of John Milton', 1, 359-83.

39 Ibid.

40 Rambler no. 90, eds Bate and Strauss, 4, 113.

41 Ibid., 114-15.

42 Rambler no. 94, eds Bate and Strauss, 4, 139.

43 This hymn (v, 153-208) is based on Psalms 19:1, 104,
and 148.

44 Cowley's imitation of Anacreon reads: 'The busie *Sun*
(and one would guess / By's drunken fiery face no
less) / Drinks up the *Sea*, and when h'as done, / The
Moon and *Stars* drink up the *Sun*' (Drinking, 11. 9-12,
in the 'Poems of Abraham Cowley', ed. A.R. Waller,
Cambridge University Press, 1905, 51).

45 See Todd, 'Poetical Works of John Milton', 2, 162n.
Richard Bentley (1662-1742), classical scholar and
textual critic, published an edition of Milton's
'Paradise Lost' in 1732 that contains numerous unjus-
tified textual emendations. Bentley incorrectly assumed that Milton's text had been corrupted through
the poet's use of an amanuensis and an editor. Pope
and other eighteenth-century satirists regarded
Bentley's 'Milton' as an excellent example of misapplied scholarship. Although Landor takes issue
both here and elsewhere with Bentley's criticisms and
emendations, both Southey and Landor engage in similar
attempts to improve Milton.

46 'Pars pro toto': 'a part for the whole'.

47 'My light', Johannes Secundus, 'Basium', iii. This
phrase occurs in two lines of Latin poetry singled out
by Landor for special praise in The Poems of Catullus;
see 'Complete Works', 11, 183.

48 Landor's criticisms refer to 11. 399-403: 'Forthwith
the sounds and seas, each creek and bay, / With fry
innumerable swarm, and shoals / Of fish that with
their fins and shining scales / Glide under the green
wave, in sculls that oft / Bank the mid-sea'.

49 See Todd, 'Poetical Works of John Milton', 2, 387n.
    Although the annotation of Benjamin Stillingfleet
    (1702-71) is primarily concerned with classical paral-
    lels in Milton's poetry, this commentator also notes
    relationships with later authors.
50 Ibid., 507n.
51 Ibid., 515n.
52 See Henry Hallam, History of Poetry from 1600 to 1650,
    'Introduction to the Literature of Europe in the Fif-
    teenth, Sixteenth, and Seventeenth Centuries', New
    York and Boston, 1863, 3, 261-4.   Landor's disparage-
    ment of Sir Henry Hallam, the historian (1777-1859),
    both here and elsewhere in the 'Imaginary Conversa-
    tions', is the result of ill-feeling that originated
    when the two men met at the home of a mutual friend
    (Forster, 'Landor', 2, 372).   Landor wrongly attribu-
    ted to Hallam a scathing review of the 'Pentameron and
    Pentalogia' (1837) that appeared in the 'British and
    Foreign Review' (October 1838), 501-21.   His Reply To
    A Reviewer, suppressed by Forster while both Hallam
    and Landor were alive, is printed only in Forster's
    'Landor', 2, 373-87.
53 See n. 3 above.
54 Milton, 'Lives', ed. Hill, 1, 171.
55 Ibid., 183.
56 Giovanni Battista Andreini (1579?-1654), Italian Re-
    naissance dramatist, based his tragedy 'L'Adamo'
    (1613) on the story of the Fall and Redemption of Man.
    Milton, according to Voltaire, saw a performance of
    this play while in Milan during his Italian journey
    (1638-9) and immediately conceived the idea of writing
    a tragedy on the same subject.   He later composed one
    act and part of a second.   See Milton, 'OEuvres com-
    plètes de Voltaire', ed. Louis Moland, new ed., Paris,
    1877-85, 8, 22-4.
57 Marco Girolamo Vida (1485-1566), Italian Renaissance
    prelate and humanist, author of the 'Christiad'
    (1535), a heroic Latin poem on the life of Christ.
58 Jacopo Sannazzaro (1456-1530), Italian Renaissance
    poet and courtier, author of the 'Arcadia' (1504), a
    pastoral romance.
59 See Johnson, Milton, 'Lives', ed. Hill, 1, 185-6.
60 Ibid., 184-5.
61 Ibid., 178.   Johnson adapts Dryden's critical remark
    that Shakespeare 'needed not the spectacles of books
    to read Nature' (An Essay of Dramatic Poesy, 'Essays
    of John Dryden', ed. W.P. Ker, Oxford: Clarendon
    Press, 1900, 1, 80.
62 Ibid., 181.

63 See Todd, 'Poetical Works of John Milton', 2, 554-7n.

64 The 'Malebolge', the gulfs of the eighth circle in the
    'Inferno'.

65 See Epicurus, Leontion, and Ternissa, No. 14 above,
    n. 4.

66 Shelley's 'The Cenci', a tragedy about a father's in-
    cestuous passion for his daughter and his subsequent
    murder by her hired assassins, was published in 1819.
    Based on events that occurred in 1599, Shelley's play
    met with condemnation in England.   Landor appears to
    feel that Shelley's poetic treatment of the subject
    was a success.

67 Francis Beaumont (1584-1616) and John Fletcher (1579-
    1625), Elizabethan playwrights who collaborated from
    about 1606-16 in the production of plays.

68 Landor's allusion is to the loss of Samson's locks
    wherein lay the source of his mighty strength (Judges
    16).

69 Jean de la Fontaine (1621-95), French poet, author of
    'Les Fables' (1668, 1678-9, 1693).

70 For Montaigne, see Postscript to 'Gebir', No. 2 above,
    n. 9;   for Charron, see Letter to Emerson, No. 9
    above, n. 12.

71 Jacques Bénigne Bossuet (1627-1704), French bishop,
    historian, controversialist, and orator.

72 Phocion (fourth century BC) and Pericles (c. 500-429
    BC), Athenian generals, statesmen, and orators.   Both
    men were greatly admired by Landor.

73 Marcus Antonius (143-87 BC) and Hortalus Quintus Hor-
    tensius (114-50 BC), famous Roman orators.

74 Of that Sort of Dramatick Poem which is called Trage-
    dy, 'Samson Agonistes'.   See Todd, 'Poetical Works of
    John Milton', 3, 209-12.

75 Ibid.

76 Jean Racine (1639-99), French dramatist who wrote
    during the French classical period.

77 See Preface to 'Samson Agonistes'.

78 Ibid.

79 Elizabeth I (1533-1603), queen of England and Ireland
    from 1558 to 1603.

80 Frans Hals (c. 1580-1666), Dutch painter of portraits
    and groups.   For Morland, see Southey and Porson I,
    No. 10 above, n. 39.

81 Raphael (1483-1520), Italian Renaissance painter, was
    commissioned by Pope Julius II to paint a cycle of
    frescoes in a series of rooms ('stanze') in the Vati-
    can.   The decorations in the Stanza della Segnatura
    and Stanza d'Eliodoro are almost entirely Raphael's,
    and the Stanza dell'Incendio, though designed by the
    artist, was largely decorated by his assistants.

82   Titian (c. 1487/90-1576), Italian artist of the Vene-
     tian High Renaissance who achieved renown as a por-
     traitist.

83   Pierre Corneille (1606-84), French dramatist and cre-
     ator of French classical tragedy; Friedrich Schiller
     (1759-1805), German dramatist, poet, and literary
     theorist.

84   Pedro Calderón de la Barca (1600-81), Spanish drama-
     tist and poet.

85   See Dryden's Absalom and Achitophel (1681), The Medal
     (1682), Mac Flecknoe (1684), and his verse transla-
     tions of Persius and the 'Satires' of Juvenal (1693).
     Pope published satirical verse in a miscellany enti-
     tled 'Cytherea' (1723), the 'Dunciad' (1728, 1729,
     1742, 1743), and a series of miscellaneous satires,
     Imitations of Horace.

86   See Dryden's A Song for St. Cecilia's Day (1687) and
     Pope's Ode for Musick, on St. Cecilia's Day (1708).
     Joseph Warton comments: 'It is observable, that this
     Ode of Pope [Ode for Musick], and the Alexander's
     Feast of Dryden, conclude with an epigram of four
     lines; a species of wit as flagrantly unsuitable to
     the dignity, and as foreign to the nature, of the
     lyric, as it is of the epic muse' ('Essay on the
     Genius and Writings of Pope', 5th ed. cor., London,
     1806, 1, 60).

87   See Dryden's Alexander's Feast; or the Power of
     Musique.   An Ode, in Honour of St. Cecilia's Day
     (1697).   Landor's allusion is to Handel who scored
     the poem in 1736.   Jeremiah Clarke provided music
     (now lost) for the first performance on 22 November
     1697.

88   See Preface to 'Fables Ancient and Modern', in the
     'Poems and Fables of John Dryden', ed. James Kinsley,
     Oxford University Press, 1962, 529.

89   Ibid., 536.

18 Archdeacon Hare and Walter Landor
1853

Julius Charles Hare (1795-1855) was one of Landor's dear-
est friends.   He had been personally responsible for
seeing the 'Imaginary Conversations' (1824-9) through the
press when the author was resident in Italy, and Landor
had expressed his gratitude by dedicating his collected
'Works' (1846) to him as well as to the editor, John
Forster.   Landor visited Archdeacon Hare and his wife at
Herstmonceux, Sussex, a year before this Conversation appeared in 'Last Fruit off an Old Tree' (1853), and it is
more than likely that several of the subjects discussed by
the two old friends in June 1852 found their way into this
Dialogue.   The first part of Archdeacon Hare and Walter
Landor is devoted to orthography, a subject that interested both, and the remainder to matters of literary concern, aptly described by one writer as a 'compilation of
Landor's most mature critical judgments' (Super, 'Landor',
409).   Portions of this Conversation appeared previously
in the 'Examiner' (17 February 1849, 101; 7 December
1850, 783) and in a letter from Landor to Robert Southey
(Forster, 'Landor', 2, 534).   This brief excerpt in which
Landor comments on the Fancy and the Imagination is taken
from the 1853 text.

Walter Landor....   Every year there is more good poetry
written now, in this our country, than was written between
the 'Metamorphoses' and the 'Divina Commedia'.   We walk
no longer in the cast-off clothes of the ancients, often
ill-sewn at first, and now ill-fitting.   We have pulpier
flesh, stouter limbs, we take longer walks, explore wider
fields, and surmount more craggy and more lofty eminences.
From these let us take a leisurely look at Fancy and Imagination.   Your friend Wordsworth was induced to divide
his minor Poems under the separate heads of these two;

probably at the suggestion of Coleridge, (1) who persuaded him, as he himself told me, to adopt the name of 'Lyrical Ballads'.   He was sorry, he said, that he took the advice.   And well he might be; for *lyre* and *ballad* belong not to the same age or the same people.   It would have puzzled Coleridge to have drawn a strait boundary line between the domains of Fancy and those of Imagination, on a careful survey of these pieces; or perhaps to have given a satisfactory definition of their qualities.

Archdeacon Hare. Do you believe you yourself can?

Walter Landor. I doubt it.   The face is not the same, but the resemblance is sisterly; and, even by the oldest friends and intimates of the family, one is often taken for the other, so nearly are they alike.   Fancy is Imagination in her youth and adolescence.   Fancy is always excursive; Imagination, not seldom, is sedate.   It is the business of Imagination, in her maturity, to create and animate such Beings as are worthy of her plastic hand; certainly not by invisible wires to put marionettes in motion, nor to pin butterflies on blotting-paper.   Vigorous thought, elevated sentiment, just expression, developement of character, power to bring man out from the secret haunts of his soul and to place him in strong outline against the sky, belong to Imagination.   Fancy is thought to dwell among the Faeries and their congeners; and they frequently lead the weak and ductile poet far astray.   He is fond of playing at *little-go* (2) among them; and, when he grows bolder, he acts among the Witches and other such creatures; but his hankering after the Faeries still continues.   Their tiny rings, in which the intelligent see only the growth of fungusses, are no arena for action and passion.   It was not in these circles that Homer and AEschylus and Dante strove.

Archdeacon Hare. But Shakespeare sometimes entered them, who, with infinitely greater power, moulded his composite and consistent Man, breathing into him an immortality never to be forfeited.

Walter Landor. Shakespeare's full strength and activity were exerted on Macbeth and Othello; he trifled with Ariel and Titania; he played with Caliban: (3) but no other would have thought of playing with him, any more than of playing with Cerberus. (4)   Shakespeare and Milton and Chaucer have more imagination than any of those to whom the quality is peculiarly attributed.   It is not inconsistent with vigour and gravity.   There may be a large and effuse light without

the [gay] motes that people the sunbeams.
[Milton, 'Il Penseroso', l. 8.]

Imagination follows the steps of Homer throughout the
Troad, (5) from the ships on the strand to Priam and
Helen on the city wall: (6) Imagination played with the
baby Astyanax at the departure of Hector from Andro-
mache, (7) and was present at the noblest scene of the
Iliad, (8) where, to repeat a verse of Cowper's on
Achilles, more beautiful than Homer's own,

> his hand he placed
> On the old man's hand, *and pusht it gently away.* (9)
> ['Iliad', xxiv, 637-8.]

No less potently does Imagination urge AEschylus on,
from the range of beacons to the bath of Agamemnon; (10)
nor expand less potently the vulture's wing over the lac-
erated bosom on the rocks of Caucasus. (11) With the
earliest flowers of the freshly created earth Imagination
strewed the nuptial couch of Eve. (12) Not Ariel, nor
Caliban, nor Witches who ruled the elements, but Eve, and
Satan, and Prometheus, are the most wonderous and the most
glorious of her works. Imagination takes the weaker hand
of Virgil out of Dante's who grasps it, and guides the
Florentine exile through the triple world.

Archdeacon Hare. Whatever be your enthusiasm for the
great old masters, you must often feel, if less of so
strong an impulse, yet a cordial self-congratulation in
having bestowed so many eulogies on poetical contemporaries, and on others whose genius is apart from poetry.

Walter Landor. Indeed I do. Every meed of Justice is
delivered out of her own full scale. The poets, and
others who may rank with them, indeed all the great men,
have borne toward me somewhat more than civility. The
few rudenesses I have ever heard of, are from such as
neither I nor you ever meet in society, and such as warm
their fingers and stomachs round less ornamental hearths.
When they to whom we have been unknown, or indifferent,
begin to speak a little well of us, we are sure to find
some honest old friend ready to trim the balance....

Walter Landor. It has been my fortune and felicity,
from my earliest days, to have avoided all competitions.
My tutor at Oxford (13) could never persuade me to write
a piece of Latin poetry for the Prize, earnest as he was
that his pupil should be a winner at the forthcoming
'Encaenia'. (14) Poetry was always my amusement, prose
my study and business. I have published five volumes of
'Imaginary Conversations': cut the worst of them through
the middle, and there will remain in this decimal fraction

quite enough to satisfy my appetite for fame.   I shall
dine late; but the diningroom will be well-lighted, the
guests few and select....

NOTES

1 Wordsworth first informed Coleridge in a letter dated
   5 May 1809 of his intention to classify his shorter
   poems if republished during his lifetime.   When
   Wordsworth's collected edition of shorter poems appeared in 1815, he prefaced it with a justification of
   his classifications, emphasizing in particular those
   of Fancy and Imagination.
2 'Little-go' is a nickname for lottery.
3 The imaginary creatures Ariel and Caliban appear in
   'The Tempest' and Titania is queen of the fairies and
   wife of Oberon in 'A Midsummer Night's Dream'.
4 According to Hesiod, Cerberus is a huge dog with fifty
   heads and a voice like bronze who guards the entrance
   to Hades ('Theogony', 311).
5 Country of the Trojans.
6 'Iliad', ii-iii, 244.
7 Ibid., vi, 391-493.
8 See The Abbé Delille and Walter Landor, No. 11 above,
   and n. 6.
9 Cowper's verse, incorrectly quoted by Landor, reads:
   '... he placed his hand / On Priams hand, and push'd
   him gently away' ('The Iliad and Odyssey of Homer',
   translated into English blank verse by W. Cowper,
   London, 1791, 1, 655.
10 'Agamemnon', 1-1398.
11 'Prometheus Bound'.
12 'Paradise Lost', iv, 708-10.
13 William Benwell (1765-96).
14 'The annual Commemoration of founders and benefactors
    at Oxford 1691' ('OED').

Reviews

19 The Poems of Catullus
1842, 1853

When John Forster assumed the editorship of the 'Foreign
Quarterly Review' in 1842, he sent Landor review copies of
recent editions of the works of Catullus, Horace, Pindar,
Theocritus, and Petrarch, hoping to elicit from him a
series of critical essays on his favourite writers.   Although Landor gathered materials on all five poets, he
completed essays only on Catullus (1842), Theocritus
(1842), and Petrarch (1843).

This review of Frederick William Doering's revised edition of 'C. Valerii Catulli Veronensis Carmina', Altona,
1834, first published in the July 1842 'Foreign Quarterly
Review' and reprinted with minor revisions in 'Last Fruit
off an Old Tree' (1853), is a thoroughly disorganized
work.   Landor commences with an ill-assortment of miscellaneous notes on the bucolics of Virgil, medieval and
modern Latinists, and Milton's 'Paradise Regained',
'L'Allegro', and 'Comus'.   He then takes Catullus' poems
in order and submits them to verbal and textual analysis.
On occasion he takes issue with the editor, makes his own
textual emendations, and comments on problems of versification and language.   The conclusion, reprinted from
'Last Fruit' (1853), contains the critical principles by
which Landor believed poetry should be judged.   He then
applies these principles in his criticism of Shakespeare,
contemporary English poets, Catullus, and other classical
writers.

...   In selecting a poet for examination, it is usual
either to extol him to the skies, or to tear him to pieces
and trample on him.   Editors in general do the former:
critics on editors more usually the latter.   But one poet
is not to be raised by casting another under him.   Catullus is made no richer by an attempt to transfer to him

what belongs to Horace, nor Horace by what belongs to
Catullus. Catullus has greatly more than he; but he
also has much; and let him keep it. We are not at
liberty to indulge in forwardness and caprice, snatching
a decoration from one and tossing it over to another.
We will now sum up what we have collected from the mass
of materials which has been brought before us, laying down
some general rules and observations.

There are four things requisite to constitute might,
majesty, and dominion, in a poet: these are creativeness,
constructiveness, the sublime, the pathetic. A poet of
the first order must have formed, or taken to himself and
modified, some great subject. He must be creative and
constructive. Creativeness may work upon old materials:
a new world may spring from an old one. Shakespeare
found Hamlet and Ophelia; he found Othello and Desdemona:
nevertheless he, the only universal poet, carried this,
and all the other qualifications, far beyond the reach of
competitors. He was creative and constructive, he was
sublime and pathetic, and he has also in his humanity condescended to the familiar and the comic. There is
nothing less pleasant than the smile of Milton; but at
one time Momus, at another the Graces, hang upon the neck
of Shakespeare. (1)   Poets whose subjects do not restrict
them, and whose ordinary gait displays no indication of
either greave or buskin, if they want the facetious and
humorous, and are not creative, nor sublime, nor pathetic,
must be ranked by sound judges in the secondary order, and
not among the foremost even there.

Cowper, and Byron, and Southey, with much and deep tenderness, are richly humorous. Wordsworth, grave, elevated, observant, and philosophical, is equidistant from
humour and from passion. Always contemplative, never
creative, he delights the sedentary and tranquilizes the
excited. No tear ever fell, no smile ever glanced, on
his pages. With him you are beyond the danger of any
turbulent emotion, at terror, or valour, or magnanimity,
or generosity. Nothing is there about him like Burns's
'Scots wha ha'e wi' Wallace bled', (2) or Campbell's
'Battles of Copenhagen and Hohenlinden', (3) or those exquisite works which, in Hemans, rise up like golden spires
among broader but lower structures, 'Ivan' and 'Casa-
bianca'. (4)   Byron, often impressive and powerful, never
reaches the heroic and the pathetic of these two poems;
and he wants the freshness and healthiness we admire in
Burns. But an indomitable fire of poetry, the more vivid
for the gloom about it, bursts through the crusts and crevices of an unsound and hollow mind. He never chatters
with chilliness, nor falls overstrained into languor; nor

do metaphysics ever muddy his impetuous and precipitate
stream.   It spreads its ravages in some places, but it is
limpid and sparkling everywhere.   If no story is well
told by him, no character well delineated, if all resemble
one another by their beards and Turkish dresses, there is
however the first and the second and the third requisite
of eloquence, whether in prose or poetry, vigour.   But no
large poem of our days is so animated, or so truly of the
heroic cast, as 'Marmion'. (5)   Southey's 'Roderick' (6)
has less nerve and animation: but what other living poet
has attempted, or shown the ability, to erect a structure
so symmetrical and so stately?   It is not enough to heap
description on description, to cast reflection over reflection: there must be development of character in the
development of story; there must be action, there must be
passion; the end and the means must alike be great.

The poet whom we mentioned last is more studious of
classical models than the others, especially in his 'Inscriptions'. (7)   Interest is always excited by him, enthusiasm not always.   If his elegant prose and harmonious
verse are insufficient to excite it, turn to his virtues,
to his manliness in defence of truth, to the ardour and
constancy of his friendships, to his disinterestedness, to
his generosity, to his rejection of title and office, and
consequently of wealth and influence.   He has labored to
raise up merit in whatever path of literature he found it;
and poetry in particular has never had so intelligent, so
impartial, and so merciful a judge.   Alas! it is the will
of God to deprive him of those faculties which he exercised with such discretion, such meekness, and such humanity. (8)

We digress; not too far, but too long: we must return
to the ancients, and more especially to the author whose
volume lies open before us.

There is little of the creative, little of the constructive, in him: that is, he has conceived no new varieties of character; he has built up no edifice in the
intellectual world; but he always is shrewd and brilliant; he often is pathetic; and he sometimes is sublime.   Without the sublime, we have said before, there
can be no poet of the first order: but the pathetic may
exist in the secondary; for tears are more easily drawn
forth than souls are raised.   So easily are they on some
occasions, that the poetical power needs scarcely be
brought into action; while on others the pathetic is the
very summit of sublimity.   We have an example of it in
the *Ariadne* of Catullus: (9) we have another in the
Priam of Homer. (10)   All the heroes and gods, debating
and fighting, vanish before the father of Hector in the

tent of Achilles, and before the storm of conflicting passions his sorrows and prayers excite.   But neither in
the spirited and energetic Catullus, nor in the masculine
and scornful and stern Lucretius, no, nor in Homer, is
there anything so impassioned, and therefor so sublime, as
the last hour of Dido in the AEneid. (11)   Admirably as
two Greek poets have represented the tenderness, the anguish, the terrific wrath and vengeance of Medea, (12)
all the works they ever wrote contain not the poetry which
Virgil has condensed into about a hundred verses: omitting, as we must, those which drop like icicles from the
rigid lips of AEneas; and also the similies which, here
as everywhere, sadly interfere with passion.   In this
place Virgil fought his battle of Actium, which left him
poetical supremacy in the Roman world, (13) whatever mut-
inies and conspiracies may have arisen against him in
Germany or elsewhere.

The *Ariadne* of Catullus has greatly the advantage over
the *Medea* of Apollonius: for what man is much interested
by such a termagant?   We have no sympathies with a woman
whose potency is superhuman.   In general, it may be ap-
prehended, we like women little the better for excelling
us even moderately in our own acquirements and capacities.
But what energy springs from her weaknesses! what poetry
is the fruit of her passions! once perhaps in a thousand
years bursting forth with imperishable splendour on its
golden bough.   If there are fine things in the 'Argonautics' of Apollonius, there are finer still in those of
Catullus.   In relation to Virgil, he stands as Correggio (14) in relation to Raffael: a richer colourist, a
less accurate draftsman; less capable of executing grand
designs, more exquisite in the working out of smaller.
Virgil is depreciated by the arrogance of self-sufficient
poets, nurtured on coarse fare, and dizzy with home-brewed
flattery.   Others, who have studied more attentively the
ancient models, are abler to show his relative station,
and readier to venerate his powers.   Although we find him
incapable of contriving, and more incapable of executing,
so magnificent a work as the 'Iliad', yet there are places
in his compared with which the grandest in that grand poem
lose much of their elevation.   Never was there such a
whirlwind of passions as Virgil raised on those African
shores, amid those rising citadels and departing sails.
When the vigorous verses of Lucretius are extolled, no
true poet, no sane critic, will assent that the seven or
eight examples of the best are equivalent to this one:
even in force of expression, here he falls short of
Virgil.

When we drink a large draught of refreshing beverage,

it is only a small portion that affects the palate.   In
reading the best poetry, moved and excited as we may be,
we can take in no more than a part of it.   Passages of
equal beauty are unable to raise enthusiasm.   Let a work
in poetry or prose, indicating the highest power of
genius, be discoursed on; probably no two persons in a
large company will recite the same portion as having
struck them the most forcibly.   But when several passages
are pointed out and read emphatically, each listener will
to a certain extent doubt a little his own judgment in
this one particular, and hate you heartily for shaking it.
Poets ought never to be vext, discomposed, or disappointed, when the better is overlooked, and the inferior is
commended.   Much may be assigned to the observer's point
of vision being more on a level with the object.   And
this reflection also will console the artist, when really
bad ones are called more simple and natural, while in fact
they are only more ordinary and common.   In a palace we
must look to the elevation and proportions; whereas a low
grotto may assume any form and almost any deformity.
Rudeness is here no blemish; a shell reversed is no false
ornament; moss and fern may be stuck with the root out-
ward; a crystal may sparkle at the top or at the bottom;
dry sticks and fragmentary petrifactions find everywhere
their proper place; and loose soil and plashy water show
just what nature delights in.   Ladies and gentlemen who
at first were about to turn back, take one another by the
hand, duck their heads, enter it together, and exclaim,
'What a charming grotto!'

In poetry, as in architecture, the Rustic Order is
proper only for the lower story.

They who have listened, patiently and supinely, to the
catarrhal songsters of goose-grazed commons, will be loth
and ill-fitted to mount up with Catullus to the highest
steeps in the forests of Ida, and will shudder at the
music of the Corybantes in the temple of the Great Mother
of the Gods. (15

NOTES

1 In Greek mythology Momus is the personification of
   criticism and fault-finding; the Graces, usually
   three in number, personify grace and beauty.
2 Scots, wha hae wi' Wallace bled (1793), a revolutionary song written by Robert Burns and entitled Robert
   Bruce's march to Bannockburn - To its ain tune.
3 The Battle of the Baltic (1801) and Hohenlinden
   (1802), martial lyrics of the Scots poet Thomas Campbell (1777-1844).

4   Felicia Dorothea Hemans (1793-1835), English poet and
    friend of Sir Walter Scott and William Wordsworth, en-
    joyed immense popularity in England and America during
    her lifetime.   Landor praised Ivan and Casabianca
    (1808) and Campbell's Hohenlinden in letters written
    toward the end of his life.

5   Sir Walter Scott's 'Marmion' (1808), a romantic tale
    of chivalry in narrative verse, has, as its historical
    setting, the events surrounding the battle of Flodden
    Field (1513) where the English defeated James IV of
    Scotland.

6   See Letters to Southey, No. 4 above.

7   See To the Rev. Cuthbert Southey ..., No. 8 above,
    n. 19.

8   Southey suffered a nervous breakdown in his mid-
    sixties which resulted in the loss of his memory four
    years before his death on 21 March 1843.

9   See Catullus, lxiv.

10 See 'Iliad', xxiv, 470-676.

11 See 'Aeneid', iv, 305ff.

12 See Apollonius Rhodius, 'Argonautica', iii-iv, and
    Euripides, 'Medea'.

13 Octavian overwhelmed the combined fleets of Antony and
    Cleopatra at Actium in 31 BC thereby ending the Roman
    republic and ushering in the Roman empire.

14 Antonio Allegri Correggio (c. 1494-1534), one of the
    great Italian masters of the High Renaissance.

15 The Corybantes were castrated priests of the Asiatic
    mother goddess, Cybele, whose rites were celebrated
    with wild dances and music.   The centre of her cult
    was Phrygia.   Landor's allusion is to Catullus' poem
    lxiii, in which Attis, a young male athlete, enters
    the forests of Mount Ida, is captured by the frenzy of
    the rites of Cybele, and, in his madness, castrates
    himself.

20 The Idyls of Theocritus
1842, 1853

This review of 'Theocritus, Bion, Moschus, ex recognitione
Augusti Meinekii', Altona, 1835, first appeared in the
October 1842 'Foreign Quarterly Review' and was later reprinted with minor revisions and two major deletions (see
notes 20, 21 below) in 'Last Fruit off an Old Tree'
(1853). It is a masterpiece among Landor's formal critical writing and, unlike the Catullus, is notable for its
order and proportion. In the first part, after praising
the edition under review and the efforts in general of
contemporary German editors of Theocritus, Landor brings
forward such relevant problems as establishing the authen-
ticity of certain poems, the origin of the term 'idyll',
the known facts of Theocritus' life, and Greek and Latin
versification. He then proceeds in the second part to
examine in order each of the thirty idylls. He concludes
the review with a brief though shrewd critical assessment
of English pastoral poetry. The following selection,
about one-half of the total work, is reprinted from the
1853 text and contains several excellent examples of Landor's re-creative criticism.

Within the last half-century the Germans have given us
several good editions of Theocritus. That of Augustus
Meinekius, (1) to which the very inferior and very different poems of Bion and Moschus are appended, is among the
best and the least presuming. No version is added: the
notes are few and pertinent, never pugnacious, never
prolix. In no age, since the time of Aristarchus, (2) or
before, has the Greek language been so profoundly studied,
or its poetry in its nature and meter so perfectly understood, as in ours. Neither Athens nor Alexandria saw so
numerous or so intelligent a race of grammarians as Germany has recently seen contemporary. Nor is the society
diminished, nor are its labours relaxed, at this day....
275

IDYL I.   Of all the poetry in all languages that of
Theocritus is the most fluent and easy; but if only this
Idyl were extant, it would rather be memorable for a weak
imitation of it by Virgil, and a beautiful one by
Milton, (3) than for any great merit beyond the harmony of
its verse.   Indeed it opens with such sounds as Pan himself in a prelude on his pipe might have produced. (4)
The dialogue is between Thyrsis and a goatherd.   Here is
much of appropriate description; but it appears unsuit-
able to the character and condition of a goatherd to offer
so large a reward as he offers for singing a song.   'If
you will sing as you sang in the contest with the Libyan
shepherd Chromis, I will reward you with a goat, mother of
two kids, which goat you may milk thrice a-day; for,
though she suckles two kids, she has milk enough left for
two pails' [ll. 23-5].

We often hear that such or such a thing 'is not worth
an old song'.   Alas! how very few things are!   What precious recollections do some of them awaken! what pleasurable tears do they excite!   They purify the stream of
life; they can delay it on its shelves and rapids; they
can turn it back again to the soft moss amidst which its
sources issue.

But we must not so suddenly quit the generous goatherd:
we must not turn our backs on him for the sake of indulging in these reflections.   He is ready to give not only a
marvellously fine goat for the repetition of a song, but a
commodity of much higher value in addition; a deep capacious cup of the most elaborate workmanship, carved and
painted in several compartments.   Let us look closely at
these [ll. 26ff].   The first contains a woman in a veil
and fillet: near her are two young suitors who throw
fierce *words* one against the other: she never minds them,
but smiles upon each *alternately*.   Surely no cup, not
even a magical one, could express all this.   But they
continue to carry on their ill-will.   In the next place
is an old fisherman on a rock, from which he is hauling
his net.   Not far from him is a vineyard, laden with
purple grapes.   A little boy is watching them near the
boundary-hedge, while a couple of foxes are about their
business: one walking through the rows of vines, picking
out the ripe grapes as he *goes along*; the other devising
mischief to the boy's wallet, and *declaring* on the word of
a fox that he will never quit the premises until he has
captured the breakfast therein deposited.   The song is
deferred no longer: and a capital song it is: but the
goatherd has well paid the piper.   It is unnecessary to
transcribe the verses which Virgil and Milton have imitated.

Nam neque Parnassi vobis juga nam neque Pindi
Ulla moram fecere, neque Aonia Aganippe.

[For no heights of Parnassus or of Pindus, no Aonian
Aganippe made you tarry ('Eclogues', x, 11-12).]

Virgil himself, on the present occasion, was certainly not
detained in any of these places.   Let us try whether we
cannot come toward the original with no greater deviation,
and somewhat less dulness.

Where were ye, O ye nymphs! when Daphnis died?
For not on Pindus were ye, nor beside
Penëus in his softer glades, nor where
Acis might well expect you, once your care.
But neither Acis did your steps detain,
Nor strong Anapus rushing forth amain,
Nor high-brow'd Etna with her forest chain.
['Idyls', i, 65-9.]

Harmonious as are the verses of Theocritus, the Greek
language itself could not bear him above Milton in his
'Lycidas'.   He had the good sense to imitate the versification of Tasso's 'Aminta', (5) employing rhyme where it
is ready at hand, and permitting his verses to be longer
or shorter, as may happen.   They are never deficient in
sweetness, taken separately, and never at the close of a
sentence disappoint us.   However, we can not but regret
the clashing of irreconcileable mythologies.   Neither in
a poem nor in a picture do we see willingly the Nymphs
and the Druids together: (6)   Saint Peter comes even more
inopportunely: and although, in the midst of such scenery, we may be prepared against wolves with their own heads
and '*maws*' and '*privy paws*', yet we deprecate them when
they appear with a bishop's: (7)   they are then an over-
match for us.   The ancients could not readily run into
such errors: yet something of a kind not very dissimilar
may be objected to Virgil.

Venit Apollo,
'Galle! quid insanis?' inquit.

[Apollo came. 'Gallus,' he said, 'what madness
this?' ('Eclogues', x, 21-2).]

When the poet says, 'Cynthius aurem vellit et admonuit'
['The Cynthian plucked my ear and warned me' ('Eclogues',
vi, 3-4)], we are aware that it is merely a form of
phraseology: but among those who, in Virgil's age, be-

lieved in Apollo, not one believed that he held a conversation with Gallus. (8)   The time for these familiarities
of gods with mortals had long been over,

Nec se contingi patiuntur lumine claro.

[Nor endure the touch of clear daylight (Catullus,
lxiv, 408).]

There was only one of them who could still alight without suspicion among the poets.   Phoebus had become a
mockery, a byword: but there never will be a time probably when Love shall lose his personality, or be wished out
of the way if he has crept into a poem.   But the poem
must be a little temple of his own, admitting no other
occupant or agent beside himself and (at most) two wor-
shippers.
     To return to this first Idyl.   Theocritus may be cen-
sured for representing a continuity of action in one
graven piece, where the girl smiles on two young men alternately.   But his defence is ready.   He would induce
the belief that, on looking at the perfection of the workmanship, we must necessarily know not only what is passing, but also what is past and what is to come.   We see
the two foxes in the same spirit and enter into their
minds and machinations.   We swear to the wickedest of the
two that we will keep his secret, and that we will help
him to the uttermost of our power, when he declares
(φατι) that he will have the boy's breakfast [1. 51].
Perhaps we might not be so steadily his partisan, if the
boy himself were not meditating an ill turn to another
creature.   He is busy in making a little cage for the
cicada [11. 52-4]. (9)   Do we never see the past and the
future in the pictures of Edwin Landseer? (10) who exer-
cises over all the beasts of the field and fowls of the
air an undivided and unlimited dominion....

     IDYL II is a monologue, and not bucolic.   Cimaetha, an
enchantress, is in love with Delphis.   The poem is curious, containing a complete system of incantation as practised by the Greeks.   Out of two verses, by no means remarkable [11. 82-3], Virgil has framed some of the most
beautiful in all his works. (11)   Whether the Idyl was in
this particular copied from Apollonius, (12) or whether he
in the Argonautics had it before him, is uncertain.   Neither of them is so admirable as,

Sylvaeque et saeva quierant

AEquora.
At non infelix animi Phoenissa; neque unquam
Solvitur in somnos, *oculisve aut pectore noctem
Accipit*: ingeminant curae, rursusque resurgens
Saevit amor.

The woods and stormy waves were now at rest,
But not the hapless Dido; never sank
She into sleep, never received she night
Into her bosom; grief redoubled grief,
And love sprang up more fierce the more represt.
['Aeneid', iv, 523-4, 529-32.]

IDYL III.   A goatherd, whose name is not mentioned,
declares his love, with prayers and expostulations, praises and reproaches, to Amaryllis.   The restlessness of
passion never was better expressed.   The tenth and eleventh lines are copied by Virgil, with extremely ill success.

Quod potui, puero *sylvestri* ex arbore *lecta*
Aurea mala decem misi, cras altera mittam.

[I have sent my boy - 'twas all I could do - ten
golden apples, culled from a tree in the wood.   Tomorrow I will send a second ten ('Eclogues', iii, 70-
1).]

How poor is *quod potui*! and what a *selection* (lecta) is
that of crabs; moreover, these were *sent* as a present
(misi), and not offered in person.   There is not even the
action, such as it is, but merely the flat relation of it.
Instead of a narration about sending these precious crabs,
and the promise of as many more on the morrow, here in
Theocritus the attentive lover says, 'Behold! I bring you
ten apples.   I gathered them myself from the tree whence
you desired me to gather them: tomorrow I will bring you
more.   Look upon my soul-tormenting grief!   I wish I
were a bee that I might come into your grotto, penetrating
through the ivy and fern, however thick about you' (ll.
10-14].   Springing up and away from his dejection and
supplication, he adds wildly,

Νῦν ἔγνων τὸν Ἔρωτα: βαρὺς θεός ἦ ῥα λεαίνας
Μασδὸν ἐθήλαζε, δρυμῷ δέ μιν ἔτρεφε μάτηρ. (13)

Now know I Love, a cruel God, who drew
A lioness's teat, and in the forest grew.
[ll. 15-16.]

Virgil has amplified the passage to no purpose.

Nunc scio quid sit amor: duris in cotibus illum
Ismarus aut Rhodope aut extremi Garamantes
Nec *generis* nostri puerum nec *sanguinis* edunt.

[Now know I what Love is; on flinty crags Ismarus bare
him - or Rhodope, or the farthest Garamantes, a child
not of our race or blood ('Eclogues', viii, 43-5).]

Where is the difference of meaning here between *genus* and
sanguis? And why all this bustle about Ismarus and Rhodope and the Garamantes? A lioness in an oak forest
stands in place of them all, and much better. Love being
the deity, not 'the passion, *qui* would have been better
than *quid*, both in propriety and in sound. There
follows,

Alter ab undecimo tum me jam ceperat annus.

[My eleventh year finished, the next had just greeted
me (l. 39).]

This is among the most faulty expressions in Virgil. The
words *tum me jam* sound woodenly: and *me ceperat annus* is
scarcely Latin. Perhaps the poet wrote *mihi*, abbreviated
to *mi*; *mihi caeperat annus*. There has been a doubt re-
garding the exact meaning: but this should raise none.
The meaning is, 'I was entering my *thirteenth* year'.
Unus ab undecimo would be the twelfth: of course *alter* ab
undecimo must be the thirteenth. Virgil is little more
happy in his translations from Theocritus than he is in
those from Homer. It is probable that they were only
school-exercises, too many and (in his opinion) too good
to be thrown away. J.C. Scaliger, zealous for the great
Roman poet, gives him the preference over Homer in every
instance where he has copied him. (14) But in fact there
is nowhere a sentence, and only a single verse anywhere,
in which he rises to an equality with his master. He
says of Fame,

Ingrediturque solo et caput inter sidera condit.

[And walks the ground with head hidden in the clouds
('Aeneid', iv, 177).]

The noblest verse in the Latin language....

IDYL VI.   This is dramatic, and is addressed to
Aratus. The shepherds Damaetas and Daphnis had driven
their flocks into one place, and, sitting by a fountain,
began a song about Polyphemus and Galatea.   Daphnis acts
the character of Galatea, Damaetas of Polyphemus.   The
various devices of the gigantic shepherd to make her
jealous, and his confidence of success in putting them
into practice, is very amusing.   His slyness in giving a
secret sign to set the dog at her, and the dog knowing
that he loved her in his heart, and pushing his nose
against her thigh instead of biting her [ll. 29-30], are
such touches of true poetry as are seldom to be found in
pastorals.   In the midst of these our poet has been
thought to have committed one anachronism.   But where
Galatea is said to have mistaken the game, when

φεύγει φιλέοντα καὶ οὐ φιλέοντα διῶκει
Καὶ τὸν ἀπὸ γραμμᾶς κινεῖ λίθον,

... Seeks him who loves not, him who loves, avoids:
And makes false moves,
[ll. 17-18.]

she herself is not represented as the speaker, nor is
Polyphemus, but Daphnis.   It is only at the next speech
that either of the characters comes forth in person: here
Damaetas is the Polyphemus, and acts his part admirably
[ll. 21-40].
IDYL VII.   The last was different in its form and
character from the five preceding: the present is more
difficult still.   The poet, on his road to Alexandria
with Eucritus and Amyntas, meets Phrasidamus and Antigen-
es, and is invited to accompany them to the festival of
Ceres, called Thalysia.   He falls in with Lycidas of
Cidon, and they relate their love-stories.   This Idyl
closes with a description of summer just declining into
autumn (ll. 135-46.]   The invocation to the Nymphs is in
the spirit of Pindar [ll. 147-57.]
IDYL VIII. (15) The subject is a contest in singing between Menalcas and Daphnis, for a pipe.   Here are some
verses of exquisite simplicity, which Virgil has most
clumsily translated.

Ego hunc vitulum, ne *forte* recuses, &c.

[I'll stake this cow.   Now, don't draw back ('Eclogues', iii, 29ff.]

De grege non ausim quidquam deponere tecum,

Est mihi namque domi pater, est *injusta* noverca,
Bisque die numerant ambo *pecus* ... *alter et haedos*.

[From the herd I'd dare not stake anything with you.
I have at home a harsh father and stepmother; and
twice a day both count the flock, and one of them the
kids as well (ll. 32-4).]

It is evident that Virgil means by *pecus* the sheep only;
pecora at this day means an *ewe* in Italian.   Virgil's
Menalcas had no objection to the robbery, but was afraid
of the chastisement.
     The Menalcas of Theocritus says, 'I will never lay what
belongs to my father; but I have a pipe which I made
myself' [ll. 18-20]; and according to his account of it,
it was no ordinary piece of workmanship.   Damaetas, it
appears, had made exactly such another, quite as good, and
the cane of which it was made cut his finger in making it
[ll. 21-4].   They carry on the contest in such sweet
hexameters and pentameters as never were heard before or
since: but they finish with hexameters alone.   The prize
is awarded to Daphnis by the goatherd who is arbitrator.
He must have been a goatherd of uncommonly fine discern-
ment: the match seems equal: perhaps the two following
verses turned the balance.

     Ἀλλ' ὑπὸ τᾷ πέτρᾳ τᾷδ' ᾄσομαι ἀγνὰς ἔχων τυ,
     Σύνομα μὰλ' ἐσορῶν τὰν Σικελὰν ἐς ἅλα.
     [ll. 53-6.]

Of these, as of those above, we can only give the meaning: he who can give a representation of them, can give a
representation of the sea-breezes.

     It never was my wish to have possest
          The land of Pelops and his golden store;
     But only, as I hold you to my breast,
          Glance at our sheep and our Sicilian shore.

....

     IDYL XII.   We now arrive at the first of those Idyls
of which the genuineness has been so pertinaciously dis-
puted. (16)   And why?   Because forsooth it pleased the
author to compose it in the ionic dialect.   Did Burns,
who wrote mostly in the Scottish, write nothing in the
English?   With how much better reason has the competitor
of Apollonius and Callimachus (17) deserted the doric
occasionally!   Meleager, (18) and other writers of inscriptions, mix frequently ionic forms with doric.   In

fact, the most accurate explorers must come at last to the
conclusion, that even in the pastoral portion of these
Idyls, scarcely a single one is composed throughout of un-
mingled doric. The ear that is accustomed to the exuberant flow of Theocritus, will never reject as spurious this
melodious and graceful poem. Here, and particularly toward the conclusion, as very often elsewhere, he writes in
the style and spirit of Pindar, while he celebrates the
loves extolled by Plato....

IDYL XV. The Syracusan Gossips. Never was there so
exact or so delightful a description of such characters.
There is a little diversity, quite enough, between Praxinoë and Gorgo. Praxinoë is fond of dress; conceited,
ignorant, rash, abusive in her remarks on her husband,
ambitious to display her knowledge as well as her finery,
and talking absurdly on what she sees about her at the
festival of Adonis. Gorgo is desirous of insinuating her
habits of industry. There are five speakers: Gorgo,
Praxinoë, Eunoë, an old woman and a traveller, beside a
singing girl, who has nothing to do with the party or the
dialogue. 'Gorgo: Don't talk in this way against your
husband while your baby is by. See how he is looking at
you. Sprightly, my pretty Zopyrion! I am not talking
of papa. Praxinoë: By Proserpine! he understands you.
Gorgo: Papa is a jewel of a papa.' [ll. 11-15.] After a
good deal of tattle, they are setting out for the fair,
and the child shows a strong desire to be of the party.
'Gorgo: I can't take you, darling! There's a hobgoblin
on the other side of the door; and there's a biting
horse. Ay, ay, cry to your heart's content. Do you
think I would have you lamed for life? Come, come; let
us be off' [ll. 40-2]. Laughter is irrepressible at
their mishaps and exclamations in the crowd. This poem,
consisting of one hundred and forty-four verses, is the
longest in Theocritus, excepting the heroics on Hercules. (19) The comic is varied and relieved by the song
of a girl on Adonis [ll. 100-44]. She notices everything
she sees, and describes it as it appears to her. After
an invocation to Venus, she has a compliment for Berenice,
not without an eye to the candied flowers and white
pastry, and the pretty little baskets containing mossy
gardens and waxwork Adonisses, and tiny Loves flying over,

Οἷοι ἀηδονιῆες ἐφεζόμενοι ἐπὶ δένδρων
Πωτῶνται, πτερύγων πειρώμενοι ὄζον᾽ ἀπ᾽ ὄζω.

Like the young nightingales, some nestling close,

Some plying the fresh wing from bough to bough.
[ll. 121-2.]

IDYL XVI.   The Graces.   Here Hiero (20) is reminded
how becoming is liberality in the rich and powerful;   and
here is sometimes a plaintive undersong in the praise.
The attributes of the Graces were manifold;   the poet has
them in view principally as the distributors of just rewards.   We have noticed the resemblance he often bears to
Pindar: nowhere is it so striking as in this and the
next.   The best of Pindar's odes is not more energetic
throughout: none of them surpasses these two in the chief
qualities of that admirable poet;   rejection of what is
light and minute, disdain of what is trivial, and selection of those blocks from the quarry which will bear
strong strokes of the hammer and retain all the marks of
the chisel.   Of what we understand by sublimity he has
little;   but he moves in the calm majesty of an elevated
mind.   Of all poets he least resembles those among us
whom it is the fashion most to admire at the present day.
The verses of this address to Hiero by Theocritus, from
the thirty-fourth to the forty-seventh, are as sonorous
and elevated as the best of Homer's;   and so are those beginning at the ninety-eighth verse to the end....

IDYL XXII.   This is the first heroic poem in Theocritus: it is in two parts.   First is described the fight
of Pollux and Amycus [ll. 53-134]:   secondly, of Castor
and Lynceus [ll. 137-204]. (21)   Of Amycus the poet says
that 'his monstrous chest was *spherical*': ἐσφαίρωτο
[l. 46.]
Omitting this, we may perhaps give some idea of the
scene.

In solitude both wandered, far away
From those they sail'd with.   On the hills above,
Beneath a rocky steep, a fount they saw
Full of clear water;   and below were more
That bubbled from the bottom, silvery,
Crystalline.   In the banks around grew pines,
Poplars, and cypresses, and planes, and flowers
Sweet-smelling;   pleasant work for hairy bees
Born in the meadows at the close of spring.
There, in the sunshine, sat a savage man,
Horrid to see;   broken were both his ears
With cestuses, his shoulders were like rocks
Polisht by some vast river's ceaseless whirl.
[ll. 34-50.]

Apollonius and Valerius Flaccus have described the
fight of Amycus and Pollux: (22)   both poets are clever,
Valerius more than usually: Theocritus is masterly....

IDYL XXIV.   Heracliskos, or the Infant Hercules.
There are critics of so weak a sight in poetry as to as-
cribe this magnificent and wonderful work to Bion or
Moschus.   Hercules is cradled in Amphitryon's shield
[11. 1-9].   The description of the serpents, of the
supernatural light in the chamber [11. 10-22], and the
prophecy of Tiresias [11. 73-100], (23) are equal to
Pindar and Homer.
   IDYL XXV.   Hercules the Lion-killer.   This will bear
no comparison with the preceding.   The story is told by
Hercules himself, and the poet has taken good care that it
should not be beyond his capacity....

IDYL XXVII.   Daphnis and the Shepherdess, has been
translated by Dryden. (24)   He has given the Shepherdess
a muslin gown bespangled.   This easy and vigorous poet
too often turns the country into the town, smells of the
ginshop, and staggers toward the brothel.   He was quite
at home with Juvenal, imitating his scholastic strut, deep
frown, and loud declamation: (25)   no other has done such
justice to Lucretius, to Virgil, to Horace, and to
Ovid: (26)   none is so dissimilar to Theocritus.   Wherever he finds a stain, he enlarges its circumference, and
renders it vivid and indelible.   In this lively poem we
wish the sixty-fifth and sixty-sixth verses were omitted.
....

IDYL XXX.   The Death of Adonis.   Venus orders the
Loves to catch the guilty boar and bring him before her.
They do so: he makes his defence against the accusation,
which is, that he only wished to kiss the thigh of Adonis;
and he offers his tusk in atonement, and, if the tusk is
insufficient, his cheek.   Venus pitied him, and he was
set at liberty.   Out of gratitude and remorse, he went to
a fire and burnt his teeth down to the sockets.   Let
those who would pillage Theocritus of his valuables, show
the same contrition: we then promise them this poem, to
do what they will with.
   The Inscriptions, which follow, are all of extreme
simplicity and propriety.   These are followed by the
poems of Bion and Moschus.   Bion was a native of Smyrna,
Moschus (his scholar) of Syracuse. (27)   They are called
authors of Idyls, but there is nothing of idyl or pastoral

in their works.   The worst of them, as is often the case,
is the most admired.   Bion tells us that the boar bit the
thigh of Adonis with his *tusk*;   the *white thigh with the
white tusk*;   and that Adonis grieved Venus by breathing
softly while the blood was running [i, 7-9].   Such faults
as these are rarely to be detected in Greek poetry, but
frequently on the revival of Pastoral in Italy.

Chaucer was born before that epidemic broke out which
soon spread over Europe, and infected the English poetry
as badly as any.   The thoughts of our poets in the Elizabethan age often look the stronger because they are com-
plicated and twisted.   We have the boldness to confess
that we are no admirers of the Elizabethan *style*.
Shakespeare stood alone in a fresh and vigorous and vast
creation: yet even his first-born were foul offenders,
bearing on their brows the curse of a fallen state. (28)
Elsewhere, in every quarter, we are at once slumberous and
restless under the heaviness of musk and benzoin, and sigh
for the unattainable insipidity of fresh air.   We are re-
galed with dishes in which no condiment is forgotten, nor
indeed any thing but simply the meat;   and we are ushered
into chambers where the tapestry is all composed of dwarfs
and giants, and the floor all covered with blood.   Thomson, in the 'Seasons', has given us many beautiful descriptions of inanimate nature;   but the moment any one
speaks in them the charm is broken.   The figures he introduces are fantastical.   The 'Hassan' of Collins is
excellent: he however is surpassed by Burns and Scott:
and Wordsworth, in his 'Michael', is nowise inferior to
them. (29)   Among the moderns no poet, it appears to us,
has written an Idyl so perfect, so pure and simple in expression, yet so rich in thought and imagery, as the
'Godiva' of Alfred Tennyson. (30)   Wordsworth, like
Thomson, is deficient in the delineation of character,
even of the rustic, in which Scott and Burns are almost
equal.   But some beautiful Idyls might be extracted from
the 'Excursion', which would easily split into *laminae*, (31) and the residue might, with little loss, be
blown away. (32)   Few are suspicious that they may be led
astray and get benighted by following simplicity too far.
If there are pleasant fruits growing on the ground, must
we therefore cast aside, as unwholesome, those which have
required the pruning-knife to correct and the ladder to
reach them?   Beautiful thoughts are seldom disdainful of
sonorous epithets: we find them continually in the Pastorals of Theocritus: sometimes we see, coming rather ob-
trusively, the wanton and indelicate;   but never (what
poetry most abhors) the mean and abject.   Widely different from our homestead poets, the Syracusan is remarkable

for a facility that never draggles, for a spirit that never flags, and for a variety that never is exhausted. His reflections are frequent, but seasonable; soon over, like the shadows of spring clouds on flowery meadows, and not hanging heavily upon the scene, nor depressing the vivacity of the blythe antagonists. (33)

NOTES

1 Augustus Meinekius (1790-1871), German classical scholar.
2 Aristarchus of Samothrace (c. 217-145 BC) achieved renown for his critical and textual studies of Hesiod, Homer, and Pindar, and is considered the father of scientific scholarship.
3 See Virgil, 'Eclogues', x, and Milton, 'Lycidas'.
4 Pan, the Greek god of shepherds and their flocks, is noted for his pipe playing and is usually described as being partly goat-like in appearance.
5 Tasso's 'Aminta' (1572) is a pastoral drama of simple plot and lyrical charm. The melodies of Tasso's verse influenced opera and cantata for the next two centuries.
6 Milton, 'Lycidas', ll. 50-3.
7 Ibid., ll. 108-31.
8 Gaius Cornelius Gallus (69-26 BC), soldier, poet, and friend of Virgil.
9 Crickets.
10 Sir Edwin Henry Landseer (1802-73), popular English animal-painter.
11 'Aeneid', iv, 523-4, 529-32.
12 See Apollonius Rhodius, 'Argonautica', iii, 439ff.
13 We have given not the editor's but our own punctuation: none after θεός: for if there were any in that place, we should have wished the words were βαρὺν θεόν. [L]
14 See the 'Poëtice' (1561) of Julius Caesar Scaliger (1484-1558).
15 The two first lines are the least pleasant to our ear of any in this melodious poet.... [L]
16 Landor's note on the title of this Idyll is omitted.
17 Apollonius Rhodius (c. 295-15 BC), author of the 'Argonautica' and pupil of Callimachus (c. 305-c. 240 BC) of Cyrene, Hellenistic poet who advocated the short, finished poem such as those composed by Theocritus.
18 Meleager (fl. 100 BC), poet and philosopher, master of the epigram.
19 See Idyll XXV, How Heracles Slew the Lion. Although

this Idyll is the longest, Landor is incorrect in
asserting that Idyll XV is the next longest.   See
Idylls I, II, V, VII, and XXII.

20 Hieron II (c. 306-215 BC), general-in-chief when
Theocritus sought his patronage, later king of Syracuse.

21 According to Greek myth, Amycus, king of the savage
Bebryces and a mighty boxer, challenged the Argonauts
when they visited his country.   Polydeuces (Pollux)
accepted the challenge and defeated Amycus.   In another exploit, Castor, Polydeuces' twin, joined his
brother in the abduction of Phoebe and Hilaeira,
daughters of Leucippus.   They were pursued by Leucippus' nephews, Idas and Lynceus, and in the ensuing
struggle Castor and both pursuers were killed.

22 See 'Argonautica', ii, 1-97 by Apollonius Rhodius and
'Argonautica', iv, 200-314 by the Latin poet Gaius
Valerius Flaccus (d. c. AD 90).

23 After Alcmena, mother of Heracles (son of Alcmena and
Zeus) and Iphicles (son of Alcmena and Amphitryon, her
husband), put her babes to sleep in Amphitryon's
shield, Hera, jealous wife of Zeus, sent two serpents
to destroy little Heracles.   Zeus filled the room
with light, and Heracles strangled the serpents.   The
next day Alcmena sent for the blind prophet Teiresias
who foretold a life of glory for Hercules, including
his famous twelve labours, and his ultimate death
(ll. 1-85).

24 Dryden's Daphnis and Chloris appeared in his second
miscellany, 'Sylvae' (1685).

25 Dryden published a complete translation of Juvenal and
Persius in 1693.

26 Dryden translated selections from Horace, Lucretius,
and Ovid between 1680 and 1700.   His monumental
'Works of Virgil' was published in 1697.

27 Bion (fl. probably c. 100 BC) and Moschus (fl. probably c. 150 BC).

28 See particularly Shakespeare's narrative poem Venus
and Adonis (1593).

29 Hassan; or, the Camel-driver, a poem from William
Collins' 'Persian Eclogues' (1742); Michael (1800), a
pastoral poem in blank verse by William Wordsworth.

30 Tennyson's Godiva (1842) is a short epyllion in the
manner of Theocritus; that is, a brief epic such as
Theocritus' Idyll XXIV, The Little Heracles.

31 'Laminae': 'fragments'.

32 In the 1842 text Landor remarks on the false simplicity in vogue among contemporary poetasters and then
includes two parodies of the ultra-simple style of

Wordsworth's followers.   See 'Complete Works', 16,
61-2.
33 Landor subjoined The Hamadryad, one of his best-loved
Hellenics, to the 1842 text in an attempt to demonstrate 'that order of simplicity which is simple in
the manner of Theocritus' (1842 text).   See 'Complete
Works', 14, 283-90, for the poem.

21 Francesco Petrarca

1843, 1853

Landor's Francesco Petrarca, a review of 'Le rime del
Petrarca con note letterali e critiche del Castelvetro,
Tassoni, Muratori, Alfieri, Ginguené', 2 vols (Florence,
1842) (a reprint of the first edition, 1832) and Thomas
Campbell's 'The Life of Petrarch', 2 vols (London, 1841),
is a masterful example of the nineteenth-century biographical and critical essay. Written sympathetically, wit-
tily, and with insight gained from the reviewer's own
domestic tragedies, this masterpiece is unique among
Landor's critical writings. It first appeared in the
July 1843 'Foreign Quarterly Review' and was reprinted
with minor revisions in 'Last Fruit off an Old Tree'
(1853). About one-half of the review as it appeared in
1853 is reproduced below. The modern system of numbering
Petrarch's poems is followed in the text and is based on
'Francesco Petrarca: Rime, Trionfi, e poesie latine',
eds F. Neri, G. Martellotti, E. Bianchi, and N. Sapegno,
La letteratura italiana Storia e Testi vol. 6, Milan and
Naples, 1951.

Scarcely on any author, of whatever age or country, has
there so much been written, spoken, and thought, by both
sexes, as on the subject of this criticism, Petrarca.
   The compilation by Mr. Campbell (1) is chiefly drawn
together from the French. It contains no criticism on
the poetry of his author, beyond a hasty remark or two in
places which least require it. He might have read Sismondi and Ginguené more profitably; (2) the author of the
'Introduction to the Literature of Europe' (3) had already
done so; but neither has he thrown any fresh light on the
character or the writings of Petrarca, or, in addition to
what had already been performed by those two judicious
men, furnished us with a remark in any way worth
notice....
290

Whoever is desirous of knowing all about Petrarca, will consult Muratori and De Sade: (4) whoever has been waiting for a compendious and sound judgment on his works at large, will listen attentively to Ginguené: whoever can be gratified by a rapid glance at his works and character, will be directed by the clear-sighted follower of truth, Sismondi: and whoever reads only English, and is contented to fare on a small portion of recocted criticism in a long excursion, may be accommodated by Mrs. Dobson, (5) Mr. Hallam, and Mr. Campbell.

It may seem fastidious and affected to write, as I have done, his Italian name in preference to his English one; but I think it better to call him as he called himself, as Laura called him, as he was called by Colonna and Rienzi (6) and Boccaccio, and in short by all Italy: for I pretend to no vernacular familiarity with a person of his distinction, and should almost be as ready to abbreviate Francesco into Frank, as Petrarca into Petrarch. Beside, the one appellation is euphonious, the other quite the reverse....

Francesco Petrarca, if far from the greatest, yet certainly the most celebrated of poets, was born in the night between the nineteenth and twentieth day of July, 1304. His father's name was Petracco, his mother's Eletta Canigiani. Petracco left Florence under the same sentence of banishment as his friend Dante Alighieri, and joined with him and the other exiles of the Bianchi army in the unsuccessful attack on that city, the very night when, on his return to Arezzo, he found a son born to him: it was his first. To this son, afterward so illustrious, was given the name of Francesco di Petracco. In after life the sound had something in it which he thought ignoble; and he converted it into Petrarca....

When he was seven months old he was taken by his mother from Arezzo to Incisa, in the Val-d'Arno, where the life so lately given was nearly lost. The infant was dropped into the river, which is always rapid in that part of its course, and was then swollen by rain into a torrent. At Incisa he remained with her seven years. The father had retired to Pisa; and now his wife and Francesco, and another son born after, named Gherardo, joined him there. In a short time however he took them to Avignon, where he hoped for employment under Pope Clement V. (7) In that crowded city lodgings and provisions were so dear, that he soon found it requisite to send his wife and children to the small episcopal town of Carpentras, where he often went to visit them. In this place Francesco met

Convenevole, who had taught him his letters, and who now
undertook to teach him what he knew of rhetoric and
logic. (8)   He had attained his tenth year when the
father took him with a party of friends to the fountain of
Vaucluse.   Even at that early age his enthusiasm was excited by the beauty and solitude of the scene.   The
waters then flowed freely: habitations there were none
but the most rustic: and indeed one only near the rivulet.   Such was then Vaucluse;   and such it remained all
his lifetime, and long after.   The tender heart is often
moulded by localities.   Perhaps the purity and singleness
of Petrarca's, his communion with it on one only altar,
his exclusion of all images but one, result from this
early visit to the gushing springs, the eddying torrents,
the insurmountable rocks, the profound and inviolate solitudes, of Vaucluse.

The time was now come when his father saw the necessity
of beginning to educate him for a profession: and he
thought the canon law was likely to be the most advanta-
geous.   Consequently he was sent to Montpellier, the
nearest university, where he resided four years;   not en-
gaged, as he ought to have been, among the jurisconsults,
but among the classics.   Information of this perversity
soon reached Petracco, who hastened to the place, found
the noxious books, and threw them into the fire: but,
affected by the lamentations of his son, he recovered the
Cicero and the Virgil, and restored them to him, partially
consumed.   At the age of eighteen he was sent from Montpellier to Bologna, where he found Cino da Pistoja, (9)
to whom he applied himself in good earnest, not indeed for
his knowledge as a jurisconsult, in which he had acquired
the highest reputation, but for his celebrity as a poet.
After two more years he lost his father: and the guar-
dians, it is said, were unfaithful to their trust.   Probably there was little for them to administer.   He now returned to Avignon, where, after the decease of Clement V.,
John XXII. occupied the popedom. (10)   Here his Latin
poetry soon raised him into notice, for nobody in Avignon
wrote so good;   but happily, both for himself and many
thousand sensitive hearts in every age and nation, he soon
desired his verses to be received and understood by one to
whom the Latin was unknown.

Benedetto sia il giorno, e 'l mese, e l'anno!

Blest be the day, and month, and year!
['Rime', lxi, 1.]

Laura, daughter of Audibert de Noves, was married to

Hugh de Sade; (11) persons of distinction. She was
younger by three years than Petrarca. They met first on
Good Friday, in the convent-church of St. Claire, at six
in the morning. (12) That hour she inspired such a passion, by her beauty and her modesty, as years only tended
to strengthen, and death to sanctify. The incense which
burnt in the breast of Petrarca before his Laura, might
have purified, one would have thought, even the court of
Avignon; and never was love so ardent breathed into ear
so chaste. The man who excelled all others in beauty of
person, in dignity of demeanour, in genius, in tenderness,
in devotion, was perhaps the only one who failed in at-
taining the object of his desires. But cold as Laura was
in temperament, rigid as she was in her sense of duty, she
never was insensible to the merits of her lover. A light
of distant hope often shone upon him, and tempted him onward, through surge after surge, over the depths of passion. Laura loved admiration, as the most retired and
most diffident of women do: and the admiration of Petrarca drew after it the admiration of the world. She also,
what not all women do, looked forward to the glory that
awaited her, when those courtiers, and those crowds, and
that city should be no more, and when of all women, the
Madonna alone should be so glorified on earth.

Perhaps it is well for those who delight in poetry that
she was inflexible and obdurate; for the sweetest song
ceases when the feathers have lined the nest. Incredible
as it may seem, Petrarca was capable of quitting her: he
was capable of believing that absence could moderate, or
perhaps extinguish, his passion. Generally the lover who
can think so, has almost succeeded; but Petrarca had contracted the habit of writing poetry; and now writing it
on Laura, and Laura only, he brought the past and the
future into a focus on his breast. All magical powers,it
is said, are dangerous to the possessor: none is more
dangerous than the magic of the poet, who can call before
him at will the object of his wishes; but her countenance
and her words remain her own, and beyond his influence.

It is wonderful how extremely few, even of Italian
scholars, and natives of Italy, have read his letters or
his poetry entirely through. I am not speaking of his
Latin; for it would indeed be a greater marvel if the
most enterprising industry succeeded there. The thunderbolt of war .. 'Scipiades fulmen belli' ['The son of the
house of Scipio, thunderbolt of war' (Lucretius, 'De Rerum
Natura', iii, 1034)] .. has always left a barren place
behind. No poet ever was fortunate in the description of
his exploits; and the least fortunate of the number is
Petrarca. Probably the whole of the poem (13) contains

no sentence or image worth remembering.   I say *probably*:
for whosoever has hit upon what he thought the best of it,
has hit only upon what is worthless, or else upon what belongs to another.   The few lines quoted and applauded by
Mr. Campbell, (14) are taken partly from Virgil's
'AEneid', and partly from Ovid's 'Metamorphoses'. (15)   I
can not well believe that any man living has read beyond
five hundred lines of 'Africa':   I myself, in sundry expe-
ditions, have penetrated about thus far into its immeas-
urable sea of sand.   But the wonder is that neither the
poetry nor the letters of Petrarca seem to have been, even
in his own country, read thoroughly and attentively;   for
surely his commentators ought to have made themselves masters of these, before they agitated the question, some
whether Laura really existed, and others whether she was
flexible to the ardour of her lover.   Speaking of his
friends, Socrates and Laelius, (16) of whose first meeting
with him I shall presently make mention, he says,

> Con costor colsi 'l glorioso ramo
> Onde forse anzi tempo ornai le tempie,
> In memoria di quella ch' i' tant' amo:
> Ma pur di lei che il cor di pensier m'empie
> Non potei coglier mai ramo nè foglia;
> Si fur' le sue radici acerbe ed empie,
> ['Trionfi d'Amore', iv, 79-84.]

I can not render these verses much worse than they actually are, with their '*tempo*' and '*tempie*', and their
'radici *empie*', so let me venture to offer a translation:

> They saw me win the glorious bough
> That shades my temples even now,
> *Who never bough nor leaf could take*
> From that severe one, for whose sake
> So many sighs and tears arose ..
> Unbending root of bitter woes.

There is a canzone to the same purport, to be noticed
in its place;   and several of his letters could also be
adduced in evidence.   We may believe that, although he
had resolved to depart from Avignon for a season, he felt
his love increasing at every line he wrote.   Such
thoughts and images can not be turned over in the mind and
leave it perfectly in composure.   Yet perhaps when he had
completed the most impassioned sonnet, the surges of his
love may have subsided under the oil he had poured out on
his vanity.   For love, if it is a weakness, was not the
only weakness of Petrarca: and, when he had performed

what he knew was pleasing in the eyes of Laura, he looked
abroad for the applauses of all around....

In the bosom of Petrarca love burned again more ardent-
ly than ever. It is censured as the worst of conceits in
him that he played so often on the name of Laura; and
many have suspected that there could be little passion in
so much allusion. A purer taste might indeed have corrected in the poetry the outpourings of tenderness on the
name; but surely there is a true and a pardonable pleasure in cherishing the very sound of what we love. If it
belongs to the heart, as it does, it belongs to poetry,
and is not easily to be cast aside. The shrub recalling
the idea of Laura was planted by his hand; often, that he
might nurture it, was the pen laid by; the leaves were
often shaken by his sighs, and not unfrequently did they
sparkle with his tears. He felt the comfort of devotion
as he bent before the image of her name. But he now saw
little of her, and was never at her house: it was only in
small parties, chiefly of ladies, that they met. She excelled them all in grace of person and in elegance of
attire. Probably her dress was not the more indifferent
to her on her thinking whom she was about to meet: yet
she maintained the same reserve: the nourisher of love,
but not of hope....

... Simone Martini, the first of the moderns who gave
roundness and beauty to the female face, neglected not the
graceful air of Laura. Frequently did he repeat her
modest features in the principal figure of his sacred compositions; and Petrarca was alternately tortured and consoled by the possession of her portrait from the hand of
Martini. (17) It was painted in the year 1339, so that
she was thirty-two years old; but, whether at the desire
of her lover, or guided by his own discretion, or that in
reality she retained the charms of youth after bearing
eight or nine children, she is represented youthful, and
almost girlish, whenever he introduces her.
With her picture now before him, Petrarca thought he
could reduce in number and duration his visits to Avignon,
and might undertake a work sufficient to fix his attention
and occupy his retirement. He began to compose in Latin
a history of Rome, from its foundation to the subversion
of Jerusalem. (18) But, almost at the commencement, the
exploits of Scipio Africanus seized upon his enthusiastic
imagination, and determined him to abandon history for
poetry. (19) The second Punic war was the subject he

chose for an epic. Deficient as the work is in all the
requisites of poetry, his friends applauded it beyond
measure. And indeed no small measure of commendation is
due to it; for here he had restored in some degree the
plan and tone of antiquity. But to such a pitch was his
vanity exalted, that he aspired to higher honors than
Virgil had received under the favor of Augustus, (20) and
was ambitious of being crowned in the capitol. His
powerful patrons removed every obstacle; and the senator
of Rome invited him by letter to his coronation. (21) ...

... But Petrarca stood far above all the other poets of
his age; and, incompetent as were his judges, it is much
to their praise that they awarded due honour to the puri-
fier both of language and of morals. With these indeed
to solicit the wife of another may seem inconsistent; but
such was always the custom of the Tuscan race; and not
always with the same chastity as was enforced by Laura....

There is much resemblance in the character of Petrarca
to that of Abélard. Both were learned, both were dispu-
tatious, both were handsome, both were vain; both ran incessantly backward and forward from celebrity to seclusion, from seclusion to celebrity; both loved unhappily;
but the least fortunate was the most beloved. (22)
Devoted as Petrarca was to the classics, and prone as
the Italian poets are to follow and imitate them, he
stands apart with Laura; and if some of his reflections
are to be found in the sonnets of Cino da Pistoja, and a
few in the more precious reliquary of Latin Elegy, he
seems disdainful of repeating in her ear what has ever
been spoken in another's. Although a cloud of pure incense rises up and veils the intensity of his love, it is
such love as animates all creatures upon earth, and tends
to the same object in all. Throughout life we have been
accustomed to hear of the Platonic: absurd as it is
everywhere, it is most so here. Nothing in the volumi-
nous works of Plato authorizes us to affix this designation to simple friendship, to friendship exempt from passion. On the contrary, the philosopher leaves us no
doubt whatever that his notion of love is sensual. (23)
He says expressly what species of it, and from what be-
stowers, should be the reward of sages and heroes.

Dii meliora piis!

[The gods grant higher rewards to the upright, tr
H.B.]

Beside Sonnets and Canzoni Petrarca wrote 'Sestine';
so named because each stanza contains six verses, and each
poem six stanzas, to the last of which three lines are
added.   If the terza rima is disagreeable to the ear,
what is the sestina, in which there are only six rhymes to
thirty-six verses, and all these respond to the same
words!   Cleverness in distortion can proceed no further.
Petrarca wearied the popes by his repeated solicitations
that they would abandon Avignon: (24) he never thought of
repeating a sestina to them: it would have driven the
most obtuse and obstinate out to sea; and he never would
have removed his hands from under the tiara until he entered the port of Civita-Vecchia. (25)   While our poet
was thus amusing his ingenuity by the most intolerable
scheme of rhyming that the poetry of any language has exhibited, his friend Boccaccio was occupied in framing that
very stanza, the ottava rima, which so delights us in
Berni, (26) Ariosto, and Tasso.   But Tasso is most harmonious when he expatiates most freely, 'numerisque fertur
lege solutis' ['(Pindar) is borne along in measures freed
from rule' (Horace, 'Odes', iv, 2, 11-12)]: for instance,
in the 'Aminta', where he is followed by Milton in his
'Lycidas'....

...   In January the poet left Parma for Vienna, where on
the 25th (1348) he felt the shock of an earthquake.   In
the preceding month a column of fire was observed above
the pontifical palace.   After these harbingers of calam-
ity came that memorable plague, to which we owe the immortal work of Boccaccio; (27) a work occupying the next
station, in continental literature, to the 'Divina Commedia', and displaying a greater variety of powers.   The
pestilence had now penetrated into the northern parts of
Italy, and into the southern of France; it had ravaged
Marseilles; it was raging in Avignon.   Petrarca sent
messenger after messenger for intelligence.   Their return
was tardy; and only on the 19th of May was notice brought
to him that Laura had departed on the 6th of April, at six
in the morning; the very day, the very hour, he met her
first.   Beloved by all about her for her gentleness and
serenity, she expired in the midst of relatives and
friends.   But did never her eyes look round for one who
was away?   And did not love, did not glory tell him, that
in that chamber he might at least have died?...

In the year of the jubilee (1350) he went again to
Rome.   Passing through Florence, he there visited

Boccaccio, whom he had met at Naples.   What was scarcely
an acquaintance grew rapidly into friendship; and this
friendship, honorable to both, lasted throughout life, unbroken and undiminished.   Both were eloquent, both richly
endowed with fancy and imagination; but Petrarca, who had
incomparably the least of these qualities, had a readier
faculty of investing them with verse, in which Boccaccio,
fond as he was of poetry, ill succeeded.   There are
stories in the 'Decameron' which require more genius to
conceive and execute than all the poetry of Petrarca, and
indeed there is in Boccaccio more variety of the mental
powers than in any of his countrymen, greatly more deep
feeling, greatly more mastery over the human heart, than
in any other but Dante.   Honesty, manliness, a mild and
social independence, rendered him the most delightful companion and the sincerest friend....

    ...   In the winter following (1359) Boccaccio spent
several days at Linterno, and the poet gave him his Latin
Eclogues in his own handwriting.   On his return to Florence, Boccaccio sent his friend the 'Divina Commedia',
written out likewise by himself, and accompanied with
profuse commendations.
    Incredible as it may appear, this noble poem, the glory
of Italy, and admitting at that time but one other in the
world to a proximity with it, was wanting to the library
of Petrarca.   His reply was cold and cautious: (28) the
more popular man, it might be thought, took umbrage at the
loftier.   He was jealous even of the genius which had
gone by, and which bore no resemblance to his own, excepting in the purity and intensity of love: for this was a
portion of the genius in both.   He was certainly the very
best man that ever was a very vain one: and vanity has a
better excuse for itself in him than in any other, since
none was more admired by the world at large, and particularly by that part of it which the wisest are most desirous to conciliate, turning their wisdom in full activity
to the elevation of their happiness.   Laura, it is true,
was sensible of little or no passion for him; but she was
pleased with his; and stood like a beautiful Cariatid of
stainless marble, at the base of an image on which the
eyes of Italy were fixed.
    Petrarca, like Boccaccio, regretted at the close of
life, not only the pleasure he had enjoyed, but also the
pleasure he had imparted to the world.   Both of them, as
their mental faculties were diminishing, and their animal
spirits were leaving them apace, became unconscious how
incomparably greater was the benefit than the injury done

by their writings.   In Boccaccio there are certain tales
so coarse that modesty casts them aside, and those only
who are irreparably contaminated can receive any amusement
from them.   But in the greater part, what truthfulness,
what tenderness, what joyousness, what purity!   Their
levities and gaieties are like the harmless lightnings of
a summer sky in the delightful regions they were written
in.   Petrarca, with a mind which bears the same proportion to Boccaccio's as the Sorga bears to the Arno, (29)
has been the solace of many sad hours to those who probably were more despondent.   It may be that, at the time
when he was writing some of his softest and most sorrowful
complaints, his dejection was caused by dalliance with
another, far more indulgent than Laura.   But his ruling
passion was ungratified by her;   therefor she died unsung,
and, for aught we know to the contrary, unlamented.   He
had forgotten what he had declared in Sonnet 17.

E, se di lui fors'altra donna spera,
    Vive in speranza debile e fallace,
    Mio, perche sdegno ciò ch'a voi dispiace, &c.

If any other hopes to find
    That love in me which you despise,
    Ah! let her leave the hope behind:
I hold from all what you alone should prize.
['Rime', xxi, 5-7.]

It can only be said that he ceased to be a visionary:
and we ought to rejoice that an inflammation, of ten
years' recurrence, sank down into a regular fit, and
settled in no vital part....

...   Happily there is preserved the friendly letter he
wrote to Boccaccio on his return;   the last of his writings. (30)   During the greater part of his lifetime,
though no less zealous than Boccaccio himself in recover-
ing the works of the classics, he never had read the
'Divina Commedia';   nor, until this period of it, the
'Decameron';   the two most admirable works the continent
has produced from the restoration of learning to the present day.   Boccaccio, who had given him the one, now gave
him the other. (31)   In his letter of thanks for it, he
excuses the levity of his friend in some places, attributes it to the season of life in which the book was written, and relates the effect the story of Griseldis (32)
had produced, not only on himself, but on another of less
sensibility.   He even learned it by heart, that he might

recite it to his friends; and he sent the author a Latin
translation of it. (33) ...

On the 18th of July, 1374, Petrarca was found in his
library, his brow upon a book he had been reading: he
was dead.

There is no record of any literary man, or perhaps of
any man whatsoever, to whom such honors, honors of so many
kinds, and from such different quarters and personages,
have been offered.   They began in his early life; and we
are walking at this hour in the midst of the procession.
Few travellers dare to return from Italy until they can
describe to the attentive ear and glistening eye the
scenery of the Euganean hills.   He who has loved truly,
and, above all, he who has loved unhappily, approaches, as
holiest altars are approached, the cenotaph on the little
columns at Arquà.

The Latin works of Petrarca were esteemed by himself
more highly than his Italian. (34)   His Letters and his
Dialogues 'De Contemptu Mundi', (35) are curious and valuable.   In the latter he converses with Saint Augustin, (36) to whom he is introduced by *Truth*, the same
personage who appears in his 'Africa', and whom Voltaire
also invokes to descend on his little gravelly Champ de
Mars, the 'Henriade'.   The third dialogue is about his
love for Laura, and nobly is it defended.   He wrote a
treatise on the ignorance of one's self and others
(*multorum*), (37) in which he has taken much from Cicero
and Augustin, and in which he afterward forgot a little of
his own.   'Ought we to take it to heart', says he, 'if we
are ill spoken of by the ignorant and malicious, when the
same thing happened to Homer and Demosthenes, to Cicero
and Virgil?' (38)   He was fond of following these two;
Cicero in the number of his epistles, Virgil in eclogue
and in epic.

Of his twelve eclogues, which by a strange nomenclature
he also called bucolics, many are satirical. (39)   In the
sixth and seventh Pope Clement is represented in the
character of Mitio.   In the sixth Saint Peter, under the
name of Pamphilus, reproaches him for the condition in
which he keeps his flock, and asks him what he has done
with the wealth intrusted to him.   Mitio answers that he
has kept the gold arising from the sale of the lambs, and
that he has given the milk to certain friends of his.   He
adds that his spouse, very different from the old woman
Pamphilus was contented with, went about in gold and
jewels.   As for the rams and goats, they played their
usual gambols in the meadow; and he himself looked on.

Pamphilus is indignant, and tells him he ought to be
flogged and sent to prison for life.   Mitio drops on a
sudden his peaceful character, and calls him a faithless
runaway slave, deserving the fetter and the cross.   In
the twelfth eclogue, under the appellations of Pan and
Arthicus, are represented the kings of France and England. (40)   Arthicus is indignant at the favors Pan receives from Faustula (Avignon).   To king John the
pope (41) had remitted his tenths, so that he was enabled
to continue the war against England, which ended in his
captivity. (42)

Petrarca in all his Latin poetry, and indeed in all his
Latin compositions, is an imitator, and generally a very
unsuccessful one; but his versification is more harmonious, and his language has more the air of antiquity, and
more resembles the better models, than any had done since
Boethius. (43)

We now come to his Italian poetry.   In this he is less
deficient in originality, though in several pieces he has
imitated too closely Cino da Pistoja.   'Mille dubj in un
dì', (44) for instance, in his seventh canzone ['Rime',
ccclx].   Cino is crude and enigmatical; but there is a
beautiful sonnet by him addressed to Dante, which he wrote
on passing the Apennines, and stopping to visit the tomb
and invoke the name of Selvaggia. (45)   Petrarca, late in
life, made a collection of sonnets on Laura; they are not
printed in the order in which they were written.   The
first [I] is a kind of prologue to the rest, as the first
ode of Horace is.   There is a melancholy grace in this
preliminary piece.   The third [III] ought to have been
the second; for, after having in the first related his
errors and regrets, we might have expected to find the
cause of them in the following; we find it in the third.
'Di pensier in pensier' [CXXIX], 'Chiare fresche, e dolci
acque' [CXXVI], 'Se il pensier che mi strugge' [CXXV],
'Benedetto sia il giorno' [LXI], 'Solo e pensoso' [XXXV],
are incomparably better than the 'Tre Sorelle' [LXXI-
LXXIII], by which the Italians are enchanted, and which
the poet himself views with great complacency.   These
three are upon the eyes of Laura.   The seventh canzone
[LXXII], the second of the 'Sorelle', or, as they have
often been styled, the 'Grazie', is the most admired of
them.   In this however the ear is offended at *'Qual all'
alta'* [1. 65].   The critics do not observe this sad caco-
phony.   And nothing is less appropriate than

Ed al foco *gentil* ond'io *tuit'ardo.*

[And fires, though all engrossing, pure as mine (LXXII,
66 tr L.D.).]

The close is,

Canzon! l'una Sorella è poco inanzi,
E l' altra sento in quel medesmo albergo
Apparecchiarsi, *ond' io più carta vergo.*

[My lay, thy sister-song is gone before,
And now another in my teeming brain
Prepares itself: whence I resume the strain
(LXXII, 76-8 tr L.D.).]

This ruins the figure.   What becomes of the *Sorella*, and
the *albergo*, and the *apparecchiarsi*?   The third is less
celebrated than the two elder sisters.
    Muratori, the most judicious of Italian commentators,
gives these canzoni the preference over the others: (46)
but it remained for a foreigner to write correctly on
them, and to demonstrate that they are very faulty.   I
find more faults and graver than Ginguené has found in
them: (47) but I do not complain with him so much that
the commencement of the third is heavy and languid, (48)
as that serious thoughts are intersected with quibbles,
and spangled with conceits.   I will here remark freely,
and in some detail, on this part of the poetry of
Petrarca.
    Sonetto 21 [XXXIV].   It will be difficult to find in
all the domains of poetry so frigid a conceit as in the
conclusion of this sonnet,

    E far delle sue braccia a se stess' ombra.

    [And with her arms weaving herself a shade (1. 14
    tr J.A.).]

Strange that it should be followed by the most beautiful
he ever wrote:

    Solo e pensoso, &c.

    [Alone, thought-sick, I pace where none has been
    (XXXV tr J.A.).]

    Canzone 1 [XXIII].

Ne meho ancor m' agghiaccia
L'esser coverto poi di bianche piume,
....
Ond' io presi col suon color di cigno!

[Nor less was my alarm,
When next my frame white down was seen to shroud,
... For the sad snowy swan both form and language lent,
(ll. 50-1, 60 tr M.M.).]

How very inferior is this childish play to Horace's ode,
in which he also becomes a swan. (49)
    Canzone 3 [XXXVII].   Among the thousand offices which
he attributes to the eyes is *carrying the keys*.   Here he
talks of the *sweet eyes* carrying the keys of his *sweet
thoughts* [ll. 33-5.]   Again he has a peep at the keyhole
in the seventh.

    Quel core ond'hanno i begli occhi la chiave.

    [That heart ...
    Of which the warders are those beauteous eyes
    (LXXII, 30 tr L.D.).]

He also lets us into the secret that he is really *fond* of
complaining, and that he *takes pains* to have his eyes always full of tears.

    Ed io son un di quei che' il pianger *giova,*
    E par ben ch' io m' *ingegni*
    Che di lagrime pregni
    Sien gli occhi miei.

    [And I am one from sadness who relief
    So draw, as if it still
    My study were to fill
    These eyes with softness, ...,
    (XXXVII, 69-72 tr M.M.).]

    Sonetto 20 [XLI].   Here are Phoebus, Vulcan, Jupiter,
Caesar, Janus, Saturn, Mars, Orion, Neptune, Juno, and a
chorus of *Angels*: and they have only fourteen lines to
turn about in.
    Canzone 4 [L].   The last part has merit from 'E perche
un poco' [ll. 57ff].
    Sonetto 39 [LXI].   In this beautiful sonnet, as in al-
most every one, there is a redundancy of words: for instance,

    Benedetto sia il giorno, e 'l mese, e l'anno,
    E la stagione, e 'l tempo.

    [Blest be the day, and blest the month and year,
    Season and hour
    (ll. 1-2 tr J.A.).]

Sonetto 40 [LXII] is very serious. It is a prayer to God that his heart may be turned to other desires, and that it may remember how on that day He was crucified.

Sestina 3 [LXVI]. With what derision would a poet of the present day be treated who had written such stuff as,

E *nel bel* petto l'*indurato* ghiaccio
Che trae del mio si *dolorosi venti*.

[And in that lovely breast be harden'd ice
Which forces still from mine so dolorous winds
(ll. 29-30 tr M.M.).]

Sonetto 44 [LXVIII]. 'L'aspetto sacro' is ingenious, yet without conceits.

Canzone 8 [LXXIII]. As far as we know it has never been remarked (nor indeed is an Italian Academia worth a remark) that the motto of the Academia della Crusca, (50) 'Il più bel fior ne coglie' is from

E, le onorate
Cose cercando, il più bel fior ne coglse

[(And) seeking there
Honour, and culling oft its garland fair
(ll. 35-6 tr M.M.).]

Sonetto 46 [LXXIV]. Here he wonders whence all the ink can come with which he fills his paper on Laura.

Sonetto 51 [LXXIX]. In the fourteenth year of his passion, his ardour is increasing to such a degree, that, he says, 'Death approaches ... *and life flies away*'.

Che la morte s'appressa ... *e'l viver fugge.*
[l. 14.]

We believe there is no instance where life has resisted the encounter.

Sonetto 59 [LXXXVIII]. This is very different from all his others. The first part is poor enough: the last would be interesting if we could believe it to be more than imaginary. Here he boasts of the impression he had made on Laura, yet in his last Canzone he asks her whether he ever had. (51) The words of this sonnet are,

Era ben forte la nemica mia,
E lei vid' io ferita in *mezzo al core*.

[Love found my beautiful enemy brave indeed -

Yet in her heart's heart even she will bleed
(ll. 13-14 tr J.A.).]

But we may well take all this for ideal, when we read the
very next, in which he speaks of being free from the
thraldom that had held him so many years [LXXXIX].

Sonetto 66 [XCVII].   The conclusion from 'Ne mi lece
ascoltar' [ll. 9ff], is very animated: here is greatly
more vigor and incitation than usual.

Canzone 9 [CV].   It would be difficult to find anywhere, except in the rarest and most valuable books, so
wretched a poem as this.   The rhymes occur over and over
again, not only at the close, but often at the fifth and
sixth syllables, and then another time.   Metastasio has
managed best the redundant rhymes.

Sonetto 73 [CIX].   The final part, 'L'aura soave'
[ll. 9ff], is exquisitely beautiful, and the harmony complete.

Sonetto 84 [CXXIII].   'Quel vago impallidir' is among
the ten best.

Canzone 10 [CXXV].   In the last stanza [ll. 66ff]
there is a lightness of movement not always to be found in
the graces of Petrarca.

Canzone 11 [CXXVI].   This is incomparably the most
elaborate work of the poet, but it is very far from the
perfection of 'Solo e pensoso' [XXXV].   The second and
third stanzas are inferior to the rest [ll. 14-39];   and
the fera bella e mansueta [the fair and gentle beast (l.
29 tr J.W.)] is quite unworthy of the place it occupies.

Canzone 13 [CXXIX] is extremely beautiful until we come
to

Pur lí medesmo assido,
Me freddo, pietra morta in pietra viva.

[I sit me down on the cold rugged stone,
Less cold, less dead than I
(ll. 50-1 tr L.D.).]

Sonetto 94 [CXLV].   'Pommi ove'l Sol' is imitated
from Horace's 'Pone me pigris' ['Odes', i, 22, 17], &c.

Sonetto 98 [CXLVIII].   Four verses are filled with the
names of rivers, excepting the monosyllables non and e.
He says that all these rivers can not slake the fire that
is the anguish of his heart: no, nor even ivy, fir, pine,
beech, or juniper.   It is by no means a matter of wonder,
that these subsidiaries lend but little aid to the exertions of the fireman....

Sonetto 111 [CLXII].   No extravagance ever surpassed the invocation to the rocks in the water, requiring that henceforward there would not be a single one which had neglected to learn how to burn with his flames.   He himself can only go farther in.

Sonetto 119 [CLXXI], where he tells us that Laura's eyes can burn up the Rhine when it is most frozen, and crack its hardest rocks.

Sonetto 132 [CLXXXIV].   In the precarious state of her health, he fears more about the disappointment of his hopes in love than about her danger.

Sonetto 147 [CC].   His descriptions of beauty are not always distinct and correct: for example,

Gli occhi sereni e le *stellanti* ciglia
La bella bocca angelica .. di perle
Piena, e di rose .. e di dolci *parole*.

[That star-stained forehead, that most tranquil-eyed,
That mild angelic mouth where rose-mist glows
Against pearl glimmer, whence rich musics glide -
(ll. 9-11 tr J.A.).]

In this place we shall say a little about *occhi* and *ciglia*.   First, the sense would be better and the verse equally good, if, transposing the epithets, it were written

Gli occhi stellanti e le sereno ciglia.

The Italian poets are very much in the habit of putting the *eyelashes* for the *eyes*, because *ciglia* is a most useful rhyme.   The Latin poets, contented with *oculi*, *ocelli*, and *lumina*, never employ *cilia*, of which indeed they appear to have made but little account.   Greatly more than a hundred times has Petrarca inserted eyes into the first part of his sonnets;   it is rarely that we find one without its *occhi*.   They certainly are very ornamental things;   but it is not desirable for a poet to resemble an Argus.

Canzone 15 [CCVI].   The versification here differs from the others, but is no less beautiful than in any of them.   However, where Love appears in person, we would rather that Pharaoh, Rachel, &c., were absent.

Sonetto 156 [CCXI].   He tells us on what day he entered the labyrinth of love.

Mille trecento ventisette *a punto*
Su l'ora prima il dì sesto d'Aprile.

[In thirteen hundred twenty seven - O vow
Still vivid! - April! - sixth sun! - First hour! -
(ll. 12-13 tr J.A.).]

This poetry has very unfairly been taken advantage of,
in a book

Written by William Prynne Esquier, the
Year of our Lord six hundred thirty-three. (52)

Sonetto 158 [CCXIII].   He has now loved twenty years.
Sonetto 160 [CCXVI].   The first verse is rendered very
inharmonious by the cesura and the final word having syllables that rhyme.   Tutto 'l dì *piango*, e poi la notte
quando, lagri*mando*, and consu*mando* [All the day I cry and
then the night, when, / ... weeping/ ... wasting (ll. 1,
4-5 tr J.W.)], are considered as rhymes, although rhymes
should be formed by similarity of sound and not by identity.   The Italians, the Spaniards, and the French,
reject this canon.
Sonetto 187 [CCXLV], on the present of two roses, is
light and pretty.
Sonetto 192 [CCL].   He fears he may never see Laura
again.   Probably this was written after her death.   He
dreams of her saying to him, 'do you not remember the last
evening, when I left you with your eyes in tears?   Forced
to go away from you, I would not tell you, nor could I,
what I tell you now.   *Do not hope to see me again on
earth*' [ll. 9-14].   This most simple and beautiful sonnet
has been less noticed than many which a pure taste would
have rejected.   The next is a vision of Laura's death
[CCLI].   There are verses in Petrarca which will be uttered by many sorrowers through many ages.   Such, for instance, are

Non la conobbe il mondo mentre l'ebbe,
Conobbila io chi a pianger quì rimasi.

[None knew her worth until the glory went -
I only knew, whose heart forever grieves
(CCCXXXVIII, 12-13 tr J.A.).]

But we are hard of belief when he says

Pianger cercai, *non già del pianto onore*.

[My overwhelming aim
Was only ... to give full vent
To my sick heart and not to flatter fame
(CCXCIII, 12 tr J.A.).]

There are fourteen more Sonnets, and one more Canzone in the first series of the 'Rime'; but we must here close it. Of the second, third, and fourth series we must be contented with fewer notices, for already we have exceeded the limits we proposed. They were written after Laura's death, and contain altogether somewhat more than the first alone. Many of the poems in them are grave, tender, and beautiful. There are the same faults, but fewer in number, and less in degree. He never talks again, as he does in the last words of the first [CCLXVI, 12-14], of carrying a laurel and a column in his bosom, the one for fifteen, the other for eighteen years.

Ginguené seems disinclined to allow a preference to this second part of the Canzoniere. (53) But surely it is in general far more pathetic, and more exempt from the importunities of petty fancies. He takes the trouble to translate the wretched sonnet (33, part 2) [CCCI] (54) in which the waters of the river are increased by the poet's tears, and the fish (as they had a right to expect) are spoken to. But the next is certainly a most beautiful poem, and worthy of Dante himself, whose manner of thinking and style of expression it much resembles. There is a canzone in dialogue which also resembles it in sentiment and feeling;

Quando il soave mio fido conforto, &c.

[When she, the faithful soother of my pain
(CCCIIX tr L.D.).]

The next again is imitated from Cino da Pistoja: what a crowd of words at the opening!

Quel antiquo mio dolce empio signore.

[My long-time gentle ruthless lord
(CCCLX tr J.W.).]

It is permitted in no other poetry than the Italian to shovel up such a quantity of trash and triviality before the doors. But rather than indulge in censure, we will recommend to the especial perusal of the reader another list of admirable compositions. 'Alma felice' [CCLXXXII], 'Anima bella' [CCCV], 'Ite rime dolenti' [CCCXXXIII], 'Tornami a mente' [CCCXXXVI], 'Quel rosignuol' [CCCXI], 'Vago augelletto' [CCCLIII], 'Dolce mio caro' [CCCXL], 'Gli angeli' [CCCXLVI], 'Oime! il bel viso' [CCLXVII], 'Che debb' io far' [CCLXVIII], 'Amor! se vuo' [CCLXX], 'O aspettata' [XXVIII], 'Anima, che diverse'

[CCIV], 'Spirto gentil' [LIII], 'Italia mia' [CXXVIII].
Few indeed, if any, of these are without a flaw; but they
are of higher worth than those on which the reader, unless
forewarned, would spend his time unprofitably.   It would
be a great blessing if a critic deeply versed in this literature, like Carey, (55) would publish the Italian poets
with significant marks before the passages worth reading;
the more worth, and the less.   Probably it would not be a
mark of admiration, only that surprise and admiration have
but one between them, which would follow the poet's dec-
laration in Can. 6 [LXXI], that 'if he does not melt away
it is because fear holds him together' [ll. 31-6].   After
this foolery he becomes a true poet again, 'O poggi!' &c.
[ll. 37ff], then again bad, 'You see how many colors love
paints my face with' [ll. 52-3].

Nothing he ever wrote is so tender as a reproach of
Laura's, after ten years' admiration, 'You are *soon* grown
tired of loving me!'   He replies, (56)

Io non fui d'amor voi lassato unquanco, &c.

[Yet was I never of your love aggrieved (LXXXII tr
T.W.).]

There is poetry in Petrarca which we have not yet ad-
verted to, in which he has changed the chords καὶ τὴν
λύρην ἅπασαν [then (I changed the) lyre as well ('The
Disobedient Lyre', no. 23 from 'The Anacreontea', l. 6)];
such as 'Fiamma dal ciel [CXXXVI], 'L'avara Babilonia'
[CXXXVII], 'Fontana di dolore' [CXXXVIII].   The volumes
close with the 'Trionfi'.   The first, as we might have
anticipated, is 'Il Trionfo d'Amore'.   The poem is a vile
one, stuffed with proper names.   The 'Triumph of Chastity' is shorter, as might also be anticipated, and not
quite so full of them.   At the close, Love meets Laura,
who makes him her captive, and carries him in triumph
among the virgins and matrons most celebrated for purity
and constancy.   The 'Triumph of Death' follows.

This poem is truly admirable.   Laura is returning from
her victory over Love; suddenly there appears a black
flag, followed by a female in black apparel, and terrible
in attitude and voice.   She stops the festive procession,
and strikes Laura.   The poet now describes her last moments, and her soft sleep of death, in which she retains
all her beauty.   In the second part she comes to him in a
dream, holds out her hand, and invites him to sit by her
on the bank of a rivulet, under the shade of a beech and a
laurel.   Nothing, in this most beautiful of languages, is
so beautiful, excepting the lines of Dante on Francesca,
(57) as these.

E quella man già tanto desiäta,
A me, *parlando* e *sospirando, porse.*

[Speaking and sighing, she held out to me -
... The hand that I so greatly had desired,
('Triumph of Death', II, 10-11 tr E.W.).]

Their discourse is upon death, which she tells him
should be formidable only to the wicked, and assures him
that the enjoyment she receives from it, is far beyond
any which life has to bestow. He then asks her a question, which he alone had a right to ask her, and only in
her state of purity and bliss.

She sigh'd, and said, 'No; nothing could dissever
My heart from thine, and nothing shall there ever.
    If, thy fond ardor to repress,
I sometimes frown'd (and how could I do less?)
If, now and then, my look was not benign,
    'Twas but to save my fame, and thine.
And, as thou knowest, when I saw thy grief,
    A glance was ready with relief.'

    Scarce with dry cheek
    These tender words I heard her speak.
'Were they but true!' I cried. She bent the head,
    Not unreproachfully, and said,
'Yes, I did love thee; and whene'er
I turn'd away my eyes, 'twas shame and fear;
A thousand times to thee did they incline,
But sank before the flame that shot from thine.'
[II, 88ff.]

He who, the twentieth time, can read unmoved this canzone, never has experienced a love which could not be requited, and never has deserved a happy one.

NOTES

1 The English poet Thomas Campbell.
2 See Simonde de' Sismondi, 'De la littérature du Midi
   de l'Europe', 4 vols (1813), and Pierre Louis Ginguené, 9 vols, 'Histoire littéraire d'Italie' (vols 10-
   14 'Histoire' ... continued by F. Salfi), 14 vols
   (1811-35).
3 Henry Hallam (1777-1859), English historian and author
   of the 'Introduction to the Literature of Europe in
   the Fifteenth, Sixteenth, and Seventeenth Centuries',
   4 vols (1837-9).

4 See 'Le rime di Francesco Petrarca ... S'aggiungono le
   considerazioni rivedute e ampliate d'A. Tassoni, le
   annotazioni di G. Muzio, e le osservazioni di L.A.
   Muratori' (1711) and subsequent editions, and [J.F.
   P.A. de Sade], 'Mémoires pour la Vie de F. Pétrarque',
   3 vols (1764-7).
5 'The Life of Petrarch collected from Mémoires pour la
   Vie de Petrarch' (by Susannah Dobson), 3rd ed., 2 vols
   (1797), compiled and translated from de Sade's
   'Mémoires'.
6 Probably either Giacomo Colonna, a friend of Petrarch's early years or Giovanni, Cardinal Colonna,
   Giacomo's brother, in whose service Petrarch was employed from 1330 to 1347.   Cola di Rienzo (1313-54)
   was a Roman tribune whose efforts to establish a popular government in Rome were supported by Petrarch.
   Cola was killed in an uprising on 8 October 1354.
7 Bertrand de Got (1264-1314), Clement V, pope from 1305
   to 1314, the first of the Avignon popes.
8 Petrarch always fondly remembered his first teacher,
   Convenevole da Prato, who, like his father, was also
   an exile from Florence.
9 Cino da Pistoia (1265-1337).
10 Jacques Duèse (d. 1334), John XXII, pope from 1316 to
   1334.
11 The identity of Petrarch's 'Laura' remains unknown.
12 6 April 1327.
13 'Africa'.
14 'Then he [Masinissa] tosses about upon his bed/ ... He
   is on fire - sadness, fear, anger, and madness keep
   wakeful watch / Often, weeping while he embraces his
   beloved though absent, /Often embracing the bed, he
   bestows upon it sweet words. / After no restraints
   prevail against his violent grief, / He begins again
   and eases his suffering by long laments, / "Too dear
   to me, sweeter than all life to me, / Sophonisba,
   farewell"' ['Africa', v, 527-35, tr. Hazel E. Barnes].
   See Campbell, 'Life of Petrarch', 2, 333n.
15 Some faint verbal reminiscences are found in 'Aeneid',
   iv, 296ff, 529ff, and vi, 450ff.
16 'Socrates', Ludwig van Kempen; 'Laelius', Lello di
   Pietro Stefano dei Tosetti.
17 Simone Martini (1283-1344), Sienese painter who painted a portrait of Laura in 1336.
18 'De viris illustribus'.
19 'Africa'.
20 Augustus (Octavian, 63 BC-AD 14), first of the Roman
   emperors, was an author himself as well as a patron of
   learning and man of letters.

21 Petrarch was crowned poet laureate of Rome on 8 April
    1341.

22 Pierre Abélard (1079-1142), French philosopher and
    theologian who fell in love with his student, Heloïse,
    the niece of Fulbert, a canon at Notre Dame in Paris.
    When Fulbert learned that their love had resulted in a
    child and a secret marriage, he had Abélard emascula-
    ted.   Heloïse then became a nun and Abélard a monk
    (c. 1114).   The lovers are now united in a tomb in
    the cemetery of Père-la-Chaise at Paris.

23 A mysterious and indistinct idea, not dissipated by
    the closest view of the original, led the poetical
    mind of Shelley into the labyrinth that encompassed
    the garden of Academus.   He has given us an accurate
    and graceful translation of the most eloquent of
    Plato's dialogues ['Symposium'].   Consistently with
    modesty he found it impossible to present the whole to
    his readers; but as the subject is entirely on the
    nature of love, they will discover that nothing is
    more unlike Petrarca's.   The trifles, the quibbles,
    the unseasonable jokes, of what is exhibited in very
    harmonious Greek, and in English nearly as harmonious,
    pass uncensured and unnoticed by the fascinated
    Shelley.   So his gentleness and warmth of heart in-
    duced him to look with affection on the poetry of
    Petrarca; poetry by how many degrees inferior to his
    own!   Nevertheless, with justice and propriety he
    ranks Dante higher in the same department [see Shel-
    ley's 'Defense of Poetry'], who indeed has described
    love more eloquently than any other poet, excepting
    (who always must be excepted) Shakspeare [sic].
    Francesca and Beatrice open all the heart, and fill it
    up with tenderness and with pity.   [L]

24 Papal Seat, 1309-77.

25 Civita Vecchia is a seaport town and episcopal see of
    Italy located about thirty-five miles from Rome.

26 'Ottava rima' is a stanza of eight eleven-syllable
    lines rhyming ababacc.   Francesco Berni (1497-1536)
    is an Italian poet whose revision of 'Orlando Innamor-
    ato' by Boiardo received great praise when it was pub-
    lished posthumously in 1541 with the title 'Rifuci-
    mento'.

27 'Decameron'.

28 'Familiares', XXI, 15.

29 Petrarch's house in Vaucluse, in southern France, was
    on the south bank of the river Sorgue; Boccaccio's
    villa, outside Florence, was near the Mugnone, a tri-
    butary of the Arno.

30 'Seniles', XVII, 4.

31 Boccaccio's 'Decameron' came to Petrarch from an un-
    known source, probably early in 1373.   See 'Seniles',
    XVII, 3.
32 See the 'Decameron':   The Tenth Story of The Tenth
    Day.
33 'Seniles', XVII, 3.
34 It is incredible that Julius Caesar Scaliger, who has
    criticized so vast a number of later poets quite for-
    gotten, and deservedly, should never have even seen
    the Latin poetry of Petrarca.   His words are:
    'Petrarch, so far as I know, first dared to raise his
    voice to heaven out of the muddy barbarism, and as we
    have said elsewhere, because I had not been permitted
    to see anything of his work, I shall leave the correc-
    tions of this man - like many other things - to the
    scholars' [tr. Hazel E. Barnes].   See 'Poetics libri
    septem', 3rd ed. (1586), p. 769.   [L]
35 The 'Secretum', Petrarch's 'Secret Book', depicts the
    poet's inner struggles between the secular and monas-
    tic ideals of life.
36 St Augustine (Aurelius Augustinus, AD 354-430), bishop
    of Hippo in Roman Africa from 396 to 430, and one of
    the great theologians of the Latin Church;   author of
    the 'Confessions' (c. 397), 'On Christian Doctrine'
    (426), 'The City of God' (426), and other writings.
37 'De sui ipsius et multorum ignorantia'.
38 See 'De sui ipsius et multorum ignorantia', 'Francesco
    Petrarca: Prose', eds G. Martellotti, P.G. Ricci, E.
    Carrara, E. Bianchi, La letteratura italiana Storia
    e Testi, vol. 7, Milan and Naples, 1955, 710.
39 'Bucolicum carmen'.
40 John II (1319-64), king of France (1350-64), and
    Edward III (1312-77), king of England (1327-77).
41 Étienne Aubert (d. 1362), Innocent VI, pope from 1352
    to 1362.
42 John II was defeated and captured by the English led
    by Edward, the Black Prince, at the battle of Poitiers
    (19 September 1356).
43 Anicius Manlius Severinus Boethius (c. AD 480-524),
    Roman philosopher, statesman, and Hellenist, who, when
    imprisoned on the charge of treason, wrote the famous
    'De Consolatione Philosophiae'.
44 This poem, attributed to Cino in the nineteenth cen-
    tury, is now considered spurious.   Ginguené asserted
    the same supposed indebtedness of Petrarch to Cino in
    'Histoire', 2, 327-8, 543-4.
45 Landor has mistakenly recalled two of Cino's poems as
    one.   See CLXXVII and CLXXVIII in 'Le rime di Cino da
    Pistoia', ed. Guido Zaccagnini (1925).

46   'Le rime del Petrarca' (1832), 1, 100.

47   See Ginguené, 'Histoire', 2, 525-34.

48   Ibid., 530.

49   Horace, 'Odes', ii, 20.

50   The 'Accademia della Crusca' or 'Furfuratorum',
     founded in 1582, was the most famous of the numerous
     literary academies established in Italy in the six-
     teenth century.

51   There is no indication of this in the last canzone in
     either part of 'Le rime del Petrarca' (1842 [1832]).

52   Cf. Abraham Cowley's An Answer to a Copy of Verses
     sent me to Jersey, ll. 15-16: 'Written by
     Esquire, the/Year of our Lord six hundred thirty
     three'.   Landor's allusion is to William Prynne's
     encyclopedic 'Histrio-Mastix; The Players Scourge'
     (1633), an attack on the immorality of all aspects of
     the theatre.   I have not found any specific refer-
     ence to Petrarch's love poetry in this work.

53   See Ginguené, 'Histoire', 2, 534ff.

54   Ibid., 538-9.

55   Henry Francis Cary (1772-1844), English clergyman,
     schoolfellow of Landor, and translator of Dante's
     'Inferno' (1805) and the 'Divine Comedy' (1814).

56   These two words and the line of Petrarch's verse that
     follows were apparently left out by the printer of
     the 1853 text.

57   See 'Inferno', v, 73-142.

Poems

22 To Southey
1833, 1834, 1837, 1846

The twin odes, Nos 22 and 23, composed toward the end of
1833, are the first of a series of poetic tributes from
Landor to his contemporaries. The ode to Wordsworth, accompanied by a list of corrections for the completed Southey poem, first appeared in an undated letter from Landor
to Lady Blessington (10-14 December ? 1833). To Wordsworth was published on 1 February 1834 in the 'Athenaeum',
and was reprinted with minor revisions in Joseph Ablett's
'Literary Hours' (1837) and with several changes in 'Works
of Walter Savage Landor' (1846). To Southey was published on 4 January 1834 in the 'Athenaeum', and was also
reprinted twice more before Landor's death, each time with
minor revisions, in 'Literary House' (1837) and 'Works of
Walter Savage Landor' (1846). The variants in these
poems are recorded by Stephen Wheeler in 'Complete Works',
15, 141-4. Both poems are reprinted from the 1846 text.

Indweller of a peaceful vale, (1)
Ravaged erewhile by white-hair'd Dane;
Rare architect of many a wondrous tale,
Which, till Helvellyn's head lie prostrate, (2) shall
    remain!

From Arno's side I hear thy Derwent flow,
And see methinks the lake (3) below
Reflect thy graceful progeny, more fair,
And radiant than the purest waters are,
Even when gurgling in their joy among
The bright and blessed throng
Whom, on her arm recline, (4)
The beauteous Proserpina
With tenderest regretful gaze,
Thinking of Enna's yellow field, surveys. (5)

Alas! that snows are shed
Upon thy laurel'd head,
Hurtled by many cares and many wrongs!
Malignity lets none
Approach the Delphic throne;
A hundred lane-fed curs bark down Fame's
hundred tongues.
But this is in the night, when men are slow
To raise their eyes, when high and low,
The scarlet and the colourless, are one:
Soon Sleep unbars his noiseless prison,
And active minds again are risen;
Where are the curs? dream-bound, and whim-
pering in the sun.

At fife's or lyre's or tabor's sound
The dance of youth, O Southey, runs not round,
But closes at the bottom of the room
Amid the falling dust and deepening gloom,
Where the weary sit them down,
And Beauty too unbraids, and waits a lovelier
crown.

We hurry to the river we must cross,
And swifter downward every footstep wends;
Happy, who reach it ere they count the loss
Of half their faculties and half their friends!
When we are come to it, the stream
Is not so dreary as they deem
Who look on it from haunts too dear;
The weak from Pleasure's baths feel most its
chilling air!

No firmer breast than thine hath Heaven
To poet, sage, or hero given:
No heart more tender, none more just
To that He largely placed in trust:
Therefore shalt thou, whatever date
Of years be thine, with soul elate
Rise up before the Eternal throne,
And hear, in God's own voice, 'Well done.'

Not, were that submarine
Gem-lighted city mine,
Wherein my name, engraven by thy hand,
Above the royal gleam of blazonry shall stand;
Not, were all Syracuse
Pour'd forth before my Muse,
With Hiero's cars and steeds, and Pindar's lyre (6)

Brightening the path with more than solar fire,
Could I, as would beseem, requite the praise
Showered upon my low head from thy most lofty
   lays.

NOTES

1 In June 1832 Landor visited Southey at Greta Hall in
   Keswick, Cumberland.
2 Although Helvellyn, one of the highest mountains in
   the English Lake District, is only 3,118 feet in
   height, its peak rises impressively above the outline
   formed by the other mountains in the vicinity.
3 Derwentwater, perhaps the loveliest lake in the Lake
   District.
4 So Milton: 'Par. Lost', B. iv, v. 333, 'sideling
   [side-long] as they sat, recline / On the soft downy
   bank, demaskt with flowers'.   [L]
5 Persephone (Latin Proserpina), according to Greek
   myth, was the daughter of Zeus and Demeter who, while
   gathering flowers one day in the fields of Enna in
   Sicily, was abducted by Hades.   Demeter's grief finally convinced Zeus to allow Persephone to return to
   the earth for six (eight) months each year.
6 The Greek poet Pindar (518-438 BC) wrote his first
   Pythian ode in honour of his patron Hieron I, tyrant
   of Syracuse (478-467/6 BC), winner of the chariot
   race, probably in 470 BC.

23 To Wordsworth
1833, 1834, 1837, 1846

Those who have laid the harp aside
    And turn'd to idler things,
From very restlessness have tried
    The loose and dusty strings,
And, catching back some favorite strain,
Run with it o'er the chords again.

But Memory is not a Muse,
    O Wordsworth! though 'tis said
They all descend from her, and use
    To haunt her fountain-head:
That other men should work for me
In the rich mines of Poesie,

Pleases me better than the toil
    Of smoothing under hardened hand,
With attic emery and oil,
    The shining point for Wisdom's wand,
Like those thou temperest 'mid the rills
Descending from thy native hills.

Without his governance, in vain
    Manhood is strong, and Youth is bold.
If oftentimes the o'er-piled strain
    Clogs in the furnace, and grows cold
Beneath his pinions deep and frore,
And swells and melts and flows no more,
That is because the heat beneath
    Pants in its cavern poorly fed.
Life springs not from the couch of Death,
    Nor Muse nor Grace can raise the dead;
Unturn'd then let the mass remain,
Intractable to sun or rain.

A marsh, where only flat leaves lie,
And showing but the broken sky,
Too surely is the sweetest lay
That wins the ear and wastes the day,
Where youthful Fancy pouts alone
And lets not Wisdom touch her zone.

He who would build his fame up high,
The rule and plummet must apply,
Nor say, 'I'll do what I have plann'd,'
Before he try if loam or sand
Be still remaining in the place
Delved for each polisht pillar's base.
With skilful eye and fit device
Thou raisest every edifice,
Whether in sheltered vale it stand
Or overlook the Dardan strand,
Amid the cypresses that mourn
Laodameia's love forlorn. (1)

We both have run o'er half the space
Listed for mortal's earthly race;
We both have crost life's fervid line,
And other stars before us shine:
May they be bright and prosperous
As those that have been stars for us!
Our course by Milton's light was sped,
And Shakspeare shining overhead:
Chatting on deck was Dryden too,
The Bacon of the rhyming crew;
None ever crost our mystic sea
More richly stored with thought than he;
Tho' never tender nor sublime,
He wrestles with and conquers Time.
To learn my lore on Chaucer's knee,
I left much prouder company;
Thee gentle Spenser fondly led,
But me he mostly sent to bed.

I wish them every joy above
That highly blessed spirits prove,
Save one: and that too shall be theirs,
But after many rolling years,
When 'mid their light thy light appears.

NOTE

1 In Greek myth Protesilaus, a Thessalian prince who

took part in the Greek expedition against Troy, was
the first to leap ashore and was immediately killed.
Laodamia, his wife, was so overcome by grief that the
gods allowed Protesilaus' shade to visit her for three
hours.   When he left she took her own life.   Wordsworth concludes his poetic treatment of the myth,
Laodamia, by describing the trees that grow out of
Protesilaus' tomb: '- Upon the side / Of Hellespont
(such faith was entertained) / A knot of spiry trees
for ages grew / From out the tomb of him for whom she
died; / And ever, when such stature they had gained /
That Ilium's walls were subject to their view, / The
trees' tall summits withered at the sight; / A con-
stant interchange of growth and blight!' [Laodamia,
11. 167-74, in 'The Poetical Works of William Wordsworth', ed. E. De Selincourt, 2nd ed., Oxford: Clarendon Press, 1952, 2, 272).

24 To Robert Browning
1845, 1846

To Robert Browning, Landor's finest literary tribute in
verse, was occasioned by the receipt of a gift copy of
Browning's 'Dramatic Romances and Lyrics' early in November 1845.   Landor privately expressed his gratitude by
post: 'My dear kind friend, Before I have half red thro
your Dramatic Romances, I must acknowledge the delight I
am receiving, - in no small doubt however, whether with
all my haste I shall be in time for the post.   What a
profusion of imagery, covering what a depth of thought.
You may stand quite alone if you will - and I think you
will....'   (W.S.L. to Robert Browning, postmarked 12
November 1845).   He publicly acknowledged Browning's
genius by printing To Robert Browning in the 22 November
1845 'Morning Chronicle'.   The poem was reprinted in 1845
on a leaflet for Browning's father, and it appeared again
with minor revisions in 'Works of Walter Savage Landor'
(1846).   The poem is reproduced from the 1846 text.

There is delight in singing, tho' none hear
Beside the singer: and there is delight
In praising, tho' the praiser sit alone
And see the prais'd far off him, far above.
Shakspeare is not our poet, but the world's,
Therefore on him no speech! and brief for thee,
Browning!   Since Chaucer was alive and hale,
No man hath walkt along our roads with step
So active, so inquiring eye, or tongue
So varied in discourse.   But warmer climes
Give brighter plumage, stronger wing: the breeze
Of Alpine highths thou playest with, borne on
Beyond Sorrento and Amalfi, where
The Siren waits thee, singing song for song. (1)

NOTE

1 Ll. 10-14 allude to Browning's poem The Englishman in
   Italy, formerly entitled England in Italy when it
   appeared in 'Dramatic Romances' (1845).

25 Catullus

1853

The three poems, Nos 25-7, first appeared in a section of
verse entitled Epigrams in 'Last Fruit off an Old Tree'
(1853).   The poems are numbered VI, CX, and CXIII respectively, and only the first has a title.   Landor prefaced
his Epigrams with this note: 'UNDER the title of "Epigrams" some will be found here which the general reader
may hardly recognise in that character....   Several of
the lighter pieces were written in early youth....'   The
poems are taken from the 1853 text.

Tell me not what too well I know
About the bard of Sirmio .. (1)
    Yes, in Thalia's (2) son
Such stains there are .. as when a Grace
Sprinkles another's laughing face
    With nectar, and runs on.

NOTES

1 The Roman poet Catullus (c. 84-c. 54 BC) had a villa
   at Sirmio, a promontory on the southern shore of Lake
   Garda.   Catullus' lines to Sirmio (XXXI) express the
   joy and gratitude of homecoming after a long journey.
2 Thalia, one of the nine Muses, was associated with the
   art of comedy.

26 [Thomas Carlyle]
1853

See headnote to No. 25.

Strike with Thor's hammer, (1) strike agen
The skulking heads of half-form'd men,
And every northern God shall smile
Upon thy well-aim'd blow, Carlyle!

NOTE

1 Thor, a god common to all the early Germanic peoples,
was a red-bearded, middle-aged warrior of great
strength whose name is the Teutonic word for thunder
and whose hammer represents the thunderbolt.

27 [Lord Byron]
1853

See headnote to No. 25.

Changeful! how little do you know
Of Byron when you call him so!
True as the magnet is to iron
Byron hath ever been to Biron.
His color'd prints, in gilded frames,
Whatever the designs and names,
One image set before the rest,
In shirt with falling collar drest,
And keeping up a rolling fire at
Patriot, conspirator, and pirate.

28 Goldsmith and Gray
1854, 1858

Goldsmith and Gray was published in the 'Examiner' on 16
September 1854, and was reprinted in 'Dry Sticks, Fagoted
by Walter Savage Landor' (1858).   The text for the poem
is 'Dry Sticks' (1858).

Sweet odors and bright colors swiftly pass,
Swiftly as breath upon a looking-glass.
Byron, the schoolgirl's pet, has lived his day,
And the tall maypole scarce remembers May.
Thou, Nature, bloomest in perennial youth ..
Two only are eternal .. thou and Truth.
Who walks not with thee thro' the dim Churchyard? (1)
Who wanders not with Erin's wandering bard? (2)
Who sits not down with Auburn's pastor mild
To take upon his knee the shyest child? (3)
These in all hearts will find a kindred place,
And live the last of our poetic race.

NOTES

1   Thomas Gray, Elegy Written in a Country Churchyard
    (1750).
2   Oliver Goldsmith, 'The Traveller' (1764).
3   See Goldsmith's 'Deserted Village', ll. 137-92.

29 To Chaucer

1863

Both poems were printed in 'Heroic Idyls, with Additional
Poems' (1863), the last book published by Landor before
his death.   The second poem is without a title.   Stephen
Wheeler's suggested title, Dante Alighieri, is misleading
because the poem is actually a poetic tribute to three of
Landor's favourite writers: Dante, Milton and Shakespeare.   Text 1863.

Chaucer, O how I wish thou wert
Alive and, as of yore, alert!
Then, after bandied tales, what fun
Would we two have with monk and nun.
Ah, surely verse was never meant
To render mortals somnolent.
In Spenser's labyrinthine rhymes
I throw my arms o'erhead at times,
Opening sonorous mouth as wide
As oystershells at ebb of tide.
Mistake me not: I honour him
Whose magic made the Muses dream
Of things they never knew before,
And scenes they never wandered o'er.
I dare not follow, nor again
Be wafted with the wizard train.
No bodyless and soulless elves
I seek, but creatures like ourselves.
If any poet now runs after
The Faeries, they will split with laughter,
Leaving him in the desert, where
Dry grass is emblematic fare.
Thou wast content to act the squire
Becomingly, and mount no higher,
Nay, at fit season to descend

Into the poet with a friend,
Then ride with him about thy land
In lithesome nutbrown boots well-tann'd,
With lordly greyhound, who would dare
Course against law the summer hare,
Nor takes to heart the frequent crack
Of whip, with curse that calls him back.
     The lesser Angels now have smiled
To see thee frolic like a child,
And hear thee, innocent as they,
Provoke them to come down and play.

30 [Dante, Milton, and Shakespeare]
1863

See headnote to No. 29.

With frowning brow o'er pontif-kings elate.
Stood Dante, great the man, the poet great.
Milton in might and majesty surpast
The triple world, and far his shade was cast.
On earth he sang amid the Angelic host,
And Paradise to him was never lost.
But there was one who came these two between
With larger light than yet our globe had seen.
Various were his creations, various speech
Without a Babel he bestow'd on each.
Raleigh and Bacon towered above that earth
Which in their day had given our Shakespeare birth,
And neither knew his presence! they half-blind
Saw not in him the grandest of mankind.

Select Bibliography

For the most comprehensive listing of works by and about
Landor, see R.H. Super's compilation in 'The New Cambridge
Bibliography of English Literature', ed. George Watson
(1969), 3, 1210-16.   For a commentary on research on
Landor, see Super's Walter Savage Landor in 'The English
Romantic Poets and Essayists: A Review of Research and
Criticism', eds Carolyn and Lawrence Houtchens, rev. ed.
(New York and London, 1966), 221-53.   Important editions
and studies are listed below:

CRUMP, CHARLES G., ed., 'Imaginary Conversations by Walter
Savage Landor', London, 1891, 6 vols.
CRUMP, CHARLES G., ed., 'Poems, Dialogues in Verse, and
Epigrams by Walter Savage Landor', London, 1892, 2 vols.
CRUMP, CHARLES G., ed., 'The Longer Prose Works of Walter
Savage Landor', London, 1893, 2 vols.
ELWIN, MALCOLM, 'Landor: A Replevin', London, 1958.
FLASDIECK, HERMANN M., Walter Savage Landor und seine
'Imaginary Conversations', 'Englische Studien', 58 (1924),
390-431.
FORSTER, JOHN, 'Walter Savage Landor. A Biography',
London, 1869, 2 vols.
FORSTER, JOHN, 'The Works and Life of Walter Savage
Landor', London, 1876, 8 vols.
KELLY, ANDREA, The Latin Poetry of Walter Savage Landor,
'The Latin Poetry of English Poets', ed. J.W. Binns,
London and Boston: Routledge & Kegan Paul, 1974, 150-93.
LANDOR, WALTER SAVAGE, 'Commentary on Memoirs of Mr. Fox'
(ptd but not pbd, 1812);   rptd as 'Charles James Fox: A
Commentary on His Life and Character', ed. Stephen
Wheeler, 2nd ed., London, 1907.
LANDOR, WALTER SAVAGE, 'Idyllia Heroica Decem Librum
Phaleuciorum Unum', Pisa, 1820.

LANDOR, WALTER SAVAGE, 'The Works of Walter Savage
Landor', London, 1846, 2 vols.
LANDOR, WALTER SAVAGE, 'Poemata et Inscriptiones',
London, 1847.
LANDOR, WALTER SAVAGE, 'The Last Fruit off an Old Tree',
London, 1853.
LANDOR, WALTER SAVAGE, 'Letter from W.S. Landor to R.W.
Emerson', Bath, 1856.
MARIANI, JOHN F., The Letters of Walter Savage Landor to
Marguerite Countess of Blessington, unpublished PhD dis-
sertation, Columbia University, 1973.
MARIANI, JOHN F., Lady Blessington's 'Ever Obliged Friend
and Servant, W.S. Landor': A Study of Their Literary Re-
lationship, 'The Wordsworth Circle', 7 (Winter 1976), 17-
30.
MERCIER, VIVIAN, The Future of Landor Criticism, 'Some
British Romantics: A Collection of Essays', eds J.V.
Logan, J.E. Jordan, and Northrop Frye, Columbus, 1966,
41-85.
PRASHER, ALICE LAVONNE, Walter Savage Landor's 'Imaginary
Conversations': A Critical Edition of the First Eight
Conversations in Volume One. [with] 'Imaginary Conversa-
tions of Literary Men and Statesmen'. By Walter Savage
Landor, Esq. The First Volume. 1824, unpublished PhD dis-
sertation, Northwestern University, 1966.
PROUDFIT, CHARLES L., ed., 'Selected Imaginary Conversa-
tions of Literary Men and Statesmen by Walter Savage
Landor', Lincoln, Nebraska, 1969.
PROUDFIT, CHARLES L., Landor on Milton: The Commentators'
Commentator, 'The Wordsworth Circle', 7 (Winter 1976),
3-12.
RUOFF, A. LAVONNE, Walter Savage Landor's Criticism of
Horace: The Odes and Epodes, 'Arion', 9 (1970), 189-204.
RUOFF, A. LAVONNE, Landor's Letters to His Family: 1802-
1825, 'Bulletin of the John Rylands Library', 53 (1971),
465-500.
RUOFF, A. LAVONNE, Landor's Letters to His Family: 1826-
1829, 'Bulletin of the John Rylands Library', 54 (1972),
398-433.
RUOFF, A. LAVONNE, Walter Savage Landor's Letters to His
Family, 1830-1832, 'Bulletin of the John Rylands Library',
58 (1976), 467-507.
RUOFF, A. LAVONNE, ed. and LEVINE, EDWIN BURTON, tr.,
Landor's Letters to the Reverend Walter Birch, 'Bulletin
of the John Rylands Library', 51 (1968), 200-61.
SUPER, R.H., 'The Publication of Landor's Works', Supple-
ment to the Bibliographical Society's 'Transactions', no.
18, London, 1954.
SUPER, R.H., 'Walter Savage Landor: A Biography', New
York, 1954; London, 1957.

SUPER, R.H., The Fire of Life, 'Cambridge Review', 86 (1965), 170-5.

SUPER, R.H., Landor and Catullus, 'The Wordsworth Circle', 7 (Winter 1976), 31-7.

VITOUX, PIERRE, 'L'OEuvre de Walter Savage Landor', Paris, 1964.

WELBY, T. EARLE, and WHEELER, STEPHEN, eds, 'The Complete Works of Walter Savage Landor' (prose, vols 1-12, ed. Welby; poetry, vols 13-16, ed. Wheeler), London, 1927-36, 16 vols.

WHEELER, STEPHEN, ed., 'The Poetical Works of Walter Savage Landor', Oxford, 1937, 3 vols.

WILLIAMS, STANLEY T., Walter Savage Landor as a Critic of Literature, 'Publications of the Modern Language Association', 38 (1923), 906-28.

WISE, THOMAS JAMES, 'A Landor Library', London, privately ptd, 1928.

WISE, THOMAS JAMES, and WHEELER, STEPHEN, 'A Bibliography of the Writings in Prose and Verse of Walter Savage Landor', London, 1919.

Index